Thomas Mitchell

Cosmogony

The Geological Antiquity of the World

Thomas Mitchell

Cosmogony

The Geological Antiquity of the World

ISBN/EAN: 9783743370678

Manufactured in Europe, USA, Canada, Australia, Japa

Cover: Foto ©ninafisch / pixelio.de

Manufactured and distributed by brebook publishing software (www.brebook.com)

Thomas Mitchell

Cosmogony

COSMOGONY:

THE GEOLOGICAL ANTIQUITY OF THE WORLD,
EVOLUTION, ATHEISM, PANTHEISM, DEISM
AND INFIDELITY REFUTED,

BY

SCIENCE, PHILOSOPHY AND SCRIPTURE,

BY

Prof. THOMAS MITCHELL.

IN TWO VOLUMES.

SYLLOGISM:
The food of plants does not exist in nature.
Plants prepare their own food.
Therefore the first plants were creations.

If God ever caused a book to be written of the origin of the world and its inhabitants, every statement of the work must have involved a philosophic necessity and a scientific conclusion. Such have we found the statements of Holy Scripture; therefore the Creator of Nature was the Author of Scripture.

NEW YORK.
THE AMERICAN NEWS COMPANY,
Publishers' Agents,

1881.

Entered according to Act of Congress, in the year 1881, by

CHARLES K. MITCHELL,

in the Office of the Librarian of Congress, at Washington, D. C.

PREFACE.

"My intercourse with highly-gifted men," says Alexander Von Humboldt in the preface to his "Cosmos," "early led me to discover that without earnest striving to attain to a knowledge of some specific branch of study, all attempts to give a grand and general view of the universe would be nothing more than a vain delusion."

The correctness of this conclusion is unquestionable, and its force may be more fully comprehended if we consider the fact that a specific branch of study, or a single science, is not only a part of the whole—the Cosmos, the universal science—but as such is necessary in order to understand and illustrate all the other parts. As well undertake to explain the whole of a masterpiece of art by leaving out a part, and especially if it be an essential part. While, however, it seems to have been Humboldt's object to give a comprehensive and connected view of the universe as of a finished work, he fails to investigate the grand *purpose* of the Cosmos itself. The temporal absorbs him. What it accomplishes in animal and human sustenance is the limit of his investigations, while the *end* for which it was made reaches into the eternal; and without taking this into the account, the disorder and derangement of the temporal is inevitably involved in the unfathomable mystery in which modern science finds and leaves the universe.

Humboldt has endeavored to deal with the mysteries

arising out of this aspect of nature in most of its details, and has crowded all the known natural science of his time into his voluminous productions. Of course his work is consistent with his undertaking, as Cosmos limits it to the universe, or the whole system of visible bodies, including the earth and the stars; but it requires the combined cosmogony of the whole, together with the science of its origin and creation, to explain its cosmical involvement.

Of the physical universe itself, in all its departments—which, for simplification, is divided into the several sciences—we have endeavored to trace the parts and phenomena to adequate causes, or a cause; and failing to find it within the limits of the universe, we have been driven to search beyond and above for its origin, and have found the true origin of nature inseparably allied with a living mind, thus demonstrating that its origin alone centers in CREATIVE FIAT, and not in natural materialism. But while the book of nature reveals as her great Original a Being of wisdom and power equal to the conception and achievement of the marvelous works which she displays, "the scripture of truth" completes the great circle of revelation by showing the nature of the purpose in its creation, and the interest and disposition of the Creator in and toward the grandest display of his handiwork—MAN.

Humboldt talks about creation, but nothing is more apparent from his writings than that he entertains no other idea of what the word implies than that which he calls Nature. Among the wonderful things discovered by science and art he says that "by the aid of powerful instruments scanning the regions of space, we see the remote nebulous mass resolving itself into worlds of stars" ("Cosmos," i. 20). If the nebulous mass resolves *itself into stars*, of course it leaves no work for a Creator to do in making stars. In order to give full credit to this opinion, we must remember that it is held by this same scientist, as well as by all others, that the stars thus formed are suns, each of which has a planetary system like our own solar system, with its planets and their satellites. Here, then, is the strongest possible expression of atheistic materialism, for which there is not the least evidence in science. To combat such an opinion would be the extreme of folly.

As an apology for his assertion, and as a reason why we should receive it without proof, he gives us the example of another scientist who had done the same thing. He says, vol. i. p. 28 : "Laplace has combined the results of the highest astronomical and mathematical bodies, and has presented them to his readers free from all processes of demonstration. The structure of the heavens is here reduced to the simple solution of a great problem in mechanics ; and yet his work has never been accused of incompleteness and want of profundity." To be sure, this is a very simple process of accounting for the structure of the sidereal heavens—namely, that white cloudy vapor should set itself at work and resolve itself into systems of planets, with vegetable and animal life and all their phenomena ; but is it not childish simplicity? One great scientist compliments another because he has not deigned to prove his scientific opinions, praises him because he has not demonstrated them, and of course falls in love with the scientific world for not calling in question their completeness and profundity. Undemonstrated profundity!—a contradiction in terms. And these are the men who stand at the head of the school of "modern scientists"!

Humboldt says, " Physics, as the term signifies, is limited to the explanation of the phenomena of the material world by the properties of matter." Do the properties of the materials out of which a steam-engine is composed explain the origin, construction, mechanism and capabilites of the machine? The explanation of one or all of these can alone be found in the mind of the inventor and builder. So is it with the machine called the Solar System, and all the constellations revolving in limitless space. The construction of each explains or manifests the power and capacity of the Mind that made it. The endowment of their simple or combined properties necessitates all phenomena, and explains the wisdom of the great Artificer of all that moves; hence "physics" explains nothing, but depends entirely upon mind for the explanation of its own existence.

The total absence of a cause in all nature—which is only a universe of effects—demonstrates the impossibility of original matter or even nature, as perfect as she now exists, having resolved themselves into anything, much less into suns and systems. Hence all phenomena came from the mind of God, the only Cause; every one of which is a finger pointing backward to its origin, cause of existence and motion, instead of to its properties as that *cause;* each of which is an effect, just as a steam-engine points to its maker for the explanation of its construction. Hence the error of Humboldt's doctrine of physics. He seems to have felt that such a definition shuts God out of the universe, because he afterward tacitly admits that there is something in nature, or manifested by it, which is beyond and superior to "physics;" and yet, in an elaborate attempt at a more satisfactory elucidation of his idea of what that something is, he covertly admits his notion of "no God," while he endeavors to disguise it by speciously arguing that "the forces inherent in matter" would, of "primordial necessity," exercise their action "according to periodical compulsion and at intervals," by the "progressive development of occult, permanent connection," in "obedience to the first impulse imparted." "THESE CONSTITUTE NATURE."

According to his definition of nature, it is as follows: "In reflecting upon physical phenomena and events, and trying their causes by the process of reason, we became more and more convinced of the truth of the ancient doctrine, that the forces inherent in matter, and those which govern the world, would exercise their action under the control of primordial necessity and in accordance with movements occurring periodically, after longer or shorter intervals. It is this necessity—this occult but permanent connection in the progressive development of forms, phenomena and events—which constitutes nature, obedient to the first impulse imparted to it." "Cosmos," p. 30.

Now, if this learned and gifted author understood or believed that a being of intelligence created all the forms of matter, by endowing the atoms with chemical and electrical peculiarities, and that these constituted the occult forces they possess, he surely could have said so in so many words. The expression "occult" comes the nearest to it, and this means "concealed," as the unknown qualities of matter. The occult sciences in the middle ages were magic, alchemy, and necromancy. If he believed it, and did not wish to exalt matter above or equal to God, why did he not describe the properties of matter as they exist, and draw the logical sequence, which necessitates the prior existence of an intelligent being, by whose efforts alone the forms and qualities of matter, simple or compound, organic or inorganic, could have originated? Why could he not have said that particles of matter exist, and are endowed with various qualities? These particles have no intelligence, and yet they perform intelligent purposes; therefore they must have received this endowment from a being capable of forming and executing purposes. He was therefore before and superior to nature. His was the mind that conceived, His the will that called into being, His the hand that shaped and gave motion and life to the vast system of nature called the universe.

Here the hand of God is as clearly manifest, and His power seen in their motions and effects, as are the genius, skill, and power of the mechanic in the invention, construction and movements of the machinery propelled by steam and electricity. Man knows that the greater machinery of suns and stellar systems, or that of the solar system, was no more capable of forming or developing themselves from particles of nebulous, vapory matter (as Humboldt affirms), than was the steam engine capable of forming and developing itself from the metals which compose it. If it is a severe tax on our mental powers to conceive and concede the existence of a Being equal to the task of creating the world, or nature, how infinitely greater is the tax imposed by that theory which claims that dumb, unintelligent matter—Nature—made herself! How infinitely greater are the credulity and superstition of those who believe the latter; and with what ill grace can these scientists (so called) taunt believers in God and the Bible with superstition!

Another Scientist Attempts a Definition.

"Nature," Schelling remarks, in his poetic discourse on art, is not an innate mass; and to him who can comprehend her vast sublimity, she reveals herself as the creative force of the universe. Before all time, eternal, ever active, she calls to life all things, whether perishable or imperishable." Here is another sublime effort to sophisticate the reader by the use of words, not as "signs of ideas," but to cover their absence, or to conceal opinions which the fear of unpopularity prevents from being clearly expressed. "Nature is the creative force of the universe; she was before all *time*." He does not say, before all *nature*: this would have revealed the fact that by "creative force" he had the conception and meant to convey the idea that force was the creator of nature, and only modestly used the word Force for God. But as nature was the force itself, being eternal she never came into existence at all; for an eternal thing never can begin to be; or if she was not eternal, and began to be, she brought herself into being by self-action. The latter conclusion would necessitate the action of a thing before it existed; while the former denies the origin of nature altogether, as an eternal thing never originated: and yet this nature was the force which brought herself into existence. This passage of Schelling may be good poetry, but it is poor philosophy and bad reasoning. "Nature called into life all things, whether perishable or imperishable;" and she did this before she existed herself, or she does not now exist.

He says: "Nature is ever active." This expression shows that its author did not entertain the conception that it was a Being of mind and intelligence, and consequent volition, as such a being could rest as well as work; could act as well as cease to act.

This "ever active force" was not a thing of life even as high as that of the lowest animal: for this has the power of volition, and may act or rest at pleasure; but this lifeless thing, denominated "nature," called all living objects, whether perishable or imperishable, into life

Here we have Schelling's poetic philosophy from which Humboldt takes his idea of "force." A thing having no life or volition itself, gives light and locomotion to all that lives and moves. Fundamental to the whole theories of atheism and evolution is the idea of progression and succession. Their language is, "Since something must be endless, an endless progression of causes and effects contains nothing intrinsically improbable." If the exact reverse of this position had been assumed, their conclusion might have been logical, thus: "Since there is no progression, retrogression, or succession—no coming into existence or going out—no one being born or dying—none beginning to live and none ceasing to live—nothing modified, changed, or changeable; but on the contrary everything moving in circles and not in lines, then might things have been eternal—without beginning or end: but the fact that progress, succession, change, modification, is the order of nature, it is fatally irreconcilable with the hypothesis of atheism; at the same time it confirms the position that nature, including all her phenomena, whether simple or complicated, had a begining, a creation, and an intelligent creator. Since, therefore, something must have been endless, it could not have been the changeable, but alone the "Infallible." To believe the contrary is the strangest credulity, the most marvelous science! Who would not be a modern scientist? And about all that is necessary to be one is, to be born in Germany and educated at the Leipsic University; or to have one's birthplace in England, and graduate at Oxford; as from these sources principally we import the godless materialism of the geological indefinite periods and the marvels of evolving before involving, unfolding before enfolding, unrolling before enrolling; in a word, of bringing things from whence they do not exist.

We are aware that we shall be complimented as "ingenious" in our manner of handling these vast subjects; but we reciprocate the compliment by ascribing the merited genius alone to these skeptical scientists, as the only defense their side of the question admits. This book evades no point, shuns no investigation, and shrinks from no conclusion; and we flatter ourselves that, though the discussion deals with the whole range of natural philosophy and science, from the grandest complication to the simplest molecules of nature, yet all may be comprehended, and that too by the common people.

That the author of these volumes has displayed an ingenuity which has put to silence all the genius and apparent reasonings of all the natural philosophers, scientists, atheists, deists, pantheists, and infidels of ancient and modern times—in a word, the whole school of materialists who have attempted to account for the origin of the universe by the principles inherent in matter—is too absurd to be entertained for a moment. But as the book produces this effect by presenting arguments from every department of natural existence, each of which demonstrates the priority of a personal God, possessed of a degree of intelligence and power equal to the Creator, and to whose direct interference the universe owes its origin and destiny, it leaves the alternative that they are correct both in premise and conclusion, and therefore TRUE.

Genius may make error appear truth, and this is the sole foundation of materialism. What is demanded to demolish the whole lying superstructure is to place the truth by its side. Truth is ever simple and ever potent, while error is ever mysterious, confused and confusing;

TABLE OF CONTENTS.

PREFACE.

                                                                        PAGE

Defect of Humboldt's Cosmos............................ 1
His definition of physics too limited..................... 6
Another scientist attempts definition..................... 8
To whom belongs the genius?........................... 18

INTRODUCTION.

To ascertain truth, prejudice must be laid aside........... 23
No antagonism between science and Scripture............. 25
The necessity of controversy............................ 27

CHAPTER I.

Independence of mind necessary to arrive at truth......... 29
Ancient philosophy, science and libraries................. 32
Aristotle on morality—Plato on virtue................... 33
Wisdom and virtue contrasted........................... 34
Difference between natural and moral virtue.............. 37

	PAGE
God the measure of everything good and grand	38
Library of Euclid—How they made books	40
Pythagoras, his learning, persecution and death	42
Socrates' manner of teaching	43
Discourse of Callias in Euclid's library	44
The ideas invented by men a real dearth	47
Euclid on astronomy, gravity—Earth a sphere	49
What Euclid knew of geography	52
All the natural science of the ancients	54

CHAPTER II.

Bible statements of Creation the most advanced science	57
Truth a system—One department explains another	59
So-called science more contradictory than religion	60
Scientists must not ignore, but prove the Bible false	62
Radical changes of modern science	64
Scripture account of Creation going back of Genesis	70
Manner of Creation—Chemical endowment of atoms by mind	72
The Eden world destroyed by the deluge	73
The geological appearances prove the flood	75
Volcanoes and earthquakes accounted for	76
Fossil and shell argument confirms the deluge	79
The glacial period never existed	79
Prof. Agassiz's cause unscientific	81
Lyell's attempt inadequate	83
The argument of uniformityism exploded	87

CHAPTER III.

PAGE

Reason, facts, science and Scripture opposed to evolution...
Why error in science gets the start of truth............... 89
Every fact has its science and philosophy................ 91
Was man created ?....................................... 94
Sophistry of geologists exposed.......................... 95
Absurdity of the theory that one vital organ produces another 97
The primordial form could not have been evolved......... 100
Conditions of life....................................... 102
Evolution reversed upon its own principles............... 105
If evolution exists, it is a rapid process.................. 106
Creation first, evolution next............................ 108

CHAPTER IV.

Christianity and evolution contrasted..................... 110
If Genesis falls, so do the rest of the Scriptures........... 111
The whole gospel is in the Scriptures of the Old Testament. 113
The Bible standard of ethics too high to be improved...... 116
The standard of Atheism also thus contrasted............. 118
Monkey origin of man Darwin's main conclusion........... 120
Savage life not the normal condition of man.............. 123
The present world designed only to be temporary......... 125
Without a knowledge of the end designed the world is an enigma... 126
Real progress must be physical, moral and mental........ 128
Mental impression physically deteriorates................ 130
The wisdom of the Creator in limiting its power.......... 132

CHAPTER V.

Materialism exposed by the laws of matter and motion.....
What is materialism?..................................... 133
An objection of mental philosophy removed............... 135
Mental organs formed of matter.......................... 138
Involuntary sleep death................................. 140
To understand nature, you must understand the Bible...... 142
Skeptical materialism defined........................... 144
The doctrine of immateriality—Annihilation.............. 145
Substantial nature of God proved by His attributes....... 147
Jesus Christ a material being, but the Christian's God... 148
Scripture argument proving the Lord Jesus the only God... 151
Christ is worthy of all honor........................... 154
If man evolved in time, why not God in eternity?........ 155
Scripture definition of the word "create"............... 158
What was the nature of the original matter?............. 161
The Atomic Theory exposed............................... 162
Changes of matter by the mind of God.................... 164

CHAPTER VI.

Mind, molecules, and the imponderable agents............
How came the atoms to be endowed with gravity?.......... 166
Man's physiological superiority compared................ 168
Power mental—Its conditions and philosophy.............. 170
The food of plants not in nature........................ 172
The vegetable primordial a perfect plant................ 174
The formation of the first plant an effect.............. 176

TABLE OF CONTENTS.   xvii

PAGE

Plant absorption of carbonic acid makes the wind blow..... 179
Why skeptics and scientists are driven to absurdity........ 181
The progenitors of each species perfect at first............ 185
The mischief of attributing results to "the laws of nature." 189
Nothing imponderable : the proof test.................... 192
Friction the law of heat and light : both matter........... 194
All organic bodies have atmospheres..................... 198
Temperature the universal agent of nature................ 200
Heat the law of motion and gravity....................... 203

CHAPTER VII.

Limit of human conception............................... 205
Electricity a created substance........................... 207
Electric attraction and repulsion of the Solar System....... 209
Electricity contains the elements of all bodies............. 211
Magnetism the agent of mind............................ 213
Inanimate things perform intelligent locomotion........... 216
Experiments by Dr. Bell................................. 218
A table moves without human contact.................... 220
A reflection from such teaching.......................... 221
Nature does not reveal the moral character of God......... 224
Man the natural image of God........................... 225
Personality of God revealed by that of man............... 228

CHAPTER VIII.

Spurious data of geological calculation................. ...
Six 24 hour days ample for the world's creation........... 230

	PAGE
The evolution world-maker enslaved by his work	232
How much of the solar system it takes to clothe and feed man	234
The carboniferous period never existed	236
The original soil a creation	238
"The world to come," solves the mystery of this	241
All appearances of the world prove its existence temporary	243
Dr. Coan's calculations erroneous	247
When geologists began to be skeptical	250
Another theory of the age of Niagara	253

CHAPTER IX.

Darwin's sophistry exposed	256
Darwin begs the question	259
There never was a natural atheist or evolutionist	261
The wonders of incubation	264
Extreme changes in organic things sudden	265
History of the coffee plant	268
If evolution were true, all plants would be produced in all countries	270
Philosophy of peculiar human features	274
Animal variations caused by climate	276
Darwin's defective reasoning	278
The most civilized would not survive	280
Their own arguments prove evolution impossible	284

CHAPTER X.

	PAGE
Defective geological data—Transparent collusion	288
Hard pressed for evidence	290
A clear case of collusion, or fraud	293
Lyell summoned to estimate the age of the skulls	296
The oil fountains proved to be creations	298
The gravel and boulder deposits by the flood	301
Lyell's ignorance or arrogance	301
Rapid changes in short spaces	304
The contest for survival between the oak and the beach	306
Better testimony than that of Lyell	308
Rapid changes of deposit	310
The Loess proves the existence of the flood	312
The chalk argument stated	313
The argument unscientific	315

CHAPTER XI.

Professors Huxley's and Tyndall's materialism false science	317
Huxley's definition of evolution	317
Conditions of life	318
The primordial a perfect creation	321
The wonderful structure of the lungs	324
Amount of the flow of blood	325
Philosophical necessities bringing the primordial into existence	327
Nature incapable of producing life	330
Similar appearance no proof of species	332

	PAGE
Prof. Tyndall's Belfast speech reviewed......................	334
Tyndall abandons disguise and becomes atheistic...........	336
Modern scientists quote heathen philosophers as guides....	338
Evolution degrades its defenders..............................	340

CHAPTER XII.

Prof. Proctor's Nebulous Fiery Origin of the Solar System unscientific...	345
The nebular hypothesis stated...............................	347
Facts of natural science prove the nebular hypothesis false.	350
Nebular matter vapor—It could not burn...................	352
If homogeneous, could not burn............................	354
If liquid fire, the earth cooled first in the center...........	357
Laws governing magnetics...................................	360
All power is mental...	363
Relation of cause and effect demonstrate creation..........	365

CHAPTER XIII.

Psychologic transmission of disease.......................	
Contiguity produces races..................................	370
Comparative order of mind................................	373
Mr. Darwin's shallow reasoning...........................	377
How the eyeless animals became such....................	379
The absurdity of natural selection........................	383
Mr. Darwin prophesies that all will be evolutionists.......	385

	PAGE
Nature cannot be arrayed against herself	387
Man one of God's machines	391
Tyndall's admiration of his ancestral matter	393

CHAPTER XIV.

Deterioration, not progress, the order of nature	396
Diseased air and mental impression	398
An approaching crisis	410
Evolution atheistic science	412

CHAPTER XV.

National degeneracy the voice of history	
Darwin's assumptions refuted	414
Heathen philosophy corruptions of Scripture	419
Lyell's inconsistency in ignoring the Bible record	423
National progress not the rule	426
Rome never equaled Greece in virtue or intelligence	429
A people never rise above their religion	433
Plato's doctrine of the divine essence, deism	435
Cook, of Boston, adopts Plato's doctrine of " life."	438
Cookism destroys moral responsibility	441
The lower animals depend upon man for subsistence and existence	444
The world with man extinct	447

INTRODUCTION.

IF the searcher after truth succeeds in compassing his object, he must divest himself of every prejudice and preconceived opinion, whether they have been adopted on the principle of authority or have resulted from his own investigations. This must be done at least to an extent that will not bias his mind in reaching conclusions. Hence an author may differ with every previous writer upon the same subject as well as with what he himself has written. Instead, however, of such a course being in the least degree reprehensible, it deserves the highest praise ; and he who does not merit it is a mere unprogressive petrifaction in the world of mind. The only conception of truth commensurate with its native dignity is that it comprehends the facts, phenomena, and object of the universe ; at least those connected with our world.

One of the commonest errors into which scientists and theologians have fallen has been the practice of blindly following each other, not in the examination of the evidences or processes by which previous authors arrived at conclusions, but by the adoption of the conclusions themselves. In order to avoid such a course only one way is open, and that is independent and impartial investigation.

If the supposition were admissible, that the authors of the works on science, systems of philosophy, or the theology of the past, were better qualified to form correct opinions than those of the present, then might there have been none but the first book on each subject written; but if the thought of the world cannot afford to be thus hampered, then such opinions, from whatever source they may have originated, should not be considered as a feather's weight in defense of any theory. That which alone has importance to us is, What evidence do they give, and are their reasonings conclusive? God has invested every man with the prerogative of judging for himself, and holds him responsible for its judicious exercise. The concurrent opinions, therefore, of all the geological evolutionists of all time, to the effect that the world came into existence by what are called "the laws of nature," furnish not a particle of evidence in support of such a theory; and yet Sir Charles Lyell fills a large portion of his "Principles of Geology" with quotations from ancient and modern writers on natural science, as authority for some of the most important principles he attempts to defend, even quoting from heathen deities. Take the following as an example: Vishnu, one of the persons in the Brahma or Hindoo deity, assumed the form of a fish, a tortoise, and a boar, of which Lyell says, "Extravagant as may be some of the conceits and fictions which disfigure these pretended revelations, we can by no means look upon them as a pure effort of the unassisted imagination, or believe them to have been composed without regard to *opinions and theories* on the observation of nature."

Of course this is not imagination, though mere nonsense, for it presents Darwin's theory of the evolution of the organic world, now adopted by Lyell. The boar was once a tortoise, the tortoise a fish, and the fish was the deity. While such has been the history of scientific discussions, so provocative of opposition, and though theology has been equally narrow in its conceits—adopting many of its tenets from heathen authors—as well as intolerant in its spirit, it has this example as its apology. The above remark of Lyell pays more respect and expresses more confidence in this opinion of a scribe of a heathen deity than can be found in his whole book in regard to the revelations of Moses, or of the living God of Moses.

No Antagonism between Science and Scripture.

The unnatural warfare against real science and philosophy—which simply means the methods of God in the physical world—can have no justifiable defense except on the preposterous supposition of antagonism in revealed truth, or that the works and teachings of God are hostile to each other, and also to himself. Those who entertain such a supposition have been either too indolent to study the book of nature, or too superstitious to learn the written book of God. Hence for many of the opinions of the theologians the Bible is no more responsible than is nature for the great mass of the opinions relating to the so-called sciences of geology and evolution. As the result of a conflict of such vast dimensions, is it wonderful that the religious world should have been cursed with its thousand years of "dark ages," or the modern scientific world with Lyell's geology and Darwin's evolution? The remedy for this evil is that such a knowledge of both the great books of Nature and the Bible shall be obtained as shall show them to be complements of each other, and therefore springing from a common source.

It is true that the theologians of our day have ostensibly repudiated the intolerance of the past; but in their new-born liberality they have adopted a sentiment still more pernicious and ruinous to the cause of Bible truth, namely, that it matters not what a man believes, if he is only sincere and honest in his faith.

If such is the fact, then it supercedes all further necessity of promulgating revealed truth, which comprehends the knowledge of God's designs with man and the world. So widely prevalent is this monstrous opinion, that when a discourse is to be delivered upon the revealed will of God, it is generally prefaced by an apology for preaching a doctrinal sermon. What would be thought of a teacher of science or philosophy who should be perpetually telling his pupils that it mattered not what were their scientific or philosophical views, or how widely those held by one might differ from those held by another, if they were only honest, sincere, charitable, and liberal minded?

Prof. Max Muller says: "The question of the descent of man may be called *the* question of the nineteenth century; and it requires all the knowledge of the century to answer it adequately."

Prof. Tyndall says: "The religious sentiment is the problem of problems of the present day."

Notwithstanding the difficulty and danger here expressed, and which no reflecting mind can fail to comprehend, the flippant saying is as ostentatious as it is common, "We have no fears for the success of Christianity," when the lamentable and momentous fact is, that Christianity fails in every instance by the adoption of any sentiment hostile to the Bible, as the man who adopts it fails to answer the end for which he was made; especially when he denies that God created him, and is not therefore the proprietor of his being, and he consequently owes Him no service. They seem to confound

Christianity with the systems and institutions of men, the very existence of which may be endangered by their organized opposition ; and because in some countries there is no such opposition, it is taken as evidence of its success ; while this very care of nations, giving it popularity, has been and is its most deadly enemy, corrupting it by the inculcation of the sentiment we have indicated, while on the other hand the fires of persecution have always proved the purification of its adherents.

The Necessity of Controversy.

Even the attempts to defend its truths by public controversy at the present day is supposed to injure them, while the example of its Founder, who provoked and engaged in controversy, stands out as one of the most conspicuous facts of his earthly history. He argued not merely with the learned Scribes, Pharisees, priests, and lawyers, but set forth his doctrines to so humble a listener as the "woman of Samaria;" the subject, too, in this instance being upon the nature of God and that of his worship. Whoever received a letter from the great Apostle of the Gentiles, or heard one of his public discourses, but heard and saw a continual stream of doctrinal controversy? Nor did he wait for the opposers of the gospel to begin the attack, but in obedience to the mandate of the Master, "Go ye into all the world, and preach the gospel to every creature," he carried the war into the camps and citadels of the enemy, disputing with the Platonic philosophers, superstitious Jews, and Pagan idolators, and never failing to produce conviction of the truth of his doctrine and of the divine authority of his mission. Nothing is more erroneous than the notion that controversy was to be limited to the first age after Christ's ascension. If it had Jews to convince then, it has more Jews now. If the gospel had Pagan idolatry to meet then, it has more Pagans now ; for in addition it has to encounter Mohammedans and Spiritualists. If it successfully met Grecian philosophy with the preaching of "Jesus and the resurrection," it has a more subtle philosophy to encounter now in the shape of evolution and geology ; the first claiming to have found the origin of the animal and vegetable life of the world in the simplest form of inanimate matter, while the second sees the nebulæ resolve itself into the solar system without the touch of an intelligent finger, thus presenting us with the most perfect form of materialistic skepticism.

"Prove all things ; hold fast that which is good."— PAUL.

COSMOGONY.

CHAPTER I.

INDEPENDENCE OF MIND NECESSARY TO ARRIVE AT TRUTH.

False Impressions of Human Knowledge and Learned Men.

THERE is, perhaps, no sentiment or supposition entertained by mankind which has acted so fatally against the progress of human knowledge and its general acquisition as its supposed profundity and vast extent, and that those esteemed learned men have explored this great ocean and made its lore their own. We do not speak of the facts of history, which to any considerable extent no man lives long enough even to read, but a knowledge of nature—her inorganic structure, organic classification, her motions; the laws by which they are governed; the nature of those laws; the extent of reciprocal dependence; the grand object her combined machinery accomplishes, and how all became endowed with these forces and susceptibilities; where is the limit between the natural (her capabilities) and the supernatural (that of which she is incapable): in a word, *the philosophy of science.*

Nomenclature—the simple names of things, either similar or dissimilar—is no part of this knowledge. A man might be able to memorize the name of every existing object, and yet not know the chemical relation of any two of them. Neither is mathematics a part of such knowledge. It is simply the art of using conventional signs whereby the comparative size, distance, and rapidity of the motion of the objects of nature may be ascertained and stated. A man may have in his memory the figures representing the sizes, distances from each other, and the velocities of every one of the objects of nature, and yet not have a knowledge of the peculiar qualities of any of these objects or of the influence which it is capable of exerting upon another, affecting its phases and motions, or have the least conception of the necessities involved as to the time or manner of such endowment. Indeed, there have been men who by mental arithmetic could solve any problem in figures put to them, and yet were almost idiotic upon every other subject, and utterly incapable of forming an abstract idea.

Nor is the commitment to memory of historic facts, knowledge; but this comes by thought, reflection, and investigation of the teaching of those facts by which the statesman learns by their repeated concurrence to depend upon them to produce substantially the same results. Hence we say "history repeats itself." Neither is language a part of such knowledge. It has been correctly said that "words are signs of ideas;" but it must be remembered that they are only such by conventionality. A child may learn to repeat words, and read them; and while others are able to comprehend the ideas thus conveyed, the speaker or reader may not apprehend a single one of the ideas himself. The art of language simply qualifies its possessor to obtain other men's ideas, spoken, written, or printed; and if a single one of these ideas were only contained in a book written in a language foreign to every living man, then it would be lost unless some one so far mastered that language as to be able to translate it into another which was known. But even this might be purely mechanical, so far as the translator was concerned. Language, therefore, can be considered in no other light than as a means of acquiring knowledge.

It is probably a fact that there is not an idea of any considerable importance, written or printed, as a part of human knowledge in any foreign language which has not been translated into English. It is not necessary, therefore, that an English student should study a dead language, or a living one other than his own, in order to be the most profound scholar, advanced scientist, and philosopher that ever lived. Indeed, if he excel as a linguist, as did Burritt, life is consumed, and no time is left wherein to acquire knowledge. It is clearly inferable from Burritt's biography that he could not make a public or private speech, unless it was first written, being so deficient in the practical use of his own tongue; and never did he pretend to have discovered a single idea in any foreign language or tongue which had not been already translated into English. We may state another important fact touching the subject, which is, that the last edition or work of a scientist or philosopher contains all he knows upon the subject; and we may go still further, and say that the last extended work of this character contains all the knowledge extant up to that time. In relation to the number and size of the books necessary to contain the whole of the knowledge thus discriminated, we have no hesitancy in asserting that it could be printed in a single volume not larger than Webster's Unabridged Dictionary. We will go still further, and say that the book may be cut down at least one-half by leaving out that part of so-called natural science and philosophy which is purely speculative, utterly destitute of evidence ; and further still it may be cut down one half more by leaving out the purely hypothetical which have not been established by logical argument or demonstration.

Here then is a book one fourth the size of Webster's Dictionary having ample space to print the full discussion legitimately connected with every phenomenon of nature, the known teaching of every fact, the relative chemical effects of all compound bodies, agencies of dissolution, specific gravities—in a word, the whole philosophy and science of the universe, including the necessities of its origin and that of the existence of its "Great Original." If this be so, then no man need be intimidated by the existence of vast libraries of books through which he must wade in order to have a perfect knowledge of everything known about the natural science and philosophy of the universe.

Ancient Philosophy, Science, and Libraries.

That the notion of the vast progress of modern science may be exposed by comparison, we introduce here a condensed view of what was known before the commencement of the Christian Era, and by heathen philosophers and scientists, which will also serve to confirm our position as to the limited compass in which it could all be written and printed. In the year 284 B. C. Ptolemy Philadelphus founded a library at Alexandria of 400,000 valuable books in manuscript, which was nearly destroyed when Julius Cæsar set fire to Alexandria, 47 B. C. A second library was formed from the remains of the first, at Alexandria, by Ptolemy's successors, consisting of 700,000 volumes, which was totally destroyed by the Saracens, by the command of Omar, A. D. 642.

Notwithstanding these vast collections of writings, it will be seen by what we are about to reiterate that all the real science, mixed with a vast proportion of speculation, was comprehended in a very few books.

Aristotle on Morality—Plato on Virtue.

"Lysis had the advantage of receiving the instruction of men of the first order both in genius and learning. Such were Isocrates and Aristotle, all friends of Apollodorus. One day Appollodorus thus addressed his son: 'Hitherto I have made no attempt to fortify you in virtue systematically; I have contented myself by making you practice it. It was proper to dispose your mind for the reception of these lessons, as we prepare the earth before we scatter the seeds by which it is enriched. You shall now call me to account for the sacrifices I have sometimes required from you; and I will enable you to justify to yourself those you may be obliged to make hereafter.'

" Aristotle had brought with him several works, some of which he had merely outlined, that treated mostly on the science of morals, and upon which he commented as he read: All modes of life, all our actions, have a particular end in view; and all those ends tend to one general object, which is happiness. It is not in the end we propose, but in the choice of means, that we deceive ourselves. How often do honor, riches, power, and beauty prove more hurtful than useful to us? How often has experience taught us that disease and poverty are not in themselves injurious. Thus, from the idea we form of good and evil, as much as from the inconstancy of our will, we almost always act without knowing what it is we ought most to desire, or what it is we ought most to dread.

"To distinguish real from apparent good is the object of morality, which unfortunately does not proceed like the sciences limited to theory. If we wish our decisions to be wise and just, let us consider our own feelings, and acquire a just idea of our passions, virtues, and vices. Of all the qualities of the mind, wisdom is the most eminent, and prudence the most useful. As there is nothing so great in the universe as the universe itself, the sages who ascend to its origin, and study the incorruptible essences of all beings, are entitled to the first rank in our esteem. Such were Anaxagoras and Thales. They have transmitted to us admirable and sublime ideas, but which are of no importance to our happiness; for wisdom has only an indirect influence on morals: wisdom consists wholly in theory, prudence in practice. [Xenophon says Socrates gives the name of wisdom to the virtue which Aristotle here calls prudence. Plato likewise occasionally gives it the same appellation.] .

Wisdom and Virtue Contrasted.

"In a family we see the master confide to a faithful steward the minute particulars of domestic government, that he may apply himself to more important affairs. Thus wisdom, absorbed in profound meditations, relies on prudence to regulate our propensities, and to govern that part of the soul in which, as I have said, the moral virtues reside.

"This moral part of the soul is continually agitated by love, hatred, anger, desire, fear, envy, and a multitude of other passions, all the seeds of which we bring into the world. Their motions, which are caused by the attraction of pleasure or fear of pain, are almost always irregular and fatal. In the same manner as the want of exercise or the excess of it destroys the body, so does a passionate emotion, either too weak or too violent, lead astray the mind, leaving it short of or urging it beyond the mark it ought to have in view; whilst a well regulated emotion conducts it naturally to the object. It is the medium therefore between two vicious affections that constitutes a virtuous sentiment. Let us give an example: Cowardice fears everything and errs by deficiency; presumption fears nothing and errs by excess; courage, which adopts the medium between the two, fears only when it is necessary to fear. Thus, passions of the same nature produce three different affections, two vicious and one virtuous. Thus do moral virtues arise from the very bosom of the passions, or rather they are no other than passions restrained within due limits.

"Aristotle now showed us a writing in three columns, where most of the virtues were placed between two extremes: liberality between avarice and prodigality; friendship between aversion or hatred and complaisance or flattery, etc. A man may be more or less cowardly, more or less liberal, but there is only one manner in which he can be perfectly liberal and courageous; accordingly we have very few words to signify each virtue, but a considerable number for every vice. Hence the Pythagoreans say that evil partakes of the infinite and good of the nature of the finite. But by what means shall we discover this good, which is almost imperceptible amid the evils that surround it? Prudence, which I shall sometimes call reason, because, uniting the light of experience to the natural light of reason, it rectifies the one by the other. The function of prudence is to point out to us the path in which we are to walk, and to restrain as much as possible such of our passions as might induce us to wander from it.

"Prudence on all occasions deliberates on the advantages we should pursue, advantages difficult to know, and should be relative not only to ourselves but to others. Deliberation should be followed by a voluntary choice, without which it would deserve only pity or indulgence. The choice is free whenever we are not constrained to act against our judgment by external force, or hurry away by inexcusable ignorance. Thus an action, the object of which is honorable, should be preceded by deliberation and by choice to make it, properly speaking, an act of virtue; and this act, by frequent repetition, forms in our mind a habit which I shall call virtue. Nature neither gives nor denies us any virtue: she grants us only faculties, leaving the use of them to ourselves. And while she has sown in our hearts the seeds of every passion, she has implanted likewise those of every virtue. We receive, consequently, at our birth an aptitude more or less approaching a virtuous disposition, a propensity more or less strong toward what is good and just.

"Hence we perceive an essential difference between what we sometimes denominate natural virtue and virtue properly so called. The former is that propensity I have mentioned; a sort of instinct, unenlightened as yet by reason, wavering between good and evil; the latter is the same instinct, constantly directed toward good by right reason, and always acting with knowledge, choice, and perseverance. I conclude from hence that virtue is a habit formed, in the first instance, and afterward guided by prudence, or a natural impulse toward good, transformed by prudence or reason into habit. It is in our power, then, to become virtuous, since we all possess the possibility to become so; but it does not depend on us to become the most virtuous of men, unless that individual has received from nature the disposition requisite to such a degree of perfection.

"Since prudence, or right reason, forms in us the habit of virtue, all the virtues become her work; whence it follows that in a mind docile to her dictates not a virtue but presents and places itself in its proper rank, and not one will be found in opposition to another. In such a mind, too, we must discover a perfect harmony between reason and the passions, since the former commands and the latter obeys.

"If such virtue be not yet matured, the sacrifice it may require will afflict us; if complete, those sacrifices will afford us the purest joy; for virtue has its voluptuousness. It is impossible for children to be virtuous, as they are unable to distinguish or prefer real good; yet as it is essential to cherish in them the propensity to virtue, they should be early accustomed to virtuous actions.

Difference between Natural and Moral Virtue.

"Let us consider virtue in its relation to ourselves and others. The virtuous man finds his enjoyment in dwelling and living with himself. You will find in his soul neither the remorse nor tumult which agitate the vicious. He is happy in the recollection of the good he has done, and in the prospect of that he may yet do. He enjoys his own esteem by obtaining the esteem of others; he seems to act only for them. His whole life is spent in useful activity; he therefore possesses happiness, which consists only in a series of virtuous actions. This is the happiness arising from an active life dedicated to the duties of society. But there is another kind of happiness of a superior order, exclusively reserved for the small number of sages who, far from the tumult of worldly affairs, resign themselves to a life of contemplation.

"In the conversations held in presence of Lysis, Isocrates pleased his ear, Aristotle enlightened his mind, and Plato inflamed him. Plato sometimes explained to him the doctrine of Socrates, or laid before him his own ideal republic; at others, he made him sensible that no real elevation, no perfect independence can exist but in a virtuous mind; that happiness consists in the knowledge of the sovereign good, which is no other than God. Thus, while other philosophers held out no recompense for virtue but the public esteem and the transient happiness of this life, Plato presented him with the nobler support of that promised in the future. Virtue, says he, proceeds from God; you can only acquire it by knowing yourself, by obtaining wisdom, and preferring yourself to what only appertains to you.

God the Measure of Everything Good and Grand.

"Follow me in my reasoning, Lysis. Your person, your beauty, your riches, are yours, but do not constitute you. Man consists wholly in his soul [himself]. To learn what he is and what he ought to be, he must consider himself in his intellectual powers—in that part which sparkles a ray of divine wisdom, a pure light, which will insensibly lead him to the source from whence it emanates. When he has fixed his eyes on this, and shall have contemplated that eternal standard of perfection, he will feel that it is most important to his interest to imitate it in his own conduct, and to assimilate himself to the divinity, at least so far as it is possible for so faint a copy to approach so sublime a model. God is the measure of everything; there is nothing good or estimable in the world but what has some conformity to him. He is sovereignly wise, holy, and just; and the only means of resembling and pleasing him is by filling our minds with wisdom, justice, and holiness. Called to this high destiny, place yourself in the situation of those who, as the sages say, by virtues unite the heavens with the earth. Let your life afford the happiest conditions to yourself, and the sublimest spectacle to others—that of one in whom all the virtues are in perfect harmony.

"I have often spoken to you of the consequences arising from these truths, bound together, if I may venture the expression, by reasons of iron and of adamant ; but I must remind you, before I conclude, that vice, besides that it degrades, is sooner or later consigned to the punishment it merits. God, as it has been said before our time, passes through the whole universe, holding in his hand the beginning, the middle, and the end of all beings. Justice attends his steps, ready to punish offenses committed against the divine law. The humble and modest man finds his happiness in observing this law : the vain man disregards it, and God abandons him to his passions. For a time he retains his consequence in the eyes of the vulgar, but vengeance quickly overtakes him ; and if she spares him in this world she pursues him with redoubled fury in the next. It is not therefore by obtaining honors and the applause of men that we should endeavour to distinguish ourselves, but by laboring for the approbation of that dreadful tribunal which shall judge us hereafter.

"Such were the discourses of Plato and Aristotle.

"Pisistratus, two centuries past, had collected a library and opened it to the public, but it was afterward carried away by Xerxes into Persia. In my time several Athenians had collections of books ; but the most considerable was that of Euclid [Euclid lived three hundred years before the Christian Era], who had received it from his ancestors, and who was worthy to possess it, since he understood its value. On entering this library I was struck with surprise and pleasure. I found myself in the midst of the greatest geniuses of Greece, living in their works, with which I was surrounded. Their very silence increased my respect. An assembly of all the sovereigns of the earth would have appeared to me less awful, and I exclaimed, How much knowledge is here, which is denied the Scythian! I have since said, more than once, Alas! how much knowledge useless to man!

Library of Euclid. How they Made Books.

"I shall not speak of all the various kinds of substances which have been used to write upon. The skins of sheep and goats, and various sorts of linen, were successively employed. Paper has since come into use, made from the interior filaments of the stalk of a plant which grows in the marshes of Egypt or amid the stagnant waters left by the Nile after its inundations. It is made up into rolls, at the extremity of which is suspended a ticket containing the title of the book. The rolls are written only on one side, and to accommodate the reader are divided into several compartments or pages. There are copyists by profession, who pass their lives in transcribing the works which fall into their hands; and others, for the sake of information, take this trouble on themselves. Demosthenes told me one day, that, in order to form his style he had eight times transcribed the history of Thucydides with his own hand. Copies are multiplied by this means, but are seldom very common, being expensive—a circumstance which greatly retards the progress of knowledge. I have known Plato to pay a hundred mine (£375 sterling) for three small treatises by Philolaus. The Greeks are versed in every species of literature, as will appear by the accounts I am about to give of the library of Euclid.

"I shall begin with the class of philosophy. The works of this class date no higher than the age of Solon, who lived near two hundred and fifty years ago. Prior to that time the Greeks had theologians, but no philosophers. Little anxious to study nature, the poets collected, and in their works gave a sanction to the reigning falsehoods and superstitions of the people. But in the time of this legislator, and toward the fiftieth Olympiad, an astonishing revolution took place in the minds of men. Thales and Pythagoras laid the foundation of their philosophy; Cadmus of Miletus wrote history in prose; Thespis first gave a settled form to tragedy, as did Susarion to comedy. Thales of Miletus in Ionia, one of the seven sages of Greece, was born in the first year of the thirty-fifth Olympiad. In the early part of his life he filled with distinction the employments to which he was called by his birth and wisdom.

"A thirst for knowledge soon induced him to travel into foreign countries. On his return, devoting himself exclusively to the study of nature, he astonished Greece by predicting a solar eclipse, and communicated the knowledge of geometry and astronomy, which he had acquired in Egypt. He enjoyed his reputation in peace, lived free, and died without regretting life. In his youth his mother pressed him to marry, and again repeated her solicitation several years after. The first time he said it was too soon; the second time, it was too late. Many of his sentences are still remembered, which I shall repeat, as they may give an idea of his philosophy, and show with what precision the sages of that age endeavored to answer the questions proposed to them. What is it that is most beautiful? The universe, for it is the work of God. What is the most powerful? Necessity, because it triumphs over all things. What is the most difficult? To know one's self. What is most easy? To give advice. What is there that can best console us in misfortunes? The sight of an enemy more unfortunate than ourselves. What method must we take to lead a good life? To do nothing we would condemn in others. What is necessary to happiness? A sound body, an easy fortune, and an enlightened mind.

"Celebrated as the name of Pythagoras is, the particulars of his life are little known. It appears that in his youth he took lessons of Thales and Pherecydes, of Ayros; that he afterward resided a long time in Egypt, and if he did not actually visit the kingdoms of Upper Asia, he had at least some knowledge of sciences cultivated in those countries. The profoundness of the Egyptian mysteries, and the abstract meditations of the sages of the East were equally well adapted to inflame his ardent imagination, as the austere mode of life which the greater part of them had embraced was congenial with the firmness of his character. On his return to his country, finding it enslaved by a tyrant, he went far from slavery to settle at Crotona, in Italy. This city was then in a deplorable situation; the inhabitants, vanquished by the Locrians, had lost all sense of their native powers, and sought no other resource under their misfortunes than the excess of pleasure.

Pythagoras—his Learning, Persecution and Death.

"Pythagoras undertook to reanimate their courage by recalling to their memory their ancient virtues, and his instructions and example brought about their reformation. He endeavored to render the good he had effected permanent, by educating the youth in the principles to which he owed his success. Knowing that nothing inspires more energy in a state than wisdom and purity of morals, nor in an individual than perfect self-denial, he planned a system of education, which, to render the mind capable of receiving truth, taught it to be independent of the senses; and he founded that celebrated institution which still stands pre-eminent among all other philosophical sects.

"Toward the end of his life, and in extreme old age, he had the affliction to see almost all that he had done rendered ineffectual by the jealousy of the leading citizens of Crotona. Obliged to take flight, he wandered from town to town until death terminated his misfortunes, reduced envy to silence, and procured honors to his memory, which were carried to an extravagant length from the remembrance of the persecution he had suffered. The Ionian school owes its origin to Thales; the Italian to Pythagoras: both of these schools have given birth to others, which have all in their turn produced great men. Euclid, when collecting their productions, had been attentive to rank them according to the different systems of philosophy. After some treatises, which were attributed to Thales, followed the works of those who have taught his doctrine, and were successively at the head of his school. These were Anaximander, Anaximenes, Anaxagoras, who first taught philosophy at Athens, and Archelaus, who was the first master of Socrates. Their writings treat of the formation of the universe, or the nature of things, of geometry and astronomy.

Socrates' Manner of Teaching.

"The different works that next followed were more

connected with morals; for Socrates and his disciples bestowed their attention less on nature in general than on man in particular. Socrates has left nothing in writing but a hymn in honor of Apollo, and some fables of Æsop which he put into verse while he was in prison. I found here both these little pieces, with the works that have proceeded from his school. The latter are almost all in the form of dialogues, in which Socrates is the principal interlocutor, it being the object of his disciples to record his conversations. I saw the dialogues of Plato, Xenophon, etc. The Italian school has produced a much greater number of authors than the Ionian. Besides treatises ascribed to Pythagoras and which do not appear to be authentic, Euclid was in possession of almost all the writings of the philosophers who have followed or modified his doctrine. The Italian school, he said, had diffused more knowledge over the world than the Ionian, but it had committed errors from which its rival was exempt. The two great men who founded them stamped the character of their genius on their works: Thales, distinguished for profound sense, had for his disciples sages who studied nature in the simplest manner; and his school produced Anaxagoras, and the soundest theology; Socrates, the purest morals.

"Pythagoras, under the influence of a lively imagination, established a sect of pious enthusiasts, who at first beheld nothing in nature but harmonies and proportions; and passing from one species of fiction to another, gave birth to the Elean school and the most abstract metaphysics.

Discourse of Callias in Euclid's Library.

"The works of these writers were also accompanied by many others: and whilst I was congratulating Euclid on possessing so valuable a collection, I saw a man, venerable from his countenance, his age and deportment, enter the library. His hair flowed upon his shoulders, and his brow was bound with a diadem and a crown of myrtle: this was Callias, the hierophant, or high priest of Ceres, the intimate friend of Euclid, who introduced me to him. After some moments' conversation, I returned to my books with an eagerness which did not escape Callias. He asked me whether it would give me pleasure to acquire some idea of the doctrines they contained. I will answer you with vivacity, as one of my ancestors formerly did Solon: I have quitted Scythia, I have traversed immense countries, and braved the tempest of the Euxine Sea, only to come and seek instruction among you. I am going to devote myself to these writings of your sages: and from their labors shall undoubtedly learn those sublime truths essential to the happiness of man. Callias smiled at my determination, whether with a mixture of compassion or not, we shall judge by the following discourse.

"'I once dreamed,' said Callias, 'that I was suddenly transported into a high road, in the midst of an immense multitude, composed of persons of all ages, sexes, and conditions. We pressed forward with rapid steps, each with a bandage over his eyes; some uttering shouts of joy, but the greater part oppressed with chagrin and weariness. I interrogated those around me; and was answered by some, We are as ignorant as yourself, but we follow those who go before us, and others follow us. Some again replied, What signify these questions to us? You see these people who press upon us, and we must on our part repulse them. Those who were more enlightened said, The gods have ordained us to run this race, and we obey their commands, without either participating in the idle joy or sharing in the fruitless sorrow of the multitude. I was hurrying away with the crowd, when I heard a voice exclaiming, This is the path of knowledge and of truth. I turned and hastily followed it, when a man, seizing me by the hand, took off my bandage and led me into a forest, where I could see no better than when I was blinded. We soon lost all traces of the path in which we were before, and met with a great number of persons who had likewise lost themselves. The guides of each never fell in with one another without coming to blows, for it was the interest of each to seduce as many followers as possible from the rest; they carried torches in their hands, and kept shaking them in order to dazzle us with the sparks. I often changed my conductor, and as often fell among precipices; frequently, too, I found myself stopped by a thick wall, in which cases my guides disappeared, leaving me in all the horror of despair. Exhausted by fatigue, and lamenting I had ever quitted the road followed by the multitude, I awoke.

"'O my son,' pursued Callias, 'men lived for many ages in a state of ignorance which left their reason at peace! Contented with the confused traditions transmitted to them concerning the origin of things, they lived happy without seeking to enlarge the sphere of their knowledge. But for these last two hundred years, agitated by a secret inquietude, they have endeavored to penetrate the mysteries of nature, of which they had heretofore entertained no doubts; and this new malady of the human mind has substituted great errors for great prejudices. When it was discovered that the Supreme Being, the universe, and man, were sublime objects of meditation, the mind of the observer seemed to acquire new elevation: for nothing inspires more elevated or more extensive ideas than the study of nature; and as the ambition of the mind of man is as active and insatiable as that of the heart, they wished to measure space, to fathom infinity, and to pursue the windings of that chain which in the immensity of its folds embraces all things and beings.

"'In examining this enormous collection before us, where excess of delirium is joined to the depth of wisdom, where man has at once displayed the strength and weakness of his reason, remember, my son, that nature is concealed under a veil which the united efforts of man can never penetrate ; and that the science of philosophy consists in discerning the point where mystery begins and its wisdom in revering that mystery. Ask the different philosophers, What is God? they will answer you, That which has neither beginning nor end ; a pure spirit ; a subtle matter—air ; a fire endowed with intelligence ; the world—no, the soul of the world to which he is united, etc. O, my son ! adore God, and seek not to know him. Waste not your time in studying the nature of the universe, but employ it as becometh you, and worthily fulfill the little space that is allotted you. Ask them, What is man ? they will answer, Man exhibits the same phenomena and the same contradictions as the universe, of which he is the abstract.

The Ideas invented by Men a Real Dearth.

"'The abundance of ideas which men have invented on the most important subjects of philosophy is in effect a real dearth ; and that pile of learning you have before your eyes, those pretended treasures of sublime knowledge, are nothing more than a wretched heap of errors and contradictions. O my son, what strange knowledge have these celebrated men, who pretend to have brought nature under subjection ! How humiliating would be the study of philosophy, if, after beginning with doubts, it must terminate in parodies! Let us, however, do justice to those who have advanced them. In general they loved and sought the truth; and thinking to discover it by means of abstract ideas, they were led astray by too implicitly following reason, with whose boundaries they were unacquainted.

"'It still remains for me to mention to you a system, as remarkable from its singularity as from the reputation of its author. The vulgar see nothing round the globe they inhabit but a vault shining with light during the day, and sparkling with stars during the night, and that these are the limits of the universe; but some of our philosophers acknowledge no bounds, and they have been enlarged in our time to a degree that overawes and terrifies the imagination. The first idea was that the moon was inhabited: afterward that the stars were so many worlds, and that the number of these worlds must be infinite, since none of them could serve as a boundary or circumference to the others. What an extensive view does this open at once to the human mind! How has this sublime theory aggrandized the universe in our eyes! Though we employ eternity itself to traverse the immeasurable space, still shall we find infinity! And if it be true that the mind expands with our ideas, and assimilates in some measure with the object it penetrates, how greatly must man pride himself in having fashioned what is in itself so inconceivably profound!'

"'Pride himself!' exclaimed I, 'and wherefore, most venerable Callias? My mind is overwhelmed at the very idea of this boundless greatness, before which all other greatness is annihilated. You, myself, all mankind, are no more in my eyes than insects in an immense ocean.'

"At these words Callias looked earnestly at me, and after a moment's reflection replied, ' My son, the insect which obtains a glimpse of such infinity partakes of the greatness which owerwhelms it." And, he might have added, because of the possession of this very faculty of observation, is absolutely greater than all this space and the inanimate, sightless, unknowing bodies within it: the comparative sublimity of the mechanism is displayed in the physiological structure of the most tiny animalcule that sees, feels, and moves of itself.

Euclid on Astronomy—Gravity—Earth a Sphere.

"'It must be allowed,' said Euclid, 'that we have made but few observations on this science, and still fewer discoveries in it. If we possess some accurate notions respecting the course of the stars, we owe them to the Egyptians and Chaldeans, who taught us to form tables which fix the periods of our public solemnities and of our rustic labors.'

"I testified my surprise that the Greeks, possessed of so much genius as they were, should be obliged to go in quest of information to distant countries.

"' Perhaps,' replied Euclid, ' we are not endowed with the talent of discovery, and our excellence may consist in embellishing and improving that of others. Besides, it is but lately that we have turned our attention toward the heavens, whilst the Egyptians and Chaldeans have persevered in calculating their motions for an incredible number of ages; and the decisions of astronomy must be founded on observations.'

"I requested he would give a general idea of the present state of the science. Euclid then took a sphere, and reminded me of the use of the different circles of which it was composed. He showed me a celestial planisphere, on which I discovered the principal stars distributed into different constellations. 'All stars,' added he, 'revolve in the space of one day from east to west round the poles of the earth. Besides this motion, the sun, the moon, and the five planets have another which carries them from east to west in certain intervals of time. The sun passes through the 360 degrees of the ecliptic in one year, which contains, according to the calculation of Meton, 365 days and 5-19 of a day.

"'Each revolution of the moon contains 29 days, 12 hours, 45 minutes. The 12 lunations consequently give 354 days, and something more than the third of a day. In our civil year, which is the same as our lunar, we neglect this fraction, and suppose only 12 months, some of 30, others of 29, and in all 354 days. We next make our civil agree with our solar year, by means of seven intercalary months, which in the space of seventeen years we add to the 3d, 5th, 8th, 9th, 10th, 16th and 19th years. We learned from the Babylonians,' continued he, ' to divide the day into twelve parts, varying in length according to the difference of the seasons. These parts or hours, which name we now begin to give them, are marked for every month, on dials, with the length of the shadow corresponding to each of them. You know that, for any given month, the shade of the gnomon, when a certain number of feet in length, gives such or such a time of the day before or after noon ; and that when any business is fixed upon for the morning or evening, we appoint the time by referring to the tenth or twelfth foot of the shadow ; and this is the origin of the expression, What shade is it ?

"'You know likewise that our slaves are sent from time to time to consult the public dial, to inform us of the hour. It has been remarked that, at the time of the solstices, the sun does not rise at the same point of the horizon; from whence it has been concluded that he has latitude as well as the moon and planets. The planets have celerities peculiar to themselves, and unequal years. Mercury and Venus complete theirs in the same time with the sun; Mars finishes his in two years, Jupiter in twelve, and Saturn in thirty. The moon borrows her light from the sun; the eclipses of the sun and moon no longer terrify the people, since our astronomers are able to predict them. It is demonstrated that some of the heavenly bodies are larger than the earth; but I know not whether the diameter of the sun be nine times greater than that of the moon, as Eudoxus has asserted.'

"After long traveling in the sky we returned to the earth. I observed to Euclid that we had not brought back many important truths after so long a journey. 'We shall be more fortunate, no doubt,' continued I, 'by confining ourselves to the globe we inhabit.' Euclid asked me how so ponderous a mass as the earth could maintain its equilibrium in the air. It is the same with the earth perhaps as the planets and stars. 'But,' said he, 'precautions have been taken to hinder them falling by attaching them to spheres extremely solid, but transparent; these spheres turn, and the heavenly bodies revolve with them, but we see nothing around us by which the earth can be suspended; why, therefore, does it not plunge into the depth of the surrounding fluid? Some say the reason is because it is not on every side environed by air; the earth is like a mountain, the foundations or roots of which extend themselves into the infinite profundity of space. We occupy the summit of this mountain, and may sleep in safety upon it. Others flatten the under part of it, that it may rest on a greater number of columns of air, or float upon the waters.

"'But in the first place it is almost proved to be of a spherical form; and if we make choice of air to sustain it, that is too weak; if of water, it may be asked, What does that rest upon? Our natural philosophers have lately discovered a more simple method of calming our apprehensions. By virtue of a general law, say they, all heavenly bodies tend toward one great point, which is the center of the universe, the center of the earth. All the constituent parts of the earth, therefore, instead of flying off from this center, are continually pressing against each other to approach it.'

What Euclid Knew of Geography.

"When I inquired what were the countries known to the Greeks Euclid wished to refer me to the historians I had read; but I urged him with so much earnestness that he at length continued as follows: 'Pythagoras and Thales first divided the heavens into five zones: two frozen, two temperate, and one extending to a certain distance on each side of the equator. In the last century Parmenides transferred the same division to the earth; and it is marked on the sphere you have before you. Man can only subsist in a small part of the surface of the terraqueous globe; the extremes of heat and cold not suffering him to inhabit the regions near the poles, or those adjoining to the equinoctial line; they have multiplied only in temperate climates. To the north of the Euxine Sea we find the Scythian nations, some of which cultivate the earth, and others wander over their vast dominions. The countries still further are inhabited by different nations and tribes, and among others by the Anthropophagi.' 'Who are not Scythians,' said I, eagerly. 'I know it,' replied he; 'and our historians have properly distinguished them;

beyond this barbarous people we suppose there are immense deserts.

"'To the east, the conquests of Darius have made us acquainted with the nations which reach as far as the Indus. It is said that beyond that river there is another country, as extensive as all the rest of Asia, which is India : a very small part of it is subject to the kings of Persia, who annually draw from it a considerable tribute in gold-dust; but of the rest we have no knowledge.

"'Toward the northeast, beyond the Caspian Sea, dwell several nations, the names of which have been transmitted with the additional circumstance that some of them sleep six months together. [This must have grown out of the six months polar nights.] You will judge from these stories of our geographical knowledge. To the westward we have penetrated as far as the Pillars of Hercules, and have a confused idea of the nation inhabiting the east of Iberia, but to the interior parts of the country we are utter strangers. Beyond these pillars is a sea called the Atlantic, which, from appearance, extends as far as the eastern parts of India. It is frequented only by the ships of Tyre and Carthage, which are afraid to venture out of sight of land. After passing the straits some of them go southward, and sail along the coast of Africa ; others again go northward, to exchange their merchandise for the tin of Capiterides islands, the position of which is unknown to the Greeks.

"' Several attempts have been made to extend geography to the southward. It is pretended that by order of Nicos, who reigned about two hundred and fifty years ago in Egypt, some vessels manned with Phœnicians took their departure from the Arabian Gulf, made the circuit of Africa, and returned after a voyage of two years to Egypt, by the Straits of Cadir [Cadiz] ; but these enterprises, supposing this account to be true, have been no further prosecuted. Commerce was unable to repeat such long and dangerous voyages, in the hope of precarious advantages. Merchants have contented themselves with frequenting the eastern and western coasts of Africa; and on the latter the Carthaginians have established a considerable number of colonies. It is asserted likewise that several great nations exist in that part of the earth, but we are not told their names. Our mathematicians pretend that the circumference of the earth contains four hundred thousand stadia. [A stadium is a furlong]. I know not whether the estimate be just, but I am very sure we are scarcely acquainted with one quarter of its circumference.'"

It may be said that astronomy was not materially advanced from the days of Euclid, 300 B. C., until the sixteenth and seventeenth centuries, by the appearance of Copernicus, 1530; Kepler, 1619; and Galileo, 1632.

We have in this brief sketch all the ideas of nature, which they call the "philosophy of science," entertained by these philosophical scientists. Aristotle's classification of animals, founded simply upon the possession of peculiar organic features, cannot properly be called natural science; the only natural science connected with organic existence is that of the identity and phenomena of species. The origin of species does not come within the limits of natural science, as nature had nothing to do with it—nature commenced when creation was finished. Thus there was a period of 340 years, from 640 B. C., the time of Thales, to 300 B. C., the time of Euclid, during which these seven most prominent students of nature in ancient times flourished : Solon, 562; Pythagoras, 500; Socrates, 432; Xenophon, 410; Plato, 388; Aristotle,

383 ; Euclid, 300. It is evident that each of these successive philosophers was acquainted with what his predecessors knew of nature ; and Euclid, the last, understood it all, and in his library it was all recorded in books. It is also a fact that all these men went to Egypt, and were schooled in the learning of the Egyptians. They were also well acquainted with the science and philosophy of the Persian and Chaldean shools : all of which was also conserved in the library of Euclid.

In the discourse of Callias, who had mastered the contents of these books, and knew the little of real worth they contained, when sifted from the mass of literary rubbish, we hear his decision, which cuts down the mass to such small dimensions that it could easily have been printed in an ordinary-sized book : we mean, what they contained of the true science and philosophy of nature. Says he, "In examining this enormous collection before us, the excess of delirium is joined to the depth of wisdom. Man here has displayed at once the strength and weakness of his reason, leaving nature concealed under a veil. The abundance of ideas which men have invented on the most important subjects of philosophy, *is in effect a real dearth ;* and the pile of learning you have before your eyes, those pretended treasures of sublime knowledge, are nothing more than a *wretched heap of errors and contradictions.*" If we compare Lyell's philosophy of the earth, called "Geology," with that of these philosophers, his is the "wretched heap ;" Darwin's "Descent of Man" with Plato's "Formation of the World," Darwin's is the "wretched heap," and Prof. Proctor's philosophy of astronomy, of fiery origin, with the astronomy of Euclid, Proctor's is the "wretched heap."

This then is all the knowledge the ancients had of natural science. We feel assured that no one will dissent from our conclusion, that as Lyell, Darwin, and Proctor are the most intelligent representatives of these different hypotheses, and their last defenders, that their writings contain all the ideas of natural science which have ever been entertained concerning the philosophy of nature, circumscribed within nature itself. If this be correct, we see that these books would form but an exceeding small library. But these must be still further cut down by leaving out all the speculations, all the opinions unsupported by evidence, all the quotations of each other as authority, and all the substantial repetitions they contain, and we hesitate not to say that a single book would contain what remains. From such data and calculation it is evident that all the real science and philosophy of the known facts of nature could be printed in a few small volumes.

In this chapter, therefore, we end where we began, by the opinion that were such a book published, men following the ordinary vocations of life would have ample time to make themselves masters of its contents, and therefore might be ranked as the most advanced scientists and philosophers of the present age, and therefore of the world. Let these men once rise to the dignity of conscious mental power, with brains sustained by strong muscular development, and it would be a fatal check to the groundless speculations of these scientific pretenders, whose ambition seems to be governed by no higher principle than that of public notoriety, and this at the expense of truth, and especially in opposition to the teachings of the Holy Scriptures.

CHAPTER II.

BIBLE STATEMENTS OF CREATION THE MOST ADVANCED SCIENCE.

THOUGH the ancient astrologists or astronomers were ignorant of the globular form of the earth, even down to a late day in Grecian history, yet this was stated to be its form in the Bible long before, and in such language as the following: "When he (God) prepared the heavens, when he set a *compass* upon the face of the earth" (Prov. 8 : 27); striking out its globular dimensions. "He sitteth upon the *circle* of the earth" (Isa. 40 : 22); then the earth was a sphere. "He walketh in the *circuit* of heaven" [atmosphere] (Job 22 : 14). Then it also was a circle. It is but a late discovery of science that the winds blow in circles, and that the great trade-wind of the torrid zone blows from the same quarter throughout the year: on the north side of the equator, in the direction of N.E. to S.W., and on the south side, from S.E. to N.W., showing that it moves continually in a circle, which movement is probably governed by the ecliptic motion of the earth. This scientific fact is stated in the Bible thus: "The wind goeth toward the south and turneth about unto the north; it whirleth about continually, and the wind returneth again according to his circuits" (Eccl. 1 : 6). When ancient astronomy was pressed with the question as to what the world stood on, it answered, Four elephants; and sometimes, On a great rock. When asked to explain what the rock stood on, the answer returned was such as the evolutionists give when asked, Whence came the primordial? "Why, rocks all the way down." The Bible statement, however, is unequivocal upon this phenomenon, and in perfect accord with the most advanced astronomical science of our day, giving expression to the wonderful results of universal gravity thus: "He hangeth the earth upon nothing" (Job 26 : 7). The running of locomotives and trains of cars is an event of such magnitude that it would be reasonable to expect that a Being who has caused the prominent events of human history to be written in advance would have made mention of it, and such is the fact; hence we read, "The chariots shall be with flaming torches, in the day of his preparation. The chariots shall rage in the streets. They shall jostle one against another in the broadways: they shall seem like torches, they shall run like lightnings" (Nahum 2 : 3, 4). It is not horses and chariots, but chariots which thus run.

The electric telegraph, the greatest scientific discovery of our age or of any other, is also of such importance to the world that it would be strange if no allusion should have been made to the possibility of sending lightning dispatches and returning answers. Hence God said to Job, "Canst thou send lightnings, that they may go, and say unto thee, Here we are. We answer the call, and are ready for the dispatch" (chap. 38 : 35). It is just as we might suppose: if the God of nature is the God of the Bible, then all of his statements are not only in harmony with each other, but are those of the most advanced science, whether of a moral, mental, physical, or religious character. But the impossibility of there being any community between the cosmological science of the Bible and evolution or chronological geology imposes upon those who believe in its system of revealed religion the necessity of entering the arena of scientific investigation, with a thorough knowledge of the questions it involves, that they may be able to say with Paul, "I am set for the defense of the gospel, and become able to defend it against all opposition."

Truth a System—One Department Explains Another.

Truth is a circle—a system requiring at least some knowledge of the whole in order to be able to comprehend any part; whence it follows that those whose researches have been confined to one of its divisions must be extremely liable to arrive at erroneous conclusions. For instance, man is constitutionally a moral and religious being as well as an animal; and as these several endowments indicate the object of his being, it follows that each must be studied if we would obtain proper views of his nature and destiny; and it is equally a fact that all these come within the scope of natural philosophy, and constitute the Science of Man. If this be so, we would ask, By what right is a man entitled to the distinction of an advanced philosopher or scientist whose investigations have been limited to the mere animal nature of man, which can be considered in no other light than the necessary foundation upon which is erected his intellectual and moral nature? What idea of a mansion could a man have whose mind was absorbed and contented with a knowledge of the foundation?

Nothing is more erroneous than the notion that the revealed religion of the Bible should be held responsible for and confounded with all the religious sentiments entertained in all time. The only question with which its defenders have to do is, "What saith the Scriptures?" "To the law and to the testimony, if they speak not according to this word it is because there is no light in them" (Isa.). In what an attitude would the philosophers and scientists of to-day appear were they held responsible for all the notions of the past called science and philosophy, or even for all those entertained at the present time? Is it possible to reduce all these so-called interpretations of nature to anything like a system?

So-called Science More Contradictory than Religion.

On the contrary it is an undeniable fact that what has been called philosophy from the dawn of civilization down to the present day reveals a more absurd and ludicrous picture than all the notions and theories entertained by the religionists of the world who claim the Bible as authority. The philosophers ask with an air of self-complacency, How are we to understand what are the teachings of the Bible amid such diversity of interpretation? But may we not retort with equal pertinency, What are we to receive as scientific truth—not to be modified or abandoned in the future—among the diversity of interpretations, held, too, by the most advanced scientists of the age, and relating to fundamental principles? As an example, take Sir Charles Lyell's last work, "Principles of Geology," between which and his former works there are palpable contradictions of the interpretations of nature. Which are we to receive as science? Among the many "geneses" of the world called science, which is the true one? One contends that our globe was once in a gaseous state: that by the gases entering into combination, evolving heat, a glowing, fusing, fiery mass was produced, which, whirling in space, and cooling, until a palpable crust was formed upon the surface, assumed the shape it now has. This then was the first genesis of the world, and was once believed by Lyell himself, and is the theory of Mr. Hopkins, of Cambridge, England, once president of the Geological Society. Next comes the evolution genesis of Darwin; and Lyell adopts that also. Now, which of these scientific interpretations of nature's method of bringing herself into existence are we to accept? There is also the glacial theory of Prof. Agassiz, which, if it did not bring the world into existence, brought it from a nascent state into a condition suitable for the abode of man, or showed it to have been in such a state while man inhabited it. Thus we have the self-burning, self-freezing, and the self-evolving genesis of the world from nebulæ; and Lyell has also adopted the ice-theory. Surely the men who thus differ in the interpretations of science should be the last to demand uniformity in the interpretations of revealed religion, or else reject the Bible altogether. Upon the same grounds and with greater consistency should not believers in the Bible reject all science until its professed defenders shall agree as to what it is? Instead of assuming such positions, scientists should study the Bible, and interpret it according to its own rules, without regard to the opinions of those who profess to believe it, requiring only that its author shall make himself understood. The same course should be pursued by religionists in investigating the phenomena of nature: dismissing all mere authoritative opinions, and with perfect independence search for facts in order to discover truth. To pursue any other course is certain to result in the unnatural disintegration of the grand circle of truth. We venture the opinion that when (if ever) both the written and phenomenal revelation of the world come to be understood, all will be found to be in the most beautiful harmony.

So far as man's eternal future is concerned the Bible makes it depend upon a resurrection from the dead, who are by that act endowed by their Maker with a perfect physical and an immortal nature, therefore one no more susceptible of death, consequently having "eternal life." This re-creation involves no greater knowledge or power than that necessitated in his original creation. Nor can such men as Lyell and Darwin with consistency object to this view of man's reproduction when they suppose that the human species has been exterminated and reproduced a number of times, and may be again, or give credit to the heathen philosophy to this effect. Now, if inanimate nature is able to accomplish such a work, cannot the great God re-create a man once, and so perfect that he will be exempt from the liability of death?

Scientists must not Ignore, but Prove the Bible False.

It is not enough that these scientists should ignore the Bible: they must demonstrate its teachings to be false by showing its statements touching nature to be absolutely contradictory to it, or, what is the same thing, that the text has been so corrupted by successive translations that it cannot be depended upon as the original revelation. Such a task, however, imposes not only the obligation to submit it to an impartial and thorough investigation, but to produce the original copies and manuscripts which have been thus corrupted, and even then these would be the true. The manner usually adopted by these scientists is that of piling up inference upon inference, conjecture upon conjecture, without the presentation of a principle by which their correctness may be tested. As an inducement to search the Scriptures we suggest that to their astonishment they will find, clearly recorded therein, the prominent events developed by the march of empire from the earliest times of authentic history even down to our own day, demonstrating these Scriptures to have emanated from a mind seeing the end from the beginning. Here, men of science, is indicated a standard of knowledge for your attainment, reaching which, you will be able to speak with authority, and understanding both sides of the questions involved in the discussion, earn for yourselves the distinguished title, Men of Science; but until this is accomplished should you not be a little more modest in so unceremoniously setting the Bible aside and of excluding God from his universe? You may also be assured that the day for the success of your speculation, falsely called science, is at an end, and that there are students who have a knowledge both of the Bible and nature, and are thus qualified to strip the sophistry from the teaching of your so-called facts, and to expose the collusion with which many more of them are connected. For those which remain—the facts of real science and philosophy—we have no fears that they will be found discordant with the truths of the Scripture.

If an infinitely wise Being inspired men to write the future history and destiny of the world, this certainly implies his ability to preserve the original manuscripts, by which the correctness of the translations which have been made may always be tested; at least those translations which, according to the history of making them, seem to be the furthest removed from the possibility of ignorant or designed corruption. If the author of the Scriptures has permitted the infusion of men's ideas with his own in this book, so as fatally to corrupt every copy, while the eternal destiny of man depends upon the correctness of the instruction therein contained, how can he avoid the severest reflections both upon his goodness and wisdom? If such a supposition cannot be entertained, and this record contains the reasons why it is that the world is deranged, and why its maker thus cursed it, and narrates the circumstances how it was done, and this exactly corresponds with such manifestations as are apparent in nature, then is it not clear that ignorance of this design and the history of its execution might lead to the erroneous supposition that it was always as physically deranged, including man, as now, and that as derangement at all is inconsistent with the wisdom displayed in its making, that it is improving and will become perfect? Hence the baseless theory of evolution. We are free to admit that if there can be produced a single fact in nature or philosophy in palpable contradiction to any statement or theory of this written revelation when expounded by itself, then such statement cannot be true, and the claim for its inspiration must be abandoned.

Radical Changes of Modern Science.

In order to show the radical changes through which the science of geology has passed, and the arrogant position assumed by Sir Charles Lyell in condemning the opinions of the earlier geologists for appealing to the Mosaic record of creation and the deluge in confirmation of their conclusions, we introduce the following from "Principles of Geology," p. 233:

"The earlier speculators in geology availed themselves of this as of every obscure period when the planet was in a nascent or half-formed state, or when the laws of the animate and inanimate world differed essentially from those now established; and in this, as in many other cases, they succeeded to no small extent in diverting attention from the class of facts which, if fully understood, might have led the way to an examination of the phenomena. At first it was imagined that the earth's axes had been for ages perpendicular to the plane of the ecliptic, so that there was a perpetual equinox and uniformity of seasons throughout the year ; that the planet enjoyed this 'paradisical' state until the era of the flood ; but in this catastrophe, whether by the shock of a comet or some other convulsion, it lost its equipoise, and hence the obliquity of its axes, and with that the varied seasons of the temperate zone and the long nights and days of the polar circle."

With reference to this opinion, we say, there is not the remotest ground for it in the Bible ; and the contrary is clearly implied. It is written (Gen. 1 : 14): "And God said, Let there be lights in the firmament of the heaven to divide the day from the night ; and let them be for signs and for *seasons*, and for days and years." Hence the days, seasons and years were the effect of the relative motions and positions of the sun and the earth ; the very fact of seasons presupposes a change of temperature, and as this change results from the increasing and decreasing obliquity of the earth to the sun, it must have occurred in the Eden world. It might have been increased at the flood, giving the polar circle its extreme long nights and low temperature, and we think it was ; not, however, by the shock of a comet or any other mysterious natural cause, but that the Being who made it thus cursed or deranged it for a purpose, which purpose is elsewhere revealed. The scientist, therefore, who held to the perfect equinox theory, did not understand the astronomical fact and philosophy here stated.

Lyell continues : "When the progress of astronomical science had exploded this theory, it was assumed that the earth at its creation was in a state of igneous fluidity, and that ever since that era it has been cooling down, contracting its dimensions and acquiring a solid crust,"

We may also remark, in regard to this supposition, that there is not in the Bible the least allusion to the world's ever having been in this state of liquid fire, which, if it existed, would have illuminated the surface of the earth more than a dozen suns.

Instead of this, it is stated that the first thing God created was light, which implies that all was dark before; and the normal temperature of dark matter is cold. Had the earth been a sphere of liquid fire, with its accompanying light, the first act of the Creator would have been to put out the light by quenching the fire, as he could not have created the world out of fire. If, therefore, those scientists who conceived and defended the gaseous, fiery geological theory, had consulted and followed the Bible account, they would have been saved from the blunder of adopting it.

One of these rash scientists was Lyell himself. He continues: "But the progress of geological investigation has generally dissipated this idea, at first so universally established. [It should be remarked, that what Lyell means by "*established*," is *believed* without evidence and afterward abandoned.] Should doubts and absurdities still remain, they should be ascribed to our limited acquaintance with the laws of nature, not to revolutions in her economy. [And his present idea of the laws of nature is that they existed before organized bodies and produced them, while the fact is, they grow out of the organizations themselves, whether of animate or inanimate nature, and the organizations were the work of the Creator, as we have shown elsewhere.] They should stimulate to further research, not tempt us to indulge our fancies in speculating about imaginary changes of internal temperature, or the unsettled state of the surface of the planet before it was prepared for the habitation of living beings." If Lyell and his school are thus unacquainted with the laws of inanimate nature, how much more must they be with those of living organic beings?

Again he says: "To return to the general argument pursued in this chapter, it is assumed, for the reasons above explained, that a slow change of species is in simultaneous operation everywhere throughout the surface of the habitable globe, of both sea and land. I shall now conclude the discussion of a question with which we have been occupied since the beginning of the first chapter—namely, whether there has been any interruption from the remotest periods of one uniform and continuous system of change in the animate and inanimate world. For this reason all theories are rejected which involve the sudden and violent catastrophes and revolutions of the whole earth and its inhabitants." Here we have the distinct and broad avowal that the geologists of the present day have rejected three of their own previously established theories of the genesis of the earth, and now reject all theories involving sudden and universal changes, and any others except those operating at the present day, of course carrying with it the Bible doctrine of the creation and flood; and it is these same slow changes, taking place every day around us, which brought the world into existence, as from remotest time there have been no other, or there never have been other changes than those now operating in nature. As, therefore, God is not now creating men, he never did create any; hence man owes him no worship, and is under no responsibility to him. Even if there is a God, he never had anything to do with the world.

The present position of science, being thus defined by its most advanced advocate, relieves us of all danger of misunderstanding its sentiments. This theory of slow uniformity which Lyell aims to establish from the beginning to the end of his book shows that the sole animating principle of what is now called the science of geology is that the world was never created, but evolved, with all its inhabitants, by just such movements as are now taking place everywhere on the globe. He appears also to be animated by the mere love of speculation, which, even if true, would be utterly incapable of conferring the least possible benefit upon mankind. On the other hand, by one fell swoop it destroys the only trustworthy record of historic man, relieving him from responsibility to any supposed proprietor of his being, and at death blots him out of existence. Hence geology does the same work as atheism to every man who adopts its conclusions. Such sentiments necessitate a defense of the Bible which shall render escape from the opposite conclusions impossible. To ignore the controversy is to yield the whole ground. How strange that such acknowledged blunders should be made the occasion of this arrogant onslaught! It however renders the task easier, turning, by the potent weapons of the revelations of nature and the Bible, its other speculations against the inventors.

In the work above referred to Lyell occupies a number of pages with extracts from ancient and modern authors whose opinions he places side by side with the records of Moses, attributing to him equally the authorship of what is there recorded, though Moses claims they were either written by the finger of God or spoken by his mouth. Lyell attempts to belittle the Noachian flood by giving accounts from heathen tradition of other floods, leaving us to infer that they are entitled to equal if not greater credit. If the dates fixed for the occurrence of these other floods and creations are subsequent to that given in Genesis for the deluge, then they are mere variations of its account; and every one of them is of later date! It must be remembered that the Hebrews alone of all nations had the Scriptures prior to the Christian era, except the Septuagint version from Hebrew into Greek, made at Alexandria 277 B. C. by order of Ptolemy Philadelphus, King of Egypt. Hence whatever discrepancies there may be between the heathen accounts of floods and that of Genesis, the latter should be taken as correct. The deluge occurred in the year 1556 of the world, and we propose to show that these scientists have overlooked, designedly or otherwise, the principal fact stated in this record, and which will be seen to account adequately for all the discoveries of geology. This fact is stated thus: "And the fountains of the great deep were broken up" (Gen. 7 : 11).

In order to form a proper idea of the magnitude of the effects produced on the globe by the deluge, it must be taken in connection with the work of the third day of creation, recorded thus: "And God said, Let the waters under the heaven be gathered together into *one place*, and let dry land appear; and it was so. And the dry land he called earth, and the gathering together of the waters he called seas." We understand this collection of the waters to have been in the heart of the earth. It is also referred to in the book of Proverbs (8 : 29) thus: "When he gave to the sea his decree that the waters should not pass his commandment: when he appointed the foundations of the earth." It is also made the burden of inspired song (Ps. 24 : 1, 2): "The earth is the Lord's, and the fullness thereof; the world, and they that dwell therein. For he hath founded it upon the seas, and established it upon the floods." If the Bible contemplated the world to be flat, these expressions might also conceive the water lying below and the earth above, but when, as we have seen, it recognizes the earth as being a sphere, then the *under* or *within* signifies its heart. Around this great fountain of seas or floods God laid the strata composing the crust of the earth, equally on every side, beginning with that the most firmly compressed, as the foundation next to the waters. At the creation everything was made in the most beautiful proportion. Every tree was rounded, with all its grains, or strata if you please, laid to correspond with its form ; and as the world is round, it is reasonable to suppose all its grains, layers, or strata were laid to conform to its shape, that of the greatest specific gravity occupying the lowest position ; and so in regular order each stratum of a lighter texture would superimpose, and so on until the soil was reached, as the lightest under the atmosphere. This order would also be followed in grading the density of the air, regularly diminishing in ascension until the highest ether was reached.

Scripture Account of Creation going back of Genesis.

This structure of the new-made world most beautifully corresponds with its primitive record as given by its author. It may not be generally understood, but there is an inspired account of creation contained in the 8th chapter of Proverbs, going still further back than that of Genesis, relating, however, exclusively to the inanimate earth, and particularly to its stratification and the collection of the matter from space, as the great chaotic deep out of which all things were afterward formed. This account forcibly sets forth the prior existence of God thus : "I was set up from everlasting, from the beginning, or ever the earth was." Genesis begins by admitting its existence, though devoid of any of the forms it was made to assume during the six days' work :

"When there were no depths." Genesis also admits their existence, thus: "And darkness was upon the face of the *great deep*." "When there were no fountains abounding with water." Genesis finds these also: "And the spirit of God moved upon the face of the waters."• "Before the hills or mountains were settled." To form these the Creator endowed every atom of the world with the two principles of gravity, or density, and chemical affinity. According to the first they sank to the greatest depth, and according to the second they adhered to each other, forming strata of varied texture. The account goes on: "While as yet he had not made the earth [this was the third day's work of Genesis], nor the open places, nor the highest parts of the dust of the world [the most ethereal gases], When he prepared the heavens [composed the atmosphere], When he set a compass upon the face of the depth [striking out the globular form of the world], When he established the clouds above [made the air to evaporate and hold water], When he strengthened the fountains of the *great deep;* when he gave to the sea his command that the waters should not pass; when he appointed the foundations of the earth." Here were the great fountains or seas confined within the foundations of the earth, and of course within its center, which foundations, forming the crust of the earth, were violently broken up at the flood by another command of the same being, letting the seas from the great fountain rush out to drown the world.

It will be seen that this account begins the order of the formation of the world with the substance called "the highest part of the dust of the world." These, being the gases, would be the first formation after electricity, which is a creation, because manifesting design and adaptation, as we have shown elsewhere by its being a universal agent. The gases must have been the first formation, as all things else are formed of them; and the gases were formed from electricity. The next formation of a more dense character is here called the "heavens;" or in Genesis, the "firmament," in which the birds flew, and which is the atmosphere; and as this is a combination of gases, it would be the next formation. When he strengthened the fountains of the deep, or condensed the waters, he formed them of the gases, and which would follow in the scale of specific gravity. The last formation mentioned in this wonderfully scientific account is, "the foundation of the earth." This was the granite, the hardest and heaviest stratum, incasing the waters equally on every side, and upon which every other stratum in the ascending scale was laid. Now as the lowest stratum was formed from the next immediately above, and so of each of the others, it must have contained all the chemical properties of that stratum, and so of each higher stratum, until electricity is reached, which we have shown contains all the chemical properties of all the other forms of matter in the universe, of course in their most sublimated state.

Manner of Creation—Chemical Endowment of Atoms by Mind.

We speak of these formations succeeding each other, but it is not necessary that the movement should have consumed successive periods, either longer or shorter. God issued his command to the great deep of chaotic fluid, and willed that certain work should be done, comprehended in the expression, for example, "Let dry land appear." Now by his own spirit-energy and according to his knowledge, he endowed every atom of this matter with peculiar chemical and electrical attractions and re-

BIBLE STATEMENTS OF CREATION.   73

sistances, and in degrees of more or less strength of affinity for each other, compelling those having the greatest amouut of adhesive force to combine, thus forming strata of the greatest specific gravity, while those having less of this force would form those of less firmness, etc. In this endowment there was another, providing for necessary classification. As the various combinations are composed of different proportions of the gases and electricity, their atoms must have been endowed by mental energy with these proportionate qualities, forcing them to seek their affinities, and thus, combining, formed all the compound substances of the world. It will be seen that every atom thus endowed would commence its motion at the same instant, thereby forming every stratum from the foundation rock to the surface soil simultaneously. Those particles endowed the most powerfully with chemical and electrical force would speed their way with the greatest rapidity to reach their equilibrium or center of gravity, and there, combining, be at rest. This endowment was the work of mind, giving rise to the motion of matter, while the motion was the birth of the laws of nature; but creation was first, and nature or the phenomena of matter followed, working out this inherent endowment. Here we are furnished with a historic genesis worthy of science, worthy of philosophy, and worthy the name and ability of its great Author.

The Eden World Destroyed by the Deluge.

From the creation up to the deluge the world was so beautiful in comparison with that which has survived that we are able to form but an imperfect view of it from its present appearance. That world was free from those derangements manifested in pestilential vapors, storms, hurricanes, lightnings, thunders, earthquakes, and meteoric disorder of every description. The equal distribution of land over the earth's surface prevented those extreme and sudden changes of temperature of which it is now susceptible. So luxuriant was the soil that it brought forth spontaneously whatever its inhabitants needed, or with just labor enough to give men healthy exercise. In a word, it was still the Eden-world —the blooming Paradise, in the eastern part of which was situated the Garden of Eden, the cradle of human kind. It is not wonderful that in such a world men should have attained a longevity ranging from five hundred to nine hundred years.

If we take thirty years, the length of a generation at the present day, and five hundred as the length of generations up to the flood, as the data of calculation, there would have come into existence seventeen generations of post-diluvians to one of ante-diluvians; and supposing all to have been equally prolific, the population would increase seventeen fold faster before than after the flood; and the age of the world before the flood, being about one-fourth of what it is now, would give about three times as many people living at the time of the flood as there are at present inhabiting the globe. Such also must have been the ratio of increase of all other animals as well as of vegetables.

In the destruction of the old world by the flood, all that was necessary was simply that the Being who made the "fountain of the great deep" should increase the temperature of the pent-up waters ten degrees, or less, and the entire crust of the globe would explode, whether it was one mile or one thousand miles in rocky thickness: indeed, nothing could withstand such a hydrostatic force. If it is desired to see what would be the appearance of the earth thus broken up, drill a hole in a round stone, fill it with water and plug the hole, then increase the temperature of the water by heating the stone, and the exploded fragments will give the result. If the pressure was equal on every side, the explosion would be universal and violent in proportion to the degree of the resistance.

The Geological Appearance Proves the Flood.

So, if the crust of the earth was thus broken up, no matter by what scientific cause, the land would as generally disappear by its submergence as the bulk of water in the globe was greater in proportion than the land ; all being hurled promiscuously together, the water, being of less specific gravity than many of the earthly strata, would prevail in greater excess upon the surface of the subsequent earth, the land sinking in whatever chasm opened for its reception. The locality and attitude of the rocks which had formed the beds of the rivers, lakes, and oceans would be changed, being found not only on the surface at the level of the sea, but forced up mountainously high, of course carrying with them the shells and fossils which had accumulated from the beginning of creation. These beds of shells might be found deposited in seams of any kind of rocky strata or mixed with other earths, as well as dividing different strata, one mass of displaced rock having been thrown upon another or turned upside down, the soil lying below and granite above. In these upheavals, corresponding to the depressions, sand-hills and other drift matter would be found upon the earth's surface at any altitude, cast up from water-bottoms. Hills of gravel would appear containing large boulders rounded by the violent commotion and rush of the waters during the one hundred and fifty days of the world-wide and world-deep deluge. There would also be found strata containing fossils adhering to and imbedded in them; for there must have been, then as now, rocky formations so soft that shells could imbed themselves in them while down deep in the earth, but which would almost immediately harden on being brought to the surface and in contact with the atmosphere. Rocks are now dug from quarries and used as building stone which, when first taken out, are so soft that they are sawed into squares almost as easily as clay, but by a few weeks' exposure to the air become as hard as limestone or granite. A house of worship in Ilion, New York, is built of such stone.

From such a breaking up of the crust of the earth it would also result that there would be subterranean streams, even rivers, running irregularly and promiscuously, and forming lakes, into whose basins would be carried and deposited drift of every description within their reach, which, opening into seas, would carry thence shells and fish and various other inhabitants and deposits of the waters.

Volcanoes and Earthquakes accounted for.

It is also evident that in volcanic localities sea and lake bottoms with their fossil accumulations might be thrown to the surface by volcanic action, the continuous commotion and friction of these vegetable and mineral substances setting free large quantities of gas, which would gather force until an earthquake and volcanic eruption would result, building up a mountain of lava.

From the subsidence of the deluge there would be produced great openings between hills and mountains, excavated by the dashing down from above the world of waters which by the fiat of God had belched forth from the "fountain of the great deep," and had deluged the world, covering its highest mountains. The surface rock thus cut might have been of the soft texture to which we have alluded, so that by these mighty torrents the deepest chasms on the surface of the earth might have been cut in a few days, before they had time to harden by atmospheric influence. This fact would always baffle the skill of man to estimate the time required to wear the chasm or the rocks, or to enable him to draw even an approximate inference founded upon any known phenomena of the ordinary movements of nature. Instead of being merely possible—this violent breaking up of the crust of the earth—every thing or appearance of nature goes to confirm it as a fact. One of the most prominent of these evidences is the attitude of the rocky strata of the earth. How seldom are any of these found lying upon a level with the plane of the earth's surface, which, no matter how or by what agency they were formed, would be their natural position. Instead of this they are found lying at every angle, and even standing perpendicular, as the Palisades on the Hudson River, which, however, is exactly what would have been the case if the strata had once laid on a level with the circle of the earth, and by some catastrophe involving a power equal to the effect had been broken up to give the waters within a free passage to the surface.

So great and universal was this catastrophe, deranging the whole geological structure of the globe, that we can by its present appearance form but an imperfect conception of its pristine regularity, symmetrical proportions, and finished workmanship. That such was the extent of its derangement by the deluge is confirmed by an inspired apostle, thus : " For this they willingly are ignorant of [including the geologists], that by the word of God, the heavens were of old and the earth standing in the water and out of the water [this comprehends the whole world]; whereby the world that then was, being overflowed with water, perished." (2 Peter 3 : 5, 6.) The supposition that the world only underwent a slight change by the deluge, or such as would follow a rain storm extensive enough to cover it with water, and then gradually subsided, there is no consistency or even truth in such a declaration. "The *world* that then was *perished*." Previous to the flood there were brooks, rivers, and large lakes called seas upon the surface of the earth; but from the brief history of the Eden-world with which we have been furnished it is fair to presume there was as much more land upon the surface in comparison with the water as there is now more water than land. In relation to this question we read : "And God said, Let the waters bring forth abundantly the moving creatures that hath life. And God created great whales and every living creature that moveth, which the waters brought forth abundantly after their kind, and fill the waters in the seas." (Gen. 1 : 21, 22).

Such was the condition of the world for the first 1,556 years of its existence. There had probably never been any rain during that period, which we infer from the following language : "And the Lord God created every plant of the field and every herb before it grew : for the Lord God *had not caused it to rain* upon the earth, but there went up *a mist* from the earth, and *watered the whole face of the ground.*" (Gen. 2 : 5, 6). The evaporating and condensing atmosphere was so perfect that the nightly mists and dewfall (and it was all over the earth the same, watering the *whole ground*) rendered rain for fructifying purposes unnecessary, this condition for vegetable growth being most favorable.

BIBLE STATEMENTS OF CREATION. 79

Fossil and Shell Argument Confirms the Deluge.

In these waters during this period were deposited the vast quantity of shells, whose fossil remains present one of the most important evidences of the extreme age of the world, in geological calculation. Shells buried deep in water are protected from the decomposing atmospheric agencies, and therefore will prodigiously accumulate. In making a proper estimate of these enormous deposits it should be borne in mind that shell-fish are very prolific, come quickly to maturity, and are of short life. The few years required to produce large beds of oysters illustrate this fact.

So mightily was the earth rent asunder by the watery convulsion that it is not strange to find portions of its crust within the polar circle which once belonged to the equatorial region, the deep-laid granite blocks piled mountainously high: for the distance from the equator to the poles is no greater than from the center of the earth to its surface. The Bible accounts of the creation and flood and of the effects produced by the latter not only establish their truth, but present the only adequate cause to account for the facts, and show it to have been both philosophical and scientific. Having rejected this record, the geologists have ransacked all nature in search of possibilities—of igneous, aqueous and glacial agencies—of internal and external temperatures, all the way from a world of liquid fire to a world covered with ice.

The "Glacial Period" Never Existed.

That our readers may have a proper idea of this last, called the great glacial period, amounting to almost a universal deluge of ice, we quote in the first place from a chart entitled, "The Ages of Nature, Geology, and

Paleontology," compiled by Deacon Dye, and published in 1874. Says the chart: "The post-tertiary, glacier, or northern drift period, brings us to one of those backward-looking times when man, if he was on earth, might have well and justly despaired of its future. Following the wonderful upheaveals and gigantic developments of mammalian life, a cold glacial or barren period ensued, and under its vigorous climate life in the Northern Hemisphere succumbed. There is good reason for believing that North America during the drift period was covered with immense sheets of ice, in places thousands of feet in thickness. All Canada, the British provinces, nearly all New England, and a large part of the United States directly west were so covered, the glaciers moving toward the ocean in the most direct line, their general direction being toward the south. [This implies there was a depth of water sufficient to float them, even across the highest lands, to the Pacific, and therefore over the Rocky Mountains; and this would make a deluge over all the earth.] Large quantities of granite and boulders have been carried from Canada and Lake Superior hundreds of miles distant into central Ohio and Indiana. The northern shores of Long Island are strewn with boulders, red sandstone, and granite from Connecticut. In Europe a similar condition of things existed, over all Switzerland and a considerable portion of Spain and Italy. From Norway to Great Britain an immense glacier extended, by which large boulders were transported across the German Ocean. Traces of ancient glaciers are found in Russia, Prussia, and in the Carpathian and Caucasus Mountains; in Scotland and Wales; in America, Europe, and Asia down to the 44th and 42d parallels of latitude, and up to the altitude of 5,000 feet. Immense blocks are at Bradford, Massachusetts. One is 30 feet each way, and its weight is estimated at 4,500,000 pounds."

Upon this subject Lyell says : " Some ice islands have been known to drift from Baffin's Bay to the latitude of the Azores, and from the South Platte to the immediate neighborhood of the Cape of Good Hope ; so that the area over which the effects of moving ice may be *experienced* [A pretty strong term, Sir Charles ; why did you not say *seen?* Was it because you wanted to settle this speculation as a geological fact, about which no further questions should be asked?] comprehends a large portion of the globe."

Prof. Agassiz's Cause Unscientific.

In his report of the Hassler expedition, dated June 1, 1872, at Conception Bay, Professor Agassiz says : " The southern portion of the South American continent and the islands adjacent are profusely strewn with erratic boulders, and mountains up to a certain height are worn by contact with glacier action, and rocks bearing marks of the grinding movement of the ice of the great glacier period are continually met with, all going to show that the movement was from a south-northerly direction: or, in other words, from the equator. [The bursting of the earth at the flood which threw these boulders in every direction was from the center or the equator.] After having traced what seems to me palpable evidence of an ice mantle once spreading over the south part of this continent, the effect of which I have seen from Montevideo on the Atlantic to Telcohuana on the Pacific coast, the question naturally arises, How far the southern extremity of Africa, as well as New Zealand and Australia. were involved in the extension ? and what produced the great glacier period ? which up to this time remains unexplained; but if the European continent should be suddenly elevated 3,000 feet, most of its surface would be covered by perpetual snow. The same would result to the North American continent if it was lifted 8,000 feet above its present level."

The Professor might also have added: A corresponding elevation of every continent or island would produce the same effect—that is, all would be covered with perpetual snow and ice. Another thing said to be a fact by these ice theorists is that all the continents were mantled by ice in some places thousands of feet thick. Now Agassiz has touched the only principle by which the ice could have been produced, that of the elevation of all the earth from three to eight thousand feet, thus bringing the level of the earth to that of those mountains which are covered with perpetual ice and snow.

At the time of the agitation of the slavery question in Congress, when members used to make what were called spread-eagle speeches, it was said that a certain orator got the eagle up so high that he couldn't get him down. The Professor has settled the question as to what produced the great glacier period, and has elevated the continents into the region of perpetual snow and ice, and there he leaves them; but the perpetual ice does not now exist to a continental extent, therefore it was not perpetual. This elevation to 8,000 feet of the continents would give the earth 16,000 feet greater diameter; and the waters of the seas were above this, for they floated the ice that ground streaks in the rocks as high as 5,000 feet; and to carry islands of ice over the Cape of Good Hope the water must have been at least three thousand feet higher than the cape. The great glacier period, with its ice-boats for erratic transportation, has been invented in order to account for the fact that boulders are found in one place which belong to another. Having denied the existence of the flood, which scattered these in every direction, this is their only alternative: that the whole earth had swelled up, oceans and all, about 8,000 feet on every side, making the world 16,000 feet greater in diameter. To produce such an effect, one of two things was necessary: first, that the elevation of the surface thus must have left a corresponding vacuum in the center of the globe; but this being contrary to the universal law of gravity, which presses every particle of matter toward this center, science declares such a cause did not produce the elevation. The only other possible cause known to nature is the expansion of every element, compound or simple, of which the earth is composed, and this implies the expansion of every atom of which these elements are formed. But heat expands and cold contracts all matter; and as during the great glacier period the surface of the earth was intensely cold, so cold indeed that it was mantled with ice thousands of feet in thickness, we say the result would have been to shrink or contract the whole land and water to its smallest possible dimensions.

Hence Agassiz's theory of the cause of the glacier period is impossible, and therefore it never existed; and we see that its occurrence is forbidden by two of the best known laws of science—namely, gravity and temperature.

Lyell's Attempt Inadequate.

In "Principles of Geology" vol. i., p. 235, Sir Charles Lyell gives the following results of a labored investigation of the cause of the diffusion of heat over the globe, in order to account for a temperature low enough to have produced the great glacier period. He says:

"We may warn the geologists to be on their guard,

and not hastily to assume that the temperature of the earth in the present era is a type of that which most usually obtains, since it contemplates far mightier alterations in the position of land and sea, at different epochs, than those which now cause the climate of Europe to differ from that of other continents in the same latitudes. It is now well ascertained that zones of equal warmth both in the atmosphere and in the waters of the oceans are neither parallel to the equator nor to each other. It is also well known that the *mean* annual temperature may be the same in two places which enjoy very different climates, though the seasons may be nearly uniform or violently contrasted, so that the lines of equal temperature do not coincide with those of equal annual heat or isothermal lines. The deviations of all these lines from the same parallel of latitude are determined by a multitude of circumstances, among the principal of which are the position, direction, and elevation of the continents and islands, the position and depth of the sea, and the direction of winds and currents."

To illustrate these differences he gives us what may be regarded as a striking case, thus: "On comparing the two continents of Europe and America, it is found that places in the same latitude have sometimes a mean difference of temperature amounting to 11°, or even in a few cases to 17° Fahr.; and some places on the same continents, which have the same mean temperature, differ from 7° to 17° in latitude."

Since the establishment by our Government of telegraphic stations for the purpose of making simultaneous weather reports, it has been ascertained that there is but a very slight variation of annual heat and cold at any one place. It is also well known that the length of seasons for raising crops in any latitude does not depend upon mean temperature. Now, what relation is there between these slight variations of temperature, even of 17°, as the result of more land than water, and that required to produce the extreme cold of the great glacier period?

Suppose the whole earth was covered with water, would that lower the temperature to a degree that would mantle it with ice? Every one knows that upon the deck of a vessel in mid-ocean there is about the same temperature as in the same latitude upon land, taking the motion and direction of the wind into the account. No, such a theory is utterly inadequate to account for the results, and it is put forward only as a shift, to account for the fancied ice-carrying speculation which never occurred. Lyell introduces it because it is a slow, ordinary movement of nature, begging his geological brethren to believe it might have been colder once because there was less land than sea!

Agassiz knows of no other cause to have produced the great covering of the world with ice than its *sudden* upheaval, and therefore a catastrophe—a sudden and entire enlargement of the earth—and that, too, by cold, which contracts all bodies.

According to Mr. Darwin's theory, these animal scientists have reached the hard necessity of devouring each other, and the only question is, which is the fittest to survive? Behold the geological hydra, ever ready to swallow its own heads! It is certain that if this great glacier period ever existed the sun was the only means of thawing it; but this was impossible, since the sun had not sufficient heating power to prevent its freezing. As long as the land and water, covered with ice thousands of feet thick, remained at this elevation, the globe would remain thus expanded, and the power of the sun, instead of contracting, which was necessary to make it warmer, would expand it still more, and therefore the great Glacier Period, if it ever existed, never could have ceased to exist; and as it does not now exist, it follows that it never did exist.

The law of equilibrium, governing all the forces and movements of nature, forbids the existence of this aqueous period. According to this, rains, streams, and rivers gradually change the configuration of every continent, forming hills from mountains and smaller ones from larger, thus filling up the surrounding depressions. These are continually wearing away by aqueous forces in all its forms of water, ice, and snow. The surface rock is split into fragments by the expansive power of frost, and ground into atoms. Rains and running currents pulverize these stones into fine dust and finally wash it into the oceans, thus leveling the heights of the land above the seas as well as grinding the shores under the water as far down as there is motion to the water. From this operation of nature two consequences must follow if no catastrophes occur. The first is, the depths of the oceans will be filled, and secondly, the whole earth will be covered with water—even the highest mountains. In fact, if, as Lyell expresses it, there has been a uniform movement from the remotest time, and as there has always been this same aqueous wearing away of the land standing out of the water, then there was never any dry land, or land above the level of the sea; for if the seas formed instead of destroying the land, still they could not have formed land above their own level. But as land does exist above the level of the sea, it must therefore always have so existed, or from remotest time. With such a period in which to operate, had the aqueous and atmospheric forces carried but a single atom each year from the land and deposited it in the ocean bed, every atom would have been submerged a hundred billions of years ago. You may smile at the definite period; but it seems a relief to indulge occasionally in geological calculation.

The Argument of "Uniformitarianism" Exploded.

Here then we have the results of the spacious doctrine of "Uniformitarianism," for the adoption of which Lyell has sacrificed all his volumes of "Catastrophism," for the reason, as it seems to us, that he thought he saw the evolution of inanimate nature by the slow movements of senseless matter, as Darwin thought he saw organic nature thus arise. But we have seen that the tendency of inanimate nature is toward dissolution and disintegration instead of formation, while the machinery of animal evolution could never have had a start, leaving Tyndall fulminating in his backward vision, and mournfully ejaculating, "Whence came the Primordial form?"

> O science! hast thou come to this?
> Where are thine exalting lessons of yore?
> Lifting man to things above him,
> Ennobling all with thoughts of highest
> Fame, replete with moral aspirations.
> Man, whence thy godlike reason,
> Measuring up and onward endlessly?
> Still among the nobler works of nature's
> God, soaring ever and anon—high,
> Deep, wide, making inquest of
> Every chain of thought, whence its
> Spring in nature, or in mind above,
> Whether the causes center in the great
> First, last, mightiest of all, finding
> Nature as a burnished mirror reflect
> The Maker by the world that's made,
> Spangling all heaven in nightly
> Beauty, noiselessly swinging in

Equal balance, hanging yet on naught.
Go thou ! begin the noble search for
Truth, nor think a beast thy brother.
'Tis base humility formed in pride—
If thy mind canst take the thought?
Science grovels not so low : 'tis its
Want. *Science true* doth but ennoble,
Whether buried in the tiny plant—
Spectroscopic unit, rolling worlds, or
Central systems. Here use thy powers,
Question all that is. List for the response,
And heed the voice of God.

CHAPTER III.

REASON, FACTS, SCIENCE, AND SCRIPTURE OPPOSED TO EVOLUTION.

Why Error in Science gets the Start of Truth.

BECAUSE of the limitation of human knowledge attained at any given period, there are facts and phenomena whose philosophy are unknown; in consequence of which a certain teaching connected with these may be used, by the simple honestly and by the intelligent dishonestly, for the purpose of overthrowing well-settled convictions upon any subject. This leaves to those holding them no alternative other than that of patient submission, until opportunity is afforded to subject them to a more profound investigation than those have done who use them for such purposes.

One of these heresies of natural science, as we shall denominate them, is, that *the less produces the greater.* If this statement be not true, the whole specious theory of evolution falls to pieces together. Another of these put forth by Professor Tyndall is, that he sees in inorganic matter the faculty of organizing a thing of life; hence he asks: "Whence came the primordial form of all the faculties of plant and animal life, including organic man?" and answers that it came from lifeless nebulæ. In the discussion of this question all mere scientists are agreed that there has not been an eternal succession of organic or inorganic things upon earth; there must therefore have been a first. As, however,

Hutton, a Scotch geologist, who wrote about a century ago, said, "I can see no traces of a beginning and no prospect of an end;" and as atheism adopts this view and claims that there has been an endless succession of living things, it is of importance that the supposition be shown to be error. The *fact of succession* itself demonstrates this, and the conclusion is mathematical, which may be stated thus: Mankind, as one of these living things, exist; they succeed each other in coming into existence. Any number of things may be counted, either from the first to the last or the last to the first: in this case, if we begin with the last man born into the world and count backward, we must arrive at the first: therefore, there was a first. The force of the argument cannot be evaded by the assumption of the evolution sophism, that man came from a lower animal form and by the smallest shades of gradation; and to give evolutionists the fullest advantage of the hypothesis we will admit, for the sake of argument, that the first man proper did evolve from the monkey as he appears at present, and that, too, through all the missing links, no matter how numerous they may be. We will go still further, and admit that the first monkey evolved from the lowest, simplest insect that could move of itself, and that every intervening animal only differed in such nice shades that no two standing nearest could be distinguished from each other. Indeed, we will carry these connecting links through every living plant, commencing with those which are part animal and part plant, down to the first cell of the first vegetable which had the faculty of producing another cell, and which we call *growing*. Now we have arrived at the first vital thing upon our globe; and do we not see, if we begin again with the last human being born into the world, and continue the count of each unit, that we finally arrive at the first vital cell, therefore that there was a first? We will leave our atheistic or evolutionist friends to explain to us the process whereby dead atoms or dead nature began and finished this thing of life, or of *vitality*, which means, "So disposed as to live," or to admit that before this there was a *living being* capable of performing this work.

So far as the teaching of such facts are concerned, it makes no difference whether man is the indirect offshoot of something else in animal or plant form, or whether he was always a veritable and perfect man; for if simple matter has the faculty of producing the lowest plant capable of reproducing itself, which implies life, and life implies perfect organization—that is, the existence and relative combination and embodiment of every organ essential to living, all of which also implies a degree of construction so perfect that each will perform its functional part of the vitality, the result of all being *life*:— then, we repeat, it may have produced man as man, a being endowed with the two fundamental principles of life and reproduction; therefore each involves the same amount of skill and power in bringing them into existence, whether large or small, visible or invisible to the naked eye. Indeed it is in the minute animalcule that the most exquisite skill is displayed.

Every Fact has its Science and Philosophy.

From the analogies of what are known we are led to conclude that every fact of nature has a philosophy and science peculiar to itself or its class, and to which its production and development must be attributed.

In order to do this, philosophy and science must be shown to have been adequate to such results; and of course this can only be done by a student of nature, who has a knowledge of all the necessities and provisions demanded. This precludes from the argument the assumption that because there is a seeming analogy between cause and effect, and which might be shown to be the real one were it better understood.

Candor and truth require us in such a case to investigate every phase of a fact of existence until all the natural principles it involves are fully known, before any conclusion should be reached or announced, as to the manner of such existence. Until this is accomplished, it can be considered only in the light of a speculation or a hypothesis.

In the attempt of the geological evolutionists to give a chronology of the world, and of man inhabiting it, discrepancies of thousands of years are common. Indeed it could not be otherwise, considering the fact that they have so far deviated from the manner of reasoning above stated, that conclusions are often drawn from the most superficial knowledge of facts, as well as from an assumption that they are such, when often they are not facts at all.

The position seems to us impregnable, that the time consumed in the accomplishment of a work so relates to the nature of the work, whose facts are its manifestations, that the one cannot be correctly interpreted without taking the other into the account. It is therefore indispensable that scientists, whose legitimate business is demonstration, should go to the very bottom of things, not only acquainting themselves with geology, but also with cosmogony, metaphysics, and the theology of the Bible. These studies, involving a classification of the works of nature and its object, are so connected that the one department cannot be even well understood without a knowledge of the others: the one presents the phenomena, the others make known the design, the plan, the origin, and the end to be accomplished. Men may investigate the phenomena, the moving machinery of the organic and inorganic world alone, and here, properly speaking, is the limit of natural science, without taking into the account the end to be accomplished by it ; but they can no more arrive at correct conclusions concerning it than they can judge of a house by observing the materials being collected for the purpose of building one, without taking its erection into the account. So with the world, unless the design for which it was made is understood—and this knowledge nature does not reveal—all is involved in confusion.

It is a knowledge of this grand relationship of facts and their science or moving principles, including God, man, and the world, which alone reveals the harmony of all. If investigation is to be confined strictly within the limits of science, then nothing must be taken for granted, and nothing assumed or inferred unless supported by logical evidence. This renders inadmissible any deduction of a skeptical character, as to the manner of creation, unless demonstrated in every way to be adequate to the production of the fact or its phenomenon. Hence the assumption that this or that development consumed this or that length of time, and could be demonstrated if we were better acquainted with the philosophical or scientific principles involved, is a most servile begging of the question upon which the whole theory is based. The most unequivocal proof is therefore demanded, for the act attempted is reprehensible according to the importance of the questions at issue ; and as in this case it involves the truth of the Bible, the creation of the world, and the existence of its creator, it becomes simply atrocious.

Was Man Created?

If I am asked who made me, I answer, God; by which I mean a Being as much my superior in the scale of intelligence and power as I am superior to anything I myself can make; and if the thing made is the greatest in my power of achievement, it must be the limit of my comprehension. If asked again what other reason I can assign for entertaining such an idea, I answer, It is because I cannot approximate the conception of the organic principles of life near enough to enable me to make a single inch of the stem of the simplest plant, or slip of one that if set in the soil would grow to maturity, producing seed which would reproduce successive generations. If I might know the precise chemical properties the plant contains, yet I could not combine them in the exact proportions demanded by the laws of vegetable life. The time, too, which nature allots for the work, limited as it is to a few hours, renders it impossible of performance on my part; for if it were not finished in a brief space of time the decomposing forces of the atmosphere would destroy the parts first made. Consider the complication of the work this simple, natural object involves! It contains not only the organic mechanism of growth common to plants, but has another department, whose function is to produce seed after its kind; and without which, when it dies by age or violence, the existence of the species is ended, and successive generations do not follow.

It is obvious, therefore, that to make a plant involves as much thought in conception and genius in execution as to construct a locomotive engine, which, when once set in motion, would not only run forever, but while running would evolve other locomotives, as perfect as itself, endowing each with the mechanical faculty of evolving from themselves successive generations of such machines. Now, if I cannot make this simple plant, can a being or thing of less intelligence do it? or, more impossible still, can the plant make itself? and, to add to the preposterousness of the evolution absurdity, can a thing of less intelligence than itself have made it? Is it not, then, impossible that this hypothesis can obtain even a theoretical starting-point in nature, otherwise than by outraging common-sense and reason, ignoring the commonest principles of philosophy, and setting all science at naught? And yet the evolutionists evade all this under the sophistical plea that it is none of their concern to be interested about the origin of things, knowing perfectly well that their theory cannot be harmonized with such an origin as the necessities of the work demand.

Sophistry of Geologists Exposed.

We introduce the following, which shows that the geologists and evolutionists are intensely interested about the origin of organic existence. Sir Charles Lyell, "Principles of Geology," p. 73, says: "Hutton's treatise, 'Theory of the Earth,' was the first in which geology was declared to be in no way concerned about questions as to the origin of things." This theory was published in 1788. Here we have the statement that up to this period there had not been a naturalist who did not acknowledge the creation of the world, all of whom were therefore interested in the origin of things; and from tradition or otherwise we may add that there had not appeared, even among heathen mythologists, one who did not also admit the fact of a universal deluge. Skeptical geology, then, dates no further back than Hutton, its father, not a hundred years ago.

Lyell says (p. 5) of himself: "An attempt will be made in the sequel of this work to demonstrate that geology differs as widely from cosmogony as speculations concerning the mode of the first creation of man differ from history." Taking into account the seemingly designed ambiguity in this allusion, we may remark, as to apparent historic differences about the account given of the creation of man and the world by Moses and those of heathen tradition, which latter bear upon their face the marks of being corruptions of that account, that there is no difference about the essential fact that man and the world were created, and by a previously existing intelligent Being; and not a historic intimation is given that the world evolved by dead matter from dead matter. There is, then, just as wide a difference between the views of the philosophers and naturalists of ancient times, down to Hutton's day, and those of Lyell, as there is between his views and all those of the past, and also between all those of the past and all the deductions of modern science and philosophy, the former being more consonant with truth.

On p. 14 Lyell also says: "But the most common and serious source of confusion [referring to the historic opinions of the naturalists] arose from the notion that it was the business of geology to discover the mode in which the earth originated." Lyell having adopted evolution, and knowing perfectly well its inadequacy to account for the first existence of things, by this sophism attempts to ignore it, and yet no one acquainted with even this geologist's works but knows he does attempt, and even declares it to be the object of his whole book, to show that the world and its inhabitants came into existence by the same uniform operation of nature as that which now exists, and that there never has been any other. He therefore admits that his only object in writing his "Principles of Geology" is to show that the manner of the world's coming into existence was exactly that which now moves and controls her works, and that it did not come into existence by a creation as described by Moses.

Mr. Darwin, "Descent of Man," p. 220, vol. 1, speaking of the conversion of the great naturalists to his views, says: "Those naturalists who admit the principle of *evolution*, and this is admitted by the greater number of rising men," etc. What an altitude of intellectual greatness these rising men have reached, with Darwin as the star in the van, may be gathered from the following admission, p. 154: "Undoubtedly it would be very interesting to have traced the development of each separate faculty from the state in which it exists in the lower animals to that in which it exists in man; but neither my ability nor knowledge permits the attempt." Though inability is here admitted, yet it is taken for granted that all the faculties have existed in succession, and in the nicest shades of difference, all the way from a single one in the simplest organic thing to perfect maturity in man; which also implies that the aggregate faculties of the whole animal and vegetable kingdoms sprang from a single primordial faculty, the simplest of all; also that a single faculty could have produced another, as well as that it could have produced the compound faculties of which all living things and beings are endowed.

Absurdity of the Theory that One Vital Organ Produces Another.

The idea is that the heart of a man separated from his body and every other faculty could produce lungs, and the lungs of themselves could produce brains, etc.

The claim, however, is that this could only have been done by very small degrees; but this only adds difficulty to the work of preserving from decomposition during the process, the things or faculties coming toward life, the impossibility of which appears on its very face. In addition to this we have what may be termed the backing-out position, thus stated by Hooker, and adopted by all the evolutionists: "No science doth make known the principles upon which it buildeth." Of course, evolution, having no principles upon which it is built, seizes with avidity such an absurd assertion; but we have already shown that the evolutionists are absorbingly interested in tracing the origin of man from the monkey, the monkey from the fish, the fish from a plant, and all plants from a single species: then, when the common progenitor or first faculty of it is reached, which is claimed to be only another link in the natural chain, they declare that they are not interested to go any further, and indeed that it is none of their business to explain the origin of things. This is beautiful. We have just seen that Darwin could trace all organizations to this first faculty, provided he had the ability, admitting this to be the common origin; and Lyell does not admit the least inability in tracing the evolution of the inorganic world to just such a state of things as that which exists at the present. But we apprehend that it is not so much the want of ability on the part of Darwin to explain how one faculty produced another, and in which respect he is infinitely lacking, as because the whole theory is erroneous and absurd, out of which no man can bring truth or even its appearance, except upon the principle of evolution, which brings things out of others not containing them.

If Hooker meant to admit that every science doth

make known the fact that it is absolutely inadequate to account for the principles of motion in organic existence, it is acknowledging the prior existence of an intelligent Being, to whose skill and power all the principles of life and motion which the universe manifest are to be attributed. It is a fact that the natural sciences, designated by different names, are so interwoven and dependent on each other that no one of them can be understood and explained without reference to the others; hence any erroneous conclusion drawn from one may be exposed by another. In illustration of this principle take the claim of evolution that all the faculties of organic life originated from a single faculty, therefore that one produced another. But physiology says no: it requires all these faculties combined in a single body in order to make it live, and until it lives it cannot produce a faculty or a rudiment of one, or the smallest atom. Evolution says rudiments are first produced, and by continuous reproduction develop into faculties. Physiology says no: it requires the exercise of a faculty in order to develop it, and this is the result of life and motion, but the rudiment did not live and could not move, hence it could have had no exercise. If evolution says it consumed a whole year for the primordial or first living thing to come into existence—and it says hundreds of years were required for this work—chemistry answers no: for the reason, first, that a thing of life must live in order to be proof against decomposition, and this quality lasts as long as it lives, but when it dies it immediately begins to decompose, and in a few days all the vital organs are destroyed; Secondly, as it requires all the vital faculties to make life possible, therefore that faculty made at the beginning of the year would decompose before the last was completed, at the last of the year. Here, then, are facts in two of the best known sciences proving that evolution is *no science*. This is not simple evidence, but absolute demonstration. The primordial did not possess all the organs or faculties essential to life—the lungs, heart, etc.—and therefore it did not live. If it possessed them all in rudimental form, nascent lungs, heart, etc., such lungs could not breathe, and such a heart could not perform its function in the circulation of the blood; they were therefore neither lungs nor heart at all.

The Primordial Form could not have been Evolved.

Hence, as the primordial never came into existence by evolution, and as this is claimed as the first link in the chain—and the peculiarity of this chain is that one link produces another from beginning to end—therefore there never was a second link, or any chain at all. And if the primordial was a living form, and should produce offspring only composed of rudiments of faculties, or a single rudiment in the place of one whose function was essential to life, still the thing would not live; hence, again, the chain would cease to exist with the first link. The only alternative is that God created the first progenitors of animals, male and female, and the first plant of every species of living creatures and things, endowing each with the faculty of reproducing its kind, *all living*, just as did their parents; and according to the universal voice of nature these were the only possible primordials.

For the sake of the argument, however, we will admit that all living things did evolve, including the lesser work of the inorganic solar system, from homogeneous or nebulous matter, as the evolutionists claim. Here, then they may indulge their imagination and employ their ingenuity to their heart's content; and we may even wish that Mr. Darwin were in the possession of his desired knowledge, to enable him to trace the first faculty as it appeared in the lower animal through every shade of descent or degree of advancement until it became a full development in man, as he claims was the fact.

It will not be questioned that everything in nature answering a fixed purpose is so far perfect as to enable it to perform that purpose. Now, reasoning from the analogies of nature and her necessities, let us endeavor to ascertain the form of the primordial, and the possibility of its having come into existence by evolution. In the first place, we may remark that if naturalists know it came into living being by the unassisted play of atoms, they must know equally well the manner in which the atoms started the operation. If I know that a man built a house, I know by its necessities the method he pursued in the work. If it be answered that as a house is not a thing of life, we can therefore comprehend the work, we reply, Neither was the primordial a thing of life until it possessed every vital organ the function of which was essential to life, and just as perfect as they now exist in every air-breathing animal. We do not mean to permit you to evade this task, and as it is self-imposed we ask you to meet it honestly, or frankly give up the claim of the truth of evolution.

We know it would be easy for you to show how the vital organs or faculties repaired the ordinary decay of the living animal, at least the facts connected with the operation; but what you must show is, how it was possible for the simple atoms of which the living faculties were built up to enable the animal to begin to breathe with rudimental lungs, and hence to live. We grant that, were all the animal faculties organized and connected in a body just as every animal has them, the atmospheric pressure would inflate the lungs, just as it does those of every new-born child, and it would live ; and no animal could otherwise live, as the existence and perfect formation of every one of these faculties is itself a condition to life—a part of life itself.

Conditions of Life.

Life is not a single thing, substance, or faculty, but results from combination, just as steam power results from the organic boiler and engine connected in a certain manner.

The fact is, the common-sense of every man, including the evolutionists, is shocked with the suggestion that atoms of matter have any such power as is here necessitated, as the ability to do the work must have been first involved in the atoms before it could have evolved the work of forming all or any of the vital organs. Hence involution was before evolution, and must have been the work of supernatural power.

So far as language goes, the primordial or common progenitor seems to be a nondescript—it is a thing which is, and yet is not. It is said to have been organic ; but this implies the prior existence of something capable of organizing it : and that must have been an organization itself, unless the idea that a simple element did the work, which we have shown was impossible. Besides, it is the undeviating work of the gases or elements to decompose all animal and vegetable bodies, and the only thing by which their destroying work is restrained is animal and plant life. Instead, therefore, of the gases entering into combination to form the progenitor and get it ready to live, it was their work to dissolve it into its elements. Now, as there must have been an organic thing to organize the progenitor, therefore the first was not the first. The only other solution to the dilemma is that the primordial is only another name for the God of creation. It is said to be a progenitor ; but as male and female are essential to offspring, the one must have been two. It required a creator to make Eve of Adam ; but evolution obtains a pair from one.

If the progenitor was a plant, as the theory necessitates—for it was the simplest form of life—then it was organized according to the laws of vegetable life, and could not have grown from seed, for as yet there had been no plants to produce seed : and if it did come from a seed, it only renders the organic work more difficult for evolution or any power to perform, as it must have produced the seed, incorporating into its structure every faculty, function, or phase of peculiarity necessary to form the plant growing from it, of course in embryo. Besides, this would prove that the first plant progenitor was not the first, as it came from seed. As this plant, like all others, was composed of about ninety-five per cent. of the gases of the air, it must have come to maturity surrounded by air, and set in soil ; but as soil is formed by the decomposition of vegetation, and as yet there had been no vegetation to decompose, therefore there was no soil. Of course this reasoning is based on the assumption that nature always works upon the same uniform principle, and for which the whole school of evolutionists most strenuously contend. Thus : we are furnished with the most favorable circumstances, or environment, as Tyndall calls it, that the nature of the case admits for bringing the primordial into existence, but yet its commencement is impossible. We are not to be diverted from the question by these wild speculators or induced to go in search of lost links in the chain of existence; for here we see that there can be no chain, because there is not the first link, and the peculiarity alleged for this chain is that one link produces another.

Huxley gives us the following definition of evolution: "The hypothesis of evolution supposes that in any given period in the past we should meet with a state of things more or less similar to the present, but less similar in proportion as we go back in time; that the physical form of the earth could be traced back in this way to a condition of things in which its parts were separated as little more than a nebulous cloud making part of a whole in which we find the sun and the other planetary bodies also resolved; and that if we traced back the animal and vegetable world, we should find preceding what now exists animals and plants, not identical with them, but like them, only increasing their differences as we go back in time, and at the same time becoming *simpler and simpler* until finally we should arrive at that gelatinous mass which, so far as our present knowledge goes, is the common foundation of all life. [Hence God is not such foundation.] The tendency of science is to justify the speculation that that also could be traced further back, perhaps to the general nebulous origin of matter. [The nebulæ was matter itself.] The hypothesis of evolution supposes that in all this vast progression there would be no breach of continuity, no point at which we could say, 'This is a natural process, and this is not a natural process.'"—*Tribune Report.* It will be seen by this definition that evolution is founded on the supposition that animals and vegetables grow simpler and simpler in their physical structure as we go back in time and toward the matter in which the first originated, and that that was a nebulous cloud.

Evolution Reversed upon its Own Principles.

Now, if we show the exact reverse of this to be true, science and philosophy—that is, if one living thing evolved from another—then the further you go back in time the more complex and perfect will each preceding thing be, necessitating the conclusion that the first was the most exquisite and wonderful organization of all, and that each has grown simpler and simpler until man comes into being, who is the very simplest of all. We say if we prove this, then evolution cannot be true science. We state it as a self-evident truth that evolution presupposes prior involution. For example, an egg cannot evolve a chicken unless its embryo was first involved in the egg. A seed cannot evolve a tree unless the embryo tree was involved in the seed. If the polyp, which reproduces by ova as well as buds, evolved the serpent, it must have involved the embryo serpent. If the serpent evolved the fish, the serpent must have involved the embryo fish. If the fish evolved the bird, the fish must have involved the embryo bird. If the monkey evolved the man, the monkey must have involved the embryo man. Here we see that the polyp not only involved the embryo of its own kind, but embryos within embryos of the serpent, fish, bird, monkey, and man, each losing an embryo in succession as man is approached, and therefore each degenerating to a simpler and simpler organic thing, leaving man the very simplest of all. Supposing, then, the polyp to have been the primordial, or common progenitor, it must have had incorporated into its organic structure, in embryonic perfection, every individual of every species of plant and animal kind, including that of the whole planetary system. But this wonderful involvement of the mechanism of the universe, being the most perfect of all, is the furthest from being a subject of evolution. This is confirmed by the fact that the subjects of its offspring instead of progressing must have retrograded in the exact ratio as man was approximated. Secondly, as it involved the living and moving universe with all its wonderful dynamics, it could only have received the endowment by a prior existing Being of intelligence and power equal to the direct creation of such a universe. We have already alluded to the fact, which should be kept in mind, that according to evolution it is the successive generations which advance organic being, from which it follows that if the first living thing attempted to be brought into existence had not arrived at maturity the first season, no matter how near it approximated to it; the unfinished parts would have decomposed before another season came round, undoing all that was done. Such a work, therefore, is, in the nature of things, limited to as short a process as that which is implied in the account of creation in Genesis.

If Evolution Ever Existed, it is a Rapid Process.

The ratio of time required, as is here shown, to bring the common progenitor into existence, would evolve the lowest monkey into the grandest model of human kind in a single season; and such a feat would admit of no just comparison with that implied in bringing the first organic thing from inorganic atoms, as there is infinitely greater superiority and difference between the lowest living form and the most magnificent inanimate orb. Indeed, such a ratio of speed would evolve an angel from a man in a single season, and in the same time every species of living things in the scale of being into the next higher. This, by the way, would make the whole process one of catastrophism instead of evolution, supposing it had an existence at all; and how does it appear, if we admit the claim of its advocates that the process of organic evolution, as well as of the inorganic world, consumed centuries and epochs in the accomplishment of the work?

What we mean by embryonic possession is that all the elements of a tree were involved in the seed from which it grew; for if the organic function endowing the tree with the ability to form the seed had not been incorporated, then the seed might evolve the tree, with every other essential attribute, but the species would be extinguished at the death of that tree; and were this the original progenitor, it would not have been a progenitor at all, as nothing could have come from it. Suppose, further, that the chemical substance giving each species of fruit its peculiar flavor had not been involved in the organism of the first seed, the consequence would have been that the tree would have produced a certain fruit in appearance, with every other property except flavor, but lacking this it could not be identified as any particular kind of fruit. From these simple illustrations it will be seen that the law of real evolution is limited to reproduction after its kind, knowing nothing whatever of the skillful endowment *involved* in the atoms and combinations, which alone give the starting point to organic things, leaving them only to be accounted for as objects of direct creation; and while this reproductive evolution requires no intelligence, the organization of the simplest thing of the universe manifests phenomena no human intellect is able to fathom, or power of nature to produce.

Here is embodied the most supreme wisdom; now, whence was it derived, or what allied it with everything of life and motion, animate or inanimate? How came universal nature to be endowed with this stupendous wisdom and power, manifested in her wonderful existences and adaptations? The atheist may answer, the seed evolved the tree and the tree the seed; but this is an attempt to reason in a circle when there is no circle, for there was a beginning and will be an end, and it is only an evasion of the inquiry, betraying the weakness and defenselessness of his cause. It were just as proper to say the steam moves the engine and the engine exhausts the steam, while the only true answer the question admits is that the steam-engine was made for a purpose and answers that purpose, just as everything in nature answering a purpose was also thus made. Every one must see that it is upon this point evolution must be sustained, if at all; but in the absence of definition, as the only alternative they wish it to be inferred that the intelligence manifested is one of the natural elements the seed contains, like the coloring matter, flavor, etc.; but these are the arrangements and endowments of the particles, while the intelligence is the power that arranged and endowed, which was therefore abstract and existed before. Every movement and phenomenon of nature only unfolds and fulfills the original and grand design of Him "who created all things by the word of his power."

Creation First, Evolution Next.

Thus, in universal nature we have two distinct powers manifested, though a single source. First, creation, comprehending the world and the representatives of all organic species, endowed with the faculty of reproducing their kind. Secondly, limited evolution, or the compulsory unfolding of such endowment.

The application of these facts of nature demonstrate

that Darwinism could never have obtained a start; and having no existence it follows that no array of supposed or real facts or theoretic speculations, no matter how plausible their seeming or upon whatever authority for the time being they may seem to rest, or whether they can be otherwise explained, are entitled to the least weight. As well suppose such evidence to be of sufficient force to overthrow the phenomena of nature that the rays of the sun produce light and heat, or that the elements when thrown out of balance seek their equilibrium. This argument rests on the impregnable foundation that the facts and philosophy of nature must be in harmony, and therefore any seeming conflict arises from a want of the knowledge of such facts and their true scientific teaching. If we are unable to understand the teaching of a certain fact or class of facts claimed to belong to one science, and from which certain ideas are supposed to be taught, wrong inferences may always be exposed by applying to them the well-known principles of other sciences, all of which must harmonize with truth, though not always with appearances. If this reasonable and reliable rule had been steadily followed in the interpretation of nature, the world would have been relieved of much of its error and bigoted intolerance, and scientists would have investigated every phase of the facts and phenomena of organic and inorganic existence, including those belonging to every science—an investigation essential to enable them to judge correctly of any—and this implies a perfect knowledge of material atoms and the laws by which they are governed. Without such knowledge it is mere presumption to attempt an estimate of their capabilities or incapabilities, or to say what may or what may not result from them without the aid of mind.

Speak, dead Nature, didst thou to being bring
A man, a beast, a plant, or living thing?
Say! from thy dead silence who thee woke,
Or broke thy spell eternal? it was God that spoke.
Man, hush thine arrogance, thy pride be still;
Carve not for thee a destiny so ominous of ill!
To shiver in the darksome world below,
And not the genial voice of God to know.

CHAPTER IV.

CHRISTIANITY AND EVOLUTION CONTRASTED.

If Genesis Falls so do the Rest of the Scriptures.

THE evolutionists seem to think that in denying the truth of the record of the man who wrote Genesis, and in order to make a new genesis of the world, it is not necessary to oppose the other parts of the Bible, especially the New Testament. We propose, however, to show that these are so connected that to reject one is to reject the other. If the account of creation in Genesis falls, Christ and the Apostles follow; if the Book of Genesis is erroneous, so also are the Gospels. We are also free to acknowledge that, if Moses was the author of the writings attributed to his pen, though learned in all the wisdom of the Egyptians, whose mythology even the evolutionists esteem as of very high authority, yet in his cosmological science he might have made very serious mistakes; but if a God of infinite wisdom conceived and dictated them, then He is their author, and there can be no inharmony between their teaching and the rest of the Bible, nor conflict with the true science and philosophy of the world.

The account Moses himself gives (assuming him to have been the writer of the Biblical record of creation) of the authorship of these writings is that God wrote some of them with his own finger on tables of stone, and the rest Moses wrote as God spoke the words. In the second place, the New Testament declares that

"Moses was a prophet mighty in word and in deed," and quotes his writings as inspired Scripture, without criticism or mutilation, or even insinuating that they had been changed or corrupted from their original purity, and never intimating a doubt as to God's being their author, but, on the contrary, denominates them "the scriptures of truth." Even Jesus Christ himself makes these acknowledgments.

We are free to confess that one of our motives in this connection is to compel these modern scientists to abandon what we conceive to be a heartless assent to the truth of the rest of the Scriptures after the rejection of the Mosaic writings; or to Christianity after rejecting the divine origin of the Scriptures, even those written by Moses. Let them have moral courage enough to hoist their true colors. It is our profound conviction that he who does not accept the divine authority of the Scriptures cannot be conversant with the grounds upon which rest the arguments in their defense; it is not for the want of capacity to understand, but the want of honest investigation and humility enough to admit the truth when seen. We have fully argued this question in another work,* showing that as the Scriptures came by direct inspiration and revelation, they must contain God's ideas and purposes with regard to man and the world; from which it follows that it has been as necessary for him to have preserved the ideas and words which describe this purpose free from corruption or change, as to have at first inspired them; guarding the translations while passing from one language into another, and even miraculously preserving and providentially spreading that version, if there are differences, the most perfectly describing these truths and designs; but we make

---
* "Philosophy of God and the World."

the assertion that there is not one truth or doctrine taught in any version (made prior to the last fifty years of the Christian era), which is left out of any other ever published; neither is there a single truth or doctrine taught in any one version which is not taught in all the others; and we hold ourselves responsible to vindicate this position.

Words are signs of ideas, and the words of Scripture are the signs of God's ideas. All of the words, therefore, which he has ever employed to make known his mind and will to man must be contained in what is called "King James's version." The opinion that this version or any other contains the ideas and doctrines of men mixed with those of God leaves the world essentially without a divine revelation; for who is to decide which is divine and which human? In confirmation of this position we have such passages as the following: "The *words* of the Lord are *pure words:* as silver tried in a furnace of earth, purified seven times. *Thou shalt keep them, O Lord*, thou shalt preserve them from this generation for ever." (Ps. 12:6, 7). Bigots have tried to corrupt and destroy the Bible, but the Lord has preserved it from the furnace of fire and from the attempt of "*this*" *present* generation to destroy it by declaring it corrupt.

The Whole Gospel is in the Scriptures of the Old Testament.

It is evident that if Paul preached the whole gospel, it was contained in Moses and the Prophets; and if any one will study the types of the law and the predictions of the prophets he will find that they embrace the entire Christian system, and that those pointing out the work of its founder at his first mission will find its exact fulfillment in the events through which he passed.

In his plea before King Agrippa, Paul says : " Having therefore obtained help of God, I continue unto this day witnessing both to small and great, *saying none other things than Moses and the prophets did say should come.*" (Acts 26 : 22). And at this time there was no New Testament. To the same import is Christ's own testimony thus : "Think not that I am come to destroy, but to fulfill. For verily I say unto you, till heaven and earth pass, one jot or one title shall in no wise pass from the law, till all be fulfilled. Heaven and earth shall pass away, but my word shall not pass away.". How, then, can the Scriptures of Moses be corrupted either by ignorance or design ? The emphatic language is," Not one jot or tittle," which certainly includes as much as a word which changes an idea, "In any wise," either by translation or interpretation. These are the expressions of the author who holds the copyright.

Now, to suit the notions of geologists, but which the science of nature does not require, if the meaning of the words and consequently the ideas which are employed by Moses in describing the creation and deluge be so changed, can such opinions be regarded in any other light than mere arrogant human invention ? And if written in a book called a translation of the Scriptures, it can never secure the protection of God to keep it in existence, or His providence to give it circulation. Indeed, every copy of such a book can be seized and burned, but the Bible cannot be thus exterminated. Its author also said : "If they hear not Moses and the prophets, neither will they be persuaded, though one rose from the dead." (Luke 16 : 31). Here the writings of Moses and the prophets are not only indorsed, but it is declared that to believe them secures the salvation of the gospel ; they must therefore contain the whole system. After His resurrection Christ meets the disciples and discourses to them thus: "O fools, and slow of heart, to believe all that the prophets have spoken! Ought not Christ to have suffered these things, and to enter into his glory? And beginning at Moses, and all the prophets, he expounded unto them in all the Scriptures the things concerning himself. And he said unto them, These are the *words* which I spake unto you while I was yet with you, that all things must be fulfilled which were written in the law of Moses, and in the prophets, and in the psalms concerning me. Then opened he their understanding, that they might understand the Scriptures. And he said unto them, Thus it is written, and thus it behooved Christ to suffer, and to rise from the dead the third day." (Luke 24 : 25-27, 44-46.)

Moses wrote between 2143 and 2183 of the world, during the forty years' journey in the wilderness. He could therefore have known nothing of the creation or the deluge, only as God inspired him to look back and see it as he saw it when it occurred. This account was not handed down by tradition; for Christ never countenanced tradition. He said to the Jewish teachers: "Ye have made void the law by your tradition" (Mark 7 : 13); and he declared, as we have seen, that the writings of Moses were Scripture; and God inspired Paul to write: "*All Scripture* is given by inspiration of God" (2 Tim. 3 : 16). Christ and the apostles, as well as most of the prophets, quote the record of the Mosaic account of the creation of the world and its deluge by the flood, and that without change of language or criticism. As to the latter Christ says: "For as in the days that were before the flood, they were eating and drinking, marrying and giving in marriage, until the day that Noah entered into the ark, and knew not until the flood came and took them all away : so shall also the coming of the Son of Man be." (Matt. 24 : 38, 39.)

Speaking of this record, Peter says : "And if God spared not the old world, but saved Noah, the eighth person, a preacher of righteousness, bringing in the flood upon the world of the ungodly," etc. (2 Pet. 2 : 5.) Again he says : "For this they willingly are ignorant of, that by the word of God the heavens were of old, and the earth standing out of the water and in the water: whereby the world that then was, being overflowed with water, perished." (2 Pet. 3 : 5, 6.) Here is affirmed, by Christ and the apostles, the argument that the writings of Moses are inspired scripture, and especially his record of the creation and flood. Whoever, therefore, denies the statements of Moses equally denies those of Christ and the apostles.

The Bible Standard of Ethics too High to be Improved.

A system of philosophy or ethics adapted to elevate mankind indefinitely must present a standard for imitation so high that it will not only develop the highest manhood and citizenship, but to such a degree that it can never be superseded by society or individuals becoming more perfect than the standard, and yet so practicable that every item of it may be understood and imitated by all. That such is the moral code of Jesus Christ, and that it stands alone in its simple grandeur, has never been questioned. For the benefit of those who may not be familiar with this standard, let us transcribe an epitome of it : "Ye have heard that it hath been said, An eye for an eye, and a tooth for a tooth. But I say unto you, That ye resist not evil ; but whosoever shall smite thee on the right cheek, turn to him the other also. And if any man will sue thee at the law, and take away thy coat, let him have thy cloak also. Give to him that asketh thee, and from him that would borrow of thee, turn not thou away. Ye have heard that it hath been said, Thou shalt love thy neighbor and hate thine enemy. But I say unto you, Love your enemies, bless them that curse you and persecute you : that ye may be the children of your Father which is in heaven ; for he maketh his sun to rise on the evil and on the good, and sendeth rain on the just and on the unjust. For if ye love them that love you, what reward have ye ? do not even the publicans the same ? And if ye salute your brethren only, what do ye more than others ? do not even the publicans the same? Be ye therefore perfect, even as your Father which is in heaven is perfect."

After denouncing the great crimes by name, he lays down a principle so broad and yet so simple that every accountable being may understand and expound it for himself, and which is therefore of universal application : " As ye would that men should do unto you, do ye even so unto them." It is true these actions are only ethical; but as they are to be performed under the immediate observation of God and with a single eye to his glory— "For whatsoever ye do, do all to the glory of God," thus comprehending the prompting motives—they make the whole life one of devout and honest Christian worship. We say Christian worship ; for they are also to be done for Christ's sake.

Here, then, is the highest standard for the development of mankind, mentally, morally, physically, socially, and religiously, which it is possible to conceive ; and if the actions enjoined were universally followed the necessity for civil law and prisons would be obviated, as not a species of vice or wrong could exist. And if the acts were performed with a desire to please God, it would show that the nature of the men who performed them was fashioned like that of Christ himself, and hence mankind fitted to be loyal subjects of his eternal kingdom.

The first of these conditions of fitness is the highest civilization, the second is Christianity. The first does not include the second, but the second does include the first. In other words, a man may be the highest possible type of morality and not be a Christian. God or Christ may not be in all his thoughts. He loves his fellow-men, and discharges all his obligations toward them ; but he does not love his Maker, and therefore discharges no obligation he owes him. " Thou shalt love the Lord thy God with all thy heart, and thy neighbor as thyself." He lives in perpetual violation of the first part of the command, and keeps the second. Hence he is just as much a sinner in the sight of God as though he had disobeyed all of his commands. It is not necessary for a man to violate all the laws of a civil state in order to be a criminal. If he is a murderer he need not be a thief in order to be an offender.

The Standard of Atheism also thus Contrasted.

The standard of human development set up by the evolutionists, or atheists, is in the widest possible contrast to this. Prof. Tyndall declares its object to be to " lift the life to a higher level." But the Bible lifts its warning voice against the prostitution of the godlike powers of man to such an ignoble purpose as groveling among the lower animals in search of his progenitor. It is recorded in the first chapter of Romans, which we here introduce with a few comments.

" For the invisible things of God are clearly seen from [or by] the creation of the world, even his eternal power and godhead; so that they are without excuse. Because that when they knew God [as Darwin, Tyndall, Lyell, and Huxley did once at least, so far as to see from the works of nature the revelation of a personal creator—a godhead of eternal power] they glorified him not as God [by descending in search of gods of power in inorganic matter, and among the lower animals for the origin of their own existence]; but became vain in their imaginations, and their foolish heart was darkened. Professing themselves to be wise, they became fools, and changed the glory of the incorruptible God into an image made like to corruptible man [like man, of course, is a monkey; all the god from whom man came was a monkey, and it from a lower creeping thing. Behold how they have degraded God, their Maker!], and to birds, and four-footed beasts, and creeping things [among which they search for their ancestors]; and changed the truth of God into a lie ["God made man in his own image" is the truth; that he came from these creeping things is the lie], and worshiped the creature more than the Creator."

Professor Tyndall gives us an expression of his reverence for the matter out of which he sprung in his Belfast speech, thus: "I can see in that matter upon which we in our ignorance pour such opprobrium the potency of life and promise of being." It seems as though Paul was inspired to write of the coming of the evolutionists, and to characterize their worship as the lowest form of idolatry: the corrupting, coarse, foolish wisdom and degrading tendency of their groveling, brutal ideas of the godless origin of man. It is a law of nature that if we habitually mingle with those beneath us in morals and intellect, we either bring them up to our standard or we go down to theirs. Thus a man may so give his time and attention to horses that they become objects of his devotion. We once knew a very wealthy man who by such association had descended so near the level of a horse that he gave in his stable a great supper to his friends. So, if a man devotes himself to the study of matter and the lower forms of life, and especially if by so doing he hopes thereby to find evidences to relieve his mind of the conviction that God made him, and that he came up from these four-footed beasts and creeping things, it will be natural for his foolish heart (his desire to have it so) and his mind, his intellect, to become so darkened as finally to believe the wicked lie, and no longer see in nature the necessity for the existence of a creation or a creator. From thenceforth he pays his devotions to the creature; and instead of seeing in himself, as he once did, the handiwork of the great Creator, he would fain trace his descent down through monkeys, four-footed beasts, birds, serpents, and the lowest creeping things. The highest form of idolatry sees God represented in the images of art or nature, while the lowest sees no God beyond and superior to nature: the worshiper himself being the highest manifestation of wisdom, he becomes absorbed in his own selfish admiration.

Monkey Origin of Man Darwin's Main Conclusion.

That Mr. Darwin, the father of this theory, believes himself to have thus descended, is evinced by the following: "The main conclusion arrived at in this work, namely, that man is descended from some lowly organized form, will, I regret to think, be highly distasteful to many persons. For my own part I would as soon be descended from that little monkey who braved his dreaded enemy in order to save the life of his keeper, or from that old baboon, who, descending from the mountains, carried away in triumph his young comrade from a crowd of astonished dogs, as from a savage who delights to torture his enemies." ("Descent of Man," vol. ii., p. 386.)

He does not care to remember that the savage had become a savage by his ancestors refusing to retain God in their thoughts as he himself is now doing; and as the above is the highest teaching of evolutionists, if their success were equal to their desire, in the course of a few generations they would degrade the whole human family to the level of mere savages. Hear Darwin: "Man still bears in his bodily form the indelible stamp of his lowly origin." Behold how he thus defaces the image of God; for "He created man in His own image." It is clear from such passages that no words of ours can place the evolutionists below a level warranted by their own confessions.

In his "History of Civilization," M. Guizot thus defines civilization: "Two elements, then, seem to be compressed into the great fact called civilization; two circumstances are necessary to its existence. It lives upon two conditions, and reveals itself by two systems: the progress of individuals and the progress of society; the melioration of the social system and the experience of the mind—the mental faculties of man. It may, I think, be fairly inferred that it is the spontaneous, intuitive conviction of mankind, that the two elements of civilization—the social and moral development—are so intimately connected that at the approach of one, man looks for the other." (Pp. 25, 27.)

We believe there can be but one opinion in regard to this definition, except that it is too circumscribed by leaving out the religious element. We judge, however, the author includes this in what he calls the "moral element," which history shows lies at the bottom of all phases of civilization.

Paganism produces Pagan civilization; Mohammedanism produces Mohammedan civilization; while Christianity produces Christian civilization. Without religion, therefore, there can be no progress, no civilization. This arises from the fact that moral obligation has its source in religious conviction, and the conviction results from the conception and recognition of the existence of a Supreme Being, to whom, as his Creator, man is accountable, and consequently answerable for his conduct. To ignore, therefore, the religious element, is equally to exclude the civil. Let us suppose, now, that evolution succeeds in putting aside the Christian religion by the acceptance of the idea that the Bible record of the creation and of the Creator is merely one of the many superstitions to be ignored in the cosmological history of the world; that the Christian's cherished divinity, like the rest of the gods, is a mere poetical myth; that there is no higher intellectual being in the universe than man himself, hence no higher standard toward which to advance, and in his religious aspirations none higher to worship; or if he venerates the great First Cause, which he supposes brought him into being, he must seek it in the descending lineage of ancestral baboons, snakes, and shell-fish, and even in the lowest vegetable thing of life;—suppose, we say, evolution succeeds in this, and the beginning of life is traced to its primordial, must it not, in the very nature of things, degrade to its level him who makes the discovery? It even degrades us to write of it. If this doctrine be accepted, it will turn the moral and intellectual world, with more than electric speed, back to the darkest midnight of human history, and to the most damning degradation possible to contemplate.

Savage Life not the Normal Condition of Man.

Mr. Darwin says: "The philosophy, however, of the first advance of savages toward civilization is at the present day too difficult to solve." This is a virtual admission that it never occurred; and the reason is, there were no higher beings with whom the savages were acquainted and after whom to pattern; this conduct being essential to progress. Had not the more advanced European mingled with the aboriginal American, there had never been any nobler specimens of red men; but many of them have, in the short period of five centuries, reached the highest form of civilization—that of intelligent Christianity. Indeed, the progress of man from savage to civilized life, associating with the enlightened and refined, is as natural as that society blends and modifies extreme peculiarities of physical, moral, and mental character, and as scientific as that inorganic nature—temperature, electricity, air, and indeed all the fluids—after having been thrown out of balance, seek and find their equilibrium. The equilibrium of inorganic elements is nature's normal condition; when disturbed, the equalizing work is their own. So, in organic nature, the highest civilization is her normal condition, sin is her disturbing element, and man's divergence from the Bible standard of truth is toward savage life. Had the white man carried to the red man nothing but the highest civilization—pure Christianity—and in all his dealings with him acted according to the rule, "As ye would men should do unto you, do ye even so unto them," long ere this the Indians would have risen above the highest civilization of any people of any time. It is true Columbus took along with him men who could teach the "golden rule" to the savage, but he also carried the fire-water of death and the more deadly weapons of slaughter; and no ship ever bore a missionary to the heathen but that also carried these emissaries of sin. As therefore the war of inorganic elements is deviation, unnatural—their savage life, if you please—so with organic man: his savageness is deviation from the laws of God, and therefore unnatural; and the term being a comparative one, every man is more or less savage until he takes Christ as his pattern. This restores him to his normal state. "God hath made man upright; but he has sought out many inventions." (Eccl. 7 : 29.)

Inorganic nature reveals to us the work of the God of nature—using the term God as a synonym for nature, the worship of which is *natural religion*. If, therefore, nature manifests savage and relentless cruelty; is unjust, partial, and selfish, disappointing man's reasonable hopes and demands; is generally fitful and precarious, indulging in so many freaks that no dependence can be placed on her, by those too who must subsist on her constancy or perish: then might organic man, emanating from the same source, have also been thus savage. If, on the other hand, there are found in this department of nature, corrective, modifying, and restoring influences, even for these her exceptional manifestations, so that when she exhibits these ill tempers and wayward freaks they are very soon brought under control—civilized, so to speak —then man, the head of organic nature in his normal state, was a civilized being; but, like his inorganic sister, susceptible of falling into wayward and even savage pranks. Indeed, our first parents must have been created with the most perfectly balanced mental, moral, and physical faculties, and therefore in the most perfect harmony with the mind and feelings of their Creator, as well as with those of their coming offspring.

The Present World Designed to be Only Temporary.

Notwithstanding this perfect condition both of man's nature and the world, it was designed to be only temporary. The human progenitors must have been, and as we conceive were, placed in the highest and safest condition of which they were capable and of answering the purposes of their Maker. There was one kind of knowledge which in this primitive life they could not have possessed — namely, *experience* — because it comes from action; and the effect of the first act of disobedience can only be known after the act is committed. He who commits it, feeling its effects, can then compare good and evil, and knows both, as his Maker knew them before. "And the Lord God said, Behold, the man has become as one of us, to know good and evil." (Gen. 3 : 22.) As they were endowed with a will, giving the power to obey, the power to disobey is inferred; from which it also follows that they were thus placed so high in the scale of being that it was only possible to govern them by moral force, or appeal to motive. It is absurd to suppose that the power that made man—formed him of the elements of the ground—could not have unmade, transformed him into those elements, so that he would have been as though he had not been; but this would have been extinction, not government. If a man refuses to obey, preferring to suffer the penalty,. he defies all authority, all power, and conquers, though by that act he ceases to exist.

This, then, is the philosophy of sin; and the fact with which we have to do is that sin entered into the world with its dreadful experiences; and in dealing with it we shall employ the common-sense method described by Moses, quoted by Jesus and the apostles, the wisdom of which is confirmed by the universal observation and experience of mankind; for where is he who has not knowingly committed an act as inexcusable as that of our first parents? Instead of their progressive development, we think the increasing tendency to habits of mental, moral, and physical transgression not only involves the degeneracy, but the extinction of the human family, in the absence of any other cause, or if the Creator does not previously interfere to wind up the world's history. This, however, is a part of His plan and revealed determination; and then He proposes its re-creation into a world of absolute perfection, and therefore of eternal duration, and to people it with those men and women who, while in the temporary life, submitted to let Him change and mold their whole mind into that of Christ's, including the will, thoughts, and feelings, and raising them, if dead, to immortality, or to a state so perfect that they will be exempt from the liability of death.

Without a Knowledge of the End Designed, the World is an Enigma.

Without taking into account the consummation of this great revealed plan—which is God's explanation and defense of the creation of this temporary and deranged world—no man can understand either the mental, moral, or physical disorder manifested in the organic and inorganic world. The first two chapters of the Scriptures contain the history of the creation of the present, temporary world, while the last two chapters give the prehistoric record of its re-creation and that of its inhabitants into the eternal world. "He that sat upon the throne said, Behold! I make all things new. And I saw a new heaven and a new earth; for the first heaven and the first earth had passed away." (Rev. 21: 1–5.)

Wherever, therefore, this reward as an inducement to virtue and sacrifice is known, the conditions will be accepted by some ; and these will be the highest examples of civilized manhood.

The law of imitation leaves no ground for Darwin's opinion that the primitive condition of man was savage. Let us suppose that a few families of savages were placed in the midst of a community or city of the most civilized of men. In a few generations they would become as highly civilized as the community. On the other hand, if the same number of families of the most civilized were placed with a tribe of savages, in the same number of generations they would become equally savage, and considering the inclination of man to imitate the evil instead of the good, the civilized would become savage sooner than the savage would become civilized. The few, being unable to elevate the mass to their standard, would descend to that of their neighbors ; and all in accordance with the law of natural assimilation.

The occurrence of such facts, many of which are recorded in history, are illustrative of the proneness of man rather to degenerate than to progress. It is historic that a very small portion of mankind are or ever have been savage, while most of the nations of different periods have been barbarous or semi-civilized ; and no one will dispute the fact that all have been sinners—that is, every man and woman has knowingly violated their own sense of right, as well as the physical laws of their nature. Hence sin is the unnatural and destroying element of man, while his primitive or normal state was loyalty to the laws of his being as well as to those of his Maker. The deviations were acquired, and in their extreme culmination developed the savage. The Bible account of the introduction of this disturbing element into the world is therefore not only natural, but harmonizes with the observation and common experience of mankind: while the theory that man was originally savage and is progressing toward universal civilization, is in opposition to all history and the philosophy of human nature as it is; proving that he was once perfect, and will in time become extinct—toward which time the species as a whole are rapidly approaching.

Real Progress must be Physical, Moral, and Mental.

Mankind are endowed with judgment approving goodness and a desire for knowledge. If we admit the principle that true progress comprehends the advancement of the mental, moral, and physical powers, we must admit that it equally forbids the development of either at the expense of the others, from the fact that they are so interwoven that if one suffers the others must, whether the cause is constitutional or a direct penalty resulting from a violation of the laws of health. If man is educated in the present age and has a cultivated mind—who has been, as we think, appropriately defined as "one who knows *something* about everything and *everything* about something"—such a strain has been given to his brain, as the mental organism and source of the nervous system, that it results in the shortening of life: that is, if the physical system is not vigorous enough to repair the waste of the brain resulting from its severe tax. In corroboration of this we may mention the fact that among all those who have attained remarkable longevity in modern times, there has not been an instance of superior intelligence. They have generally been negroes, or persons much secluded in society; remarkable, however, for temperance and morality, and with scarcely an exception were Christians.

If this strain shortens human life, it will not be questioned that vice and immorality cut into the vital forces and functions with a twofold greater violence, and in the same ratio limit the period of life. The assertion, therefore, of David may be considered not only a historic but a philosophic truism: "Bloody and deceitful men shall not live out half their days." (Ps. 55 : 3). Upon this subject biography is none the less explicit and general, showing that the children of great intellects fall below the common level. There are exceptions, but this is the rule. If progress was the rule, then the children of each successive generation would be, as a whole, wiser, more moral, and physically more robust.

The stability and perpetuity of inanimate nature depend upon the harmonious and peaceful operation of her laws; from which it may be argued that it equally depends upon the harmonious blending and operation of all the laws of human nature in order to secure permanent advance in each successive generation. Were such the fact, true progress might be claimed for man. When, however, we behold discord and weakness so fearfully prevalent, and every form of vice increasing, how can real progress be hoped for in the present world?

Besides, any view of human progress which leaves out the religious element is not only partial but radically defective; and we may add that no theory of natural religion, even the most refined heathenism—all of which are but corruptions of that revealed in the Holy Scriptures—can be expected to accomplish so great a work as the general elevation of mankind, when the original and uncorrupted religion has proved itself inadequate. But to elevate mankind is not its proposed work, and therefore it cannot be said to be a failure. The endowments and aspirations of humanity are so distinctive and universal that if their elementary source is to be found in any propositions of religious theory, that religion must be adapted to insure man's highest elevation, mentally, morally, physically, socially, and civilly. This constitutes the highest form of civilization, and in the very nature of things demonstrates that man was made for that religion, and it for him; and as Christianity perfectly meets each of these demands, it is therefore the most fundamental principle in human progress. We do not mean a mere national, formal, ritualistic religion, but that which is individual, bringing the sympathies of the heart, the submission of the will and the intellectual faculties into harmony with themselves, with God, and His system of righteous government, regulating every act of life, and all founded upon faith in the fulfillment of His promises of future reward—namely, eternal life in His coming kingdom.

That the Christian religion has accomplished this great work is attested by millions of intelligent human experiences. It stands, therefore, upon a better foundation than any other system of ethics, moral philosophy, or material science, all of which change: and while the deductions of natural religion are only available to the few who by long study master its nice problems, commencing by stifling their convictions of the existence of a personal God—the facts and demonstrations of Christianity are such equally to the scientist, philosopher, and people.

Mental Impression Physically Deteriorates.

Another obstacle in the way of human progress which we may mention is the power of mental impression to degenerate offspring. Its power to mark and shape is such as to render all the singularities of human feature transmissible, which fact is manifested in the birth of monstrosities ; from which it follows that the more ordinary peculiarities are also thus transmissible, such as the color of the hair, eyes, skin, curling of the hair, shape of the nose, lips, etc. These variations of physical organization are so common among families and nations—which are only families on a larger scale—that it is one of the most important principles in the division of the human species into races. Children of the same family often differ as widely from their parents and each other as from other families and nationalities. These phenomena may be inherited from grandparents, when not possessed by the parents. The feature was fixed upon the offspring directly by the mother, but was indirectly traceable to some nervous or unlovely grandmother, either dead or living at the time. The mother's memory and fear of such deformity of her child had the effect to produce it, enlisting and concentrating the molding and fashioning powers through the nervous forces of the mind, which are known to affect the circulating fluids of the whole system. According to this law, if the monster have features resembling those of a lower animal, the mind of the mother at a certain stage of gestation became fixed upon the animal, either by fear, hatred, or love, and the baleful work was done.

This is the philosophy of the increase in our day of dwarfs or midgets, as well as of their extreme littleness, and which must multiply by their public exhibition. Such features are liable to become a family inheritance, transmitted from generation to generation. If the deformities are such as to derange the reproductive organism, the subject will be infertile, and will run out in the first generation, except such as are influenced by the principle of mental impression above stated.

Upon this principle it often happens that offspring of human mothers come into the world part monkey, part dog, part hog, indeed, part any animal that has impressed the mother, as mentioned above. A fact is here involved which reverses evolution—namely, that no monster was ever born of a lower animal part human, or of a woman part angel; the principle of mental impression therefore deteriorates instead of advancing the human species. We might also remind the evolutionists that monstrosities are the product of catastrophism and not of uniformitarianism. This fact proves two things: first, that when an extreme change takes place in the generation of man it is sudden: the greatest may not occupy more time than a single year; secondly, when it occurs it deteriorates instead of improves mankind.

The Wisdom of the Creator in Limiting its Power.

That the extreme monstrosities do not reproduce their kind is an exemplifiication of the wisdom of the Creator in thus checking the otherwise too rapid degeneracy of the human species, which might baffle the purpose for which man was created, and which we have already shown. Mr. Darwin argues that monstrosities may slightly yet permanently transmit their peculiarities, and it is by a reversion of its action—which, as we have demonstrated, never works in that direction—that he obtains the only plausible grounds in favor of his theory. But his failure consists in not making the discrimination at which nature limits the transmission of deformities to those of the physical system which do not interfere with the vital and generative organs; and to do this renders offspring even of a rudamentary character impossible.

CHAPTER V.

MATERIALISM EXPOSED BY THE LAWS OF MATTER AND MOTION.

What is Materialism?

The question of materialism and its opposite, immaterialism, so prominent and assuming at the present day, seems to us to have grown out of the ancient heathen philosophy which taught the viciousness of matter, simply because it was matter. As a consequence, we find those terms generally employed to signify religious belief on the one hand and skepticism on the other. But we consider the questions here involved as purely of a philosophic and scientific character, relating to the existence, conditions, and phenomena of things, or what may be called the methods of God in nature, and as such cannot conflict with any statement contained in the written revelation emanating from the same Being.

As there is no medium between material and immaterial things, or properly between something and nothing, therefore something cannot become nothing, nor nothing something. Of course this argues equally the eternity of simple matter and the impossibility of its annihilation.

Having mentioned annihilation, it may be proper here to quote what Dr. Bernet says, thus: "The doctrine was unknown to the Hebrews, Greeks, and Latins. The ancient philosophers denied annihilation, the first notions of which are said to have arisen from Christian theology." That Mr. John Wesley did not entertain such a theological notion is evident from the following: "All matter indeed is changeable, and that into ten thousand forms; but that it is changeable does in no wise imply that it is perishable. The substance may remain one and the same, though under innumerable different forms. It is very possible any portion of matter may be resolved into the atoms of which it was originally composed; but what reason have we to believe that one of its atoms ever was or ever will be annihilated?" (Wesley's Sermons, vol. ii, p. 14.)

In reference to such a belief we may further remark that it is as creditable to ancient philosophy as to ancient theology, that neither held such an unnatural opinion. The twin sister to this notion is that material things or matter itself was made out of nothing, and rests upon no better ground than that a Mr. Hutchinson said the original word *create* signified this; in consequence of which idea this definition has found its way into our dictionaries; but we shall show that it has no such signification as used in the Bible.

Locality, motion, and organization belong exclusively to matter and its relations. As to locality, it is a fact that matter alone occupies space, or, what is the same thing, has a locality. Space itself is absolutely *nothing;* for if it were a *thing* it would have limits, size, shape, and could therefore only occupy a part of space. Remove every particle of matter from a square inch of space and you have a square inch of *nothing;* and what is true of one inch is equally true of every inch. It is just as correct to speak of empty space as of an empty house—that it has nothing in it, provided the house was a perfect vacuum. It is a fact that one modification of matter in its fluid state (and all solids become fluids and fluids solids) penetrates the cavities or pores of another, thus adding to the weight of the former; yet one square inch of any form of matter, if it is perfectly solid, fills exactly one square inch of space, and under a given temperature and pressure does not increase or decrease in size.

It is obvious that if by any process of art or nature this cube of matter were reduced to immateriality it would cease to occupy space, leaving the cube of space from which it had been immaterialized or annihilated, which is the same thing, an inch of *nothing*. Thus we see that the doctrine of immateriality conveys the strongest possible conception of annihilation, and the conclusion is equally formidable against the supposed existence of purely immaterial things or beings occupying any part of space, hundreds of millions of which might dwell in a single square inch of space and not a particle of it be filled. It is a fact that a square inch of the subtlest or most ethereal gas of the atmosphere or even of electricity may displace a solid inch of gold; but the two cannot occupy the same space at the same time. This law is called the "impenetrability of matter."

An Objection of Mental Philosophy Removed.

But it is said that thoughts, conceptions, imaginations, are things, and yet they occupy no space. This, however, is mere sophistry, for these are only exercises of material mental organs. As well say the growing of a plant is a thing separate from the plant itself, the running of water a separate thing from the water, or that the rolling of the earth is a separate existence from the earth itself, and occupies space. These exercises of the mental organs may be completely stopped by physical obstruction, pressure or disease of the brain, entirely suspending all rational exercise, rendering impossible the least intellectual acquirement, and of course preventing its commencement, if any of these existed in early childhood and had continued.

Upon this subject we quote Mr. Wesley again, who was a philosopher and a scientist as well as one of the best theologians of his day. Confounding as he does the soul, spirit, and intellectual powers, and how they may be hindered by the bodily organs, he says: "These very frequently hinder the soul in its operations; and at best serve it very imperfectly; yet the soul cannot dispense with its service, for an embodied spirit cannot form one thought but by the mediation of its bodily organs, for thinking is not, as many suppose, the act of a pure spirit, but the act of a spirit connected with a body and playing upon a set of material keys. It cannot possibly, therefore, make any better music than the nature and state of its instruments allow. Hence every disorder of the body, especially of the parts more immediately subservient to thinking, lay an almost insuperable bar in the way of its thinking justly." (Wesley's Sermons, vol. ii, p. 34.)

Upon the same subject we quote the following from the essays of the celebrated John Locke, "On the Human Understanding": "We have the ideas of matter and thinking; but possibly shall never know whether any mere material being thinks or not. It being, in respect to our notions, not much more remote from our comprehension to conceive that God can, if he pleases, superadd to matter a faculty of thinking, than that he should superadd to it another substance with a faculty of thinking; since we know not wherein thinking consists, nor to what sort of substance the Almighty has been pleased to give that power; for I see no contradiction in it, that the first eternal, thinking Being should, if he pleased, give to certain systems of created, senseless matter, put together as he thinks fit, sense, perception, and thought."

It is a fact that the immateriality of the soul was never advanced in Christian discussion until the days of Hobbes, in 1679. It seems very clear that Mr. Wesley did not believe in immaterial existences. Says he: "But it has been questioned by some whether there be any fire in hell, that is, any material fire. Nay, if there be any fire, it is unquestionably material; for what is immaterial fire? The same as immaterial water or earth; both the one and the other is absolute nonsense, a contradiction in terms. Either, therefore, we must affirm it to be material fire, or deny its existence." (Vol. ii, p. 34.)

Motion is a relative property of matter, and therefore nothing but that which is composed of some modification of matter can move or be moved; hence motion is not an abstraction or an idea simply, for we can have no idea of the motion of immateriality, or even of its existence. It may be proper to call the space from which we have supposed all matter removed, immateriality. The matter it contains may be changed from one locality to another, but the space remains eternally fixed, and this is only the condition of *nothing*. As the term motion expresses the simple fact of matter moving, it follows that the theory which dispossesses a thing or being of any modification of matter renders that thing or being immovable, and shuts it out of universal space. Hence the doctrine of immateriality teaches nothing but non-existence, as it most perfectly annihilates every thing or being to which it is applied. This is equally the voice of philosophical science, of metaphysics, according to its ancient definition, and of the Bible.

We come now to consider the proposition that organization belongs to and can only be predicated of matter. In order to demonstrate this proposition it is only necessary to consider the opposite theory, which assumes that immaterial organs may not only exist, but that they possess the faculty of self-motion, as well as the power, by direct action of imparting motion to inanimate matter. But as these organs are of the same nature as immateriality itself, they have no location in space—and this is equivalent to non-existence—and therefore they cannot move or be moved, nor endow with the faculty of motion, nor communicate it to the smallest particle of matter.

It is no more an axiom of nature that "from nothing nothing comes," than that nothing cannot move something, nor something nothing; yet these are calmly set aside by the absurd theory that all things were made out of nothing.

Mental Organs formed of Matter.

As the human mind is supposed to be immaterial, it follows that this fancied relation exists between it and the material, voluntary organs of the body. As immateriality cannot move itself, it is incapable of moving or obstructing, or in the least degree affecting any operation of the organs of the human brain; and if the human mind is pure immateriality it has no power or faculty of *exercise*, which implies its motion or that of its organs—indeed expresses this—or by the mere fiat of will of giving locomotion to the material human body.

Numerous facts are recorded demonstrating the material organization of the human mind, including the intellectual powers. The cerebrum, or intellectual brain, has received injuries by which the cranium has been depressed, immediately suspending all rational thought. Sometimes fractured portions of the skull have been lifted from the brain by surgical operation, when instantly the subjects became conscious, and in some cases have been known to finish the sentence arrested by the accident, but yet had been perfectly unconscious of all events intervening between the injury and the remedy, though years had elapsed. Such facts demonstrate the operation of the organic mind, and that such operation is essential to thought or the acquisition of human knowledge.

Another important fact in proof that the brain proper is the organized sensorium, the motions or exercise of which result in rational thought, is the phenomenon of sleep. Organic man is composed of two grand departments, the voluntary and involuntary. The cerebrum is the source of the intellectual faculties and nerves of volition, and constitutes the intellectual department; while the lesser, anterior brain, or cerebellum, is the source of the involuntary nerves, leading to all the vital organs, and constitutes the department of life. All of these are continually active, whether we wake or sleep. These commence operation when we begin to live—in fact constitute the life itself—carrying on all the functions of animal life and phenomena, so that the blood circulates, the heart beats, the liver secretes its bile, the lungs respire, and all the lesser organs continue their uninterrupted activities while life lasts, whether the mind is awake or sleeps, whether we will or not; so that man cannot end his life by voluntarily ceasing to breathe. He may hold his breath until he faints; but now, becoming unconscious, the will, the supreme governor of the voluntary instruments, relaxes its grasp, and the involuntary faculties restore him to consciousness.

Involuntary Sleep—Death.

The involuntary department obtains all the rest demanded because of the reduced consumption of the vital force by the slower motion of the vital organs, while the voluntary department, the intellectual, has its nightly sleep; but when the involuntary department goes to sleep, *that* sleep is death to both—of course reducing all to a state of unconsciousness until the resurrection or re-creation of the organic structure, which is the revealed design of man's Maker.

Here two principal physiological facts are to be observed: first, that the living, involuntary department never for a moment sleeps, except in death; second, that by the exhaustion of the sources of motion—inhaled from the air and assimilated by the vital organs from the food taken into the stomach—by continued mental activity, the mental, thinking department is also compelled to sleep, in which condition, as a consequence, all thought and consciousness are at an end. It is true that in dreams irrational thoughts occur, but this is owing to the fact that all the mental organs are not then in perfect sleep. Those which have been most excited or exercised during the day are the last to sleep at night; by this strain the brain-organs and the nerves leading from them have become most expanded, and are therefore the last to contract and sleep; and as rational thought requires the perfect wakefulness of all the mental organs, dreams are but the confused vagaries of minds partly dead, as the whole mind is dead while it is in a state of sound sleep.

For example, a man has been engaged during the

day in endeavoring to collect money, and has been unsuccessful. He lies down at night to sleep; but that part of the brain more immediately connected with such an enterprise, as acquisitiveness and secretiveness, having been most active is the most expanded, and therefore the last to contract and sleep at night.

Hence the man dreams, and his dreams are about money, but of course are devoid of sense, and these phrenological and physiological facts show why. Solomon presents this philosophy thus: "Dreams cometh from a press of business." It will be observed that it is not the living, unthinking department that sleeps thus nightly, but the mental, intellectual, thinking powers; and every time sleep is repeated the mind becomes as profoundly unconscious of all passing events as though the man was dead. It must also be remembered that it is the unthinking, vital powers which thus compel the mental faculties to cease their operation. Now, no matter what are the speculations of any class of men in regard to these phenomena, daily observation and their own daily experienced emonstrate such to be its philosophy.

These facts give us the solution of the question so often propounded, What is life? and show that it is not any one thing—not the breath, or spirit, or soul, or mind, or intellect, or even the lungs, heart, or stomach—but all of these combined in a single body. Life, therefore, is *in the combination*, and results from the organization. The demonstration is, that had a single vital organ been left out—say the lungs—life would have been impossible, because breathing could not take place. We see also that as human intelligence results from thinking, and thinking from living, therefore had the first man, Adam, not lived he could never have acquired a thought, hence he would have been as though he had not been.

These physiological facts are also in the most perfect accord with the Mosaic statements in relation to the creation of the first man. He was organized perfectly, and therefore susceptible of living, and his Maker then "breathed into his nostrils the breath of life, and man became a living soul." The breath was not the life, but was the *breath of life;* it was the first breath, and set the vital machinery in motion; the second and every subsequent breath were inhaled by the man, "the living soul" himself. The breath was one of the vital principles, the lungs were another, and neither could have given life without the other: for man could not live if he had not breathed, neither could he have breathed without lungs. Therefore, no one or more of the vital organs or principles, all of which are essential to life, was the life, the living soul, but all combined made the man such.

To Understand Nature you must Understand the Bible.

Whoever would understand the teachings of nature in the highest degree must at least understand the leading truths of the Bible. By leading truths we do not mean what any man may call such, adopting and reporting them upon second-hand authority; but such as one may find by searching the Scriptures and mastering them for himself. A man might just as well adopt and proclaim what another declares to be the teachings of nature, without comprehending a single one of her principles, or mastering a scientific problem. Such a theologian or scientist should be ruled out of the discussion of all the questions herein involved, leaving it to be prosecuted by his better qualified master. We insist that he who justifiably arrays any fact or truth of nature against any fact or truth of revelation contained in the Bible must have qualified himself for the task, either by mastering the reasons, and thus obtaining the evidences from both these sources of knowledge, which led others to the conclusions he adopts, or of acquiring them by independent investigation.

To hold the Bible responsible for all the erroneous and contradictory sentiments which have been attributed to it is as absurd as it would be to hold a modern scientist or philosopher responsible for the opinions of Plato, who, in his attempt to account for the physical derangement of the world, attributed it to the inherent vicious and implacable nature of senseless matter. So in relation to the doctrine of matter, its nature and duration, revealed alike in nature and the Bible: when both are understood, and are left to interpret themselves and each other, they are found to be in the most perfect harmony.

A study of matter puts a limit to scientific research and human capacity, and within its circle imposes on him who makes use of any of its facts or phenomena to oppose the statements or any teaching of the Bible, the necessity of having a perfect comprehension of such facts and the philosophy of their existence and a determination of the exact time required for coming into existence; which implies a knowledge of all the dynamics and possible agencies that may have been present and active in the operation. It is only by such qualification that it can be determined whether there was a being possessed of mind interested and engaged in the work, whether he possessed the requisite power to perform it, and whether he was abstract and independent or confounded with the work: did he possess the ability to bring into existence a stratum of granite a mile in thickness in a single hour, which if formed by the slow process of nature [if it is thus formed at all?] would consume a hundred thousand years, but which would in both cases bear the same marks of age?

Skeptical Materialism Defined.

The grounds of the controversy between materialism, in the skeptical sense of this word, and revealed religion originated in the supposition that in some of the modifications of matter are found or to be found all the powers and facilities required to have formed the organic and inorganic world as it is, and, of course, without the intervention of an intelligent being, who may or may not exist, but that nature reveals no necessary work for him to do. Hence the term "materialists" properly designates skeptics; but to apply it to Christians for believing that Jesus Christ was a material being, and that he is their God and the Creator of all things, and that there is to be a resurrection of the same material being that now lives and dies, is to assume the ridiculous attitude of denouncing as skeptics all the apostles and all the Bible Christians of the world. Christians believe in and worship a personal, living God who made all things; while skeptics hold that there is no such being, and that all things came into existence of themselves by evolution; or that they never came into existence, and yet they exist! The conclusions we have now reached in relation to matter and its opposite, immaterialism, may be summed up thus:

Materiality has shape, immateriality has none. Materiality has weight, immateriality weighs nothing. Materiality has tangibility, can be felt, immateriality cannot be felt. Materiality is susceptible of motion, immateriality is not. Matter occupies space, immateriality does not. Matter may be organized, immateriality cannot be organized. Matter cannot become immateriality, nor *vice versa:* otherwise, the first proposition would involve the absurdity of annihilation, and the second the equal absurdity that matter can be made out of *no matter*—in other words, that nothing can become something, and something become nothing. If matter exists, it must always have existed, and cannot cease to exist. Immateriality does not exist, and never did exist; as well suppose the existence of non-existence. Hence we have the self-evident statement, "*From nothing nothing comes.*"

Life and intelligence are the result of organic being. An immaterial mind cannot move or have exercise, which implies motion, and therefore it cannot create material things or govern them. As it cannot move itself, of course it cannot cause the motion of other things, which an act of creation or government implies. If God is immateriality, He has no weight, form, size, organs, or intelligence; He therefore has no power to move either himself or a particle of matter. He is inorganic, and fills no space. This immaterial fantasm, called God, can be found nowhere in the universe, and must be left just where He is found and what He thus is—*nowhere and nothing*.

The Doctrine of Immateriality—Annihilation.

With regard to the application of this word to describe the nature of the Deity—whose greatness is as infinitely above man's comprehension as the creation of the world is above his power of execution—instead of its being a sign of an idea, was invented by a Mr. Hutchinson, as Mr. John Wesley says, and as we repeat, to hide his ignorance and cover up his arrogance in a proud attempt to comprehend the nature of the being who made him, to tell us of what kind of stuff he was composed, so closely had he analyzed him; which is as foolish as would be an attempt on the part of a thing of man's make to explain to his fellow-things what kind of material man, its maker, was composed of, or to declare that a being great enough to make it could not be a material being at all.

Multitudes have adopted this word in its application to God, without for a moment stopping to examine its inherent absurdity. Those who assume to be thus wise —by the wisdom of the world to find out God, to comprehend the incomprehensible—naturally seek to bring analogies and plausibilities to their assistance, and they reason thus: All matter is made out of nothing: if God is matter, He must have been made or have made Himself, and that too out of nothing. He is therefore immateriality. Matter is destructible; if God is matter He is destructible; and therefore also all the immortal, resurrected saints, being the same *material* organisms which died, are not immortal, but destructible; but as God is eternal He must be immaterial. A material being must have a location in space, or his dimensions must be as boundless as space, which ideas being incompatible, He must be immateriality, which has no locality. As nothing but matter can be organic, and as God is not matter, he cannot be an organized being.

As immateriality could never have come into existence, or cease to exist, and as God is immateriality, He is therefore indestructible and eternal. Now, what is there in this apparent profound reasoning? Simply that, having reduced the being of God to *absolute nothing*, He could no more have come into existence or cease to exist than can nothing; therefore he is eternal, but an eternal *nothing*.

If it be sought to avoid this conclusion by the declaration that God is an immaterial *substance*, it in no wise relieves the argument of its philosophic absurdities, unless this substance is defined to be something which occupies space; and this admission invests it with all the essential qualities of matter, and therefore virtually overturns the whole doctrine of immaterial existences. If the doctrine of the existence of a personal organic God is beyond the grasp of created mind, does not the conception of an immaterial God become still more impossible, by reducing or elevating him into a kind of being which, by all the analogies of nature and known existences, is not only incomprehensible, but absolutely repugnant and contradictory to reason, still further from the grasp of the human mind to conceive?

Substantial Nature of God Proved by His Attributes.

It is claimed that even this God has attributes, some of which are, omniscience (all-seeing), omnipresence (all-knowing), and omnipotence (all-powerful). With some, these inhere and belong to the Divine Being, and with others they constitute the Godhead. If this view is correct, then it seems to us we need no further argument, nor to add a word to prove God to be an organized being, and as such He must have a location somewhere in space; for it is impossible to disassociate a combination of attributes and personal organization. As omnipotence, manifested in the government of the inanimate universe, is material power, it must be a material attribute, as an immaterial being cannot have a material attribute, which is a part of himself; therefore God is not immateriality.

As to the attributes of God and their description, we prefer taking the written, revealed language describing it. Hence we read: "Whither shall I flee from thy presence?" (Ps. 139 : 7.) "To him the darkness shineth as the light, darkness hideth not from thee." "Am I a God at hand, saith the Lord, and not a God afar off?" (Jer. 23 : 23.) "Can any hide himself in secret places that I shall not see him? saith the Lord. Do not I fill heaven and earth?" (Jer. 23 : 24.) "He that made the ear, shall he not hear; he that made the eye, shall he not see?"

The idea that God must be in close contact with every object He sees is infinitely more preposterous than that a man should be thus in contact. The sun is in man's presence, because he sees it, just as it is in the presence of God. A man sees everything he has made, and has a perfect knowledge of its capability and uses, by the eye of his mind, though they may all be in another continent at the time. So God may as really occupy a location in space not larger than that filled by a man, and yet see and have a perfect knowledge of everything he has made, or that exists.

If a man's mind is susceptible of having imprinted on it every object which he has ever seen, or with which he has been interested, all of which are in his presence, may not all the works of God be also thus imprinted, and be also in His presence, and He Himself be "far above all heavens?" "Known unto God are all His works from the beginning of the world." (Acts. 15 : 18.)

In reference to His power we read: "The Lord God Omnipotent reigneth." Omnipotence therefore is not an abstract attribute of the God of nature and the Bible, but is so allied with his Being that He Himself *is omnipotent.*

Jesus Christ is a Material Being, but the Christian's God.

To those who believe in Christianity and yet entertain

such heathen views of God, we propose to present a few arguments for their reflection. First, the world is as ignorant of the nature of God as the above conclusions show. "The world by wisdom knew not God : for it is written, I will destroy the wisdom of the wise, and will bring to nothing the understanding of the prudent." [Those who say, Well, if Jesus is Lord, we should be careful not to confess it, lest the heathen philosophers laugh us to scorn for having a material God.] Where is the wise ? where is the scribe ? where is the disputer of this world ? For after that in the wisdom of God the world by wisdom knew not God ; it pleased God by the foolishness of preaching to save them that believe : for the Jews require a sign, and the Greeks seek after wisdom ; but we preach Christ crucified, unto the Jews a stumbling-block, and unto the Greeks foolishness. But unto them which are called, both Jews and Greeks, *Christ*, the power of God and the wisdom of God. [The called are those who accept Jesus Christ as the embodiment of the *wisdom* and *power* of God, and therefore *God Himself*.] Because the foolishness of God is wiser than men ; and the weakness of God is stronger than men : for ye see your calling, brethren, how that not many wise men after the flesh, not many mighty, not many noble, are called. [Not many of those whose wisdom led them to adopt the heathen philosophy of the impersonal, immaterial God of nature as taught by Pantheistic mythology and modern evolution.] But God hath chosen the foolish things of the world to confound the wise ; and God hath chosen the weak things of the world to confound the things which are mighty, and the base things of the world, and the things which are despised, hath God chosen, yea, and things which are not, to bring to naught things that are : that no flesh should glory in his presence. But of him are ye in Christ Jesus, who of God is made unto us, wisdom, and righteousness, and sanctification, and redemption : as it is written, He that glorieth, let him glory in the Lord." (1 Cor. 1 : 19-31.)

The Scriptures teach, clearly, unequivocally, and as positively as language can, the truth that the One living and eternal God prepared a human body for Himself, and was about thirty-three years in the work, and consummated it when he took it from the tomb of Joseph ; that from that event He was God in the form of man, and in this form he was the Son of God, and which transaction made God "*Father*," as this was the *only begotten* Son, hence making God *Father* and *Son*, both in *one person*. God was Father in purpose, in decree, and in prediction before this, even from the foundation of the world, and Christ was a "lamb slain from the foundation of the world ; " but neither of these were facts until this investment took place, of which we have the history recorded by the evangelists and writers of the Epistles.

We do not propose to answer the apparent objections to this position, as it would require too much space for this book ; besides we have done this in another work, at least to our own satisfaction. Nor can we give more than a small number of the Scripture statements and passages which admit of no other inference. To do this fully it would be necessary to consider the import of all the names God has used to reveal Himself in the Scriptures ; likewise to show that Jesus Christ possessed and manifested all the wisdom and all the power which the organic and inorganic world exhibits, and that, too, while He was on earth, and during the time God was in and with Him, making the preparation of the human body for Himself, and consequently in his lowest and weakest form. This also we have set forth in another work.

Scripture Argument Proving the Lord Jesus the Only God.

The question is, Is this Son of God, this Jesus, God Himself? If so, he must be the object of universal worship.

In order to appreciate the Scripture argument upon this subject, it must be understood that God has purposed, and fully revealed that purpose, to make a new world out of the dissolved elements of this, called "the world to come," the new heaven and new earth, the pre-historic record of which is summed up in the last two chapters of Revelation; that this is to be His eternal kingdom, in which He and His immortal saints, having like Him been raised from the dead, shall reign forever—this is the "world without end"—that this reign is signified by His name *Lord*, meaning one who reigns; that *Jesus*, the *Lamb*, the weakest, meekest, lowliest name of God, by the immanualization of himself, *is this Almighty Lord to reign.* We may remark that it was not the body which was Jesus, or Lord, or the Son of God; but God having himself incarnated, invested with it and in it—just as the material body of man is his own—became Jesus, Christ, the Son of God, the Lord to reign; and this form of God he is to exalt to be the Lord God Omnipotent, the Lord God Almighty, and the Lamb.

In proof of these statements we quote the following words of Scripture, which to us is authority, and the only authority we admit upon religious questions:

"Let this mind be in you, which was also in Christ Jesus: who, being in the *form of God*, thought it not robbery to be equal with God: but made himself of no reputation, and took upon him the form of a servant, and was made in the likeness of men : and being found in fashion as a man, he humbled himself, and became obedient unto death, even the death of the cross. Wherefore God also hath highly exalted him, and given him *a name which is above every name :* that at the name *of Jesus* every knee should bow, of things in heaven [the angels] of things in earth [all living men], and things under the earth [the dead in their graves, under the surface of the earth when resurrected] ; and that every tongue should confess that Jesus Christ is Lord, to the glory of God the Father." (Phil. 2 : 4–11). Here the fact is stated, that the time is coming when all intelligent creatures will confess that Jesus is Lord ; and as the Father and Son are one, and as God has become Father and Son by taking the human form, therefore to glorify one is to glorify the other.

"God, who at sundry times and in diverse manners spake in time past unto the fathers, by the prophets, hath in these last days spoken unto us by his Son, whom he hath appointed heir of all things, by whom also he made the worlds ; who being the brightness of his [God's glory], and the express image of his person [God is *a person*, not two persons, and the Son is his image, and express image], and upholding all things by the word of his power [the power of the Son], when he had by himself purged our sins, sat down on the right hand of the majesty on high : being made so much better than the angels, as he hath by inheritance obtained a more excellent name than they : for unto which of the angels said he at any time, Thou art my Son, this day have I begotten thee ? and again, I will be to him a Father, and he shall be to me a Son ? And again, when he bringeth in the first begotten into the world, he saith, And *let all the angels of God worship him,* and unto the *Son* he saith, Thy throne, *O God,* is forever and ever ; a scepter of righteousness is the scepter of thy kingdom." (Heb. 1 : 1–8.) Here the only-begotten son is declared to be God, and to hold the scepter of eternal reign in his kingdom, and to be worshiped by all the angels. Upon what other principle can this be true or lawful, and not idolatry, but that God himself is invested with this human form ?

"And thou shalt worship no other God : for the Lord, whose name is Jealous, is a jealous God." (Ex. 34 : 14.) Here we see that it is so impossible for God to permit any but the Lord to be worshiped that he calls his very name "*Jealous.*" "The Lord of hosts is his name. For my name's sake, for mine own name's sake, will I do it, and I will not give my glory to another." (Isa. 48 : 2, 9, 11). If Jesus is another person than God, the Lord, He will not give him his glory. "But I had pity for mine holy name, which the house of Israel had profaned among the heathen, therefore, thus saith the Lord : I do not this for your sakes, O house of Israel, but for mine holy name's sake, and I will sanctify my *great name,* and the heathen shall know that I am the Lord, saith the Lord God." (Ez. 36 : 21–23.) Here the Lord God declares his *great name* to be Lord, and "every tongue is to confess that *Jesus is Lord,*" and this name is to be "exalted above every name ;" God has pity upon this, his *great name,* upon himself, in the form of man, suffering the death of the cross for man, taking the dead body again triumphantly from the grave. "The Lord is risen indeed, and become the first fruits of them that slept." (1 Cor. 15.) Thus, the Lord God is Lord, and *Jesus* is Lord. "There is one Lord, one faith, one God, one Father." (Eph. 4 : 5, 6.] Therefore, also, is *Jesus*

God. "Wherefore when he cometh into the world, he saith, Sacrifices and offering thou wouldst not, but a body hast thou prepared me." (Heb. 10 : 5)

Christ is Worthy of all Honor.

As we have in another work (see "Philosophy of God and the World") argued at length and exhaustively the question of the Godhead of Jesus Christ, we need not pursue it further here; and so far as ourselves are concerned we may say that we esteem it the highest possible honor to be permitted to have part in the worship of this centralized, this profundity, "God." We ask no share in the work of the self-complacent, bearing the Christian name, of disintegrating the Godhead, and then passing judgment on the fragments, saying which is greatest and which is least. Though the revelation of this "*Wonderful*," as he is designated in inspired prediction, is utterly *beyond* human comprehension (not incongruous to it), still the evidence of his nature and existence is as conclusive and overwhelming as that upon which the truth of the Sacred Scriptures themselves rest. So also there are marvelous phenomena connected with our own origin and existence, yet we do exist, and began to exist. Is it anything but infatuation to reject the idea that Jesus Christ is the embodied Deity because we cannot comprehend the manner of that embodiment? He may be allowed to make material bodies for men and angels, but not for Himself. If such strange specimens of mentality are consistent with themselves, we doubt whether they believe anything; for if they do not unless they can comprehend it, or the manner of its existence, they certainly do not believe that they themselves exist.

Though personal revelation establishes the existence

of just such a god as nature and its design require, yet He is rejected by the evolutionists, as the grossest materialists, and as Professor Tyndall, one of the ablest advocates of their theories, declare, he sees in the simplest matter the origin and potency of all things the life of the world manifests, we must meet them upon their own line of argument; for it would be certainly more consistent were we to argue that there once existed a creature like man, only so much superior as to have been the maker of the world with its inhabitants, than that these should have originated in a being of less capacity than man.

If a Man Evolved in Time, why not God in Eternity?

As it is the evolutionists who more than any other class of skeptics ignore the existence of a personal God as having or having had any relation to the existence or government of the world, we must consider their attitude more inconsistent than that of other skeptics, from the fact that they trace the descent of the greatest and most perfect organizations from the simplest conceivable beginnings. If, for example, man with all his wonderful powers and susceptibilities, physically, morally, and mentally, and even as a religious being, has through countless ages evolved from the simple movement of intelligent atoms, why may not a being have evolved from the vast machinery of all the universes and systems of worlds and stellar centers, in the incomputable eternities of the past, possessing all the knowledge and power which this little insignificant plaint (as it is called) manifests, so that he might easily have been its creator? And further, as man has the supreme dominion over the organic things from which he evolved, laying the vegetable and animal kingdoms under contribution to minister to his wants and will, inflicting pains and penalties for every act of insubordination, resulting either in subjection or destruction, why may not this great Supreme, holding control of all the organic machinery from which He Himself evolved—why may not He lay all species, races, and individuals under contribution to minister to his pleasures, purposes, and will, and inflict pains and penalties for every act of disobedience, whether of a mental, moral, or physical character, and finally resulting also in submission or extermination?

Further still, if this short-lived world, even giving it the longest period claimed for its existence, has evolved such a being as man, capable of making, and perpetually inclined not only to make things, but those of the most wonderful construction, such as the electric telegraph and locomotive engine, to minister to his interests and wants, why may not the being evolved from all the systems of worlds during the eternities of the past, be also, like him, a material organization, and, choosing himself as the model, have made, directly by his own hand, the great Omniform, or Primordial, from which the earth, the solar system, and man himself have come into existence?

If evolution be a principle of nature, why should its operations be circumscribed within the chronological and geographical limits of this little world? What reason can be assigned why such a being should not have come thus into existence, and the world have been his direct workmanship, as that man should thus have evolved, possessing to some considerable extent the power to subdue the elements by mechanical and chemical means, in order to subserve his purposes? Indeed, we do not see why it should be a greater tax on the imagination to suppose a succession of gods, with all the knowledge and power this world manifests, to have evolved from the universes of all nature and the duration of all past eternities, than to suppose that a succession of mankind, as the evolutionists claim, have evolved from and upon this little planet, of an ephemeral existence compared with the vast ages through which the evolution machine has been running; for if it commenced, that would have been a "catastrophe," the possibility of which the system does not admit. Any one of such gods might have laid the omnific golden egg, from which Time hatched the world.

This idea solves the hard problem, and gives evolution its starting point, so far as this world is concerned, but still it is one of creation.

If we have the proper conception that all power is mental, and compare that manifested by the man who created the steamship which plows the ocean, propelled by an engine of five thousand horse power, with that of which the first living plant-cell was capable, and from which man has evolved, and which cell had no life to begin with, and also that all worlds, during all past time, are likewise subjects of evolution, then why may they not have commenced also without antecedent life and from the simplest form of matter—plasma, monera, anything—and have evolved a being as personal as man, looking like him, and abundantly capable of being the creator of this our little world, as it is estimated by these same so-called scientists. We repeat, if evolution is true at all, and is capable of producing intelligent beings, and man in so short a fragment of eternity as that of the few years the world is said to have existed, why limit it to the development of man? Here, then, according to evolution, we have a personal God—the Creator of the world and man.

Should any of these, His works, question the existence of this cause, and ask who designed the designer, we answer, "Nature," and to be a little more particular, and hence a little more absurd, we may say, "Nature" had no life herself, but she gave life to all the living inhabitants of the world, beginning by small degrees and working upward. So, also, if an evolutionist asks who designed the designer, we answer, a living, personal God. If pressed further with the question, "Whence came He?" we answer, He evolved away back in duration from lifeless matter, as evolution can do anything, only give her time enough; and for the accomplishment of this work of god-making we lavishly bestow upon her boundless duration: surely this is long enough.

Here is a field in which Professor Tyndall may revel with his backward vision in search of his godless engineer to get up steam to start his first primordial into being from no primordial with such plausible grounds as Darwin gives him for confining his researches to our little globe; and if one finds, as the result of his petty evolution, man, with faculties and endowments enabling him to originate and construct the most wonderful machines, may not the other find, evolved from the material movements of an eternal succession of universes, a being of capacities and powers equal to the creation of this one little mundane sphere?

Scripture Definition of the word Create.

It is a well-known fact in the history of science and philosophy that new words are coined to describe newly discovered facts and ideas; from which it follows that if the facts are only supposed facts, and the ideas false, that such words convey no intelligent meaning. Such is the modern definition of the word "create." Some one conceived the notion that "God made all things out of nothing," and claimed, therefore, that the word create had this meaning; but though human authors employ it in this sense, the Scriptures use it simply to express the fact that God made one thing or substance out of another previously existing; and so far as the teachings of this book are concerned, the matter out of which all things were made might have been eternal. As the words *made*, *form*, and *create* are used interchangeably, descriptive of the work of bringing the heaven and the earth into existence, it follows that they have the same meaning.

The account of creation begins with the mention of matter existing in a great, dark, chaotic deep, devoid of any of the forms it was made to assume during the progress of the work. The phrase, "In the beginning God created the heaven and the earth," is a general expression covering the whole subsequent work, while the particular work done on each of the six days is afterward described: "For in six days God made the heaven and the earth, and all things that in them is." As this is the same work, and the whole of it, covered by the expression, "the beginning," it can signify no longer time; and to make these days any other than days of twenty-four hours each is to "handle the word of God deceitfully."

If there were no other evidence than the fact that the seventh of these days was the twenty-four-hour Sabbath on which God rested from His work of creation, and afterward made it a Sabbath for the rest of man and beast, it would be sufficient to establish our position; showing the absurdity of the rule of interpretation which makes six of these days indefinite periods and the other a definite one. That the words *create*, *made*, and *formed* are used as we have indicated, will appear by the following quotations: "In the beginning God *created* the heaven and the earth." (Gen. 1 : 1.) "And God *created* great whales." (Ver. 25.) "And God *made* every beast of the field after His kind." (Ver. 27.) "So God created man in His own image .... in the image of God created He him .... male and female created He them." (Chap. 2.) "And on the seventh day God ended His work which He had *made* .... and God blessed the seventh day and sanctified it, because that in it He had rested from all His works which God created and *made* .... in the day that the Lord God *made* the earth and the heavens."

In this last passage it will be observed that the word day means the same as that of beginning, also covering the whole work, and is a recapitulation.

The following passages show that the words *made*, *formed*, and *create* do not mean to make things out of nothing:

"And of the rib, which the Lord God had taken from man, made He a woman." She was not therefore made out of nothing. "And the Lord God *formed man of the dust of the ground.*" And not out of nothing.

"And out of the ground the Lord God formed every beast of the field and every fowl of the air." Not out of nothing. "For I have *created* him [man] for my glory. I have *formed* him; yea, I have *made* him." (Isa. 34 : 7.)

"This is the generation of Adam, in the day that God created him, in the likeness of God *made* He him." (Gen 1 : 31.) "And God saw everything that He had *made*, and behold it was very good, and the evening and the morning were the sixth day." "And He that sat upon the throne said, Behold, I *make* all things new."

(Rev. 21. 5.) This is the "new heaven and the new earth," which, by turning to the chapter, will be seen is to be done after the conflagration of the present heaven and earth, which reduces it to a second chaos. In predicting this Jeremiah says: "I beheld the earth and the heavens and they had no light, and lo, they were without form and void." (4 : 23.) The creation of the new heaven and earth, or the re-creation of the present world, is to take place in accordance with the promise of God to Isaiah (65 : 17) : "For behold, I create new heavens and a new earth."

These are to be created out of the dissolved elements of the present world, and not out of nothing. "For in six days the Lord made heaven and earth, and the sea, and all that in them is, and rested on the seventh day; wherefore the Lord blessed the Sabbath day and hallowed it." (Gen. 31 : 17.) "It is a sign between me and the children of Israel for ever: for in six days the Lord made heaven and earth, and on the seventh day He rested, and was refreshed."

What was the Nature of the Original Matter?

We come now to consider what was the nature of the original matter out of which all things were made, and we agree with Professor Huxley, that it was *homogeneous*, which means of the same kind or nature. Its particles therefore had no chemical or electrical variety or peculiarity, and hence had no faculty, function, or power to be in the least degree affected by each other, which is essential to molecular or atomic motion, which leads us to the conclusion that were the universe filled with such matter, not a particle of it would ever move; and as the simplest formation is two particles adhering together, this implies that they have chemical or electrical affinity, and are not homogeneous.

If, therefore, the original matter *was homogeneous*, then the motion of its particles was and is impossible ; and as such motion was essential to the very simplest as well as the grandest combination, not one of these could ever have existed. If, however, the evolutionists, seeing this fatal result to their hypothesis, should change their grounds and deny that the original matter was homogeneous, then they must take the only other horn of the dilemma, that its particles were intelligently endowed with a vast variety of chemical and electrical peculiarities. We say intelligently, from the fact that they seek each other according to these endowments or laws, and by combining formations result. As each of these formations answers a certain purpose, and as a purpose can only be predicated of mind, therefore the endowment came from an intelligent Being, and was an act of creation. Instead, therefore, of the original matter out of which the world came having been, as is variously claimed, in a fiery, icy, tumultuous, dashing condition, every atom of it had lain perfectly motionless, and without intellectual interference would have so remained.

Thus it is not only proved but demonstrated that in such a universe of matter evolution could have had no starting point.

The Atomic Theory Exposed.

This homogeneous matter, God, by His spirit, agency, or power, which was material—for it came in contact with and moved matter, which immateriality cannot do—collected from space and condensed into that consistency Moses called "the great deep." This was an act prior to the creation of the world. Atoms may be divided by mechanical operation, chemical dissolution, or theoretically by mathematical calculation, *ad infinitum;*

and yet each piece is as really matter as though it weighed a ton. Indeed, we have no more approximated the conception of a particle which may not continue to be theoretically divided than we may approximate the comprehension of eternity, infinity, or the bounds of space. Nor have we disposed of one of the essential conditions of such particles of matter. The mathematical principle also shows the error of the atomic theory, which fixes the ultimate size of atoms.

Another fact in relation to atoms is, that they are imponderable only when in this high state of sublimation, because no art of man is able to collect them in sufficient quantity to manifest specific gravity, and to detect which the scale must be placed above that area where they are in equilibrium. The fact is, the smallest atom as much occupies an area of space equal to its dimensions as the loftiest mountain or even the globe itself does. From these facts we conclude that the proper application of the term *nature*, when employed to describe the motions or phenomena of material substances, as the movements, order, or plan of nature, is limited by true science to created existences. To call the matter out of which the world was made, nature, while it was the making that gave nature her birth, is as absurd as to call the material out of which a house is built the house itself.

As absolute inertia is the law of simple or unendowed matter, and as there is no such matter within the circumference of the solar system, every particle of which is now susceptible of motion by its inherent constitution, of chemical affinity or electrical polarity, therefore, there is no uncreated matter within this area: the earth itself flies rapidly through space. The decompositions and formations of all material bodies show that there is no particle of matter which has not the power to affect and therefore move some other particle. Hence there is none connected with our world absolutely inert.

Changes of Matter by the Mind of God.

We may state this argument thus: first, matter existed without the power of motion; secondly, it now moves; thirdly, its motions are according to fixed laws; fourthly, these laws are inherent, constitutional endowment; fifthly, the motions accomplish certain uniform fixed ends; sixthly, these motions and ends are the works of nature; seventhly, the endowment was involution, the work of the Creator, the working out or unfolding of which is evolution; therefore evolution is the effect and involution the cause; but as it is only a secondary cause it is therefore an effect itself, while the sole cause resided in the mind of God.

We have assumed the existence, as a philosophic necessity, of a Being of intelligence and power equal to the involvement of that displayed in the living, moving and adjustable universe, and here is our argument in its defense. The work of a mechanic no more demonstrates his prior existence, wisdom, and power, than does the universe, the handiwork of God, proclaim His wisdom, power, and beneficence.

If a mechanic should make a rude shelter suitable only for his horse, and this hut should produce a beautiful dwelling-place for the mechanic himself, then might the Being who made the world have produced only a rude, nascent, shapeless globe, containing only the lowest types of organic things; and even these could no more have come into existence of themselves than could the rude shelter the man made for his horse: much less could the most wonderful machine man was capable of making in turn produce the man himself. This, then, is the silly fancy of evolution, bearing upon its very face the most palpable refutation of all its claims and pretensions to science ; and more preposterous still, were that possible, because it cannot bring to bear in its support the first principle or fact of philosophy.

CHAPTER VI.

MIND, MOLECULES, AND THE IMPONDERABLE AGENTS.

How came the Atoms to be Endowed with Gravity?

WE have already seen that the sole cause of power, which is matter in motion, resides in mind. The agents of mind essential to motion, and consequently to power, with which every atom and form of matter in the universe is endowed, are heat, light, electricity, chemical affinity, pressure, and gravity, each of which occupies space, and which nothing but matter can do.

The theory of atomic or molecular motion, first taught by Maschus before the Trojan war, was, "that atoms were endowed with gravity, by which all things were formed without the aid of a Supreme Being." If this ancient philosopher, or those who afterward adopted his theory, as Epicurus and others of great celebrity, had gone one step further, and asked, How came the atoms to be endowed with gravity? it would have compelled them to admit the existence of an intelligent personal Being, who not only thus endowed the atoms, but out of them organized the universe, with all the progenitors of its living creatures and productions as well as its lifeless formations. This work gave birth to nature and science.

Although the physical school of philosophers, by which is meant those who attributed the origin of things to physics and not to mind, to atoms and not to God, acknowledged their inability to explain how the universe was built up by the working of simple molecules, yet they wished it to be inferred that when it came to be better understood, the science better known, the mystery would vanish. This is also the cherished hope of the evolutionists, and all the advocates of the physical theory of life by natural forces independent of mind. When this is achieved they expect to show how everything in the whole solar system, from man down to the most insignificant organic thing visible only by the aid of the microscope, has been built up molecule by molecule.

It seems to us, however, that the legitimate teaching of the molecules and their phenomena is, that the solar system and its constituents must have been created, of course by an intelligent Being, and that if plants, animals, or inorganic bodies differ from each other in quality, it is because the qualities and allied forces of the atoms also differ, and that this difference was designed by their Maker.

Nothing in comparative anatomy, microscopic detection, or the facts of natural selection is able otherwise even to approximate a solution of the mystery.

The nebula theory of Laplace involves the same doctrine, and as material motion only derives its power from mind, it is equally erroneous. It is, however, at this point that the problem for solution lies, and as it is fundamental it must be understood to enable us to arrive at the truth. The great fact of nature is, *things move*. It matters not whether the things are men or the most minute atoms of which they are composed—for each is an organization of itself—provided it has chemical peculiarity, adapting it to a place in the simplest or the most complicated organism or formation the world contains.

The question is, Does the molecular force inhere by nature, or was it derived from an adequate cause beyond? So far as plants and animals are concerned, to answer this question intelligently we must discriminate between the original pair of each species and their successive generations. That a material body has the faculty of starting from one locality and reaching another without regard to the space traversed or time consumed, presupposes that body to be endowed with some of the organs of sense, of reasoning faculties, will, and capable of being actuated by inducement or motive. This is voluntary motion, and therefore implies the existence of the faculties and the processes essential to such motion.

Such phenomena are as true of the minutest animalcule, whose instruments of locomotion are the finest hairs, perceptible only by the aid of the microscope, as of man himself; and so far as the fact of such motion is concerned, and the intellectual processes involved, man has no superiority over the insect. Although the difference is comparative, yet it is very wide, and is manifest in the variety of motions with which each moves toward the accomplishment of an intelligent purpose or determined end. Herein man justly claims superiority, and this is due to the higher purposes and susceptibility of his being, stamping him as the masterpiece of organic skill.

Man's Physiological Superiority Compared.

It must be admitted that it is difficult to judge between the degree of perfection manifested in the human organization and that so exquisitely displayed in the smallest insect existence. If we except the structure of the human brain, supposing its organism to be fully understood as the seat of the mental faculties, there is just as much mechanical skill exhibited in the structure of the lowest insect, the entire physiological laws of which man can no more comprehend or simulate than he can understand the physical laws of the world, or make the world itself. The test of the comparative superiority of all animals endowed with the power of self-motion is the degree of their intelligence and future destiny.

A machine of human invention and construction, involving the greatest number of functions, and capable of accomplishing the greatest results, possesses the most nearly perfect organization. So, among the works, or, if you please, the inventions and constructions of God displayed in the universe, man, the thinking machine, stands forth the noblest of all. As we recede from him in the scale of comparative anatomy, or of organic life and mental power, we arrive at simple inorganic matter, and as a consequence reach a point at the greatest distance from the possibility of their existence.

Hence the molecules and a thing of life stand at opposite extremes. Thus we perceive that the wanderers toward the molecules in nebula, in search of life and motion, must forever be involved in hopeless disappointment. Otherwise it were as reasonable to claim that the elements composing the iron ore, from which the skill of man constructed the steam-boiler and engine, had the faculty of doing and did this work themselves; or, what is still more absurd, that the original molecules of which man himself is composed possessed the requisite skill for building, and did actually build up man himself. Besides, if this were a matter of fact, it involves another conclusion equally fatal to skepticism. If the simplest atoms, not even possessing the power of motion, produced man, the most stupendous mental power in the created universe, then man himself can produce an intellectual being as far superior to himself as he is to the atoms. Such a being would be capable of creating the universe; for all analogies prove that the difference between the faculties and productions of an atom and those of a man is so great as to qualify a being as much superior to man as he is to the atom to be the creator of the world itself.

If the atom or man created the universe, it would surely be more reasonable to say that it was man who did the work; for he can construct such wonderful things as steamships, while the atom can construct nothing. Or if the universe evolved from either of these it surely would be more likely to have come from man, who combines in himself the grandest evolutionary machinery to begin with. But if the universe evolved from either, it must have been first involved in one or the other. The act of involution presupposes the existence of an intelligent Being equal to the task. Hence by philosophic and scientific necessity we are compelled to admit the existence of a Being so much superior to the universe as to have been its Creator.

The endowment of the molecules, inclining them to move toward each other in formation and from each other in decomposition—in the formative act in such lines and angles as were demanded in the previous organic seed, as the center of attraction—demonstrates it to have arisen in mind, and also proves that it is the source of the origin of species, compelling each to preserve its own identity, and hence that there were at first as many progenitors as there are species, including those which have become extinct.

Power, Mental—Its Conditions and Philosophy.

The philosophy of motion, implying something moving, is equally conclusive in the settlement of this question. Whatever moves does so upon conditions, whether it be an atom, the earth, or a man. The involuntary motions of man's organism depend upon the existence of his vital organs. The voluntary motions depend upon the decision of his will. The decision of the will depends upon a motive. The motive depends upon a prior reasoning process. The reasoning process depends upon the organic brain and at least one of the organic senses, and the whole operation upon whether the man is alive. Had he never lived he would never have had a thought, a voluntary or involuntary motion; which fact demonstrates our position: therefore, all these phenomena, from the least to the greatest, are effects involved in the organic or inorganic structures and peculiar chemical and electrical endowment.

Formation by this movement consists in the combination of simple atoms or their compounds within a certain proximity, and between which affinities exist. Whatever these conditions are, and wherever they exist, combinations must take place. A tree is the product of absorption by its roots and leaves of carbonic acid from the soil and air, and which the plant decomposes, forming from it its own food. Upon these phenomena we quote the following from Medlock's "Book of Nature": "Vital power is peculiarly and exclusively distinguished by its capability of appropriating the simple chemical substances, and applying these to the production of bodies [other bodies], such as we, with all our resources at command, are utterly unable to effect, and probably ever will be. It is true that we can combine, in the due proportion of weight and volume, all the chemical constituents which are contained in the sap of plants; but life alone [a living thing alone] is able to construct either a cell or an organ from these materials.

"The fundamental work of life [or a living thing] appears to be its power of forming the vegetable or animal cell through the absorption or assimilation of new matter from without; and also by means of the nutritive matter, effecting an increase in all directions; or, in other words, it posseses the power of growth. An accurate comprehension of this department of the science is attainable only through a right understanding of the various organs of vegetation and of their functions, as well as through that of the nutritive media received from without, and the subsequent change of the latter into vegetable substances.

The Food of Plants not in Nature.

"What, then, are the nourishing media or food of plants? We can only satisfactorily and precisely answer this question by stating what the simple chemical compound parts of the different vegetable objects are; for it is an established fact that the smallest particle of their whole mass is not, and cannot be, self-produced; therefore everything which they contain must be derived from without. The principal mass of every plant is composed of cellular tissue, vascular tissue, or of woody fiber; there are also contained in the cellular membrane partly solid substances, as starch, chlorophyl, resin, salts, etc., and partly a watery sap, holding in solution sugar, gum, acids in union with metallic oxides, albumen, etc., to which are to be added, as the contents of many plants, volatile and fixed oils, with other fatty matters.

"Daily experience also shows that the chief mass of every plant, by combustion, passes into gaseous combinations; it disappears, and only the non-volatile metallic oxides and salts remain as ash, which forms an inconsiderable proportion of the weight of the plant. Are we to infer, therefore, that starch, woody fiber, gum, sugar, oil, albumen, etc., are the nourishing media of plants? If so, the soil, the water, and the atmosphere, wherein plants pass their lives, should contain these bodies, in order that the plants might simply receive them therefrom, and convey them to their proper place [and this would require the prior organization of the plant]. But such is not the case. We never meet with woody fiber, starch, sugar, albumen, etc., except in the plant itself; it must consequently possess the means [faculty] of assimilating them [mechanically manufacturing them] and of combining them out of the simple chemical [gaseous] substances [principally carbonic acid].

"Carbon, by itself, is totally insoluble in water, and hence cannot, through this medium, be introduced into the circulation of the plant. Neither can it be assimilated in its solid form, because, in accordance with the law of vegetable absorption, a plant is incapable of receiving any body into its circulation which is not in a fluid condition. All the carbon which is met with in plants must have been received by them in the form of a compound, which is soluble in water. This body is *carbonic acid*, which consists of carbon and oxygen. This is the chief constituent of the food of plants [or is that from which the plant itself forms its food].

"This material is principally received into the system of the plant through the roots, and partially through the leaves; and the *carbonic acid is decomposed in the plant itself*. The carbon is applied to the formation of the vegetable organs; and its oxygen is allowed to escape by the leaves. The root sucks up the water in its neighborhood. All the water of both land and sea holds carbonic acid in solution. It is produced from the never-failing supply of dead and decaying animal and vegetable matter on the surface of the earth, and also by the respiration of man and animals. During the development of the embryo, and while the stem does not appear above ground, and further till the leaves are produced, the root is exclusively the medium of supplying carbonic acid to the plant; after this the leaves inhale through their stomata or breathing pores carbonic acid from the atmosphere, and exhale the oxygen, which, when separated from the carbon, is never retained in vegetable bodies. The separation of the oxygen only takes place during the day, and goes on with the greatest rapidity when the plants are exposed to the full action of the solar rays.

"The atmosphere contains, in 5,000 measures of air, two measures of carbonic acid, which plants are continually abstracting from it. The equilibrium is as continually restored by the breathing of animals, by combustion, and by the decomposition of carbonaceous bodies. Although the carbonic acid of the air appears very insignificant, yet on account of the prodigious extent of the atmosphere, it is sufficient to yield an ample supply of carbon for the development of every plant on the surface of the earth. All the phenomena of the vegetable kingdom confirm this view, namely, that the great mass of carbon is received from the atmosphere, either directly by the roots, or indirectly by the leaves; and this view cannot be questioned in reference to such plants as cactus, house-leek, etc., which grow on bare rocks, walls, or roofs; or in such as grow in the water, as forget-me-not, hyacinth, water-cress, etc." (Pp. 459–461.)

The Vegetable Primordial a Perfect Plant.

We have supposed the primordial to be but a single vegetable cell; but as the whole root as well as the mature plant is composed of such cells, and as one cell cannot have a root, and as the plant depends upon the root to suck up the carbonic acid from the earth in order to grow, it must have been a mature plant, composed of both root and stem, and made before it was planted in the ground. What was true of a single plant, the progenitor of a single species, must have been equally true of those of every other species, as no species can produce another species. In accordance with these necessities we have the classic and philosophic statement: "And the Lord God made every plant of the field before it was in the earth, and every herb of the field before it grew. I have given you every herb-bearing seed which is upon the face of all the earth, and every tree in the which is the fruit of a tree yielding seed, to you it shall be for food. The herb yielding seed and the fruit tree yielding fruit after *his kind*, whose seed is in itself." (Gen. I.)

In reference to the first cell or plant, certain facts are here taught.

First. The plant must have had a root, as it is the root which draws the carbonic acid from the earth.

Second. It must have had at least a single cell of the stem or body of the plant. This was necessary to decompose the carbonic acid and from which to form its food—starch, gum, albumen, resin, sugar, chlorophyl, wody fiber, etc.—without which not another cell could have been formed, and all the primordials themselves would have died immediately.

Third. The work the first cell performed was that of life; it therefore lived before it produced the second cell, which was the first act of growth. Hence the first was an act of creation, which act not only endowed the cell with the faculty of producing or evolving all the other cells necessary to its own formation, but involved the necessity of evolving an additional department, capable of producing seed after its kind (of the same species) for its perpetuation.

Fourth. The progenitors of each species were creations, acts of mental power, involving in them everything susceptible of being evolved from them.

Fifth. This being a work which nature was incapable of performing, it was superior to it, and therefore was supernatural, or miraculous.

Sixth. This little vegetable cell had involved in its structure a chemical apparatus for the decomposition of carbonic acid and the faculty of forming all the different kinds of food which nourish plants; hence it was more wonderful than the most perfect apparatus of the artistic chemist, and performed a work of chemical composition which no human chemist is capable of performing.

The Formation of the First Plant an Effect.

Every phase of these facts and phenomena, we can easily perceive, was an effect following the original creations, the only cause being the Creator Himself. After such acts of organic and inanimate formation it is proper to say, *it is natural;* for thus nature was born. It was this endowment which gave molecular motion its birth, and which gave rise to the motion of all material atoms or systems, demonstrating the fact that power (which is the effect of matter in motion) originated in the mind of the Creator. Here, then, we reach the first and only cause, possessing all the intelligence and power manifested in the universe, involving in it every motion and phenomenon, and all of their possibilities. Its movements throughout all subsequent time are but the unfolding of these grand mental dynamics.

Like the power resulting from the motion of a machine made by man, it is found alone in the mind of the maker, including the fulfillment of the conditions by another, which the maker designed, in setting and keeping it in operation. A clock is made capable of measuring time, but combines in its structure certain conditions to enable it so to do. One of these is that it must be wound up, and he who communicates this power fulfills one of the conditions which was in the mind of the maker; but the power to make the clock and the power to wind it up were involved in both men by their Maker. What the men did was evolution, and effects of their living organism, while their power thus to act was the prior involution of these by their Maker, and of which he was the sole cause.

The comparative superiority of the machinery of nature over that made by man, although involving the same principles, is manifest in the fact that the laws of nature for the production of the tree inhere in the seed and its environment, and do not need another mind to set them in motion.

To illustrate this fact of nature, so that we may understand how largely nature is thus involved, let us take a peach-seed and the mature tree bearing seed after its kind. This seed, like all others, has incorporated in it the embryo tree; yet not an atom it possesses would ever move of itself; it is not therefore a law of nature. Neither is the soil such a law, nor yet the solar light; nor is the heat received from the sun such a law. These may all exist, yet if the seed is kept out of the soil no vegetable effect would follow. If the seed were planted in good soil, yet amid perpetual darkness, still no vegetation would result, as no plant can be brought to maturity, which means the reproduction of itself, without sunlight.

The law of vegetation therefore necessitates the astronomical motions of the earth. Suppose the earth did not revolve on its axes: in that case the half turned from the sun would be always dark and cold : hence if the seed were planted on that side of the earth, not one of its particles would ever move except to decompose, as they certainly would decompose unless the temperature was so low as to keep them frozen ; and this would be going back to motionless molecules instead of forward to organic life.

To produce germination a degree of heat is demanded sufficient to burst the shell of the seed. This requires a substance which can pass freely through the stomata or breathing pores of the shell, expanding the particles of the kernels, but not those of the shell ; for were both expanded equally, there would still be no bursting of the shell, and as a consequence no vegetable growth.

It is also a fact that atmospheric air cannot penetrate the walls of the seed, else it would have decomposed the seed in a few days after the peach had fallen ripe from the tree, just as it did the rest of the peach. This substance, then, must be some modification of electricity, whose particles are so minute that they penetrate and permeate everything in nature. Coming now in contact with the kernel of the seed, and charging each atom with an electric atmosphere, and of course expanding it, they develop motion : the movement of the atoms against each other produces friction, and the friction generates heat, the latter adding to the expansive force until the shell, unable to bear the pressure, bursts. This gives the embryonic roots of the seed access to the carbonic acid of the surrounding earth, which it absorbs, and which the embryo cells of the plant decompose, and out of which other cells are formed ; and thus the tree grows, as we have already shown.

Plant Absorption of Carbonic Acid makes the Wind Blow.

The motion of the atoms of the seed, and those of the contiguous air after the plant rises above the ground, creates heat by their friction against each other. These atoms, expanded by heat and robbed of their carbonic acid by the plant, are compelled to move off in search of their chemical and temperatural equilibrium, while those of a lower temperature, charged with the normal quantity of carbonic acid, take their place. The effect of these atomic motions is the blowing of the wind. Of course it is upon a small scale; but the same principle produces the hurricane or tornado. We have supposed this peach-seed planted on a perpetually dark side of the earth; but as sunlight is essential to vegetable maturity, the revolution of our planet on its axes becomes indispensable to the promotion of vegetable growth.

We have also supposed the seed planted in a dry soil; but as moisture is another essential element of vegetable growth, dew or rain must fall upon the soil to prepare it to do its work. But this can only come from the atmosphere, and as water is not one of the constituents of air, it must be drawn into the air by some inherent principle designed for the purpose. Of course this principle is evaporation, the water being principally taken from the oceans, lakes, and rivers. By this process the air becomes so highly saturated that the specific gravity of the moisture precipitates it to the ground; but it would fall again directly into the bodies from whence it had been taken, were it not for the motion of the clouds thus formed. Their motion is produced by the unequal expansion of the air, principally resulting from the ecliptic motion of the earth, and that upon its axes, perpetually heating and cooling unequally different spaces in the atmospheric envelope. These interdepending molecular and organic departments, which, as we have seen, comprehend the machinery of the entire system, present us with such fundamental facts of natural science as the following: First, not the simplest plant could live in any nascent or half-formed condition of the globe, or in one less perfect than that which now exists; and without vegetables for animal food, animals could not have existed. That the laws of nature are not abstractions, susceptible of having an existence prior to nature itself, but chemically inhere—were incorporated at the formation of the bodies themselves—in a word, that they are the reciprocal effects of which all the atoms of simple elements, affecting their adhesion as well as organic or lifeless formations, produce upon each other.

Either not understanding this universally interdepending philosophy of nature or unwilling to make it known because it is fatal to the doctrine of the geological antiquity of man and the world—that of evolution and atheism—the most prominent naturalists of the present day declare the laws of nature to be no part of nature, as they existed before her and brought her into being.

Says an eminent geologist: "You will learn from chemistry that all the gases combine according to regular and established laws. The gases did not make the laws, but received them from a living, intelligent lawgiver." (No. 1, *Popular Educator*.) Here we have the idea that the laws are abstractions, made and applied. We may remark that this opinion was written about twenty years ago, when evolution had not so prominently evolved from marvelous human brains as now. Hence it gives a creator some work to do: He made the laws, and the laws made the world. The same opinion is to be found in Plato's mythology: "The Supreme Being made inferior gods, and they made the world."

On the title page of "Principles of Geology," Sir Charles Lyell, quoting Playfair's illustrations of the Huttonion Theory, says: "Amid all the revolutions of the globe the economy of nature has been uniform, and *her laws* are the only things that have resisted the general movement. The rivers and the rocks, the seas and continents, have changed in all their parts; but the laws which direct these changes, and the rules to which they are subject, have remained invariably the same."

The idea is that as all nature is changeable and the laws of nature unchangeable, they are no part of nature. If a thing has the faculty of resisting the motion of another, it must be separate from the thing resisted; and as these laws resist everything in nature, and have always done so, they are no part of her, and never were; and if they have produced all the existences and phenomena of the universe, they are superior to it, or, what is the same thing, supernatural, and therefore gods or God, which gives the world a Creator and governor; but hoping to free themselves from accountability to a lawful, intelligent proprietor, they change his name from the God of nature to the Laws of nature. If the laws formed and govern the universe, and as this work manifests itelligence, they must be elevated into gods, or if combined, become a single intelligent God or personal Creator. On the other hand, if the laws result from the endowment, formations, and organizations of the universe, then they follow these, and therefore had no agency in bringing nature into existence.

Why Skeptics and Scientists are Driven to Absurdity.

That it is the hope of the skeptics, in their efforts to discover a universe without a God, to relieve themselves of moral responsibility, is shown by the intense excitement they manifest whenever their pet hobbies seem to be effectively attacked. Call in question the opinions of an astronomer, and he will not utter impertinent or arrogant remarks; but pursue the same course with the evolutionist and the chronological geologist, and they will resent it as though you had stolen their gods, or as though you had brought them face to face with their Creator, whom they had abused without stint.

A few years before he died, when about to deliver a lecture before the students at Yale College, Professor Agassiz prefaced it by saying: "If my listeners include any who believe in the creation as written in the book of Moses, he had better not hear me." We need hardly say that for such pride of opinion we have no respect, and no fear of confronting its possessor, whoever he may be. Has he or any of his school given us a better genesis of the world, more in accordance with the philosophical or scientific necessities demanded in bringing it into existence? Indeed, have they given us one which does not contain so many incongruities as to outrage common philosophy, common science, and common sense? If one of his auditors believed in the book of Moses, and that was error, it was his business to drive the error out of his mind by presenting sufficient evidence to sustain a better theory of creation. Is it the way to enlighten the mind of man to invite him not to hear you?

With all the light the nineteenth century affords, so utterly have the scientists failed to give even a common-sense theory of the manner in which the world came into existence that they wish to have it understood they are not interested in the question. They declare with Hooker: "A geologist has nothing to do with any theory of creation;" while nothing is more evident than the fact that they do attempt in all their writings and lectures to account for the existence of all things by the genius of evolution, admitting, however, that the work consumed an immense period of time. By this misconception of the philosophy of the laws of nature, as one of the fundamental principles of natural science, it is not strange that Lyell, having embraced Darwinism, should have indulged in such mysterious utterances as Hutton's definition of the laws of nature.

That all nature is the work of intelligence, and that intelligence can only be predicated of a personal being, is manifest even to the most superficial observer; but, discarding the existence of such a being, modern scientists seek to elevate a part of nature—her laws—to the altitude of intelligent entities, clothed with the power requisite to produce the universe. If belief in the existence of a Supreme Being is objectionable, belief in the entities or gods of the evolutionists must be equally objectionable; indeed, more so, for *many* are the gods of modern science. The polytheist believes too much, the atheist too little, while the Christian believes in the One living and true God; and if he had no other defense than that it requires more credulity to be a polytheist —to believe in many gods than to believe in one—on the one hand, and on the other, more stifling of nature to reject than to believe in one God, this would be sufficient.

The relations of light and heat with their phenomena also furnish a conclusive argument against the hypothesis of evolution. To our mind, the evidence is altogether in favor of the theory that the sun's atmosphere is electricity and its light electric light; and the fact that the atmospheres of bodies are composed of the same chemical properties as those forming the bodies themselves, would seem to argue that the sun itself is a great electric battery, organized for the special purpose of preserving the relations and perpetuating the motions of the bodies in the solar system.

It is well known that electricity is in itself dark and cold, which fact leaves us to infer that such also is the temperature and condition of the sun, and that light and heat are the effect of its electric rays passing through the atmosphere, whose friction sets on fire the oxygen it contains. That the rays of the sun are cold before striking our atmosphere would seem to prove them also to be dark. That they are cold would seem to be a fact inferred from the other fact, that the higher you ascend toward the sun the lower the temperature falls, and his rays correspondingly lessen their brilliancy. Aeronauts have in summer, and directly toward the meridian sun, ascended so high that they were nearly frozen.

There are two facts illustrative of these phenomena—first, that the density of the atmosphere is greatest at the surface of the earth, and decreases regularly as we ascend ; secondly, that its extent also grows less. If light and heat are thus produced, it follows that they are at the greatest intensity on the earth's surface, decreasing in proportion to distance from the earth, until above the atmosphere all is intense cold and total darkness, at which height neither the sun nor stars would be visible. Supposing the stars to be suns, as astronomy teaches, their light upon earth results from the same causes. As the satellites reflect borrowed rays, their light is also the effect of atmospheric radiation. Aeronauts have also discovered, at their greatest heights, that the luminous halo of the sun had so perceptibly diminished that they experienced not much more difficulty in gazing at it with the naked eye than in looking at the full moon from the earth. Here then we have an approximate understanding of the wonderfully complicated law of solar light and heat, comprehending the sun, solar system, and organized atmosphere of the earth with its oxygen gas, and which must have been as perfect in all their parts, to render light possible, as they are at the present day. Hence, again, we see that their origin could not have been the work of evolution.

The Progenitors of each Species Perfect at First.

A proper understanding of the laws of nature in relation to the original progenitors of each species of plant also necessitates one of two things—either that each plant was created and did not come from a seed, or that the seed was created and did not come from a plant. If the seed was first, it must have been perfectly formed, and could not have been a rudiment, for imperfect seed will not produce a perfect plant or one that will reproduce its kind. If the plant was first, it must have been a perfect organization, as it could not have lived were a single organ performing a vital function only a rudiment.

The doctrine of rudiments supposes one produces another—the first the second, etc. The fact, however, is, that not only has the rudiment of a vital organ no life, but its perfect development has none. Cut every leaf from the stem of a plant as soon as it appears, and the plant will die, because it is through the leaves that the plant inhales carbonic acid from the air, and out of which it prepares its food. It is evident that had the leaves remained rudimentary, undeveloped, the same result would have happened to the plant, showing that the rudiments of leaves were not vital or were not a part of the life of the plant. This argument assumes that every other organ of the plant was perfectly developed —that is, had the faculty of performing its part in the growth of the plant, life being the result of the combination, the function of each organ being essential to the existence of a living plant. How absurd, then, is the claim of the evolutionists, that the first organs of the first living thing was a rudiment, and therefore no vital organ at all!

This argument is so conclusive that a statement of these facts is its complete vindication; yielding this sweeps away every vestige of evolution which is in any wise held to account for the manner of living things coming into existence by the power of nature.

It is true, the tree might have been made a shrub, and in successive seasons grown to maturity; but this in no wise invalidates the force of the argument; for the shrub must have contained every element of the tree. Besides, we have the wonderful fact that most plants will grow from slips, forming their own roots; but instead of this fact furnishing grounds for the inference that any first progenitor might have come into existence from a part of a spear of grass, it teaches exactly the reverse—namely, that its organization was thus more complex, rendering its species more fertile and tenacious of life than that of animals having passed beyond those which are part each, and instead of these being the simplest they are the most wonderful organisms of all. Divide the body of a man, and neither part will become another man.

We see in this fact of nature the exemplification of the wisdom of the Creator. Vegetation being the direct or indirect food of all animals, it should have had superior chances of survival and greater power of reproduction. Upon this difference the most perfect book of nature has the following passage : "For there is hope of a tree, if it be cut down, that it will sprout again, and that the tender branch thereof will not cease, though the root thereof was old in the earth, and the stock thereof die in the ground : yet through the *scent of water* it will bud, and bring forth boughs like a plant ; but man dieth, and wasteth away : yea, man giveth up the ghost, and where is he?" (Job. 14 : 7–10.) Mark the expression : it is not that water will produce this effect ; but "through the *scent* of water"—the carbonic acid the water contains.

Suppose that element whose function it is to produce seed in the tree had not been involved in the original tree, the result would have been *that* species of tree would have become extinct in the first generation.

Suppose, further, that the organic principle, whose function it is to produce leaves, had not been incorporated in the tree or shrub, or its embryo omitted from the seed, it would have rendered the tree or shrub leafless, and thereby fruitless. Indeed, it never could have been a tree or shrub. The existence of any such plants would have been an impossibility. In contradiction to all these facts and well-known principles of natural science, evolution says that any and all of these vital organs may have been, nay, were left out of the original progenitor, or reduced to a single one, and that only a rudiment ; and yet it was capable not only of producing its kind or species, but every other kind, not only equal, but as much superior to itself as man is superior to the simplest weed of the field. It offers no relief in theory to reduce to the nicest shades the differences apparent in the vital organs of any two ; for in fact they must be as wide apart as organic or inorganic, functional or non-functional ; in a word, as different as life and death. Life evolves life, but death evolves nothing.

In summing up this argument we observe that every seed, whether original or of subsequent production, had incorporated into its structure the embryo of everything it is capable, in any conditions, of evolving. A department for the production of seed after its kind; the chemical properties for the formation of all the organic and functional susceptibilities requisite for the development of the mature tree and the continuation of its species; the sap, from which a grain of wood is produced each year; the bark, limbs, roots, leaves, form of the tree, shape of its fruit, its coloring matter and that of the leaves, flavor, attitude of the limbs, general appearance and size of the tree, with that wonderful function capable of multiplying itself an hundredfold, for the sustentation of the numerous species and races of animals dependent upon it for its food—all these were crowded into the little world of wonder.

Had not the original plants been thus endowed, on the power that made them would have been imposed the necessity of originally making all the seeds from which successive generations were to grow, and of preserving them in some great seed store-house, ready for distribution to those who wished to plant them throughout all coming time and in all countries of the world, or else have been kept constantly at the work of making seeds to meet the demands of the ages. But the Creator chose the more practical method, the facts, philosophy, and science of which are set forth in His own book, thus: "And God made every plant of the field before it was in the ground, and every herb of the field before it grew, the herb yielding fruit after his kind, whose seed is in itself. And God saw that it was good." (Gen. 1.) That each kind or species had preserved its own identity is evident from the fact that the great Naturalist asked, "Do men gather grapes of thorns, or figs of thistles?" (Matt. 7 : 16.)

Here is demonstrated the fact that the first seed of each species was a perfect organization, containing in embryo every element of the plant and its products; and if the plant was first, as it was, according to the history given by its Maker, it was also perfect in all its parts and products, admitting of no omission or improvement. Hence, at every point of the argument, we find this spurious, so-called science standing in contradiction to the experience of every student of nature whose pride of opinion does not make him her teacher, and in the most palpable conflict with the facts and well-known laws of vegetable and animal existence.

The Mischief of Attributing Results to the "Laws of Nature."

It is so common in our day to hear all natural phenomena attributed to the "laws of nature" that it is not strange that they should have come to signify a kind of myth, like Plato's subordinate deities, moving with their immaterial fingers the various substances entering into the composition of the globe and solar system. The advocates of the mongrel science of geology, chronology, and evolution profess, as we have seen, to have found in nature an amount of evidence sufficient to shut God out of her premises, and they do this as coolly and unceremoniously as they would eject a disagreeable tenant from their own premises; and in the next breath they tell us they have nothing to do with the question of the cosmogony of the world.

Nothing, however, is more manifest than their intense desire and unflagging efforts to account for it all upon the hypothesis of evolution. Thus the most superficial and far-fetched theories ever palmed off on human credulity are invented ; and, astonishing as it may appear, they are regarded by many intelligent people as plausible if not true. So complete is the sophistry in which these speculations are involved that men everywhere, partly in jest and partly in earnest, refer to the possibility of their monkey ancestry. The remedy for this infatuation is to become better acquainted with the great scientific and philosophical principles and teachings of the facts of nature than are these scientists, and to show from the relations and interdependence of her works the necessity of the existence of a personal, intelligent Creator and that of the creation of the world.

A proper understanding of what are called "the imponderable agents" relieves physical and mental science of half their mysteries. A discrimination between matter and these agents for any other purpose than accommodating classification we think unjustifiable either in science or philosophy. Our position is that every agent of nature (and everything is such an agent, without regard to the degree of its solidity, which produces an effect upon another thing), coming in contact with a denser matter, produces its motion, whether such agent be light, heat, gas, or electricity, is nevertheless composed of as solid atoms as iron or gold, and as really as these possesses specific gravity. The source of agency is the first cause, and therefore all agents are mental, and point back to mind as their creative and moving cause. But every substance, simple or compound element, which affects another, conveying motion to it or to its atoms, bears the stamp of a servant and not of proprietor.

The fact that all solids and fluids are convertible into each other, thus throwing their atoms into motion (this being true of electricity itself), demonstrates our position. The identical atoms which form plants furnish nourishment for animals, and the assimilating and appropriating principles are to be attributed to the organic differences existing between vegetables and animals. As these processes are results, and comprehend the entire phenomena, they point to the existence of a supernatural mind as the source whence all the power is derived. Hence we have the apostolic statement : " All power is of God."

By the agents of decomposition resident in the atmosphere, such as the gases, light, heat, and electricity, any solid may be reduced to the subtlest ether. Even a diamond may be made to blaze like a pine torch, and water burn like alcohol. A pound of ice exposed to the heat of the sun will be dissolved into such small particles that they will be lighter than those of the air nearest the surface of the earth, and, consequently, evaporated by heat, they ascend until they reach the location where they find their equilibrium or center of gravity ; and this is determined principally by temperature. Another example. A pound of charcoal, which in round numbers is a pound of carbon, subjected to the action of a certain degree of pressure, to the action of fire, or that of the galvanic battery, will be changed into a fluid and evaporated, or pass into the air in the form of dry heat, or by electricity dissolved into still smaller atoms, and carried proportionally higher into the atmosphere, observing the same law as those of the ice.

These particles, however, will not remain a separate bulk of carbon, but will diffuse themselves and mix with the other gases of the air, and in the exact proportion as carbon forms one of its constituents. Though carbon at its normal temperature is heavier than common air, and therefore subsides into vaults, wells, etc., and in such condition extinguishes animal life and flame, yet when expanded by the rays of the sun, or other heat or dissolving agent, as we have said, it rises into the atmosphere and becomes thus distributed. Thus our pound of coal is changed into another form and occupies another locality; but is it not matter as much as it was before?

Nothing Imponderable: The Proof Test.

It may be said, If it is matter it must have weight. To give the objection its full force we will admit that it has all been converted into heat, and heat is claimed to be *imponderable.* We answer, that as its particles have now entered into the atmosphere, of which carbon is one of the constituents, and which as a whole weighs fifteen pounds to the square inch at the level of the sea, the carbon makes its proportion of the fifteen pounds. Though its particles are heavier than those of the common atmosphere, yet by their chemical affinity for the lighter gases, such as hydrogen, they are suspended by elementary equilibrium. But suppose the pound of coal were changed into heat, would it not be a pound of heat? Let every atom it contained be again condensed by cold, and formed into coal by some power equal to the task, would there not be still a pound of matter? These particles may therefore be thus formed and transformed, but each maintains its own specific gravity unaltered.

Carbon and oxygen form carbonic acid. This is the food of the tree, and therefore that of which it is formed, and the tree may be burned into charcoal, and though the volume of the carbon in the atmosphere is much larger than when in the form of the coal, yet it is vastly less than when first expanded by the fusion or the dissolution. The fire, the pressure, or the galvanism produced the disturbance or motion of the atoms; this motion created friction; the friction evolved heat; the heat expanded the atoms into gas; but during every stage of the phenomenon were they anything else than particles of carbon? or at any stage of the operation did they collectively weigh less than a pound!

It may be objected again that if heat is substance, so is cold; that if two bodies, one hot and the other cold, are placed in contact, the temperature of both will become equalized, the hot body giving off its heat and the cold one its cold reciprocally.

Although this theory looks plausible, yet we think it defective science. The equalizing of temperature is accounted for not upon the supposition that the hot body loses its heat, which is a part of itself, but that as the particles of the cold body thus in contact are themselves moved by the expansion, the friction gives them a higher temperature. An ounce of red-hot iron is brought in contact with a cold house; the house is burned to ashes: did this mass of heat come from the little piece of iron? Hence the experiment of weighing a piece of iron hot and cold, showing no difference in its specific gravity, furnishes no proof that heat is not matter or that cold is matter; the demonstration being in regard to the heat, that if you heat to fusion a pound of iron or coal while on the scale, and keep it at that temperature long enough, every atom of it will go off into heat, and the balance will show that the heat weighed a pound.

The reason why the supposed imponderable agents have not been found to have appreciable weight consists in the fact that all the attempts to detect it have been made on the surface of the earth; whereas, if we would find the specific gravity of any substance, the scale must be placed above that locality in which it exists in equilibrium of density and temperature. To illustrate : if the earth were a globe of water, a piece of gold dropped anywhere upon its surface would sink until it found the exact center of the globe, or, scientifically speaking, "the center of gravity." Here the gold would have lost its specific gravity—it would weigh *nothing*, not as much as a feather—for the attraction of gravitation and atmospheric pressure as well as the weight of the water are equal on every side. The question therefore is, Is this gold not matter because it has no weight at this locality?

Though at this location the piece weighs nothing, yet if you place the scale one foot in any direction from this center—and any direction is above it—the piece of gold, say a cubic inch in size, will weigh more than in any other place in the globe, and its weight will diminish at every increase of the distance from this center. In confirmation of this principle, it is found that the same thing will weigh less on the top of a high mountain than at the level of the sea ; so that it would be a good speculation to buy gold on the Alps and sell it in the deepest valley below. So likewise the expanded and heated particles of any consumed or decomposed substance will ascend to a locality where their gravity and pressure are equal on every side, and where they weigh nothing, this being their center of gravity. Here they are *imponderable*, as the gold was ; but place the scale for weighing them above this locality, and all will be found to be *ponderable*.

Friction the Law of Heat and Light—both Matter.

The arguments which prove heat to be matter also prove light to be such. If light were an abstract immateriality it could exist in an atmospheric vacuum, but a thousand experiments have demonstrated that it will not so exist. Light therefore is composed of particles of matter in a state of fusion. In order to illustrate this phenomenon it is only necessary to consider still further the pound of coal, and to heat it to a luminous state. This more rapid decomposition of its atoms produces a corresponding increase of friction, and the result is not only heat, but light. It must be remembered that flame consumes or decomposes compounds rapidly or slowly according to its intensity, and in this case the light is simply particles of carbon fed by the surrounding oxygen.

If the coal were only heated by the rays of the sun the particles would be moved so slightly that no light would result; but if a torch with a flame of sufficient intensity were applied, the atoms would be thrown into such rapid disturbance, and such a corresponding degree of friction produced, that they would become lighted, or *light*. The consumption of the coal was not the work of the torch applied to it, for this only moved those atoms with which it came in contact—simply gave a starting motion—for a single match will start the conflagration of a city as well as light a candle. These disturbed atoms disturbed contiguous atoms, and these in turn disturbed others, and by the friction of their motion produced the heat and light running along together until the candle or city was consumed.

The normal condition of matter is cold, dark, and motionless; and these were its condition before the creation of the world. By the mind of the Creator all its ultimate atoms were endowed with chemical and electrical affinities, which all are known to possess, giving them the faculty of affecting, and therefore moving each other, the slower movement of which became heat, and the more rapid light. These inherent endowments constitute the law of heat and light. These qualities of the atoms would in time produce inorganic formations, but never one of organic life. The representatives, therefore, of each organic species must have been organized of these atoms, and of course by so many acts of creation.

These facts of science show that heat and light are not the product of immaterial agents; for these, if they have any existence, cannot produce friction, as this only results from the motion of matter in contact. These facts also presuppose the existence of the compositions and organizations, as consumption, dissolution, or disorganization can only follow prior formation and organization. Light and heat, therefore, are not separate and distinct agencies from nature itself, but are integral parts of her grand machinery. It were just as reasonable to separate cold from ice, moisture from water, decomposition from inertia, or manifestation from light, where there are eyes to see.

Take another illustration : A tallow candle is lighted by a friction match, which was itself ignited by the motion of its atoms, started by rubbing it against another body. Let us now suppose that the whole candle has been converted into light and heat, except a small amount of ashes, every particle of which was carbon and oxygen in a state of fusion, and when the consumption was effected the particles became again motionless, dark, and cold, proving that the identical atoms are light and heat when in a certain relation and degree of motion, but dark and cold when inert. The same dissolution would have been produced if the candle had been exposed to the rays of a summer sun : every day portions of it would have been melted and carried off into the air, until the whole candle and even the wick would have ascended and mingled with the same gases of the atmosphere of which it had been composed; but the process in this case would have been so slow, and the corresponding friction so slight, that the particles would have been heated, but not ignited; and the amount given off by the dissolution would have been precisely the same as when the consumption resulted from the light of the match, only in a longer period of time.

The inflammable and ponderable agencies of nature are therefore matter rendered hot and luminous by the motion of their atoms, the primary sources of which are the organized or compounded atmosphere, central sun, and the interdepending planetary system, compelling each other to perform all the motions assigned them by the Creator, evolving the mechanism *He involved in them.* Take away the sun, and the essential regular motions of the earth would immediately cease, extinguishing all the vegetable and animal life of the world. Remove the planets, and the sun itself would no longer be held in its place by their reciprocal force. In a word, all would go back to cold, dark, and dead inertia; and yet the sun only heats and lights, and therefore perpetuates the motions of the atoms of which the solar system is composed.

That heat and light are atoms of the consuming bodies we also have verified by our senses. In a close room, in which charcoal is burning, men or animals can live but a few moments, which is owing to the fact that the air becomes filled with heated, expanded particles of carbon or charcoal. What is true of the consumption of coal, in respect to its own atoms going off thus tested by the senses, is equally true of everything else. The reverse of this phenomenon is produced by freezing. If you freeze the most putrid organic matter, not a particle of it escapes into the air so that it could be detected by the most acute sense of smell.

All Organic Bodies have Atmospheres.

That all organic bodies, or their atoms, have surrounding atmospheres peculiar to themselves is a fact of great importance in the elucidation of much of the phenomena of natural science. It is by virtue of these atmospheres that substances are distinguished from each other. These are composed of the same chemical properties as those of the things or beings they surround, and are the active agents in affecting both the formation and decomposition of the bodies within them. These gaseous atmospheres fill all the spaces between the particles of bodies, from the smallest atom to those within the solar system. It is these molecular spaces which render all bodies or simple elements susceptible of condensation by external pressure or internal contraction.

According to another property of matter called impenetrability, these atmospheres cannot be forced into the spaces occupied by others without displacing them. It is within these that the electric and chemical properties are located which compel the atoms to cohere and to preserve their distances from each other, and which constitute the great law of universal gravity. It is also in this atmospheric constitution of material compounds or their molecules that the natural forces or laws are located. In these atmospheres are also held those peculiar properties called scent, by which, through the sense of smell, we are enabled to determine the quality and identity of organic things. That every human being is thus surrounded is demonstrated by the fact that a dog is able to trace the footsteps of his master. By this also the dog tracks his game.

Thus has every animal and plant an atmosphere peculiar to itself, which is composed of the same gaseous properties as itself; which, indeed, arises from the decomposition and reformation of the organizations within. It is also a fact that electricity in some of its modifications largely permeates these atmospheres, whether surrounding suns, planets, animate or inanimate bodies, and even infuses itself into the molecules, being so sublimated that all other forms of matter are sufficiently porous to admit it.

Another law of electricity is that it endows everything with the phenomena of polarity; whether worlds or the smallest atoms, each has its negative and positive pole. If we were familiar enough with the electric constitution of things, it is probable we should be able to trace the law of force to a unit. We mean in the nature of things, after the things had received creative endowment and organization, and that all the imponderable agents, so-called, enter alike into the motion of the smallest atom and the rolling of a world. From what we already know, most of the phenomena of nature may be traced to the agency of *heat*. As we have seen, heat is the result of friction, friction the result of matter in motion, matter in motion the result of its expansion and condensation, condensation the result of external pressure or internal contraction. If two pieces of wood are pressed and rubbed against each other, heat is the result. A piece of iron exhibits the same phenomenon by hammering, and if the process is continued long enough and with force enough it will become red hot, thus also manifesting the phenomenon of light. This process also gives rise to the phenomena of attraction and repulsion.

Heat a piece of steel to a certain degree, cool it suddenly, and the particles will become electrically deranged, but if cooled slowly they will arrange themselves, with their negative and positive poles lying in the direction of the grains of the steel. Thus arranged, the cohesive attraction of the magnetic atoms holds the body more firmly together than when lying crosswise the grains. When steel is heated and suddenly cooled it becomes hard and brittle, but if gradually cooled it is soft and flexible. This is owing to the fact that sudden cooling does not give the electric poles of the atoms sufficient time to arrange themselves parallel with the grains, and in the degree that it becomes hard it becomes brittle, which is owing to the fact that the atoms, with their electric poles, lie in every direction; hence it is no stronger in one direction than in another. It also manifests a greater outward attraction than before, drawing surrounding particles of metal to itself. This is owing to the fact that some of the poles of the atoms are turned outward, exhibiting their strength in this direction instead of holding each other together. The hardening of all other metals is also produced by hammering, or the compression of their atoms. This explains the fact that a cannon will only endure a certain number of discharges, each of which acting as a blow hardens its atoms.

Temperature the Universal Agent of Motion.

In corroboration of these facts, showing the universality of material motion by the agency of heat, we give below some extracts from *Chambers's Journal:*

"Among the papers read before the Royal Society was one by Mr. W. Crookes, F. R. S., which treats of the action of heat on gravitating masses, and in its details of highly refined and accurate experiments, demonstrating that substances are repelled by heat and attracted by cold. The experiments were made with a balance formed of a beam of straw, with a pith-ball at each end.

A lighter balance could hardly be devised. It was tried in common air and in a vacuum, and from its behavior certain conclusions were drawn. A similar series of experiments were made with a cross-beam bearing two brass balls, and with corroborative results. It is therefore clear that density and temperature play an important part in the production of the phenomena; and if so, what then? Why, that the answer connects itself with one of the grandest problems of science, that nature offers evidence of the repulsive action of heat and the attractive action of cold, and that, too, on the grandest scale.

"By the radiation of heat from the sun may be explained the phenomena of comets and the shape and changes of nebula, and as Mr. Crookes remarks: 'To compare small things with great, to argue from pieces of straw up to heavenly bodies, it is not improbable that the attraction now shown to exist between a warm and a cold body will equally prevail when for the temperature of melting ice is substituted the cold of space. For a pith-ball a celestial sphere, and for an artificial vacuum a stellar void.

"'In the radiant molecular energy of cosmical masses may at last be found that agent, acting constantly according to certain laws, which Newton held to be the cause of gravity.' From this it will be seen that Mr. Crookes has started an investigation which in its results may explain the theory of the universe: [So says the editor, but we published this theory more than twenty years ago.]

"Another remarkably interesting report (says the same writer), on the voyage of the Challenger discovery-ship up to the time of her arrival at the Cape of Good Hope, and which has been published by the Admiralty, to the same effect, and to all who desire further knowledge of physical and oceanic phenomena it will be especially acceptable.

"The particulars are furnished by Captain Nares, commander of the vessel. They comprise the temperature of the sea in different latitudes, the extent of warm and cold areas, the depth of the water, and the form of the bottom; and these, being represented in colored diagrams, can be clearly understood. By a little study of these diagrams any one may see that the Atlantic is, so to speak, cut up into a series of basins, among which three are very remarkable: from New York to Bermuda, from Halifax to Bermuda, and from Bermuda to St. Thomas. Soundings taken in the neighborhood of Bermuda prove it to be a solitary peak in the midst of the sea, having a base of not more than one hundred and twenty miles in diameter.

"The southern and eastern boundary of the gulf stream was determined within three hundred miles of the Azores, 2,250 miles from the source of that great stream, which, as Captain Nares remarks, has not lost one particle of its heat in traveling that enormous distance. That this heat plays an important part in the physics of the globe may be imagined, seeing that the whole mass of warmed water is estimated at two hundred millions of square miles in extent and one thousand feet in thickness."

In connection with these facts and their import, we may add that as contiguous water as well as air moves in circles, it may also be found that in its circulation this great stream follows the elliptic motion of the earth, and therefore in a more indirect manner distributes the heat of the sun over the globe, equalizing the otherwise extreme temperature of the poles and equator—a theory much more likely correct than Lyell's supposition, that the unequal distribution of land on the surface of the globe accomplishes this work.

It is also a fact that these gravities may not only be modified but completely changed in their several localities by the action of heat and cold. For example : the steam in a boiler may be heated and compressed to a solidity equal to that of the iron of which the boiler itself is formed. If the boiler should burst, the steam would ascend to its level of expanded air, which would be its center of gravity, and would weigh nothing unless it was forced above this center. It would now contract by cold and descend, if not obstructed, and reach the very center of the earth, again supposing it to be a globe of water, and that the temperature of the steam or its water would be higher than that of any other substance with which it came in contact on its passage.

Heat the Law of Motion and Gravity.

The same change is produced on the surface of the globe of water by the action of the sun as by being heated in the boiler : its surface waters are thrown into warmer currents, and colder ones rise to take their place, precipitating the warmer ones until in time every square inch of the water of the globe would in turn occupy the exact center of gravity.

Thus we have aqueous and igneous phenomena keeping the whole matter of the world in a state of agitation, effectually overcoming all other forces and agents of nature. By this investigation we see how far may be unraveled the mysteries of natural science ; and as nature and her phenomena are only agents, there must be a proprietor before and above all.

We might accumulate evidence upon this subject

almost without limit, but we must content ourselves without the indulgence. We are, however, sure that we have said enough to furnish the key to most of the mysteries of nature.

The only reason we can assign for the course pursued by the evolutionists, searching among the simplest molecules and animalculæ for the starting point in organic things, is the hope that within this supposed mythical region the error would not be so easily discovered, and the drapery stripped from the shrines, or laws, or gods of nature at which Lyell, Darwin, Tyndall, Huxley, and the rest of their school pay their sordid devotion.

CHAPTER VII.

LIMIT OF HUMAN CONCEPTION.

In discussing these questions we assume that there existed before the world, or nature—by which we mean the same—and as philosophic necessities, *matter, space,* duration, and God, the latter an intelligent personal Being, of whom man is the express personal image.

The question, Where did this Being come from, or how did He come to exist? is as impossible for man to answer as for him to fix the line beyond which there is no space, or to define the chronological period, running to a point beyond which there is no duration. If this Being had attempted to simplify the answer in order to bring it within the comprehension of the greatest created mind, he would have remained as ignorant as though no such effort had been made, simply because of his inability to grasp the conception.

Equal want of success would attend the effort to teach a dog natural science, philosophy, or the metaphysics involved in the connection between life and mind. Why? Simply because he is a dog. The same failure would result from the effort to teach a monkey the alphabet or the multiplication table, and this simply because he is a monkey. Indeed, there is an infinitely greater disproportion between man and his Maker than that existing between man, the dog, or the monkey; the just comparison in the latter case being between man and the machine he has or can make. In a word, the question involves the absurd idea of the thing made endeavoring to comprehend the origin and greatness of its maker. The monkey, however, might follow the example of the evolutionists, who in this direction go one step further, and because of this circumscription of capacity deny he was made at all, and with equal propriety contend that there is a limit to space, an end to duration, that matter does not exist, and that there is no God. In harmony with this view we have the Bible statement: "The world by wisdom knew not God."

As original matter had no motion, there could have been no power, for power is the result of matter in motion; and as the universe manifests the phenomena of power, it must have been derived from some other source, and as there always existed a Being of wisdom, it must have originated with Him. All power is mental: that displayed in the material world proves this Being capable, by an act of will, of putting material atoms in motion, which requires a physical agency or medium of communication, and of forming them into any desirable shape, either organic or inorganic. In accordance with such demands, the creation must have proceeded upon the plan of separation, compression, and endowment of the atoms.

Strictly speaking there is no difference between mental and physical power, and to draw lines of discrimination is only excusable upon the ground of scientific classification. It requires but little reflection to convince any one that the true philosophy of dynamics has its source in mind. That manifested in the creation and government of the world to the mind of the Creator, while that displayed by the works of man, or, if you please, his creations to his mind. These last, however, are but secondary and not original, as man himself is the result of the first power.

Electricity a Created Substance.

Although electricity is the most subtile of all the so-called imponderable agents, yet it is not so high in the scale as the original matter out of which all things were made. In proof of this we refer to the fact that electricity is endowed with certain fixed laws by which it is governed, and according to which it is compelled to accomplish its various offices in the universe, which endowment is its creation. It must therefore have been condensed from another form of matter not possessing these characteristics; so that out of this invisible homogeneous substance God made the visible and palpable universe. Hence we have such declarations as the following: "We understand that the worlds were framed by the word of God, so that things which *are seen* were not made of things which do appear." (Heb. 2 : 3.) Or are seen, and were therefore made of things which are not seen, but still "out of things," and not out of nothing. In the same degree that this condensed solidity increased, the ease and rapidity of its motion decreased.

To be convinced that electricity is composed of solid particles of matter, it is only necessary to have a proper view of the construction and operation of the galvanic battery. Three things are essential—copper, zinc, and acid. Arrange these according to certain mechanical rules, and electricity, or galvanism, which is substantially the same, is evolved. By the process the zinc plates are decomposed, and their particles enter into the composition of the galvanism, which therefore is composed of as solid atoms as those which form copper, zinc, and acid. Indeed, all that is required to reduce or expand any material compound into the highest sublimation of which its particles are susceptible is to subject it to a degree of heat of sufficient intensity, or to a concentrated force of electricity, when its particles will assume their original condition, but of course no higher than that of electricity, the decomposing agent. To go beyond this would be to uncreate, which power resides alone in the mind of the Creator, as the laws of nature are limited to created things.

Investigation into the susceptibility of substances to affect others, reveals the fact that the most powerful agents are the most subtile. Water may be moved by the wind, and its waves dashed in vain against some bold rock jutting into the ocean; but let the electric flash be loosed from a powerfully surcharged cloud, and its sharp, swift bolt instantly shatters the same into fragments. Or let an accumulation of pent-up gases explode from beneath, and the very foundation of the neighboring earth is shaken, and the rock which had defied the storms of a thousand years is suddenly rent and is swallowed up in the yawning chasm. It is the velocity with which a fluid moves, and not so much its specific gravity, which arms it with superior power. Even the planets are suspended and rolled in their orbits by the negative and positive magnetic forces, and the sun itself is held in the common center by their reciprocal action.

If the sun, down to its center, is not a vast body of electricity, its surface is certainly thus composed. This, in magnetic relation, makes it positive to all the planets and satellites in the solar system. The sun, pouring its perpetual rays on these, renders them also positives, and as two positives resist each other, the centrifugal force results, compelling all the planets to preserve their respective distances from the sun and each other; and as the planets form a balance of attractive force around the sun, it is itself held by their reciprocal attraction within the common center.

Electric Attraction and Repulsion of the Solar System.

It is a law of magnetized bodies that while positives resist, negatives and positives attract each other, inclining them to come together. Now as one-half of each planet always faces from the sun, this half is always dark and cold, and this constitutes them negatives, giving the attractive power toward the sun, or centripetal. The faces of the planets toward and from the sun being equal gives us a view of the astronomical law that upholds the universe, and shows why the planets do not fly off at a tangent or consolidate with the sun, and also why the sun is held in the common center. Here we have suspension, attraction, and repulsion, all by electricity; yet within the recourses of all this grand machinery there is not a ray of light thrown upon the inquiry as to how these orbs came to be thus endowed, adjusted, or set in motion; but in the most positive manner declare there was no capacity in the original atoms even to move themselves, much less to combine, intercombine, and organize the stupendous system.

The theory of Dr. Franklin is unquestionably correct, "That all terrestrial things contain a certain quantity of this subtile fluid; but that its effects become apparent only when a substance containing more or less than the natural quantity is brought in contact with it. This condition is effected by the friction of an electric; thus, when a piece of glass is rubbed by the hand, the equilibrium is lost, the electrical fluid passing from the hand to the glass, so that the hand contains less and the glass more than its ordinary quantity; these conditions implying the presence or absence of electricity and constituting the negative and positive." Dupay's theory supposes two kinds of electricity, called the *vitreous* and *resinous*, because the former is obtained from glass and the other from "resin," corresponding to the negative and positive of Franklin. This theory is illustrated by the fact that "two pith-balls or other light bodies, placed near each other and touched by an excited piece of glass or sealing wax, repel each other ; but if one of the balls be touched by the glass and the other by the wax, they will attract each other."

We adopt both of these theories. Indeed, they are but parts of the same science. There are phenomena connected with electrics which cannot be accounted for upon either taken alone. While the theory of Dupay has no application to the electric force passing from a cloud surcharged to one only charged, that of Franklin equally fails to account for the fact, among many others which might be mentioned, connected with animal magnetism—namely, that a weak child cannot be magnetized by a powerful man, who possesses ten times as much as the child. On the other hand, a mere child may thus affect a powerful man, completely depriving him of the power of voluntary motion.

Indeed, it seems to be a principle of universal application that electricity becomes modified or changed into another kind by the chemical properties of every different substance with which it is allied, and it pervades all things in nature. These changes, however, do not to any considerable degree impede the rapidity of its motions, though thus encumbered by bearing away the decomposed particles of the substance from which it has been loosed. Nor do these affect its control by the same laws as when in its pure state, whether as the agent of the mind or the rolling of the planets. In the philosophy of natural science it is of the first importance that we understand the nature of electricity and the laws by which it is governed, not merely the negative and positive, but its own endowment with those properties which constitute it the most powerful decomposing agent of nature.

Since the discovery by Galvani of the existence of animal electricity or its modification as connected with minerals—called "galvanism," after the electrician's name—as Dr. Wollaston has shown, most if not all the chemical effects of the galvanic battery may be produced by electricity; such as the decomposition of water by the Dutch chemists, long before the discovery of galvanism. Since that event the decomposition of the alkalies, and as a consequence other discoveries of great value, have been effected. "One of the most extraordinary facts belonging to the agency of galvanism is that the elements of decomposed bodies follow an invariable law in respect to the electric sides on which they arrange themselves. Thus, in decomposing water, or other compounds containing its elements, the hydrogen escapes at the negative pole and the oxygen at the positive. In the decomposition of salts and other compounds, this law in every instance is observed, the same kind of element being always disengaged at the same pole of the battery." (Comstock's Chemistry, p. 71.)

Electricity contains the Elements of all Bodies.

These facts show in the most indisputable manner that the phenomena of electricity must be attributed to two kinds, and not always to unequal quantities. All the elements of compounds susceptible of galvanic decomposition—and all substances are thus susceptible—possess the feature of electric polarity, which fact implies that they were not only formed from electricity, but that each simple element contains the same chemical endowment as electricity itself, which renders it not only susceptible of electrical government, but discovers an affinity between it and all other forms of organic and inorganic matter, demonstrating the fact that it contains the positives for all the negatives, and the negatives for all the positives in nature.

The conclusion from these facts and principles is that were all earthly substances, compound or simple, reduced to their highest sublimation, the product would be "electricity," with its negatives and positives, possessing chemical affinities for all other forms of matter; and these peculiarities were its creation.

It is a universal law of chemical solution that if one substance will decompose another, it must be in chemical affinity with that substance; and as electricity or galvanism will decompose all other substances, it must therefore contain the chemical properties of all others—of course in their highest ethereal degree. It is this endowment which adapts it to be a universal agent, penetrating, as it does, every element or compound of nature, whether it be the most compact formation or the finest ether. Here, then, is the first created substance, the creation of which implies its separation from original matter; its condensation to a degree below such matter, and, in the third place, these peculiar endowments.

Notwithstanding the original formation of this substance, as above set forth, if nothing further had been done by mind, still there had been no creation of the world; so that Darwinism could not have obtained a starting point, though it had had this matter, containing all the elements of nature instead of simple homogeneous atoms. The principal argument upon this point is the fact that as electricity can be thrown out of equilibrium only by substances of greater or less density, and as there were none such then existing, it must have remained in eternal quietude. The connection of mind with material motion involves such close metaphysical deduction that it is in danger of being overlooked. Of course its facts and manifestations are only to be found within the domain of the highest mental philosophy.

The creation of the world involves the necessity that simple atoms of matter, without sense or intelligence, should have obeyed the word and will of an intelligent Being, and should have moved in lines, circles, and angles, in the formation of everything in nature possessing them, to meet his desired purposes. If this phenomenon can be produced by an intelligent mind, analogy teaches that it may also be produced by every other intelligent being; but the degree of such control is in proportion to the order of the different minds. If material bodies may be thus moved without any other contact than the mental agency controlled by the will of human beings, they certainly may be by the mind and will of God. The question therefore is, Can unknowing matter be moved by the mind of man, and made to perform intelligent acts without bodily contact?

Magnetism the Agent of Mind.

Connected with what is called "Spiritualism" is the phenomenon of table-tipping, including the moving of other articles, which almost every one has witnessed, and which, through ignorance of the scientific principles involved, have been attributed to the agency of spirits. Even were this true, it would still demonstrate our argument by showing that immaterial spirits, as they are held to be, are capable of moving inanimate bodies, and of compelling them to perform intelligent acts, as the pen moves in the hand of the writer. If we touch a true principle of nature we can reason from a balance made of straws up to a stellar sphere. In like manner may we reason from these human phenomena, the mere straws of the principle, up to that upon which God endowed, separated, condensed, and formed and governs all the bodies of the universe, and this implies their motion without direct contact ; but all produced by the agency of His mind, directed by His will for the purpose.

Whether these phenomena, therefore, emanate or result from the minds of men or that of man's Maker, it is the one grand science of mind, matter, and motion. As in the motion of an atom of matter, so in every other atom or combination of atoms, there is involved what may be denominated a threefold law : First, an intelligent Being ; secondly, a material agent, as the medium of communication ; and in the third place, an effect producing motion. A common illustration of this is seen in every act of self-preservation. The mind receives an impression, through a nerve of sensation, that the hand is in contact with flame, producing pain, when, quick as a flash, a sufficient quantity of the mind's electric agent is dispatched by the will, and instantly the muscles of the arm are contracted as though brought suddenly in contact with a charged galvanic battery. The muscles being attached to the bones by their respective tendons, the hand is immediately removed from the seat of danger.

This law, it will be observed, like every other natural law, is involved in the combination, and *evolved* by the effect produced, while the cause was in the mind of the Being who made the combination. His work was the *involution*, while that of nature is the secondary work of *evolution*. In the movement of a table by these mental dynamics, let us suppose a number of persons assembled, either to witness or produce the phenomenon. Among them is one susceptible of the magnetic trance, or psychologic sleep (but, like Balaam, having his eyes open), who is known as the medium. The concentration of all the minds present becomes fixed, either by design or expectation, upon the medium and the object to be moved. No sooner is this done than the electric force of all these minds is agitated and put in motion, some by the direct power of the will and others by simple expectation ; the entire force, however, is dispatched from the brain and conducted by the nerves of the arm to the finger ends, and if these are in contact with the table the communication is unbroken and it readily moves, and moves also in the direction which those forming the circle wish or expect. If the table is not touched, the intervening air acts as the conductor of the mental force.

The presence of those who are not susceptible of the mediumistic state, and who have little faith in the phenomena, shows, however, that they have some desire or expectation, having never before witnessed the manifestation. Their minds therefore assist, acting inadvertently though irresistibly on the mind of the medium, strengthening the impression that the object sought will be accomplished ; and as they believe, so is their power in the premises. Thus the entire mental force, or that of volition, of the medium becomes concentrated upon and conveyed to the table, the movement of which is thus effected. The immediate physical effect being the production of an atmospheric vacuum, the air above and around the table becomes so far electrified that its pressure is neutralized or balanced, of course counteracting the specific gravity of the table, and consequently requiring but the slightest degree of force to suspend it or move it in any desired direction, as well as to compel it to perform intelligent locomotion.

To understand the formation of this vacuum it must be remembered that on every square inch of the surface of the table—above, below, and on either side—there is an atmospheric pressure of fifteen pounds. Let us now suppose that the surface air on the top, upon which the minds and fingers rest, becomes so far displaced by the electrical force thrown upon it that it weighs only fourteen pounds to the square inch, while the pressure beneath remains at fifteen. Do we not see that the table must move upward, just as surely as that if fifteen pounds be put in one scale of a balance and fourteen in the other, one will fall and the other rise? Do we not also see that if the mental force be concentrated on one side of the table, the result will be its movement in the direction of the vacuum thus produced? If the manipulators advance with the table, the vacuum follows by the continuous displacement of the air.

Inanimate Things Perform Intelligent Locomotion.

As the motion of the table is caused by mental force and that of volition, it is as obvious that the table must perform intelligent action as that the arms and legs of a human being move in obedience to the will, and intelligently after proper training. Thus tables are made to write intelligently, which the hand of man cannot do until it has had suitable training. This fact has been witnessed by almost every one, in the operation of the planchette, by the use of which any one may demonstrate it in his own family, without the presence of a medium. All possess the power, to a limited degree, of thus enduing with motion inanimate objects; for, being a law of mind, it must apply to all minds.

Thus we see how and from whence emanated the original power to form and combine inanimate matter, and gain some conception of the mental agency inherently allied with all organic and inorganic bodies, as we find them arranged by the great Mechanic of the universe—and the inanimate, so chemically and electrically bound together that when once set in motion they are compelled to perpetuate and carry out His designs until they are accomplished. The law of universal gravity is but another name for the inherent construction and constitution of matter by the infusion of mental dynamical force. It is the original involvement of motive power, while gravity is the evolvement or secondary power.

The principle of mind controlling atmospheric pressure is that by which Christ walked upon the water and ascended into heaven. Being the Creator of nature's laws, all that was necessary for Him to do in order to perform these acts was to remove one pound of atmospheric pressure from above His head and increase it to that extent beneath His feet. By so doing He would be carried to the outer verge of the heavens, from whence He could make gravities to convey Him majestically to any part of His universe.

We might introduce here scores of experiments which we have made and witnessed, illustrating this principle of mental science, but we prefer giving the following, which is supported by authority that no intelligent mind will question. We copy from a paper read by Dr. Bell, as the report of a committee before the superintendents of the Hospital for the Insane of the city of Boston, which was published in the *American Journal of Insanity.*

Experiments by Dr. Bell.

Dr. Bell began by expressing surprise at finding that, although there was a large number of persons whose lives were spent in investigating the reciprocal influences of mind and body, scarcely a single member had during the year bestowed a moment's attention upon a topic directly in their way, which, whether regarded as an epidemic, mental delusion, or a new psychologic science, was producing such momentous effects upon the world—whose adherents are now said to number over two millions, with an extended literature in many forms, and which had taken hold of many minds of soundness and power.

"I am aware that many were disposed to cast ridicule on those who were engaged in investigating the (so-called) spiritual phenomena, and especially when it was being prosecuted seriously by hospital directors; but if there were any class of men who had duties in this direction it was ourselves. Our reports contain the record of many cases of insanity said to have been produced by it; it was important, therefore, that its precise length, breadth, and nature should be studied, as it is well known that mystery always loses its terrific character when boldly met and exposed to the light of day.

"On returning from Washington I had a peculiar wish to verify my previous observations on witnessing what are technically known as the physical manifestations. I could not, however, doubt my former personal observations, addressed to my senses of sight, hearing, and touch, and separated, as I believe, from any possibility of error or collusion, and yet the offer made by Professor Henry of a large sum of money to any person who would make one of his tables in the Smithsonian Institution move, and the obvious incredulity of many of the brothers, had produced an ardent desire to witness a full and unequivocal experiment of this character.

"An opportunity was not long wanting : on the occasion of a well known gentleman, long connected with the insane, who had never witnessed any of these phenomena, whom I invited to accompany me to a family where a medium of considerable power was visiting. The family was one of the most respectable in the vicinity, the head of it being a gentleman with whom was intrusted millions of dollars of other people's money, as the financial manager of a large banking institution, who, with his wife, had been for years perfectly convinced of the spiritual character of these manifestations.

"The medium was a young lady of about eighteen years, of a very slight figure and weighing between eighty and ninety pounds, who had discovered herself to be a medium while visiting these relatives. A family of such character and position in society was beyond suspicion, or anything like irregularity, collusion, or fraud.

"We were so fortunate as to find the medium at home, and the circle was composed of the five individuals named. The ordinary manifestations of raps, beating musical instruments, and responses to mental questions were remarkable on this occasion, as well as the movements of the table under the contact of mere finger-ends. Finding circumstances so favorable for an exhibition of more astonishing things, I proposed to try the great *experimentum crucis* of moving the table without human contact. I arranged things to suit myself, beginning by opening the table wider than common, and inserting two movable leaves, increasing its length to about ten feet.

This gave me an opportunity to clearly discover any wires or machinery which might have been attached to it, as well as to enable me to answer positively as to their non-existence. The table was a solid structure of black-walnut, with six carved legs with castors attached, and of such great weight that I could but just move it by a full grasp of the thumb and finger of both hands.

"The persons stood three on the one side and two on the other, with a space between them and the table of about eighteen inches. Being tall, I had no difficulty of seeing between the table and all the persons present.

A Table Moves without Human Contact.

"At a request, the table commenced its motion with a moderate speed, occasionally halting and then gliding along a foot or two at once. It seemed to me that its motion would have been continuous if the hands above it had followed it in the same position which they occupied at the first. In reaching the iron rod on which the folding doors traversed, which projected a half or three-fourths of an inch from the level of the carpet, it raised at once over it, entering the other parlor, through which it passed until it came near a pier-glass which stood at the opposite side of the room. At a request, the motion was reversed, and it returned until it again reached the iron rod. Here, however, it stuck, although it heaved and creaked and struggled; but all in vain; it could not surmount the difficulty. The medium was then impressed to write, and seizing a pencil, hastily wrote that if the forelegs were lifted over the bar, they (the spirits) thought they could push the others over, which was accordingly done, and the motion continued. Once or twice during the movement of the table I requested the whole circle to withdraw a little further from it, in order to see how far the influence would extend, and it was found that when a greater distance was reached (say two feet) the movement ceased, and a delay of three or four minutes occurred before it commenced, conveying the idea that, if broken off, a certain re-accumulation of force was necessary in order to put it again in motion.

"The table finally reached the upper end of the parlor from which it started, about four feet from the meridian line of the room. I expressed my gratitude to the company for the very complete exhibition with which we had been favored, but remarked that it would be enhanced if the spirits would move the table about four feet at right angles, so that the chairs would come right again for their late occupants, which was immediately done. The performance was so perfect and satisfactory that nothing more was asked on that occasion.

"This," remarked Dr. Bell, "was the sixth time I have seen tables move without human contact, and all under circumstances apparently as free from suspicion as that just described. I might have stated that the table traveled on this occasion over fifty feet. A clergyman of extraordinary sagacious perceptions took this medium home with him, where she had never been before, and in the presence of his family alone, one of his own tables was made to go through the fullest locomotion without human contact."

A Reflection from such Teaching.

From the teaching of such facts and principles, can we come to any other conclusion than that all compound bodies, or their smallest divisible atoms, derive their power to move and to affect each other from mind, and therefore that *all power is mental?*

If evolution could furnish for its vindication such facts and demonstrations as those we have presented, allied, as they are, with the most transcendent of all sciences, that of mind, it would not only claim respectful consideration, but would take philosophically the front rank in natural science. We believe also that were those who are so prominently committed to the theories of the geological antiquity of the world and the origin of things by evolution as well informed as these laws of mind and matter render it possible for them to be, they would redeem modern science from the degradation into which these godless speculations have sunk it, and themselves from the groveling mysteries in which they must otherwise continue hopelessly to grope and flounder.

If the human mind has the power, as above recorded, to counteract on a small scale, the laws of pressure and gravity, cannot the Maker of that mind control or suspend them at pleasure? and is it not demonstrated also that He is their Creator? A man speaks to an inanimate table, and it moves toward the accomplishment of an intelligent purpose which was the mental conception of the speaker; and it was done. God speaks to the homogeneous matter of the great deep, lying dead and motionless, saying, "Let there be light." "And his spirit" (mental agent) "moved upon the face of the waters, and there was light." Were the whole operation written, it would have been: "And the motion of the mental agent created friction, and the friction created light."

God speaks again—"Let dry land appear."—and in accordance with His wish and conception sends down His electric mental agency through all the vast deep, endowing every atom with chemical affinity and electrical polarity, as well as variety of densities, pressure, or gravity; and now behold every atom seeking its equilibrium and kindred! Some sink toward the center by their comparative weight, forming the lower strata, the next lighter covering it, and so on until the soil is spread over the face of the round world. The more sublimated rush above the solids, forming the heaven, and the dry land appears. This is named earth. With these creations science was born, which gives us feeble creatures a faint conception of the mental philosophy of the great God giving birth to the dynamics of the universe.

Nothing has so excited the ambitious pride of man as the attempt to write out the history of God and the origin of things. All such efforts bear the feeble stamp of the thing made attempting to comprehend its maker, and give us the measure of their childish superficiality. Seeing this folly, the great Maker had the sentence written: "The world by wisdom knew not God."

The mythological speculations of the great men of the past concerning the "Supreme Being," as some of them called Him—and even these were polytheistic—were of a low moral standard. Not even Plato gives us an argument drawn from nature, or from its inadequacy to account for its own existence, to show that he had any conception of His being the maker of the world. As to moral character, Socrates affirms: "It was never supposed that in the gods dwelt virtue." Among the ancients no one was better qualified to pronounce such an opinion than Socrates.

While, however, such were the views entertained by the ancients respecting the character of God, history does not furnish a single example of an intelligent atheist or evolutionist—not one who rejected the personal embodiment of the godhead, or denied that nature did not reveal His underived and therefore "eternal power." The great apostle of the Gentiles referred to the teachings of this fact in nature thus : " For the invisible things of God are clearly seen from [by] the creation of the world, being understood by the things that are made ; even His eternal power and godhead."

Nature does not Reveal the Moral Character of God.

While thus in nature was lodged the indisputable evidence of the existence of a personal God, and hence the foundation for natural religion, yet it was only His eternal awfulness which overwhelmed the worshiper, while it utterly failed to reveal an idea of His being either lovely in Himself or mercifully inclined toward His creatures.

The inflexibility of natural laws, the merciless manner in which they execute their own penalties for every violation, preclude the idea of His being either good or merciful. Let the deist, so vociferous in his praises of the God of Nature and so clamorous against the God of the Bible, remember that although the former exempts from suffering all who obey His laws, yet, without distinction of person, rank, age, or sex, or of making any allowance for ignorance, He visits every infraction with merciless severity ; while the God of the Bible gives timely notice and full written information of His intent to punish, the reasons why, and the condition of escape. In view of this, it is proper to exclaim of the God of the Bible, "Behold the goodness and severity of God ; " and equally proper, "Behold only the severity of the God of Nature." Behold the mercy of the Christian's God ; behold the implacability of the deist's god."

Of the views of the ancients which have come down to us, those which approach nearest to skepticism are those of

Xenophon, a pupil of Socrates, who was the first to publish the discourses of that philosopher; and these only relate to the shape of the Supreme Being, not questioning his personal existence. "There is," says he, "one God supreme above all other gods, diviner than mortals, whose form is not like unto man's, and as unlike his nature; but vain mortals imagine that gods, like themselves, are begotten, with human sensations, voice, and corporeal members. So, if oxen or lions had hands and could work in man's fashion, and trace out with chisel or brush their conception of godhead, then would horses depict gods like horses, and oxen like oxen, each kind the diviner with its own form and nature endowing."

Here is a man, all alone in his presumption, calling in question the opinions of all the wise men of Greece, Persia, Chaldea, and Egypt, whose national deities, supposed to represent the godhead, were fashioned after the similitude of man. What do his assumptions weigh against the testimony of such an array of wisdom, inasmuch as it is all matter of opinion and conjecture?

Man the Natural Image of God.

On the supposition that God desired to make a being most pleasing to Himself, and deemed Himself to be the most perfect model, would He not fashion him like Himself? From the greatest source of divine wisdom we add the following: "And God created man in his own image, after his likeness;" and also that Jesus Christ is the Christian's God; and he is the express image of God's person, and yet the perfect likeness of man. It should be remembered that the definition Socrates gives of virtue is that it is the power philosophy inculcates, which, if attained, enables men to keep their passions under control, while vice consists in yielding to them; and although such virtue pleased the gods, yet they themselves did not possess it; and while they had gods representing every bad passion, they had none to represent human kindness and benevolence.

How could heathenism have entertained any other views of the God of Nature, looking out, as they did, upon a world convulsed by physical derangement and moral disorder—a world of conflicting elements and deadly agents, which, from the light of nature alone, seem to serve no other purpose than to disappoint man's hopes, confuse his calculations, and rudely trample down his present interests and future prospects? Behold some of these: Earthquakes to devour, floods to inundate, conflagrations to burn, hurricanes and tornadoes to devastate, lightnings to scathe, wars to kill, famines to starve, "pestilence walking in darkness and wasting at noonday," indiscriminately killing the aged and the infant, the good and bad. Add to this picture the whole troop of deadly diseases, warring against everything that lives, and you have a partial view of the disposition or moral character of the God of Nature. At the same time, no reason is given for permitting all these to exist, or apology for their origin, or what end is proposed to be accomplished by their agency.

Of such a deity, the worship by the votaries of natural religion can only be extorted by awful respect or apprehensive dread. If deists or natural religionists entertain truer or better views of God in this age, it is because they emanate from a better revelation—one which gives the reasons for all these sufferings and hardships.

Or has nature given proof of milder administration since the days of Socrates? Does not the curse continue to devour the earth as of old, and indeed with a greedier maw? Does the universal destroyer, Death, relinquish any of his merciless demands? Does he make discriminations in favor of the good, the wise, and the useful, so that these survive while the others perish? Do the disturbances of the natural elements, in seeking their equilibrium, go forth with milder tread? Even supposing the present generation to be more tolerably dealt with—the God of Nature relaxing the rigor of his arbitrary laws, conferring greater physical vigor, longer life in which to grow wiser and more virtuous, by obedience to his demands—what apology can he make to the two hundred generations of the dead for their sacrificial offering upon such an altar? Of what avail to them is it that a few better students of nature have flourished—even so wise as to have discovered that the world made itself, or that it always did and always will exist? Or that others of the same school have discovered that nature (their god) brought man into being through an ancestral line of weeds, shell-fish, and monkeys? and that this has been repeated several times, and as often have all gone back to extinction?

O ye generations of the dead, be consoled by the reflection that your metempsychosal existence has developed such grand exemplars of thought and originality—men who can comprehend the evolution, from a mere mushroom, of a world teeming with life and power, and even bring the mushroom itself into existence—men who, though thus imbued with the marvelous and wonderful, yet cannot admit the infinitely more reasonable hypothesis that the world was made by an intelligent Being equal to the task!

If nature does not reveal any just conception of her Maker, or the end He proposes to accomplish with the world and its inhabitants, and if there are satisfactory assurances entertained in relation to these questions, must they not have originated from some other and superior source, and therefore from the Bible?

Personality of God Revealed by that of Man.

It is true that we may draw some correct inferences as to the nature of this Being from the works displayed in the animate and inanimate world. From the organizations of nature we may learn the embodiment of God, which idea cannot be separated from that of substantial being. These manifest omnipotent power, and as power emanates from mind, therefore there is an Almighty. As man, the greatest example of created skill, has a local existence, so also has the Creator Himself. If in order to the possession of intelligence a living being is required, as manifested in man, such must also be the nature of God Himself. If man was made of a single element, then might the Deity be likewise so made. If made of matter and occupies space, can God be immateriality—not matter, or nothing—and occupy no space?

Thus we might reason according to all the analogies of nature and being, and find nothing to warrant the heathen conception of the Deity as expounded by Platonic philosophy, nor the least light thrown upon His real disposition toward men, though unmistakably reading from the book of nature of the existence of God as a philosophic necessity.

That the most exalted views upon all cosmical subjects entertained at the present day are radiations from Christianity, taught alone in the Bible, renders it indispensable to apply to its teachings if we would obtain a true theory of the world and the object of its creation.

To shut our eyes to this light is to involve history, science, and philosophy alike in the most profound mystery. Especially is this confusion manifest in the writings and teachings of those who set God and his written revelation aside. They find a world of confused material, embracing untold generations of living creatures, but until very late in the history of creation not a vestige of man; and even then his appearance was a mere accident. Indeed, nothing was designed, for there was no designer; but he comes into existence by a freak of unintelligent matter.

The world itself had been running along in its unknowing and unbroken career through thousands of years, ages, or epochs, turning out successive generations of beautifully organized vegetables and animals arrayed in variegated splendor, the flora odorously burdening the air, the great sun pouring his benignant rays upon the unseen flowers and groveling beasts, with not an eye raised to behold the glory. The stars shone down from their canopied heights, but not a living being knows of their existence, not one capable of distinguishing between the most transcendant beauty and the most fabulous ugliness: the animals living merely as prey for each other. Finally, man crawls into existence, through a long line of weeds, fishes, insects, birds, and monkeys, ranking only a little higher in the scale, as a monkey is supposed to be higher than a wolf. O Science! O Philosophy! if these thou art, what hast thou and thy gods done?

CHAPTER VIII.

SPURIOUS DATA OF GEOLOGICAL CALCULATION.

Six Twenty-four-hour Days Ample Time for the World's Creation.

WE have already shown that the time alloted by nature for the work of bringing organic things into existence depends upon the character of the thing created, and is limited to the possibilities of the case; further, that six literal days were not only ample, but could not have been consumed in the work of organization. A being capable of performing such a work was under no necessity of consuming long periods, much less of experimenting upon simpler forms in order to qualify Himself for making man, especially as we have the fact that prior to this He had created angels, a higher order of beings. We frankly admit that had creation been the work of senseless nature, the time required might well have been computed as an endless succession of indefinite periods; indeed, no time would have been of sufficient length. Those who suppose this to have been the work of the god *Nature*, and who study his ability, and thereby discover his inability, seem never satisfied with the figures employed; even millions of centuries are too limited for the performance of his work. Of course they thus betray their want of confidence in his creatorship, well knowing that it is a poor workman who takes a life-time to perform a work that another could have accomplished in an hour. While this course reveals minds imbued with rank skepticism in relation to God and His being the Creator of the world, it also reveals the strange anomaly of the most marvelous credulity existing in the same minds. In their imagination there exists a thing called a primordial, which from formless dead matter brought into palpable existence all the wonders of the living, moving world. If it did, it must have possessed infinite wisdom; and yet it had none. This thing, neither living nor dead, moved from nebulæ and formed itself first, and then the whole solar system with its inhabitants. Such faith should put to the blush those who doubt God's having created the world in six days, or that such a Being existed capable of self-motion, which power they give their primordial. In view of such fanciful scheming in support of the opposite theory, is the inference not inevitable that a being possessing the wisdom and power necessitated by the creation might as well have made it in six days as in any other period of time? Supposing creation to have been the work of blind fatality, it could not have known when the work was finished, and must have worked on without ceasing, adding more atmospheres to the earth, more planets and suns to the solar system, not one of which could it admit without disturbing the whole. In a word, this fortuitous god would have mixed up one world with another in endless confusion; ten thousand things, having no connection with each other, and answering no purpose, would be promiscuously thrown together; but in fact there is not known to be such a substance or thing in existence. Suppose a steamship should have evolved from the concentrated forces and agencies of inanimate nature: would all its parts and machinery exactly adjust? On the contrary, no single piece of the engine would fit another; not a plank, block, or piece of tackling would adjust to another.

The Evolution World-maker Enslaved by his Work.

It is almost enough to make one blush on behalf of the evolutionists to institute such a supposition, and yet there is not a millionth part of the skill displayed in the construction of the steamship that there is involved in the simplest plant or insect in existence. Alas for evolution! Seeing they could not restrain their god from continuous work, they have invented a notion to give him steady employment. This is the destruction and reconstruction of his own works. The god of the evolutionists is like the man's cork leg, which was so light that when once set in motion it could never stop. Waiving the question of the intelligence or even the common-sense of this theory, the best possible view that can be taken of it is, that it is rank pantheism, confounding the maker of the world with the world made, and presenting the absurdity that the maker made himself: and thus we dispose of it. That the world was brought into existence in a very short space of time is further proved by the interdependence of its animate and inanimate departments. The wisdom thus manifested seems to demonstrate the fact that the universe is one grand and perfect system, wonderfully adapted to accomplish the object designed. Among organic things there is not a species of vegetable or animal life, from man down to the lowest link in the chain, which is not calculated to administer either directly or indirectly to the health, comfort, and longevity of mankind. To suppose that the world existed for myriads of centuries, with everything it contains but man, is to charge its maker with folly, indifference to admiration, or with morbid imbecility; for who but man can form the least idea of the existence of a God, or entertain a conception of His handiwork?

To argue that man, in his final destiny, is the great object for which the world exists, pre-supposes the extreme purposelessness of its existence without him. Behold the world rolling in its splendor, with every phase of motion requisite to produce and perpetuate its vegetation, with its beautiful colors and sweet aroma, with none but a few wild beasts to gaze on their beauty or inhale their fragrance! This reciprocal dependence is seen in the fact that almost every species of organic life furnishes food for another. If it be objected that some of the largest species of animals, such as the mastodon, have become extinct, and man lives without seeming to miss them, the answer is: We are not sure that their loss has not conduced to shorten human life and impair physical power. In his primitive state these may have served man as beasts of burden, answering the place of steam-power, while the modern substitute has maimed and shortened millions of human lives; and who can tell but that the unnatural excitement and quickening of the commerce of the age has thus resulted, which in ten thousand ways has cut and is cutting into the vitality of man?

Though we are not in possession of sufficient accurate data to enable us to trace the vital ratios between all living species and man, yet he is known to depend upon so many of these for his food, raiment, and comfort, that we are left to infer that many, if not all others, only fill up less important links in the chain, and that in the absence of all other causes the extinction of any one species would finally result in the extinguishment of man himself. We are not left to conjecture, however, respecting the interdepending departments of inanimate nature, which prove them and man to be simultaneous creations.

How much of the Solar System it Takes to clothe and Feed Man.

To the question, How much of the world and solar system is thus connected and depending? we answer, in the first place, that as the sun's light is essential to vegetable life, the sun itself must have existed, not in a nascent state, but as perfect as now, before a plant could have lived. The existence of the sun necessitated the simultaneous existence of all the planets in the solar system whose reciprocal attractions and repulsions hold all in their orbits and the sun in their center. To suppose that one of these could have existed without the others would be as absurd as to suppose a balance holding two weights in equal poise would remain in that position after one was removed, or after a third had been thrown into one scale. To prove that light existed before animal life, it is only necessary to state the fact that all fossils found in the strata of the surface of the globe are furnished with eyes—a superfluous appendage on the supposition that animals existed before light. This fact, however, harmonizes with the Mosaic statement that the first act of creation was the making of light. Water also must have been a perfect formation before the inhabitants it contains existed, as they could no more then than now have lived in a thick, chaotic mass ; nor in such a mixture of elements could their finny instruments of locomotion have been of any use. Besides, the effluvia arising from this stagnant mass would have so impregnated the air as to have rendered animal life impossible. The poisoning of the air would also have followed had the waters of the sea remained motionless ; and of themselves they had no power to move from a dead level. To produce these phenomena,

SPURIOUS DATA OF GEOLOGICAL CALCULATION. 235

therefore, the evaporating power of the sun must have been as great as it is now, and the atmosphere as perfectly constituted as it is at the present day.

This law of evaporation and precipitation causes all the rivers and streams upon the surface of the earth to flow, or even to exist ; otherwise the deeper ocean-beds would have drained them dry. The expansion of the waters by the heat of the sun and moon was also a necessity, in order to produce and perpetuate their motion, seen in the ebbing and flowing of the tides, as well as its vertical currents or circles of hotter and colder water. The sun raises the temperature of every globule of water as far down as the rays penetrate, compelling the colder particles to rise by displacing the warmer ones, which sink to take their place, thus keeping in constant motion every drop of water in the great seas, and preventing the salt they contain from precipitating to the bottom and there remaining; which cause alone would render the waters putrid, and thereby destroy the life of the animal, if not of the vegetable world. That vegetable and animal life came simultaneously into existence is proved further by the fact of the absorption of the carbon of the atmosphere by vegetation, and the oxygen by the animals, thus preserving its balance and rendering the existence of these grand departments of organic life possible, as well as constituting the great law of atmospheric equilibrium. Denude the earth of vegetation, and all animals would almost instantly become extinct. The animals continuing to absorb the oxygen of the air and rejecting its carbon, it would very soon become so highly carbonized that its inhalation would extinguish animal life. On the other hand, were all animals destroyed, vegetable life would cease by reason of the air becoming overcharged with oxygen. This great law of nature, growing out of this endowment, demonstrates the fact that the atmosphere with its relative constituents of carbon and oxygen, must have been as perfect before plants and animals could have existed as it is at the present day.

It is conceivable that the atmosphere, after having been created, might have preserved its chemical balance indefinitely, or as long as no substance or thing existed which would absorb one of its gases and reject all others; but give plants, which do this very thing, a few years the start, and they would so derange or poison the atmosphere for animals that, if then brought into existence, they would immediately become extinct; in fact, not an air-breathing animal could have begun to live, though possessing all the vital organs in a perfect state of development, as the first breath of too highly carbonized air would not have set the machinery in motion.

The Carboniferous period never existed.

It is also a fact that increased carbonization of the atmosphere, though carbonic acid gas is the principal from which plants form their own food, would extinguish that life, as no plant can live and reproduce itself in pure carbon; nor can animals live in pure oxygen. We have in this natural law an argument demonstrating that what is called the Carboniferous Period, so fruitful of vegetable life, never existed, though to the decomposition of its prolific vegetation is ascribed the origin of the coal-beds. It is another fact of science that light is supported by oxygen, and that the light of the sun is essential to the healthy growth of plants; but the rays of the sun, passing through a highly carbonized air, could not have produced the light demanded for this purpose: the light upon the surface of the earth would be no more than a mere twilight. Fill a vessel with carbonized air and put it in the only window in a house, and you would have an illustration of the gloom such an atmosphere would create. Now, as these different facts of nature cannot be harmonized with the supposed existence of the carboniferous period, the conclusion is that it never did exist, and therefore all the supposed geological results, such as the formation of coal, etc., fall with the theory which assumed them.

The geological interpretation of the Mosaic six days of creation, making them indefinite periods, puts the carbonic period before the oxygen or light period; but if we turn to the account, we find that the first work of the first day, or period, was the creation of *light*. This account therefore harmonizes with the scientific necessities of the work, and proves the views of the geologists to be erroneous. Thus we see that a perfect condition of the planetary system, including every phase of motion they manifest, as well as the inanimate formations which now exist, was indispensable to the possible existence of vegetable and animal life; and as man is an animal, and as such is governed by the precise laws common to all animals, therefore an organized world adapted to other forms of life was equally adapted to the life of man. Hence the world was not made by parts, with long intervals between, but at once, and perfect; and the voice of universal nature joins that of the Bible in ascribing its origin to the acts of a single Mind, possessing the intelligence and power demanded by the work. Let it be conceded that the world was created with a degree of perfection capable of sustaining life—which implies a condition as high as that which now exists, everything in maturity—and do we not see that all bore the marks of age? For example, a tree was made a tree, with its ripe fruit ready to sustain the life of man, and its trunk would perhaps show thirty rings or grains, one of which is formed each year by the laws of nature or of natural growth. Understanding this law, a botanist would have pronounced the tree thirty years old on the day in which it was made. Adam was made a man, and not an infant to become a man; the day after this he might have been pronounced thirty years old. The two great whales made on the fifth day might have been pronounced a hundred years old on the day of their creation. A certain stratum of granite was needed as the foundation of others. God endowed the atoms with affinities and adhesive attractions requisite to such formation, which sent them in rapid haste toward each other; and in like manner was formed by Almighty fiat, and in an hour's time, each stratum above.

Suppose Sir Charles Lyell were now asked to give an estimate of the age of this stratum. Finding it to measure fifty thousand inches in thickness, and knowing similar rock to have been formed, according to natural laws, at the rate of one inch each year, he would have pronounced the whole stratum fifty thousand years old. Hence his blunder.

The Original Soil a Creation

The voice of nature declares soil to be of very slow formation, as it results from the decomposition of vegetation, mixed slightly, it may be, with pulverized rock. But in the formation of the original soil there were no vegetables to decompose; it was therefore a creation accomplished by the endowment of common matter with the same peculiarities as those of decomposed vegetation, thus forming a soil in an hour which, as now, by the natural law of decomposition, would consume thousands of years in producing. Hence the original soil was as truly a creation as the plants set therein, each of which, from the most gigantic tree of the forest to the most delicate moss of the wildwood, is furnished with a separate department or apparatus for the propagation of its kind.

That we may observe the skill here displayed, let us examine the organization of the moss. The plant consists of little bodies, forming, as it were, the spokes of a wheel, which are cases containing spores, or that part of flowerless plants which performs the function of seeds, having a very curious receptacle for the spores. When mature, these are scattered by a set of elastic spiral filaments which lie among them. When it begins to develop, the spore does not burst all at once and emit the seed it contains; but its outer coat only is ruptured, and a long tube projects from its interior, within which new cells are growing, taking their origin from the minute grains which the spore contained. These cells gradually increase into a leafy expansion, from the lower part of which root-fibers proceed, and in due time assume the appearance of the original plant, forming its own grains and fructifying itself as did its parent. An interesting circumstance touching one of these little plants is connected with Mungo Park, when in the interior of Africa. After relating how he was cruelly stripped and robbed by bandits, he proceeds: " In this forlorn and almost helpless condition, when the robbers had left me I sat down for some time, looking around with amazement and terror. Whatever way I turned, nothing appeared but danger and difficulty. I found myself in the midst of a vast wilderness, in the depth of the rainy season, naked and alone, surrounded by savage animals, and men still more savage. I was five hundred miles from any European settlement. All these circumstances crowded at once on my recollection, and I confess that my spirits began to fail me, considering my fate certain, and having no alternative but to lie down and perish. The influence of religion, however, aided and supported me. I reflected that no human prudence or foresight could possibly have averted my present sufferings.

"I was indeed a stranger in a strange land, yet I was still under the protecting eye of that God who has condescended to call Himself the stranger's friend. At this moment, painful as were my reflections, the extraordinary beauty of a small moss caught my eye [this is called Hooker's shining moss], and though the whole plant was not larger than the top of one of my fingers, I could not contemplate the delicate conformation of its roots, leaves, and fruit without admiration. Can that Being, thought I, who had planted, watered, and brought to perfection in this obscure part of the world, a thing which appears of so small importance, look with unconcern upon the situation and sufferings of creatures formed after His own image? Surely not! Reflections like these would not allow me to despair. I started up, and disregarding both hunger and fatigue, traveled onward, assured that relief was at hand, and I was not disappointed."

Had Mungo Park been an evolutionist, we venture the remark that his fate would have been inevitable. No such exalted views and aspirations are possible to their groveling, godless reflections. In this moss he would have only looked for irregularity of formation, and from this would have descended to other plants, less perfect, which produced it, until, arriving at one so simple in its construction that nature or nothing might have brought it into existence, in his grossness he would have laid down and died. And who will say it would not have been a just retribution?

Reasoning from the relations and dependence of departmental nature, it seems to us there can be but one conclusion—namely, that the origination of everything that moves, varies, or reproduces was the direct and instantaneous act of an intelligent Creator. After the act of creation, the process of formation and transformation, especially of inanimate things, though the indirect acts of God, may be very slow; but as the destiny of man is the great object for which the world was made, and as he must be consulted and persuaded, but cannot be forced to enter upon this plane of destiny—which a sufficient number in a sufficient time will do—hence the necessary delay of a few thousand years in the accomplishment of the work, involving as it does the re-creation of the world into one of perfection and eternal duration, which also has been decreed to be a sudden work.

The "World to Come" Solves the Mystery of this.

The prehistoric record of the reconstructed world is contained in the Bible, and is summed up in the last two chapters of the Book of Revelation—that is, revealed from other Scriptures. Having no idea of this plan of God, the evolutionists are necessarily bewildered in the interpretations of nature, because wholly engrossed with the present temporary and deranged condition of the world, knowing not whence it came or for what purpose it continues. Hence we hear Sir Charles Lyell stating positively his theory to be that the existence of all things, organic and inanimate, originated in the same slow process which marks their continuance. Referring to former geologists who had assumed that sudden and abrupt causes were necessary to produce the effects everywhere witnessed in nature, he says: "Never was there dogma more calculated to foster indolence and to blunt the keen edge of curiosity than the assumption of discordance between the ancient and existing causes of things."

Thus does Lyell prefer speculative curiosity with its fanciful conclusions to the ancient Mosaic account of the commencement of things by creation, and administers this sharp rebuke to all geologists before him for not cutting loose from such restraint. Again he says: "So in geology, if we could assume that it is a part of the plan of nature to preserve, in every part of the globe, an unbroken series of monuments to commemorate the vicissitudes of the organic creation, we might infer the sudden extirpation of species and the simultaneous introduction of others, as often as two formations in contact are found to include dissimilar organic fossils; but we must shut our eyes to the whole economy of existing causes, aqueous, igneous, and organic, if we fail to perceive that such is not the plan of nature." What an idea—that anything but an intelligent being can have a plan, and can work economically according to that plan! What are such expressions but consummate nonsense? In accordance with the plan of the living God, when the time arrives, we may not only infer, from the sudden creation of the world and the species inhabiting it, their sudden extirpation and reproduction, but witness the bringing into existence of the second grand world, including every organic species, with immortal man at their head, which once came from the hand of the great Creator, and which he pronounced not only good, but *very good*. Let us add a reflection for the benefit of Sir Charles and his deluded followers. It is easy to infer, from the contempt in which they hold the works of the Creator—their detraction from His honor in ascribing them to other sources—that they will be unfit subjects for that coming world, where there shall be not one whose highest delight does not consist in ascribing all honor to Him who sat upon the throne, and repeating these words: "Thou art worthy, O Lord, to receive glory, and honor, and power; for thou hast *created all things*, and for thy pleasure they are and were created." (Rev. 4: 11). The coming of such a world is not only revealed in the Bible, but likewise in the very nature of man. If all the resources of the present world were possessed and exhausted by a single man, there is not in them that which would satisfactorily supply his intellectual, moral, and religious needs even for a single day: there must therefore come one adequate to meet these demands, and this work involves his re-creation or resurrection, both of which terms are used synonymously in the Scriptures. The promise of this inheritance is the motive to induce men to obtain the necessary qualification for its possession. That this new creation of man is to be sudden, even in the "twinkling of an eye," implies that his first creation was also sudden. If evolution can raise a man from the dead after his dissolution into his elements, or can re-create him, then we might infer that he came thus originally into existence.

All Appearances of the World Prove its Existence Temporary.

The monumental series of derangements in every department of the organic and inorganic world corroborates the written revelation that it was designed only for a temporary purpose; and the wisdom it exhibits of its Creator forbids the idea of its annihilation, and therefore indicates its re-creation into one of incorruptibility, and hence of eternal duration. Not to be able to discern this grand destiny respecting man and the world, Lyell must have shut his eyes to the most philosophic and indisputable evidence, written and commemorated in every phase of dead and living nature. This, then, is the stupendous plan and economy of the 'God of nature, in the execution of which he must work as rapidly as the possibilities admit. The fact that some species of animals have become extinct affords no evidence that new species have come into existence. Such a supposition implies the absurdity that because nature can destroy she can create; that because her fires can consume a man to ashes, they can restore him again to life; that because her seas can drown they can reproduce; that because her decomposing agencies can resolve the diamond into carbon, they can reproduce the jewel. As a conclusion, Lyell says: "There never has been any interruption, from the remotest periods, of one uniform system of change in the animate and inanimate world." If this assertion is true, no room is left for God's having created the world, or for the universal deluge. It is much easier to put forth assumptions than to substantiate them by evidence. In one of the above extracts will be noticed the phrase, "If we could assume," but the writer concludes with the most positive assertion. Dr. T. M. Coan says: "Many computations have been made in respect to the actual antiquity of the various prehistoric remains that have been discovered. Sir Charles Lyell, one of the most cautious geologists, thinks that 100,000 years have been required to form the alluvial delta of the Mississippi, and it is a moderate estimate." Shutting their eyes to the fact that the subsidence of the great deluge, as the only adequate cause of accounting for the promiscuous distribution and unequal configuration of the land and water on the surface of the earth—which was capable of producing more of this land wash, or drift, in the one hundred and fifty days of its duration than the ordinary deposit of rivers would have amounted to in thousands of years—how can modern geologists come to any other than extravagant and groundless conclusions? [In reference to this Mississippi formation see page   .] If Sir Charles Lyell is one of the most cautious of geologists, it would be more amusing than instructive to see some of the calculations of the more extravagant; and before we get through it may appear that one of these is Dr. Coan himself. Again he says: "Sir Charles Lyell himself thinks we may expect to find the remains of man in the Pliocene strata; but there he draws the line and says, 'that in Miocene time had some other rational being flourished, representing him, some signs of his existence could hardly have escaped unnoticed.'" The doctor goes on to say: "It is true that few of our existing species, or even genera, have as yet been found in Miocene strata; but if man constitutes a separate family of mammalia, as he does in the opinion of the highest authorities [geological authorities, of course], according to all palæontological analogies, he must have had representatives in Miocene times. We need not, however, expect to find proofs in Europe; for our nearest relations in the animal kingdom [meaning the monkey tribes] are confined to hot, almost tropical climates, and it is in such countries that we are most likely to find the earliest traces of the human race."

If man or his ancestors evolved in one country, why not in every other country? As he lives equally in every climate, the speculation about temperature has nothing whatever to do with the question. That speculation evolved naturally from the superficial brain of this doctor, who, it is evident, has not descended far enough from his acknowledged monkey ancestors to be profound. But he continues: "It will be remembered that side by side with the remains of Arctic animals have been found others indicating a warmer climate, such, for instance, as the hippopotamus. This fact, which has always hitherto been felt as a difficulty, is at once explained *by the suggestion* of a change every 11,000 years, from a high to a low temperature, and *vice versa*. But a period of 11,000 years, long as it may appear to us, is very little from a geological point of view. We can thus understand how the remains of the hippopotamus and the bones of the musk-ox came to be found together in England and France. The very same geological conditions which fitted our valleys for the one, would, at an interval of 11,000 years, render them suitable for the other."

The finding of the remains of the musk-ox, which is an inhabitant of the country about Hudson Bay, and of the hippopotamus, a native of Africa, together in England and France, where, according to the climatic theory, neither of them belongs, presented not only a difficulty, as the doctor admits, but an insuperable barrier to geological calculation: the fact conflicts with their assumption as to the localization of species, both territorially and periodically. That is to say, one species existed at an earlier period than another, and became extinct before a different species evolved from it, but was still its representative! As the changes in the work

SPURIOUS DATA OF GEOLOGICAL CALCULATION. 247

of evolution were infinitely slow and minute, how absurd to suppose that every one of one species should have been a native of an Arctic, and those of another of a Tropical climate ! Though the fact that these animal remains were found together in England and France is conclusive against the theory of evolution, it is equally in favor of the universal acclimatization and simultaneous existence of all living animals in the Eden World, but which were drowned by the flood and thus scattered over the earth's surface.

Dr. Coan's Calculations Erroneous.

In order, however, to reconcile these facts with geology, Dr. Coan invents a theory and makes a suggestion. The invention is so simple that it is a wonder that it was not discovered before ; but better late than never. He says : " This time of 11,000 years may seem long." Though this period is almost twice the actual age of the world, yet we are glad it is so short, that we may test the theory by the chronology of the world. If, then, in 11,000 years the temperature of the tropics became as cold as the arctics, and the arctics as hot as the tropics, then the musk-ox living in the arctic regions became extinct by the tropical regions moving north, and the hippopotamus perished with cold in the once sunny south. By another whirl of the evolution machine, the musk-ox was reproduced in the tropics and the hippopotamus in the arctics ; and just as two of these animals were passing each other on the journey they were caught in the temperate zone of England and France, and dying together, were found buried side by side. Behold to what a mere suggestion, coming from an evolutionist of the wisdom of the nineteenth century, may lead ; from it what marvelous things may evolve ! It is, however, in keeping with the doctrine of natural selection, that the less produces the greater.

The evolutionists are wiser than Moses, or even than the God of Moses; they are, however, examples of that class described in the Bible, "who do not wish to retain God in their thoughts, whose minds become dark, seeking to be wise they become fools." If, as is alleged, in every period of 11,000 years there is a complete change of climate at the poles and at the equator, so that the coldest temperature of the frigid zones becomes that of the equator, let us suppose that the temperature of the arctic regions had been at its lowest degree and that of the equator at its highest 11,000 years ago. Five thousand five hundred years later there would have been, as a result, an equal temperature at these extremes, and consequently over the whole earth. Suppose, still further, that the 11,000 years had begun 6,000 years ago, the date of the creation: the result would have been that in the fourteenth century of the Christian era, or the year 5,500 of the world, the temperature at the poles and at the equator would have been equal; and at the present time, five hundred years later, the tropics would be one-twentieth colder than the poles. This is the ridiculous conclusion of Dr. Coan's celebrated "suggestion," which, when made, was regarded as of so much importance that it relieved the whole geological fraternity from the musk-ox and hippopotamus embarrassment.

The fact is, however, that there has never been a change of so much as a single degree of temperature between these sections of the globe. It is upon such speculations called facts that the spurious chronological geology and the godless so-called science of evolution are founded. Shutting their eyes to the philosophical and scientific necessities of the world's creation, how can modern geologists have their speculations appear in any better light? It is said that Voltaire attacked and ridiculed the theories of Burnet, Woodward, and other physico-theological writers of his day, because they defended the account given in Genesis, by the geological phenomena of the world, of the creation and deluge. He said they were as fond of changes of scene on the face of the globe as were the populace of a play: every one of them destroys and renovates the earth after his own fashion, as Descartes, for instance; for philosophers put themselves without ceremony in the place of God, and think to create a universe with a word. Lyell says that Voltaire ascribed the existence of shells found in the Alps to their having fallen from the hats of pilgrims coming from Syria, but that in his later writings he admitted the true origin of the shells of Turaine.

That in the latter part of his life this bitter skeptic should have begun to deal respectfully with geology has its explanation in the fact that at that time it was passing from its legitimate sphere of teaching—exhibiting the harmony between the appearances of nature and Scripture statements concerning it—into that which rejects the latter, and shuts God out of his universe. He began to see that if geology would thus undermine the confidence of men in the hated Bible, which all his life he had been openly and boldly endeavoring to do, why, then it was a good science, and therefore to be approved. Hence it is not surprising that he should have become a convert to the teachings of geology. In our day the Voltaires have all turned geologists, as a more respectable mask under which to accomplish the desired work of destroying Christianity and the Bible. Were Voltaire himself now living, we doubt not he would be elected to a professorship of geology, perhaps in a theological institution, or to fill the place of the late Professor Agassiz.

When Geologists Began to be Skeptical.

That geology was assuming a skeptical attitude in Voltaire's day is evident from the fact that Hutton, a Scotch geologist in 1788, said: "In the economy of the world, I can find no traces of a beginning, no prospect of an end." He thus, in a single sentence, set at naught the two great truths of the Bible—the history of the world's creation, and the prehistoric record of its end. The Huttonian theory taught the exclusion of all causes not belonging to the present order of nature, as he termed it. He did not understand nature sufficiently to see that the order or laws of nature originate nothing, but that they grow out of organizations, and the chemical and electrical endowment of matter, giving some of its particles an inclination to adhere, and others a disposition to resist, and that there is no cause in nature.

Because this Scotch geologist did not see the necessity for a beginning to the world or an approaching end, does it follow that all men of all time are equally poor students of nature? Because one man is blind, can no man see? Who cannot see that at some time in the past, man must have made his first appearance upon this planet, and that if he began to be, he may cease to be? How can a reasonable man affirm that the advent of man upon the earth was as ordinary an event as the reproduction of his kind? A scientific view of the world exhibits the two great principles of wisdom and power: the first in the chemical endowment of the molecules with peculiar affinities, attractions, and resistances, distributing them in the exact proportions required to produce all the combinations of the organic and inorganic, animate and inanimate world, and the intellectual power to organize and combine the first progenitors. This was creation; reproduction is the work of nature, or evolution. Another illustration of the erroneous data for calculating the age of the world is the chasm worn by the Niagara river and falls. From Professor Huxley's Nashville address, printed in the *Tribune* Extra under the heading, "Testimony of the Rocks," we take the following : " Take, for example, the cataract of Niagara. It is easy to see that the Niagara river has formed its own valley, has cut its own way back to where the falls are now for some six miles. The great cliff from which it tumbles is formed of two kinds of rock—hard rock at the top and soft rock underneath. The water undermines the soft rock, when the solid structure above falls over. Now, the rate at which that is going on has not yet been positively ascertained ; but we may be perfectly certain that the work of cutting back does not go on at the rate of a yard in a year. We have six miles of such cutting, which will give you ten thousand years for the cutting back of the Niagara, and it is much nearer the truth if I said four times that amount?"

In order to show the fallacy of this calculation, we must remember that one of the fundamental facts of geology and evolution is that this rock, as well as all the rocks of the earth, was once softer than clay ; and also that the irregular surface in the vicinity of Niagara, as well as everywhere else upon the earth, was produced by aqueous and igneous agency, which means simply the action of water and fire. The first wears away the surface, the second throws up the foundations. No one will question our right to assume that the upheaval and depression of the earth in the vicinity of Niagara occurred when this rock was rudimentary and soft. The very action which created the irregularity of the surface started the flow of the water, and over this rock it began to pour, at a point six miles down the river, admitting Huxley's theory that it wore its way back. It must be evident, therefore, that more rock would be wasted in a single day perhaps than now, after it has become hard rock, than in ten thousand years, or in Huxley's longest period—40,000 years—which he takes the liberty to change from the previous geological calculation of 10,000 years.

There is another fact which this chronological mathematician has not taken into the account. Examination of the rock along the banks of the river for these six miles shows that it lies at an inclination with the surface in the shape of a wedge, growing thinner and thinner as it recedes from the present falls, until, at the end of six miles, it runs out on the surface to an edge. Thus, at all events, we have seen it exhibited on geological charts. Here, then, at the thin edge, is the point at which Huxley says the water first began its work of cutting. Do we not see that the rock would at that time crumble away more perhaps in a single year than at its present rate in ten thousand years, and that between the two points there are no respectable grounds of comparison; and that the cutting grows less rapid as the present falls are approached?

Let us now inquire into the facts in relation to the manner of cutting out the bed of the river, and the time consumed in the work. When Lake Erie was formed—which we believe to have been at the time of and by means of the flood—its overflowing waters found outlet in the direction of Lake Ontario, whose basin it filled. No matter from what cause, the water found its lowest outlet at or near the point of the present falls. This was the beginning of Niagara river, which at first was a stream over which a man might have stepped. Of course the waters continued until they reached the lake below, whose basin was excavated by the same catastrophe (the flood), the stream widening and deepening according to the hardness or softness of the earth over which it flowed, as well as the increasing or decreasing rapidity of its current.

It is evident that had the hard rock, which begins with the "rapids" and ends in the vicinity of the falls, been laid the whole length of the river, and at the same declivity as that of the rapids, these (the rapids) would have continued the whole distance, and there would never have been any other falls. But now coming in contact with the soft rock or clay, the cut became perpendicular, and increased according to the distance of the fall of the water; while the whole bed of the river was cut out from the surface regularly and simultaneously, beginning at Lake Erie, and not at Ontario, leaving the same general appearance which the six miles now bears, with the exception that the falls have been cut back probably a few rods.

Another Theory of the Age of Niagara

If we would ascertain the true period consumed in cutting out the bed of Niagara river, we should reckon from the surface of its banks to the river's bed, taking that part where the water flows evenly, entirely avoiding the irregular vicinity of the falls. Suppose that in this part the chasm averages twenty-five feet in depth for the whole six miles, and that from the time the river began to flow it had cut its bed from the surface at the rate of one inch a year; this would give 3,500 years, whereas about 4,400 years have elapsed since the flood. Besides this, there is the absurdity of Huxley's statement, that the falls have cut their own bed from six miles below, which implies that when the river first began to flow there was no bed behind it, and therefore there could have been no river; for a river cannot exist without a bed having some depth below the two banks. That a river should begin to cut its bed at its mouth instead of its source is the height of absurdity. In view of this we ask, What becomes of Huxley's geological period of 40,000 years? Instead of calling his statement the "testimony of the rocks," it should have been called the testimony of the *sand*.

Upon this evidence the Professor proceeds to pile up inference upon inference until he declares 40,000 years to be but an infinitesimal point of the time consumed in developing the whole phenomena of the globe. Now mounted on his hobby and drawing his favorite weapon, in conclusion he gives Moses, as usual, this adroit stab: "I need not say that this view of the past history of the globe is a very different one from that which is commonly taken. [Meaning the Mosaic record.] It is so different that it is absolutely impossible to effect any kind of community, any kind of parallel, far less any sort of reconciliation between these two ideas. The one is true; the other is not." No, Mr. Huxley! this array of words and pompous expression only betray the weakness of your conclusion; and we assure you and your fellow-scientists that you must give us more plausible theories and draw ·more logical conclusions from them, or others will do so to your discomfiture. In closing this brief criticism, we may remark that we know of no more solid so-called fact than that which this

Niagara record affords in support of the assumption of the great age of the world, either in Sir Charles Lyell's "Principles of Geology," Darwin's "Descent of Man," Huxley's "Lectures in America," or Tyndall's "Fragments of Science," and none which may not as easily be shown to be irreconcilable with others supporting the same hypothesis. Each is in contradiction alike of all science, all philosophy, and all natural history, whether written in the Book of Nature or in the Bible.

CHAPTER IX.

DARWIN'S SOPHISTRY EXPOSED.

"THE question," says Mr. Darwin, "whether mankind consists of one or several species has, of late years, been much agitated by anthropologists, who are divided into two schools of monogenists and polygenists. Those who do not admit of the principle of evolution must look at species either as separate creations or as in some manner distinct entities; and they must decide what forms to rank as species by the analogy of other organic beings which are commonly thus received. It is a hopeless endeavor to decide this point on sound grounds until some definition of the term 'species' is generally accepted; and the definition must not include an element which cannot possibly be ascertained, such as an act of creation." It is evident from this that Mr. Darwin feels himself to be unable to combat a definition of species which is claimed to have originated in an act of creation; and the reason is, if man was created, he did not evolve; and if it can be shown that he did evolve, that will settle the question. That he was created is rendered an absolute necessity by all the analogies of organic being, as we have shown, and shall demonstrate by more than a score of syllogisms. By this adroit attempt at intimidation we are to be prevented from defining what species means, unless we adopt Darwin's dictum that it does not mean an act of creation. This is the very thing to be proved, and of course it can only be done by producing an array of facts and other conclusive evidence showing that inorganic things caused organizations to exist, dead things produced living ones, and out of unintelligent things came those of intelligence—the very mention of which is an expression of the grossest absurdity. But this is one of those hard necessities with which Darwinism is environed, and upon which it depends for its existence. In effect, Mr. Darwin says: Let me shut God out of creation and from the controversy, and my chances are as good as yours to show how things originated. In such a case indeed, neither could show anything of the kind. He thus begs the whole question to begin with. Is it not marvelous, therefore, that such men as Sir Charles Lyell, Tyndall, and Huxley should adopt his theories, and declare, as Tyndall did in his Belfast speech, "that the evidence in proof of the modification of species furnished by Mr. Darwin was overwhelming;" by which he means that one species becomes another by animal descent, and hence that all living things came from a single primordial form, and that form from lifeless inorganic matter.

The definition of the term "species," which the natural relation of living things and the physiological laws of organic life compel us to give is, that it signifies those animals or plants which will not reproduce by crossing with others; and by the word "race" is meant the varieties of species which, without regard to these differences, will constantly reproduce offspring. So universally do the living organisms of the world vindicate the correctness of these definitions that no room is left for Darwin's insinuation of difficulty. Every one knows that the terms "species" and "race" have been used interchangeably to designate the whole family of mankind as descended from Adam ; but since the theory of evolution has been promulgated, it has become necessary, in order to seem to furnish proof in its favor, to define them both to mean "race," and either to discard the word species altogether, or to employ it in the same sense as signifying all the plants and animals of the world.

That Mr. Darwin avoids the true definition of these terms is manifest by his assumption that sound definitions will and must be generally accepted ; and that their acceptance will prove them to be correct. How does this look in the historic light of scientific discovery, which shows that whenever a new truth has been brought out and defined, it has been generally rejected, and that, too, by the very men who were the foremost advocates of the science of which it claimed to be a part ? No, Mr. Darwin ! a *sound definition* depends solely upon the question whether it is a true definition, and not in the least upon the fact whether any man or number of men will receive or reject it ; and we shall show that the facts and laws of generated organic life render it an absolute necessity that the evolutionists must accept the definition herein maintained, though it prove fatal to their theory.

The difficulty under which the polygenists labor is seen by the following : " Mr. Darwin says sub-species is a term some naturalists have lately employed to designate forms which possess many of the characteristics of species. Now, if we reflect on the weighty arguments above given for raising the races of man to the dignity of species [here is the idea that races become species], and the insuperable difficulties on the other side in defining them [there are not only no insuperable difficulties, but none at all in definitions we are about to give], the term 'sub-species' might here be used with much propriety, but from long habit the term 'race' will perhaps always be employed." Descent of Man, p. 216.

Darwin begs the Question.

It is said again, as a conclusion: "Finally, the naturalists might argue that the natural fertility of all races has not yet been fully proved; and even if it had, it would not be an absolute proof of their specific identity." Here it is evidently implied that if the natural fertility of all races, as he calls them, was a fact, it would almost amount to demonstration of the specific identity of all species, or that each had its original progenitor, and therefore a separate creation. But if this has not been positively proved, then Mr. Darwin's book would contain the exception; for no one can be acquainted with the works of this author without being convinced that he has ransacked all nature, history, and fable to obtain evidence in defense of his theory; and the only thing his labored effort does contain having the least show of evidence, after sifting it of sophistry, in proof of the infertility of species, is, that there are individuals among all species which are sterile. This, fact, however, only proves that physical derangement exists in the generative organs of such individuals. Now if fertility is a universal fact among all the races of the human family, which all efforts at crossing have demonstrated, what is Mr. Darwin's assertion to the contrary worth? We put it with his dictation as to what kind of a definition we must or must not give to " species."

In opposition to this arrogance we have not the least hesitation in affirming that there never was an abstract idea so well ascertained and so strongly enforced by philosophic necessity and the analogies of nature, as that plants and animals required acts of creation to bring them into existence, and that each species had its specific progenitor or progenitors at that creation. This position is also vindicated by the failure of thousands of efforts to produce a new species by crossing which would persist—made, too, by the most celebrated naturalists, who believed in its possibility. Their experience settled the question until Darwin's speculations came out. Such cross-breeds as those produced the pheasant and hen; but if their progeny are permanent, the fact only proves that these and similar examples are only different races of the same original species, and that crossing brings them back to their original specific identity—it is only undoing what peculiar environment did.

As every branch of natural science is employed by the evolutionists to prove that organic existence originated without the aid of an intelligent being, this theory of the identity of species is no exception. Hence if we would successfully expose the futility of their efforts we must make use of the same arguments to prove the existence and intervention of such a being, without whom the universal voice of nature proclaims that there never would have been a beginning or a succession. Suppose no name had been given to this creator—so certainly revealed in nature, and in man especially as a part of nature—still the conception would have been as definite and profound that such a living, personal, intelligent being existed, as abstract and before her works, as that the works of man prove his abstract, intelligent, and prior existence. We venture the remark that there never was a human being of ordinary intelligence, who had arrived at maturity, whether heathen or Christian, who had not by his own intuition or reasoning received this definite conception.

There never was a Natural Atheist or Evolutionist.

It therefore follows that there never was a natural atheist or evolutionist, the latter being still more unnatural and absurd than the former; for, unphilosophic as is the notion of an eternal succession of the works in nature, the notion that there was a beginning without a creation is still more so. To prepare the mind to admit either of these requires a long process of mental training, in which convictions are stifled, reason outraged, and pride of opinion and self-indulgence gratified. It is an undeniable fact that every sensible child, beholding the surrounding objects of nature, learns very early that human skill is inadequate to the task of producing them. Perhaps the first lesson has been learned from efforts to draw pictures of flowers, birds, or animals. Here skill is brought into requisition; but the great difference apparent between the drawings and the things themselves forces upon him the conviction that it requires a hand vastly more skilled than his even to make good resemblances; then how much greater would the failure have appeared had the attempt been to make the living things themselves? Even if the parent undertook the work, still the child discerns a marked difference in the result. Now, while laboring with this conception, what would shock this child more than to be told that a thing far less skilled than himself or his parent made the flower, bird, and animal themselves, while they, though skillful and intelligent creatures, had failed even to make satisfactory pictures of them?

Take another example. A young farmer has learned something about hens' eggs and chickens. He has found out that the hen desires something of a start in a nest, as an inducement to lay her eggs in it, and he makes a chalk egg for the purpose. Of course it is not an egg because it resembles one; but even this rude effort has exhausted his skill in organic construction. It is, however, of sufficient similarity to deceive the hen, simply because she is a hen, and has not the intelligence of the farmer. He has also learned that chickens are hatched from eggs simply by the hen sitting on them a sufficient length of time, and has ascertained that even this is not absolutely necessary; but that hatching will follow if the eggs are otherwise exposed to the same temperature for the same length of time.

With the knowledge of these facts, what other conclusion could the farmer arrive at than that the hen is a natural machine, constructed by some Being capable of performing the work, for the manufacture of eggs, and the eggs involving the embryos for evolving chickens—just as a saw-mill is made for the manufacture of boards from logs, or a grist-mill for making flour from grain; and that it was just as necessary that the hen-machine should have been perfectly organized in order to turn out her work, as that the mills should have been perfect before they were capable of doing theirs? He had also observed that this result was not owing to the quality of food fed to the hen, for the same fed to hogs—hog-machines, if you please—would be turned into pigs.

The hen had an instinctive desire inclining her to sit on the eggs. This desire was not acquired by cultivation or imitation, hence it was not "natural selection," but was involved in her organization; and for the gratification of which she would patiently endure confinement and loss of flesh while sitting on the eggs for three weeks and then assiduously begin the task of bringing up a large brood of chickens. Thus, in obedience to this law of nature, the hen was induced while living to reproduce her kind. The farmer's reflections upon these wonderful facts would lead him to the conclusion that nothing less than infinite intelligence was necessary to so mix the common material of which all animals are composed that this or a similar feeling would be an inherent function, without which perhaps no creature would willingly endure the hardship and deprivation necessary to raise up future generations; and that without this compensatory gratification all races and species of animals would have become extinct at the death of the first progenitors, though each were perfect in every other respect.

Suppose, still further, that the farmer had often tried the experiment of so mixing different kinds of eggs—those of hens, turkeys, geese, etc,—setting them under each other in order to produce a new species of fowl, a half-breed—one between a hen and a turkey, looking as much like the one as the other—that the egg this new creature laid—if it laid any—were also as perfect a hybrid in form and size as itself, and that the new fowl was just as fertile in laying eggs and hatching chickens as were any of the uncrossed hens and turkeys: with these facts before him he might have concluded that all kinds of fowls had a common progenitor, but instead of its being simple, he would have concluded that it had involved in its organization the embryos of all the varieties of fowl living upon the earth, and consequently that to make it required infinitely more skill than to make any one of the kinds evolved from it. Instead of being taught the lesson of the evolutionists, that this first progenitor was the lowest and simplest in the scale of organic being, he would learn that it must necessarily have been the very highest of all, involving in its structure all the peculiarities of feature, size and color of all the fowls that had ever existed; and if it was the egg that was first, it was such a marvel of mechanical skill that none but a being of infinite wisdom and power could have brought it into existence.

The Wonders of Incubation.

The following observations on the changes that occur from hour to hour during the incubation of the hen's egg are from "Stearm's Reflections:" "The hen has scarcely sat on her eggs twelve hours before some lineaments of the head and body of the chicken appear. The heart may be seen to beat at the end of the second day. It has at that time somewhat the form of a horseshoe, but no blood yet appears. At the end of two days two vessels of blood are to be distinguished, the pulsations of which are visible; one of these is the left ventricle, and the other the root of the great artery. At the fiftieth hour one auricle of the heart appears, resembling a noose folded down upon itself. The beating of the heart is first discovered at the auricle, and afterward in the ventricle. At the end of seventy hours the wings are distinguishable, and on the head two bubbles for the brain: one for the fore and the other for the hind part of the head. Toward the end of the fourth day the two auricles already visible draw nearer to the heart. The liver appears the fifth. At the end of seven days the lungs and stomach become visible, and four hours afterward the intestines, bones, and upper jaw.

"At the one hundred and forty-fourth hour the two ventricles are visible, and two drops of blood instead of the single one which was seen before. On the seventh day also the brain begins to have some consistency. At the two hundred and nineteenth hour of incubation the bill opens, and the flesh appears on the breast. In four hours more the ribs appear, forming from the back, and the gall-bladder becomes visible. The bill becomes green at the end of two hundred and thirty-six hours; and if the chicken be taken out of its covering, it moves itself. At the two hundred and sixteenth hour the eyes appear. At the two hundred and eighty-eighth hour the ribs are perfect. At the three hundred and thirty-first hour the spleen draws near the stomach, and the lungs to the chest. At the end of three hundred and fifty-nine hours the bill frequently opens and shuts, and at the end of the eighteenth day the first cry of the chicken is heard. It now gets more strength and grows continually, till at length it is able to set itself free from its confinement."

What a loose play of the imagination must it be to see in an operation of blind, unknowing matter, the production of such a world of wonder as is thus disclosed, and which was involved in the organized egg and in the hen that produced it; and how would the astonishment be increased if the hen or egg should have given birth to a creature of more complication and superior organization to itself—as, for instance, a man from a monkey! Let us suppose still further that the farmer had learned by his experiments that a certain kind of eggs invariably produced a certain kind of fowl. He could differentiate his chickens in size and color by always setting the fowls upon the largest eggs, or upon those laid by certain colored hens; but whether large, small, white, black, or speckled, each was of the same truly identical kind of fowl as though none of these changes had been effected —just as dogs are dogs, whether large, small, white, black, or spotted.

Extreme Changes in Organic Things Sudden.

He would also have learned that these changes did not come by such slow and nice shades that those of a single generation would not be perceptible, as is claimed for evolution, but were wide and palpable, as often in a single season the greatest extremes may be reached, and in a few generations the largest fowl produced, and yet at the same time the farmer's hens were all white, black, or spotted, just as he desired to have them.

By further experimenting he would have found that a certain kind of seed would produce a certain kind of fruit-tree; but that it was necessary to plant the seed in soil, and also where it would be exposed to the light and heat of the sun, and that the soil must be made moist. The man possessed some skill, but he knew there was none in the seed; for skill implies volition, and this implies self-motion, etc. Neither is there skill in the sunlight; the sun shines by necessity, and of necessity the rain falls; and these elements, the farmer soon learns, are the principal constituents of the law of vegetable growth. But even the combination has no skill, and knows nothing of the inherent power it possesses, or whence it was derived. The tree, however, grew to maturity—that is, if the seed was perfect, as an imperfect seed will not produce a perfect tree, or one that will reproduce its kind. From these evidences of the incompetency of nature the farmer rightly concludes that the whole phenomena of producing the original plants or seed were supernatural work, and therefore that of a great Creator. He also learns an important truth of natural science, enabling him thereafter to distinguish between creation and growth, or involution and evolution. The first possessed the laws inhering in the material elements combined in the seed, and the last evolved the tree from the seed, with all its susceptibilities, including that of the reproduction of seed after its kind.

It is unquestionably good for the cause of truth that Messrs. Darwin, Tyndall, and Huxley have assumed extreme ground in this controversy, seeking to account for the coming into existence of the original "primordial form" by the simple play of material atoms independent of a creator. For a number of years naturalists have been diverging in this direction, some claiming more and some fewer representative species. Their attitude has challenged a close and profound investigation into the natural history and peculiarities of man, and this investigation has led us directly to the Mosaic account, which gives a single pair as the progenitors of each animal species, as the scientific and only solution of the problem. Here science, fact, and philosophy harmoniously blend in a conclusion, not only at variance with the theory of evolution, but absolutely repugnant to it. Now, suppose it were impossible, with our present light (which we do not admit), to show that all the apparent phenomena of localized shells and fossils could be harmonized with a simultaneous, sudden, and perfect creation: would not this overwhelming evidence forever establish the fact that such was the necessity notwithstanding? These supposed facts, or their environments, depend upon many contingencies of localization, indicating no uniform scientific principle of deposit, such as that the growth of plants or animals admit of extremely different interpretations, as increased light has done in thousands of similar instances in the past. Hence it is idle to assume that these shells and fossils teach a chronology of the organic world at all, much less one which is in conflict with that given by the God of Scripture. If, therefore, the human species are a unit, having sprung from a single pair, and yet manifest great variety in its races, does it not establish the fact that all the lower animals and vegetables are distinct species—units also?

If we make a comparison between man and those animals which in general form approach man the nearest, physiology and anatomy show his organs to be exactly like theirs, almost muscle by muscle and nerve by nerve, and performing exactly the same functions in each. Surgical experiments are repeatedly performed upon the lower animals in order to qualify practitioners for human surgery, and by these means the functions of human organs have been discovered. Physicians also have experimented with alleged medicinal substances upon the lower animals, and thus ascertained their effect upon man. But if we would obtain all the instruction anthropology affords, plants as well as animals must be investigated, because the two are subject to the laws of organic life ; and whatever questions relating to organic phenomena are proposed, the answer to the one gives the answer to the other. As it is of the greatest importance that we shall have a proper apprehension of what constitutes the exact difference between species and race, nothing vague or conjectural should be admitted in the discussion, and as we have dwelt somewhat at length upon the natural laws here involved, we propose now to introduce a few facts by way of illustration.

History of the Coffee Plant.

We begin by quoting from a lecture by A. De Quatrefages, delivered in Paris a few years since. The first example is that of the coffee plant.

" The use of coffee spread early and with great rapidity in the East, but it penetrated Europe much slower, being first introduced and used in Marseilles, France, and first drank in Paris in 1667. The seeds furnished on the occasion were brought in a small quantity by a French traveler named Thevenot. Two years afterward, Solomon Ago, ambassador of the Sublime Porte in the time of Louis XIV., induced the courtesans of that king to taste it. It was not, however, until the eighteenth century that it began to be generally used in France. So we see that coffee has not been very long in circulation, as it is scarcely a century and a half since it became an article of general consumption by the people of Europe. During many of these years Europe remained tributary to Arabia for this commodity. Indeed, all the coffee consumed in Europe came from Arabia, particularly from Mocha.

"Toward the commencement of the eighteenth century the Dutch attempted with success to import it into Batavia, one of their colonies in the Indian Archipelago. From Batavia some stalks were taken to Holland and put in a hot-house, where they succeeded equally well. One of these stalks was brought to France about the year 1710, and was placed in the Garden of Plants. It also prospered, giving birth to a certain number of stalks. In 1725, an officer of the French navy, Captain Desclieux, thought that since Holland had cultivated coffee at Batavia, he might also acclimate it in our colonies of the Gulf of Mexico. When embarking for Martinique, he took from the Garden of Plants three stalks of coffee and carried them with him.

"By reason of contrary winds the voyage was long and difficult, and the supply of water being insufficient, it was necessary to put the crew on rations. Captain Desclieux, having with others but a small quantity of water to drink each day, divided it with his coffee plants. Notwithstanding all this care, two of them died on the passage. On the arrival this one was put at once into the earth, and it prospered so well that from it have descended all the coffee-trees now spread over the Antilles and tropical America.

"Twenty years after this our western colonies exported millions of pounds of coffee. Here we see the coffee-tree starting from Africa, reaching the extremity of Asia on the east and America on the west. Hence it has nearly traveled round the world. In this voyage coffee has become modified. Passing by the tree, of which we know but little, in this report let us consider the seed

No one would confound Mocha with Bourbon, or Rio Janeiro with Martinique. Each of these seeds possesses peculiar forms, properties, and aroma, giving the certificate of its birth. Now, whence came these changes? these peculiar phenomena? The answer is, They came from differences of temperature, climate, culture, and soil. This shows that if we transport plants to considerable distances, where they encounter these differences, we obtain different races. But this is the limit of change. Coffee, in all its modifications, remains substantially identical." None of these kinds have ever approximated beans or Indian corn, or any other seed. Neither would any of the countries to which the coffee had been transplanted ever have produced it but for the fact of the transportation; and this proves that all the plants and coffee-seeds of all the world and of all time originated from a single seed or plant, whichever was created first. The same laws apply to all other plants and seeds, which demonstrates the fact that each species not only started from a single plant, but equally from a single territorial center of the globe. These facts also prove that organic productions do not move in an unbroken circle, but in a line of succession, one generation following another. Therefore, there was a first; and if you begin at the last and count backward you must arrive at the first.

If Evolution were true, all Plants would be produced in all Countries.

If the theory of evolution is the true interpretation of the organic life of the world, we should have as a consequence the fact that every island and country on the face of the earth would have equally produced and possessed every species of plants and animals susceptible of living in those particular parts of the world. The original plant would just as certainly have evolved, and in the same time, from no plant or seed, in one country as in another, the laws of nature, to whose genius the work is attributed, being not only uniform but universal in their operation. This result being contrary to the fact of universal organic distribution, proves evolution not to be true, and therefore not science. No matter what may be the supposed import of any local fossilizations, if the inferences drawn from them palpably conflict with the positive knowledge of organic distribution, then they are error and not science. But we introduce another example from the same source, and from the animal kingdom—the turkey.

"This bird is wild in America, and presents many characteristics which distinguish it from the domesticated turkeys of other countries. The wild turkey is very beautiful, and of a deep brown color, very iridescent, presenting reflections of blue, copper, and gold, which make it truly ornamental. It was because of its fine plumage that it was first introduced into France. In the beginning no one thought of the turkey as food; and the first turkey served at table was in 1570, at the wedding of Charles IX. As soon as the turkey was tasted it was found to be too good merely to look at, and it passed from the park to the poultry-yard, from thence to the farm, and from one farm to another, east and west, north and south, till at present on almost every farm turkeys are raised and have become an object of considerable commerce; but in going from farm to farm this bird has encountered different conditions of existence—of temperature and nourishment, and never the primitive conditions it had in America. As a consequence the turkey, like the coffee, has varied, so that to-day not a turkey in France closely resembles the wild stock; generally it has become much smaller. Some have become fawn-colored, others more or less white, gray, or fawn-color. In a word, almost all the localities to which turkeys have been taken have given birth to new varieties, which from the species have thus been transformed into races.

"Now, in spite of these marked changes between each other and their first parents in America, are the French turkeys any less the children of the wild turkeys of America? or are they less brothers and sisters? or have they ceased to be parts of the same species?

"What is true of the turkey is also true of the rabbit. The wild rabbit lives in the downs and woods, and resembles but little the domestic rabbit. These are both large and small, have short, black, white, yellow, and gray hair, are spotted and of uniform color. In a word, this species comprehends a great number of races; but all constituting one and the same species with the wild stock."

From these facts, which might be multiplied indefinitely, we conclude that if a pair of rabbits were left in a place where they would encounter no enemies, in a few years they would fill it with descendants, and eventually would overrun the whole country, or continent, in like manner as we have seen a single stalk of coffee so multiplied as to produce all the coffee since raised in America. The wild rabbits and their captive descendants, the wild turkeys and their domestic offspring, must then be considered as equally the descendants each of a single primitive pair. Nor does it in the least complicate the question because we do not know the history of the introduction of the wild stock into any country where their descendants dwell. These and other equally well known examples lead to no other conclusion than that all the plants and all the animals of the world, wherever distributed, have obeyed the same law, originated in a common geographical center, and hence in the "Garden eastward in Eden" (the eastern part of the Eden world). No other intelligent conclusion can be drawn from the facts thus established.

Let us now inquire as to how these facts throw light upon the question of the unity of the human species. The peculiar features they manifest are very marked. We do not know how or when mankind's progenitors became inhabitants of their several localities; but as man is an organized being, he obeys the laws governing all organized beings, and therefore the law of intermixture or crossing. As the basis of our argument, let us take the types which seem most diverse, exhibiting the most marked differences—the white man and the negro. If these types really constitute distinct species, then their union must bear the stamp we have found to characterize the crossing or union of animals of different species —to wit, in the great majority of cases, that of infertility; in the remainder, slight fertility, and this soon disappearing, with the formation of no intermediate groups. But if these extremes are races of the same species, their union will be fertile, and the fertility continue indefinitely, and numerous intermediate groups will be formed, with peculiarities so modified that if representatives of all were placed side by side it would be impossible to distinguish between any two standing nearest each other.

Now, what are the facts? It is about three centuries since the white man made the conquest of the world. Wherever he has gone he has found groups of human beings which very much differ from himself, and everywhere he has married with them; and the unions have not only proved fertile, but sometimes more fruitful than the indigenous people themselves. To show the rapidity with which mixed races multiply, bear in mind the fact that it is only about twelve generations since the European race overspread the world, and it is already estimated that one-seventeenth of the population of the globe are mixtures. In some states of South America, where the emigration of the whites was earlier, one-fourth of the population is cross-bred; and in some **states and sections they constitute more than one-half.**

It is evident from these facts of universal observation and experience, as well as the logical conclusions of science, that there exists but one species of man. These races now exist at the antipodes in America, Polynesia, and elsewhere.

The changes which do not affect offspringing, and which may therefore be transmitted, are those we have mentioned, and also extend to such peculiarities as the size of feet, length of legs, arms, etc., which in a greater or less degree are common to different nations; indeed, traces of the greatest extremes of these peculiarities may be found in every nation, and even in a single family. These have their explanation in temperature, mental impression, exposure, habit, diet, taste, and the consistency and chemical peculiarities of soil.

Philosophy of peculiar human features.

The flat nose of the African and his large nostrils result from the necessity of inhaling larger draughts of tropical air to produce the same degree of vitality, because of its greater expansion, the increased exercise giving the nostrils increased width and a larger nose. The curling of the African's hair, though universal on his continent, is common in every country of the globe. Perhaps this fact has its scientific solution in the other fact that the curls deflect the rays of the tropical sun, thus preventing their more severe penetration into the brain. In the transmission of light, it is a law that every intervening object with which a ray comes in contact is bent and diverted in another direction. Another fact illustrative of this phenomenon is that heat curls hair of every kind, and the knotted hair provided by nature for the protection of the brain from injury by the rays of a tropical sun is a created endowment of adaptation or acclimation everywhere prevalent, and which in time by degrees becomes the inheritance of offspring.

The peculiar thickness of the skull of the African affords another means of protection to the brain. In a tropical climate people would naturally cease to wear coverings on their head, which is in fact their general practice; continual exposure would increase the thickness of the skull by giving it more work to do in resisting the attack of the atmospheric elements, just as the soles of the feet become covered with thicker skin if shoes are not worn, or that of the hands by the handling of hard and heavy objects. Speaking of the color of the African's skin, Dr. Livingstone, the great African explorer, says: "When the English people think about Africa, they imagine that all the Africans are like the specimens we have in front of the tobacconist shops. This is not the case at all. *That* is the real negro, and is only to be found in the lowest of the population. The people generally are not altogether black. Many of them are of olive color or of the color of coffee and milk; and usually, those in the higher grades of society are of a lighter color. The type we see on the ancient Egyptian monuments is nearer the type of the central population." It is evident from this that it is the outdoor exposure of the lower or working classes that makes the skin blacker. It must also be remembered that it is not the skin of the human inhabitant of Africa alone which manifests deep color; but the same is true of its birds, beasts, fish, reptiles, and plants. Another fact in relation to this phenomenon is that everything grows less high colored as we approach the polar regions. Within the arctic circle is found the white bear, and nowhere else; while the black bear lives in and is native to almost every climate.

We are aware that the skin of the Esquimau is of a copper color; but before this fact can be made an objection to our argument, it must be shown that the first inhabitants of these cold regions, who had emigrated from other countries, were not blacker than, or at least as black as, the present inhabitants. It must also be borne in mind that it is not required that the colder climate shall change the black skin to white in order to adapt those wearing it to live there, any more than that the use of large nostrils is detrimental by the inhalation of cold air. Because they will admit more air it does not follow that the lungs should inhale more: nor because curly hair protects the brain from the rays of the tropical sun, that it does any harm in the arctic regions. The change involved in marking a tropical race with these peculiarities is essential to health and prolonged life; but their absence in another climate, where they are not needed, is not thus essential. Hence, they may be permanent in all climates after having once been impressed on a race; at least they will not die out in the same time they were produced.

Animal Variations caused by Climate.

Upon this subject we quote the following from "Colton's General Atlas:" "In the animal as well as the vegetable kingdom, the largest number of species are met within the warmer regions of the globe; and a gradual decrease in the number both of genera and species takes place as we recede from the equator. It is in intertropical regions also that mammiferous quadrupeds are most remarkable for their magnitude, strength, and ferocity; that reptiles are larger and more venomous; that birds are decked with the most splendid plumage, and the insect tribes are distinguished for their size and brilliancy of their tints. These effects of light and heat appear to be extended even to the inhabitants of the ocean. Sharks and some of the fish are larger and more ferocious in the seas of tropical regions, and some species of fish are adorned with gayer colors than those of temperate zones. It is also from the warm regions of the earth that the greater number of the most beautiful shells of molluscous animals are obtained, and there likewise do the coral animals and other radiata occur in the greater variety.

"Animals belonging to cold climates are provided with warm coats, which would be unsuited for the inhabitants of hot regions. Sometimes when animals of the same species inhabit countries possessing different climates, the garb of the one will differ from the other in accordance with the difference of climate. Thus, the skin of the stoat in England is comparatively thin, and of a dull grayish-brown color; but in Northern Russia and Siberia the coat of the animal is transformed into a beautiful thick fur of a clear white in every part except the top of the tail, which is of a deep black, affording under this form the well-known fur called ermine. If by accident or the agency of man, animals are removed to places uncongenial to their natures, they either perish altogether, or some change takes place to fit them for their new abode. Thus the race of sheep now inhabiting some of the valleys of intertropical America, which were originally from temperate European regions, possess instead of their warm fleece, a coat of glossy hair better adapted to the heat of the climate in which they have now become naturalized." Upon the color of the African's skin Darwin lays the greatest stress, as the distinguishing feature for establishing man's identity with the lower animals; but we ask if these facts and their teaching—which might be almost indefinitely multiplied—are not of sufficient weight to account for these peculiarities, without so changing or modifying a single species as that it shall even in the remotest degree approximate the nature of another.

Darwin's Defective Reasoning.

Another important fact in defense of evolution according to natural selection is said to be the beautiful adornment of birds and fowls, the design of which is declared to be to attract the attention of the other sex, with a view of leading to the coupling of the male and female. This conclusion is founded on the fact that Mr. Darwin can find no other use for the possession, by the peacock and butterfly, for example, of such beautiful wings and feathers. There may be quite a number of things in the universe the use for which Mr. Darwin is unacquainted; but does such ignorance justify him in assuming that any of them are for a definite purpose, and for no other reason than that they go to aid his theory? Will Mr. Darwin inform us for what purpose the beautiful and fragrant flowers of the garden, field and wildwood are so exquisitely adorned that they called forth that forcible comparison by Him who made them: "Consider the lilies of the field, how they grow; they toil not, neither do they spin; and yet I say unto you, that Solomon in all his glory was not arrayed like one of these?" (Matt. 6:20). Was this floral beauty designed to induce the marriage relation?

In his "Descent of Man," Vol. i. p. 225, Mr. Darwin says: "Now, when naturalists observe agreement in numerous small details of habits, tastes, and dispositions, between two or more domestic races, or between newly allied natural forms, they use this fact as an argument that all are descendents from a common progenitor who was thus endowed, and consequently that all should be classed under the same species." This argument may be applied with much more force to the races of man, as every one of these have substantially the same habits, tastes, and dispositions. In another chapter we have shown this conclusion to be without the least force viewed from such premises. Whatever may be the extent of the supposed gap between the lower animals and man, one thing is certain: he must rule them or be ruled by them. Were man weaker or less sagacious than the animals, he would long ago have been devoured, if indeed he could ever have obtained a starting point in existence, and upon Darwin's theory it would have been impracticable.

That man does exist, and is the ruler of all the lower animals, demonstrates the fact that there must always have been as great a gap between him and them as that which now exists. This fact is irreconcilable with the notion that there ever were animals only so much lower in the scale than man that the degree could not be easily distinguished. Evolution only admits of this, as there would have been necessitated an act of creation had there ever occurred an abrupt and great change, such even as that which now exists between monkeys and men. For the sake of argument let us admit the existence of this close relation, and do we not see that the contest for supremacy would involve perpetual warfare, and that between the savages the most savage would always prevail? Hence the lower men-monkeys would exterminate the higher men-monkeys in every encounter.

Whenever a lower animal evolved one of a higher degree, and therefore of a more pacific and civilized disposition, and who should attempt to govern his father with less brute force, the more savage brute father would invariably devour his milder child, and therefore the more unfit would survive. It must be remembered that the difference in intelligence between the two is not of such a degree as to give one the advantage of superior weapons, or that the child used weapons of which the father was incapable. In illustration of this, let us inquire, Why have the American Indians so long survived? Why has the United States Government so long petted and indulged them? We answer it has not been out of any peculiar sympathy or respect for them, but simply and solely because they are savages. Would the people of this country have tolerated the existence of an equal number of white, copper-colored, red, or black men from any other country, who should have committed as many cold-blooded atrocities upon helpless, unarmed men, women, and children as they have? No! Every man of them would have been exterminated. Only through fear of a repetition of these same cruel, savage acts have they been tolerated; hence the most unfit have survived. No; if men were savage at first, so would they have remained, just as the lower animals have done, unless domesticated; and this was not the work of the animals, but that of civilized man.

The most civilized would not survive.

It is also true that the most savage has the least regard for consequences, either of a moral or physical character. Such have also the greatest physical strength, in which respect man is vastly inferior to his animal contemporary or ancestral brothers and sisters, if they were of the lower order. Such a state of facts and their logical teaching drive us to the only alternative—namely, the revealed cosmogony contained in the Bible. Here we find the gap between man as the ruler, and all other animals as the subjects, so wide that they are under the control of his will and superior intelligence; and the truth of this record is corroborated by the facts of the world's natural history: "And God created man in His own image ; in the image of God created he them. And God blessed them, and said unto them, Be fruitful and multiply, and replenish the earth, and subdue it, and have dominion over the fish of the sea, and over the fowls of the air, and over every living thing that moveth upon the earth." (Gen. 1:27, 28).

Hence, according to the facts and nature of things, instead of the family of man having commenced with universal savage life—and that, too, animal savage life—from which it has been progressing toward civilization by such contests as above indicated, it started with the highest intellectual, moral, and physical endowments with all their susceptibilities, rendering him the fittest to survive, and he has accordingly survived. The same authorities tell us that the largest and most powerful of the lower animals have perished ; while natural history fails to show that a single species or individual of the savage animals, if left to themselves, ever lost their savage nature. That all are savage still demonstrates the fact that man could not have been the exception : were his ancestors ever brutally savage, and associated with none higher to teach him civilization, savage also must have been his children, and so have continued during all succeeding generations.

When the polygenists assume that one species produces another they put themselves in opposition to all facts, and also in contradiction to all the naturalists, botanists, and zoologists, as Buffon, Turniford, Jessie, Geoffroy, and Cuvier, who studied plants and animals outside of all discussion and without thought of evolution. But the facts of experiment thus furnished demonstrate nature to be utterly incapable of producing a new species, and the primitive pair as well, and that her operations are confined to the simple and unimportant changes modifying species, which result in different races, thus rendering the conclusion inevitable that the organization of each pair of animals and each original plant was the work of supernatural power.

Now, if in a few generations, a continent has been peopled by a single pair of animals of a given species, and covered with plants sprung from a single shoot, then, in a greater number of generations the habitable globe could also have been thus populated and clothed. And if among all the modifications of species into races there has never been produced an organic thing of life lacking a single vital organ, or one that had double the number —say one which had two sets of lungs—and transmitted the same peculiarity to offspring, it also follows that each species had its own original progenitor or progenitors, so perfect in themselves that the identity of each through all coming time was rendered a natural necessity. Therefore, polygenism is neither science, philosophy, nor Scripture, and monogenism is demonstrated by all of these to be true. Hence the original progenitors of each species had its existence in the mind and act of an independent, uncreated Creator. Any other view is alike antagonistic to philosophy, science and reason, as well as to the endless array of the cosmological facts of nature, discovered and understood by her students of all ages. Hence Mr. Darwin's definition and classification of species and races is one of the most gross and palpable errors ever advanced under the name of science.

If we would arrive at truth, is it not the simplest dictate of reason that we should consult the laws, facts, and principles connected with those animal and vegetable forms with which we are most familiar—those of historic and not of prehistoric times—and therefore commencing with the present, living generation? In other words, we must reason from the known to the unknown. Every historian knows that among the ancients each nation had its fabulous epoch, and every form of (idolatrous) religion, its mythical period; and whatever there was of science partook of the same characteristics. According to the geological mode of reasoning, these cloudy records of myth and fable are to be considered more trustworthy than those of real history. Fossils of supposed extinct species—even one of a kind, which might have been a monstrosity, having no identical unity with anything else in kind or time, evolved from others less perfect—are brought forward in defense of the theory of evolution.

Instead of this, their position demands that they should produce the most indisputable facts, showing that known, living plants and animals are the parents of new species before unknown—for instance, fowls from fish, birds from serpents, acorns from pines, pines from oaks, serpents from monkeys, monkeys from men—and this only reverses the order and strides of evolution. The facts render this necessary, if it exists at all; for it is claimed that many of the noblest animals have become extinct by the survival of the fittest, and that too, within this known period; and as the one has survived by the nicest shades of development, the other has in the same degree degenerated toward extinction. But we have shown that whatever of extinction has taken place, according to the close likeness and contest the theory defines, was of those of the most refined and fittest to survive, and has been by close, personal, deadly conflict between each pair. The philosophy, therefore, of extinct species was not that of the evolutionists any more than was the philosophy of their development; but was that of catastrophism, and by the flood, while the coming into existence was by creation.

Instead, however, of giving us absolute proof here, where it is indispensable, these gentlemen have the effrontery, by an adroit attempt to beg the whole question, to say : " Only give nature time enough, and she will evolve that which she does not possess. She will unroll that which is not enrolled, or turn out that which she has not within—such as an organic thing from inorganic matter ; " and to the disgrace of the age, multitudes of sensible people not only seem to believe it, but esteem its speculators eminent scientists. Let us ask, are not six thousand years of historic time sufficient at least to have made some sensible approximation toward such a result—that of producing new creatures? Especially when it is remembered that during this period it is declared that many species have become extinct, and by the same contests which have developed the surviving, hence in the same time.

Their own Arguments prove Evolution Impossible.

Thus, according to their own argument, evolution was always impossible. It is so slow a process that any two generations standing nearest each other—and this is as true of any two of its individuals—are so nearly identical, that before any radical change is reached the species or individual exhibiting it has itself become extinct, and the tooth of time has so marred and obliterated the features of the remaining fossils that no just comparison can be made. Those fossilized skulls, for instance, which have been pronounced a hundred thousand years old, have their exact types among the living men of our most civilized countries at the present day. Indeed, all the varieties of shape and size and of peculiarly formed heads exhibited by the whole human family may be matched by those of the living, native inhabitants of the city of New York, with phrenological developments showing every degree of mental and moral capacity and susceptibility, from that of the lowest savage up to the most civilized of the world.

Some of the facts relating to organic beings, and which show they originated in a single mind, and were objects of intelligent purpose, are as follows : All organized beings are born small and weak, and have limited existences, varying from an ephemeral age to that of a few hundred years. During these periods all increase in size and strength until reaching maturity; then decrease in power and vitality, and sometimes in size, and finally die. While living they must be nourished, and as species, reproduce their kind, either by eggs or seeds, and have a father and a mother. As mankind are included in these general laws, they are equally controlled by them. These are not only facts of science, but are established by every day's observation, and are therefore fundamental principles. How wonderfully does this show that man and the lowest insect are linked together in the great chain of organic being, the whole forming a world of God's handiwork of beautiful harmony and mutual dependence!

The reasons, to our mind, which show why anthropology or the natural history of man is discussed at the present day with such anxious intensity—its defenders making such apparently bold and successful advances against the well-known science of man—are principally these: First, the assumption of facts which are not facts; second, unwarrantable inferences drawn from real facts; third, arrogant and unqualified assertion; fourth, using an ingenious and subtle sophistry; fifth, collusion and deception, in the finding of drawings and making estimates of the age of fossils: the animating cause of all being a desire to undermine and thereby destroy in the estimation of others, the foundation upon which Christianity rests. Hence the records of the Bible are set aside with as great an air of ostentation as though they were a mere effusion of the imagination, instead of alone containing the history and object of the world's creation and destiny, as well as the principal historic and prehistoric events, civil and ecclesiastical, which have happened and are to happen from the beginning to its end, reaching, indeed, into the consummation of the design, the re-creation—"The world to come." These records declare the eternal and immortal destiny of exaltation to which man may attain, while evolution leaves him to die like the common beast of the field, without the least hope of a future existence.

Though man is governed by the physical laws common to all animals, yet he is distinguished from all these by at least three fundamental characteristics—the abstract sentiment of good and evil, the conviction that there will be something after this life, and the conscious recognition of a Supreme Being. These are so universally and naturally recognized as the inheritance of mankind that those who reject them on the honest grounds that they do not and never did possess them all, must have heads of such intellectual and moral deficiency as to class them among monsters. It is the moral attributes even more than the intellectual which distinguish mankind from the lower animals. Indeed, the Proprietor Himself made man the ruler and, under certain prescribed conditions, the absolute dispenser of all below him, conferring upon him the right of appropriating them to his purposes of pleasure or necessity. We close this chapter with a few lines suggested on beholding in the beauties of nature the resplendency of her Maker.

God, Science, and Nature.

Daughter of heaven, handmaid of the skies,
O, science, awake from dust, now arise.
Each link is golden in thy fair chain—
From God down to the lowliest name.
Each tiny creature, or the planets that roll,
The loftiest orb, or the littlest mole—
Hymns forth alike with musical voice ;
Each has its mate and each has its choice.
Nature is gushing with life all aglow,
To her great Maker with songs overflow.
Truth's mighty circle intwines all the worlds,
Serene and resplendent her banner unfurls—
Diamonds, jewels, bright polished stones—
Dug from the cavern or plucked from the thrones
Prefigure alike thy radiant sheen,
Nor shadow to mar thy fair crystalline.
Thy pictures inwrought with beauty divine,
In canopied height or deeply dug mine.
Truth all immortal to thee shall arise
The songs of all nature with harps of the skies.
If thou wouldst know the truth spread abroad,
Consult all the pages revealed by thy God—
The world as it is, and is yet to come,
Its mansions, its fields eternal and young.
Behold in thyself, what destiny's there?
What stamp of being, what nature to share,
Crowns, robes, palms immortal, and thine?
All came from the world—all came out of time.

CHAPTER X.

DEFECTIVE GEOLOGICAL DATA.

Transparent Collusion.

IN order to show still further the feeble attempt to prove the existence of man prior to the Mosaic history, we introduce some extracts from a lecture delivered in Paris, "On the Antiquity of Man," by Prof. A. De Quatrefages. They relate to the alleged simultaneous existence of man and a certain elephant, or mammoth, whose fossil remains were found so connected with dead human skeletons that it is claimed they must both have lived in prehistoric times. This period is called the Pliocene, or the most modern part of the Tertiary, about 6,000 years before the advent of man upon earth. The Prof. says: "I call especial attention to this mammoth, and we shall presently see the reason why. At different times these animals have been discovered in the frozen earth of Siberia. Now, as man is the contemporary of this mammoth, may he also be found in a fossil state?

"Down in these times, all the eminent men in natural history, geology and palæontology answered this question in the negative, and Cuvier in particular never believed in fossil man; but to-day we are led by many well-established facts to answer this question very differently, and we are forced to admit that fossil man really existed and that man was contemporary with those species of animals, especially with the mammoth. [Yes, but the mammoth only became extinct at the flood. The small portion of the earth which the flood left uncovered by water did not yield sufficient food for these monster-devourers and they became extinct.] This is certainly one of the most beautiful discoveries of modern times ! The ground for it was laid by the establishment of a certain number of facts observed in England, Germany, and France ; but the honor of having brought decisive proof which convinces everybody [He means geologists, who easily believe curious things.] belongs incontestably, to two Frenchmen, M. Boucher de Parthes and M. Edward Lartet.

"M. Boucher de Parthes, the eminent archæologist of Abbeville, while inspecting the excavations made in the earth around his native village, at Menchecourt, discovered stones fashioned in a particular manner. It was soon evident to him that these stones owed their form to human industry. Now, these polished flints, or stone hatchets [Behold how soon peculiar-shaped stones, which all stones have, change in the hand of this lecturer into polished flint hatchets !] were found in the earth associated with the bones of the mammoth ; whence he concluded that the men who had fashioned them lived at the same epoch with those great mamifers, long since extinct.

"At first this conclusion was objected to by the highest authorities in geology. This is why I attach so much importance to the facts, which entirely refute these conjectures. M. Lartet examined a burial-place of these remote times, at Aurigans, in the south of France. It was a grotto excavated in the side of a hill. At the time of discovery it was closed by a slab taken from a bed of rocks some distance from this point. In the interior were found the bones of seventeen persons, men, women and children ; and before the entrance was found the well-attested remains of a fireplace. There were traces of funeral repasts that the first inhabitants of our country were in the habit of making, and such as we find sometimes in our day among certain European peoples. In the ashes of this fireplace were found bones bearing the traces of fire and excrements of wild animals. [It must have been an immense fireplace to have held the mammoth bones, which must have been in their natural size to determine their character. This must have been a barbecue on a very large scale, to feed a funeral procession. Here, too, was found human excrement, preserved on the surface of the earth, not washed away or decomposed for eight thousand years. How this Frenchman must have drawn upon his imagination!]

"Here, consequently, man appears eating the animals in question, whose contemporaneousness had been disputed. M. Lartet crowned these beautiful researches by discovering in a cave, in the center of France, a piece of ivory on which was unmistakably represented the very mammoth to which we have just called your attention. It is very evident that this picture could only have been made by a man who lived at the same time with the mammoth. In view of Lartet's discoveries, we must admit the existence of fossil man, that is to say, the co-existence of our species with the last species of animals of which we have spoken." *Popular Science Monthly*, No. 2.

Hard Pressed for Evidence.

In the first place, we wish to direct attention to the assumed importance of this discovery—that it demonstrates the existence of man four thousand years before the days of Adam, and that before this discovery there was not a geologist who believed in fossil man; that in view of this solitary discovery every one of them is satisfied of his former error, and now admits the great antiquity of man. To credit such evidence, and from it to draw such a conclusion, exhibits such dogged persistency to make out a case that we cannot attribute it to the morbid love of the marvelous, but to the fact that being sorely pressed for evidence, it is eagerly accepted as fact, with its absurd conclusion, though it antagonizes the Mosaic account of creation as to time.

Now if these so-called facts bear unmistakable marks of having been fabricated for the purpose, then the pretentious teaching intended can be characterized by no milder term than *infamous*. It is said this mammoth existed and became extinct in what geologists call the Pliocene part of the Tertiary period, a formation more recent than chalk and consisting of sandstone, claybeds, limestone, and containing fossils, some of which are identical with existing species. This period is divided into three parts, the Eocene, Miocene and Pliocene, and is chronologically located about 4,000 years prior to the days of Adam. These mammoths became extinct in the latter part of this period, which, according to Dye in his work entitled, "The Ages of Nature, Geology, and Palæontology," is put down at 2,000 years prior to Adam. Here man existed, not in his monkey-transition state, but as veritable man. Here the mammoth lived and became extinct, and his bones have been preserved in the heart of France without decomposition for the period of 8,000 years.

The lecturer above quoted further says, "We have not only found traces of these primitive industries, but jaw-bones and entire craniums. Hence we can judge of the characteristics which distinguished our first ancestors; and, strange to tell, we find that these men, who even in France warred with stone weapons against the mammoth, have at the present day descendants presenting the same characteristics in Europe." If it is a fact, as here admitted, that the craniums of these ancient men exhibit the same phrenological developments as those of the present European, then man is not the creature of evolution, but as physically perfect at one period as at another. Hence the facts of geology and the facts of evolution demolish each other, and leave the testimony of Moses uninjured.

The question of the use of flint hatchets proves nothing more than that emigrants to new countries or regions substitute rude implements both for warfare and husbandry. In the Life of President Lincoln it is recorded that, when he was a boy living on the frontiers of Kentucky, his father dug a concave hole in a log and found a stone to fit it, with which the family used to crush the corn for making bread, answering the purpose of a grist-mill. Now suppose some such enthusiastic geologist as this Frenchman, Lartet, had exhumed from the ruins of the Kentucky log-cabin where the great Lincoln was born the remains of this rude grist-mill, and not knowing its history, would he not have declared them to be positive evidence of prehistoric times, and of fossil man, and have gravely chronicled the fact that they were contemporaneous with the flint hatchets, and were used in the Pliocene period, 8,000 years ago?

The French geologist found the bones of seventeen men, women and children, in a grotto in France, and in such a perfect state of preservation that they were thus identified and distinguished. At the entrance of the sepulcher, in an old fireplace, were found bones and ashes of extinct animals, which were therefore while living contemporaneous with the human beings of whom these bones were the remains. Imagine an old fireplace containing bones, excrements, and ashes for eight thousand years! Verily it was "old."

From these so-called facts it is assumed that these men, women, and children were buried contemporaneously, with the mammoths, and that those who had buried them had partaken of a fine repast of roasted mammoth, which they had first killed with their hatchets, of which instruments there has never one been found having a handle; but it is supposed these little pieces of sharp flint were fastened in the ends of split sticks. In a word, this funeral procession surprised the mammoth, which was about four times as large as a modern elephant, and attacked him with the sharp flints fastened in split sticks, until finally overcome by the mourners, he fell dead into the fireplace, just where it was necessary for him to fall, as no number of men forming a funeral procession could have carried him there. As he was now in the fireplace they roasted him whole. This is proved by the fact that Lartet found his bones whole. Having the beast in the fireplace, they must have had quite a time in felling trees with the flint hatchets, as a number of cords of wood would be required to roast him.

Such a barbecue, it would seem, would consume several weeks, during which time the funeral procession stayed day and night in the burying-place. Behold, what a fact of geology and evolution is here! The mouth of the grotto was covered by a loose slab of rock, of course not so good a barrier against the admission of the decomposing agents of the atmosphere as though these dead had been buried five or six feet under ground. Can there be found a single bone of a corpse, even thus buried, after the lapse of two hundred years, unless petrification has taken place? and petrification is not claimed for the seventeen bodies: they had not decomposed for 8,000 years even so as to prevent identity of sex or size.

A Clear Case of Collusion or Fraud.

But Lartet crowned these beautiful researches by discovering *in a cave*, in the center of France, a piece of ivory on which was unmistakably represented this very mammoth; and it is declared by the German lecturer that the picture could only have been drawn by a man who lived at the same time with the mammoth. But we ask, why should the finding of this picture in another cave and in another locality connect all these strange things, and all go to prove the vast antiquity of man? Why could not Lartet, supposing him to be a poor artist, have carved it himself, or have procured the aid of a palæontologist to draw the picture of the whole beast from having seen a single bone, even of a toe—as this is the qualification claimed for them—have copied the picture on the ivory, and then have voluntarily lost it in the cave and found it again, for the purpose of making this "beautiful discovery."

Did it never occur to those who accept such fables as the fossil men and ivory picture found in caves by this famous French geologist, that an equally interested individual by the name of Mohammed "found" a book in a cave at a place called Mecca, who declared this book (the Koran) was written or dictated by an angel; and how finally tens of thousands of intelligent people believed the lie? They might also be reminded of another similar circumstance: how a man by the name of Spaulding wrote a fictitious story for his own amusement, purporting to be the history of an extinct people, and called it the "Book of Mormon," which afterward was mysteriously deposited in a cave or hole in the earth near Palmyra, N. Y., and was then "found" by one Joseph Smith, who pretended it was a divine revelation. Thousands of people believe the story to-day.

There is also the later mystery of the "Cardiff Giant," which was dug out of the earth a few years since and exhibited in various places in this country, among others in Albany, N. Y., at the geological rooms. The facts concerning it are now well known. One man hired another to carve the giant out of stone, and then buried it in a certain spot on his farm, where after a few months the farmer "discovered" the wonderful fossil while digging a well, and exhumed him for exhibition.

Had those who ferreted out these facts been content with such superficial investigation as the geologists and evolutionists usually accept, this marvelous fossil, inasmuch as it was composed of a kind of stone which is claimed to have been found millions of years ago, would have been regarded as a contemporaneous formation or petrification. Hence the fossil would have demonstrated the great antiquity of man, showing also that there were giants as well as mammoths in those early days.

As an addition to these cave mysteries, we quote the following, also from Deacon Dye's chart : " The oldest remains of man that have been found are represented by skull No. 14, found by Prof. Schmerline, in the Engis Cave, Belgium. In 1860, No. 13 was found in the Muenderthal cave. Sir Charles Lyell estimates that 100,000 years have rolled by since the persons owning these skulls lived." It is necessary to state that most German professors are not on very good terms with Moses, and are famous for bold assertion and extravagant conclusion, urged on as they are by a long-acquired love of the skeptical, and by as determined a zeal to demolish the Bible as ever burned in the breast of Paine or Voltaire, but not with as honestly avowed purpose.

This Professor Schmerline, driven to sore extremity for some astonishing facts to demonstrate the great antiquity of man, with which it would be impossible to reconcile the Mosaic account of his creation, and hoping also for the notoriety such a discovery would insure, procured the skulls of two idiots or monsters, and hid them in two caves in different places, and then afterward "found" them. Now all the declarations of all the geologists and evolutionists in the world will never prevent sensible people from looking upon such discoveries with suspicion, and holding the pretentious discoveries in the merited contempt which attaches to all collusionists.

Lyell Summoned to Estimate the Age of the Skulls.

Who is summoned to examine and ascertain the age of the skulls? Is it one who questions the authenticity of many of the so-called geological facts and disputes the conclusions drawn from most of the remainder, and of all of those relating to the philosophy and science of their genesis of the world? Not at all. Such a one might ask too many questions, and might propose to procure other just such skulls on persons still living No, no! Pharaoh wants only his own magicians. "Call in the wise men of Egypt;" it is in the success of their arts he hopes; indeed, he fears nothing more than the truthful interpretations of the little rod of Moses. Sir Charles Lyell is accordingly summoned to unravel the mysteries of the wonderful skulls, and to declare their import. No more of Moses—the magic—philosopher's stone is found. The geological world stands on tip-toe to hear Lyell's amazing announcement: "One hundred thousand years since these skulls were worn." Grieve not that embalming is buried among the "lost arts!" Egyptian mummies of 2,000 years, ye are but infants; for here are charmed caves wherein human skeletons may be preserved from decomposition one hundred thousand years.

Who cannot see that this Lyell, being one of the most prominent champions of the theory of almost limitless time for the coming into existence of the inorganic, and a little less for the organic world, is the very last man who should have been invited by Professor Schmerline, the happy man who found the relics, to pronounce upon their age? No, Sir Charles, we should be unworthy of the age were we not to give expression to the demand of the good and noble of the world, to be satisfied with nothing less than infallible and diversified proof in such an important controversy—such for example, as that sunshine produces light and heat ; that heat expands and cold contracts material bodies ; that gravity keeps the solid earth in order ; that plants reproduce their kind ; that fluids seek their level, or that like causes produce like effects. Give us, in a word, such demonstrations as establish these fundamental principles of natural science, the philosophy of which is recognized, and they cannot fail to commend themselves to respectful consideration. To be satisfied with less, when such momentous issues are involved, would be not only a servile cringing of the manhood of our age, but would have been an unpardonable affront to the mental and moral night of the "Dark ages," and therefore a much graver offense against the civilization and Christianity of the nineteenth century.

Another erroneous calculation as to the great age of the world is founded upon the assumption that the coalbeds were formed by the decomposition of vegetation, ages before man was upon earth. In answer to the inquiry as to where such a prodigious mass of vegetable matter came from, we are told that in long ages past the earth's atmosphere was composed principally of carbon, the gas upon which plants feed, and they therefore grew in great abundance and luxuriance. Of course we cannot but be thankful to Dame Nature for having been so considerate in making timely provision to meet the necessities of mankind, whom she intended to evolve by a turn of her wonderful machine. The science and philosophy involved in the process of coal production are founded upon the fact that vegetation decomposes the atmosphere, retaining its carbon and rejecting its other gases. The atmosphere therefore becoming principally carbon, supports vegetables with much greater vigor and renders them more prolific.

It might as well be claimed that if the air were composed principally of oxygen, the gas which supports animal life, animals would become more vigorous and prolific. Instead, however, of this being true, no man or animal could live an hour in an atmosphere composed principally of oxygen. So with plants: although they make their food out of carbonic acid gas, yet were they exposed to an atmosphere of carbonic acid gas, they would live but a short and sickly life, never reaching that degree of maturity necessary to the reproduction of their kind. Hence, if the carboniferous period ever existed, instead of its being able to produce the vast amount of vegetation necessary to form the coal measures, it could have produced none at all. These are well-known facts of science, which are irreconcilable with the geological theory of coal production, which is therefore not true science.

We have shown that the relative component parts of the atmosphere are invariable, and that the simultaneous existence of the two great divisions of organic nature—vegetables and animals—is essential to the preservation of the equilibrium of the atmosphere, so that either may live. Sunlight is also essential to vegetable production; but in a carbonic atmosphere there could have been no light, at least nothing more than dim twilight. There was therefore never any "carboniferous period," and its invention by skeptical geologists to overthrow the Mosaic chronology of the world falls to the ground.

The Oil Fountains Proved to be Creations.

Our answer, therefore, to the question, Whence came

DEFECTIVE GEOLOGICAL DATA.

the coal? which nothing in nature needs or animals use but man, and which is a necessity for the advanced improvements and needs of the present generation of mankind, is that it came from the same Hand that made the air he breathes, the water he drinks, the food he eats, the wools and furs for his clothing. If coal possesses vegetable properties, so does the soil, and so did the original soil. To make the soil must have been an act of creation, as there had been no vegetables to decompose to form it. Coal-beds, like salt-mines, are distributed over the earth. Salt is not found upon the surface of the earth, where it would unfit the land for vegetable production, yet it is not buried so deep but that the art of man may reach it.

Neither are coal-mines found upon the surface; had they been above ground, conflagrations would have destroyed them. So also with petroleum. Had the attempt been made to store it in basins upon the earth's surface, fires would have licked it up long ere this; but coal and oil, though buried, lie within the available reach of man, and are found in quantities which have been and will continue to be sufficient to meet his wants so long as the globe remains in its present form.

When wood for fuel failed to meet the needs of mankind in successive localities, coal-mines were discovered. When oil for light and lubrication had approached exhaustion, on account of the rapid increase of population and the extension of machinery, the fountains of petroleum were opened. Petroleum lies at a depth of from three hundred to eight hundred feet, and that in solid rock, with the exception of about thirty feet of loose material upon the surface. It lies in strata of sandstone, such as grindstones are made of. These strata are cased on both sides with a few inches of flint, and are always found lying horizontally with the plane of the earth's surface, showing that they have never been disturbed by any upheaval or depression of the crust of the earth in those localities. He who rent it into fragments by breaking up the "fountain of the great deep" to bring out the waters thereof, in order to cover the surface of the globe at the flood, left these rocks enclosing the oil undisturbed.

Were these coarse-grained sandstone strata not cased with the flint, through which no liquid or moisture can penetrate, the oil would have sunk by its own gravity into the finer grained rocks below and have been forever lost to man. Or had these strata stood at the inclination or angles common to rocks in other localities, and indeed almost universal—some even standing perpendicular, as the palisades on the Hudson River—then also would the oil have sunk beyond the power of art to reach. Here, therefore, is manifested the wisdom of the God of Nature, in the creation, manner of deposit, and preservation of the coal and oil to supply the demands of human kind until his purposes are accomplished.

Two facts forbid the possible formation of petroleum from vegetable decomposition. First, there is no possibility that a particle of vegetable matter could have penetrated hundreds of feet of solid rock ; indeed, were it possible, so soon as it reached the flint casing of the sandstone, there it must have remained. As stated above, the oil lies within. The other fact is, that there is no chemical affinity between the sandstone formation and the oil. Therefore, not being produced from the sand grains within the flint casings, and being by them prevented from entering either from above or beneath, it must have been created and thus deposited.

The Gravel and Boulder Deposits by the Flood.

Lyell says: "There can be no doubt that the myriads of angular and rounded blocks could not have been borne along by ordinary rains or marine currents, so great is their volume and weight, and so clear are the signs, in many places, of time having been occupied in their successive deposition; for while some of them are buried in mud and sand, others are distributed at various depths through heaps of regularly stratified sand and gravel." Yes, and he might and should have said that each of the sand-grains and gravel atoms is also a rounded boulder, on a smaller scale, and was disintegrated by an adequate wash of water from larger fragments of broken rock with which its structure is identical.

Lyell's Ignorance or Arrogance.

"No waves of the sea raised by earthquakes, nor the bursting of lakes dammed up for a time by land-slips or by avalanches of snow, can account for these facts." Yes, Mr. Lyell! but you should not have been ignorant of the fact that there was once an *extraordinary* deluge, lasting for one hundred and fifty days, covering with water the highest mountains, and which "broke up" the crust of the earth, letting the fountains of water out to drown the world. This catastrophe was amply sufficient to break the rocks into fragments and grind them into the larger and smaller boulders; and at the subsidence of the waters they would be formed into regular and irregular strata, just as we find them. If you were not ignorant of the existence and history of this universal inundation, recorded equally in the rocks and in the "Scriptures of truth," then your egotism or arrogance is reprehensible in the last degree; for while you ignore the Bible statements concerning this greatest historic deluge of the world, still you attribute all its effects to lesser causes, not seeming to comprehend the fact that the violence of the cause will in a short time produce effects which would require a much longer time for agencies of less magnitude; and that the fact of regularity or irregularity in the effects depends entirely upon particular local circumstances.

In the November number of the *Popular Science Monthly* for 1873, we are told that a Mr. Morlot has made some interesting calculations respecting the age of geological formations in Switzerland: "The torrent of Tinvere, at the point where it falls into the lake of Geneva, has gradually built up a cone of gravel and alluvium. In the formation of the railway the cone has been bisected for a length of 1,000 feet and to a depth, on the central part, of about 32 feet. The section of the cone shows a very regular structure, which proves that its formation was gradual." He assigns about 6,000 years for the formation of the lower layer of vegetable soil. "But above this is another layer, which was formed when the lake stood at a higher level than at present, and is referred to the period of river-drift gravels, indicating an antiquity of 100,000 years." The assumption for the time consumed in building up the hill or cone rests upon the facts that the layers are somewhat regular, and that the soil which was once on the top is now at the bottom.

It is admitted that the cone was formed by the subsidence of a mighty lake. Of course the top of the cone, which is 32 feet above the railway, was once at the bottom of the great lake; and supposing it to have been as much above as it is now below, the lake would have been 64 feet deep at the level of the railway. This would give a flood which would probably have covered every hill on the surface of the earth prior to the flood—the higher mountains and deeper oceanic excavations being the work of the flood. The scientific fact that water seeks its level proves that if a hill 64 feet high in Switzerland was covered with rising water, it would also cover every other hill of the same height on the globe. Let us suppose that where this hill now stands was once a valley, and that it was in such a position that when Marlot's lake, or the Mosaic flood—both of which must have risen above the top of the highest hill—subsided, the hill was formed by the drift.

Of course the soil which lay on the surface of the higher land would drift first and form the lowest layer in the cone below, and so continue until every layer in it was formed; but that which would be last of the drift and last of the deposit would form the top layer of the cone. The Noachian flood lasted 150 days, and occupied most of the time in subsiding, which would give ample time for the formation of this cone. Of course its appearance and that of its layers would be precisely the same whether formed in 150 days or 100,000 years, the regularity and reversion of the layers being the same in either case and giving the only ground for the calculation.

This explanation also accounts for the geological structure of all similar hills, and exposes the folly of this Morlot's calculation. It is a well known fact that the time consumed in rounding off the corners of large blocks of stone on small grains of sand or gravel is long or short in proportion to the violence and density of the elements driving them along, or rushing over or through them if stationary. If fifty years were required to round a boy's marbles, of which a thousand are sold for a dollar, their manufacture would be a very unprofitable business; but the fact is, it only requires a few days' tumbling in a rolling barrel, submerged in water and sand, to accomplish the work.

Rapid Changes in Short Spaces.

We have introduced some extracts from an article published in the *Methodist Quarterly Review* for 1865, written by the Rev. Thomas Hurlburt of Sarnia, C. W. For thirty-five years the writer had been wandering over the continent of North America, as an Indian missionary, studying Indian languages and natural phenomena. In this character he explored the region from Texas to Hudson Bay, tracing the course of more rivers than almost any other man, but devoting special attention to the laws of change and general phenomena. He says: " Fluviology—river-study—is as much a science as geology or botany, and as much worthy of a niche in the great temple of human knowledge. It is from this source mainly we propose to draw our evidences of the recent order and origin of things.

" Sir Charles Lyell, on page 245, expresses the opinion that it is possible to render the delta of the Mississippi available as a chronometer by which the lapse of past pliocene time could be measured. In this opinion we most fully concur. Mr. Darwin, in his work on the 'Origin of Species,' allows us to suppose that fourteen hundred millions of generations of animal life have passed since its first creation or appearance on our globe. And Lyell and others inform us that their discoveries justify the conclusion that North America has been peopled by man a hundred thousand years.

" On page 16 of Mr. Lyell's work we find an account of some peat-bogs in Denmark, in which at great depth, forest trees and the works of man are found from a period of from four to sixteen thousand years. It must be borne in mind that these peat-bogs are all found in hollows, and that man existed before the drift filled them. The bones and works of man are found mixed promiscuously with vast amounts of the bones of extinct animals, as well as those that still exist. The peat-bogs of Denmark show these changes in forest vegetation. Near the bottom of the bogs are found Scotch firs and the works of man; above these, oaks are found and the works of man, showing an advance in civilization; and above these beech trees are found, which is almost the only tree now indigenous in Denmark.

"It is argued that, to produce this growth of peat and these several changes in the entire forest vegetation, required a vast lapse of time and great changes in the climate. In hundreds of places in the northern part of our continent I have seen these changes in the forest vegetation. In the nature of things it is impossible for these old fir forests to remain for many years. The mass that always accumulates on the trees and on the ground in these gloomy forests, impervious to sun or wind, and the rosin that exudes and accumulates on the trees, will, in time, insure their destruction by fire, just as certainly as the prairies are thus consumed. I have often seen these old forests burning, sometimes a whole hill or mountain-side enveloped in one sheet of flame.

"After their destruction there invariably comes another species of tree occupying the vacant place. In this way the destruction of the fir forests of Denmark and the substitution of the oak can be accounted for in one hundred years. Sir Charles Lyell informs us there were a few oaks and beech trees mixed with the firs from the beginning. Suppose, then, during a very dry season a fire had swept through these old forests of fir: it would destroy it and them with all their cones which contain the seeds, and as this class of trees never send up shoots from the roots, the whole would be destroyed. Not so, however, with the oak, for it will almost invariably send up shoots from the roots.

"In the prairies of the West we have counted as many as fifty times where the oak and hickory have been destroyed by fire, and would start up again from the roots before the struggle for life was over; consequently no cone-bearing trees can live in this region, except in inaccessible cliffs beyond the reach of fires. In the northern parts of our continent, where beech, oak, and hickory cannot grow, we find as soon as the firs are destroyed that poplar and birch immediately occupy the vacant ground. But in a country of mountains, bogs, and lakes, the fire cannot destroy all the firs, so, in time, a few are seen struggling up through the poplars and birches, and in time supersede them, to be again destroyed as before.

"But in a flat country like Denmark, the firs once destroyed would have no chance of survival. We give it as our opinion that no thick forests of fir can exist in our northern hemisphere for five hundred years without being destroyed by fire. If, then, the firs ceased in Denmark five hundred years after the close of the drift period, how long would it require for the beech to supersede the oak? After the fires had destroyed the firs, the oak would most readily take their place, and get the start of the beech; because of its greater tenacity of life, it would send up shoots from the roots, while both the oak and beech would have a start from the stores of beech-nuts and acorns hibernating animals had laid away in the ground or hollow trees.

The Contest for Survival between the Oak and the Beech.

"The contest would now be between the oak and the beech, and a very few centuries would determine it, soil and climate being more favorable to one than the other. Thus we see, from the rate of changes at present going on in our own country, that all the changes of forest vegetation in Denmark since the drift period may easily be accounted for in one thousand five hundred years. Nothing but beech has been known in Denmark since the historic period, and the firs, oak, and beech occupy spaces in the bogs corresponding to the periods when they severally predominated. None of these peat-bogs, as far as we recollect, are over thirty or forty feet deep.

"Mr. Sterry Hunt, Assistant Provincial Geologist in Canada West, has made the statement, based on careful examination, that these peat-bogs will produce ten times as much vegetable matter in a given time as our common forests. It is estimated that if all the timber on our common forests was compressed into coal, it would make a layer of one inch thick all over the ground. This we may suppose would represent the growth from one to two hundred years. Were our deepest peat-beds or bogs compressed and converted into coal, according to the above estimates, we would find it difficult to carry back the close of the drift period beyond four or five thousand years. [This would be about the time of the deluge.]

"The Black Forest of Germany has changed three times in the historic period: first fir, then oak, and now fir again. From such very uncertain data is the attempt made to carry back the human period far beyond the account of its origin given in Genesis. Another fact relied upon to prove the antiquity of man is the old pottery and other works of art found deep down in the sediment of the Nile. Without going into facts or figures, it will be sufficient to state that the sediment brought down by the annual floods and deposited in the valley of the Nile, amounts somewhere to about two and a half or three inches in a century, so that what was the surface in the days of Moses is now some 15 feet below.

"In digging and boring wells, works of art have been found seventy-two feet below the present surface, from which it is inferred that Egypt has been inhabited by man 30,000 years. Let it be borne in mind that the Nile, like the Ganges, Missouri and Mississippi, and other rivers of this class, has its lower course through a region of soft sediment deposited from its own waters. All such rivers, unless artificial means are used to prevent, are continually wearing away on one side and depositing sediment on the other, thus keeping all such rivers of uniform breadth. The laws that govern this constant shifting of the channel are easily explained. In times of flood, especially wherever the current impinges strongly against a bank, it will cut away on that side, but at the same time an equivalent for this loss will be found in the depositions in the eddy on the opposite side ; thus, first on one side and then on the other, it is cut away and filled up, so that in course of time these curves chase each other down stream.

Better Testimony than that of Lyell.

"I have traversed rivers where these ever-receding curves reminded one of the appearance of an auger in boring, where the curves appear to chase each other perpetually. Most of the large rivers of our globe are underlaid with sand, a tide of which is constantly rolled along the bed of the stream, and simultaneously accumulating with the depositions of sediment in times of flood on the adjoining bottom lands. In the course of a few centuries the river really runs on a ridge of sand, with banks of soft clay or mud on each side, so that all these rivers slip off from this ridge of sand, and as the adjoining clay or mud banks are more easily cut away than the sand, accounts for the fact that these rivers are uniformly deepest in the parts newly cut away ; so that a work of art lost in one of these deep places, in the course of a few centuries may be found far from the river, and deeply imbedded in river mud.

"The city of Booneville, in Missouri, was first built on the north bank, but the river left the town, having made a turn toward the south side of the valley. The inhabitants followed up the river, and built on the alluvial banks. But the town had not made much advancement before the channel changed again, and this time chose the south side, where the banks of bluffs come sloping down to the alluvial plain. Here Booneville still remains, and all this in less than fifty years. The great flood of 1844 carried away a whole section of land near Kansas City, belonging to Colonel Chick. Those who have traveled on our great Western rivers will often have seen a man with the lead, sounding the depth where shoals were apprehended. The line used is nine fathoms. In the distance of a mile the depth may vary from one to nine fathoms. When the lead does not touch bottom the man will cry out, 'No bottom ; no bottom!' The bell is rung, and all steam put on.

DEFECTIVE GEOLOGICAL DATA. 309

"The river Nile is a stream of precisely the same character as the Missouri or Mississippi. Suppose in the early days of the settlement of Egypt, old pottery, bricks and other works of art had been lost in an eddy near shore where the water might have been ten fathoms deep, the moving sand along the bottom, and the deposition of sediment in this case would be several feet in a year, until it was raised above low water. Thus it is very easy to see, from the changes actually going on at the present time, how in the course of a few centuries works of art could be buried many feet deep, and be found far from the present bed of the river. Some of these works of art, from the data adopted by Sir Charles Lyell and others, have been pronounced twenty thousand years old, and have subsequently been found, from inscriptions on them, to have been only two thousand years old. Lyell himself in one place informs us truly that all such large rivers as the Nile, Ganges, etc., are constantly changing their beds. We, however, did not need his testimony to settle this fact. In the year 1850 we stood on the banks of the Missouri River, near the city of Weston. A man standing by my side pointed to a snag about eighty rods out in the stream and said, 'When I came here seven years ago, Squire Jones had his corn-field all on this side of that snag. In that time the land has all been washed away, and is now nearly filled up again.' In three or four years after Squire Jones's corn-field was washed away, the man with the lead on the bow of the steamer might have been heard crying 'No bottom! no bottom!' in the identical place where the corn-field had been.

"Now suppose at this juncture a black boy, who might have been splitting wood on the deck, had dropped his axe overboard, and the mate had said: 'There, you clumsy black rascal, you have lost the axe; you shall have a rope's end for that;' and the boy had replied, 'Well, massa, it was an old one, and broke on de corner.' In fifty years corn may have been planted again in the same place, and then let Sir Charles Lyell, Horner, Darwin & Co. come along and sink a shaft in this part of the Missouri valley and have found the identical axe. They would then announce their discovery and infallible scientific deduction thus: It is a well-established fact that this great valley rises by the deposition of sediment at the rate of one foot in a century; fifty feet from the surface we found the American axe, showing conclusively that this great valley has been inhabited by civilized man of the Anglo-Saxon type for five thousand years. While many are wondering at the old relic and at the profound deduction of science, an old gray-headed negro comes along and says, 'Let me see dat axe.' After examining it attentively he says, 'I lost dat berry axe overboard jist fifty years ago, an' massa flog me for it.' Lyell and Horner's estimate of the first settlement of Egypt is no better than the above.

Rapid Changes of Deposit.

"That such rapid changes take place in the Mississippi region is a matter of fact. I have seen six feet of sediment that had accumulated in an eddy in the Missouri River in six months, and that so near the surface as to be left dry at low water. The accumulations would be much greater in the deep parts that were said to have 'No bottom.' On pages 43, 44 we have an account of a pit sunk at New Orleans for gas works to the depth of sixteen feet. Four layers of cypress forests were dug through, with several hundred rings in the trees, and at the depth of sixteen feet charcoal and a human skeleton were found. The cranium of the skeleton is said to belong to the type of the red Indian race. Dr. B. Dowler, indorsed by Sir Charles Lyell, estimates the age of this skeleton at fifty thousand years. No data are given by which this conclusion is reached, so we are left to our own resources. Lyell estimated the rise in the alluvial deposits of the Mississippi at one foot in a century; but it is a pretty well established fact that the delta of this river has encroached on the Gulf of Mexico at the rate of six miles in a century, and a descent of about three inches in a mile is required to drain off the waters. St. Louis is three hundred feet above the Gulf, and as it is about twelve hundred miles by the course of the river, we have just three inches average descent for the whole distance. But we will take Lyell's own estimate of one foot in a century as the average rise of the valley by the deposition of river mud. This will make the skeleton sixteen hundred instead of fifty thousand years old. This also is time enough for four cypress forests to grow and be superimposed one above the other, with several hundred grains in each.

"'That the whole lower Mississippi valley is rising rapidly by the deposition of river mud is evident from the fact that the leveling or raising the embankments of the river to keep the waters in the channel has only been resorted to for a comparatively short time, and already presents the appearance of a raised ditch. Had not Sir Charles Lyell in another instance given us his estimate of one foot rise in a century, all we could have said of him, after the facts were known, would have been that a great scientific light was in error; but for him to indorse the monstrous absurdity of Dr. Dowler shows a disposition on his part to strengthen a favorite theory by any and all means.

" Neither are flint weapons, pottery, etc., of themselves evidence of antiquity. The Cherokees, *to this day*, make pottery exactly the same as that found in the most ancient mounds of America. While in their country we were shown the material of which it was made, and had the process described. And as to flint implements and weapons, some twenty-five years age a very old Indian living north of Lake Superior, informed me that he remembered when the Indians manufactured these things. We were told where they produced the flint, and how they manufactured them. In digging a garden in a place where he said they were used to camp and where they made the flint implements, we found the ground full of chips of flint and broken weapons.

" These things, wherever found, simply indicate a rude state of society in that country. It will be seen that these facts and their real teaching as here presented are those very ones from which the geologists obtain their data for the great age of man and the world, and which is here clearly to be seen, not only justify no such conclusions, but utterly fail to furnish any evidence that reaches back as far as the deluge, and that the beds through which the small rivers and streams now flow could not have been excavated by them, or by any less a cause than the deluge itself, and that the greatest of these drift monuments indicate a simultaneous period, and that not beyond the Mosaic chronology of the flood.

The Loess Proves the Existence of the Flood.

"For instance, the *loess* found in all continents is a formation attributed to the action of this great drift. It is commonly deposited along rivers, but it is also found in open and level countries far away from rivers. In Southern Iowa this *loess* covers the open country one hundred miles from the great rivers, and is from twenty to forty feet thick, covering the whole region like a mantle of snow In digging wells in this *loess* old bogs and bones are found. On one occasion bones supposed to be those of a man were found thirty feet from the surface, and in the open country with no hill near, and resting on or near the sedimentary clay. It is not to be forgotten, as having an important bearing on the right understanding of this subject, that in nearly every case the *loess* and works of man and the bones of a vast multitude of large terrestrial animals are found in drift *loess*. These facts seem to indicate a vast and simultaneous flood covering man and his works and the larger animals in one common grave."

Another assumption founded upon just such spurious data is that of the existence of chalk and its locality. Sir Charles Lyell says: "I may also mention in this place, that the vast distance to which the white chalk can be traced east and west over Europe, as well as north and south, from Denmark to the Crimea, seems to some geologists a phenomenon, to which the working of causes now in action could present no parallel; but the soundings made in the Atlantic for the submarine telegraph have brought us that mud, formed of organic bodies similar to those of the ancient chalk, and the formation is in progress over spaces still more vast."

Why should the ancient chalk have been formed of different material or by a different process from those of modern chalk? In what other respect did the mud brought from the bottom of the Atlantic differ from chalk except that it was white mud, and therefore similar to chalk? Why did not Lyell give us a trustworthy fact as to the nature of this white mud, upon which to base the origin of chalk, such as drying some of the mud, and then pressing it into a hard lump? If it was chalk it would then tell its own story by making white marks. Who does not know that you may pulverize shells so that their grains are as fine as those of chalk? Yet it will leave no such marks on wood as those of chalk.

The Chalk Argument Stated.

Upon this chalk theory, the modest Dr. T. M. Coan of the "wonderful suggestion," which changes the temperature of the poles to the tropics every eleven thousand years, says: "To the geologist, however, these large figures have no appearance of improbability." [No figures are improbable to the geologist except those which make the world about six thousand years old.] "All the facts of geology," he continues, "tend to indicate an antiquity of which we are beginning to form a dim idea. Take, for instance, one simple formation— our well-known chalk. This consists entirely of shells and fragments of shells deposited at the bottom of an ancient sea, far away from any continent. Such a process as this must have been very slow: probably we should be much above the mark if we were to estimate the rate of the deposit at ten inches in a century. [The Doctor having no reason for this guess, we guess the deposition was twenty inches in a year.] Now the chalk is more than a thousand feet in thickness, and would have required, therefore, 120,000 centuries for its formation. [Behold how evolution obtains the greatest from the least!] The fossiliferous beds of Great Britain as a whole, are more than 70,000 feet in thickness, and many which there measure only a few inches on the continent expand into strata of immense depth; while others of great importance elsewhere are wholly wanting there; for it is evident that during all the different periods in which Great Britain has been dry land [So Great Britain has had *a number* of deluges,] strata have been forming, as is the case now elsewhere.

"We must remember that many of the strata now existing have been formed at the expense of older ones; thus, all the flint gravels in the south-east of England have been produced by the destruction of chalk. This, again, is a very slow process. It has been estimated that a cliff 500 feet high will be worn away at a rate of one inch in a century. [The estimate is simply a guess, and we pass it like the other geological data. Just think of it, for 100 years they had a land-mark so accurate that it only varied one inch.] This may seem a low rate, but we must bear in mind that along any line of coast there are comparatively few points which are suffering at one time, and that even those, when a fall of cliff has taken place, the fragments serve as a protection to the coast, until they have been gradually removed by the waves. [We should like to know where the waves float these fragments of rock to. The fact is, they lie there, and are washed by the waves, always toward the shore, until ground into sand, and serve as an effectual barrier against further encoachments on the coast. Hence the spurious calculation.] The Wealden Valley is 22 miles in breadth, and on these data [guesses] it has been calculated that the denudation must have required more than 150,000,000 years." This, we presume, is one of the methods of calculating the age of the world which the geologists are but just beginning to use.

The Argument unscientific.

If the process here explained by Dr. Coan for the formation of chalk is contrary to natural science and fact, then the estimate of time required for the process was a false one. He says, "All chalk was once shells." If so, then either the grinding action of the waves or some chemical process formed them into solid strata; but as no chemical process can convert the crumbled shells into lumps of pure chalk, the inference is that they were never so formed into chalk. This, then, leaves the formation of chalk from shell to aqueous agencies. Now as no aqueous process, assisted by any amount of hydraulic or other pressure, will convert the particles of crumbled shells into a solid lump of natural chalk, it follows that the hills of chalk were never formed by any such process. Besides, no matter how fine shells may be ground, the particles are not those of chalk, but of shells, and having no adhesive attraction or chemcial affinity, nature cannot form them into chalk.

In the second place, if the conversion of shells into chalk was by a chemical process, then the law of change common to all inanimate bodies must have been observed —namely, dissolution first and formation afterward. Now, if shells are chemically decomposed, they must be resolved into the smallest atoms of which they are composed, and any new chemical combination must begin with these particles. . It is therefore certain that all animal identity must be destroyed by the process; for each shell or fragment of a shell which may be seen even by the most powerful microscope to be such, has not been dissolved, and therefore cannot be organized chemically into another body. It is also true that the elements of nature in the same locality cannot decompose and from the atoms form the same inorganic body. Thus we see that chalk never was shells, nor shells chalk.

The mere denudation or breaking up of flint and chalk by water on the English coast leaves the particles just as they were before—simply those of flint and chalk. The nature of chalk and its existence in that locality show it to have been the result of volcanic action. It must be remembered that another hypothesis of geology is that all the solids of the earth were once fluids, or gases even, and that the hardening process first took place on the surface of the earth. Another hypothesis is that all the land on the surface of the earth now lying above the ocean level was once sea bottom, and became dry land as the result of upheaval. Hence this chalky and flinty coast of England, when first thrown to the surface, was in a soft and muddy condition, and therefore would be worn away by the waves of the ocean more in one year then than now in ten thousand years. In fact, there can be no comparison in the ratio of destruction under these extreme circumstances.

Here we see how what are called the "principles of geology" destroy each other. Especially are they irreconcilable with the perfectly well known principles of chemical affinity, dissolution and composition. That a little white mud found at the bottom of the Atlantic—of course formed by the decomposition of white marine shells—should have led Lyell and Coan into fixing a period of 150,000,000 years of chalky phenomenon merely proves the fundamental principle of evolution, which Lyell and all the other great naturalists have adopted or soon will adopt [as Darwin declares it to be true], namely, that "the least produces the greatest."

CHAPTER XI.

PROFESSORS HUXLEY AND TYNDALL'S MATERIALISM FALSE SCIENCE.

Huxley's Definition of Evolution.

It is fair to presume that if the doctrine of evolution can be established by scientific argument, Prof. Huxley is the man above all others best qualified for the task, and that while in America, standing before the most appreciative audiences, who generally sympathized with his views, he would have advanced the most conclusive arguments it affords. He assumes certain facts in relation to the theory of rudiments—and this theory is fundamental to evolution—and deduces therefrom certain conclusions; yet we think his facts admit of no such conclusions as he draws from them; and if we show that the scientific and philosophic causes assigned for their existence are inadequate, then evolution has no foundation in nature. He says:

"The hypothesis of evolution supposes, that in any given period in the past we should meet with a state of things more or less similar to the present, but less similar in proportion as we go back in time; that the physical form of the earth could be traced back in this way to a condition of things in which its parts were separated as little more than a nebulous cloud, making part of a whole in which we find the sun and the other planetary bodies also resolved; and at no point of the continuity could we say, 'this is a natural process, and this is not a natural process;' but that the whole might be strictly compared to that wonderful series of changes which may be seen going on every day under our eye, in virtue of which there arises out of that semi-fluid homogeneous substance which we call an egg the complicated organization of one of the higher animals. *That*, in a few words, is what is meant by the hypothesis of evolution. The universe has come into existence somehow or other, and the question is whether it came into existence in one fashion, or whether it came into existence in another." (*Tribune* Report.) In answer to this question, Prof. Huxley claims that the universe did come into existence either upon the above hypothesis or upon that of which Moses gives us the account in the Book of Genesis.

If we prove by the teaching of familiar facts and the well-known principles of natural science that the animal and vegetable species and races of the world did not come into existence upon the hypothesis of evolution, then it follows that they were created according to the account given in the Bible ; and whether all or any of the fossil remains discovered can be accounted for has nothing whatever to do with the question. If nature is inadequate to the task of bringing herself into existence, then the theory of evolution is false. Here the plain statement is made that from a mass of gelatinous, homogeneous matter, as the foundation of all life, and by a process inherent in itself, nature brought into existence the sun, the planets and all things organic and inorganic. Now if we show that "life" is of such a nature that it could not have come into existence in this manner, that an intelligent Being created it follows inevitably. The question therefore is : What is life ?

Conditions of Life.

It will not be questioned that whatever is essential to life is a part of life. As all air-breathing animals possess in common what are called the "vital organs," which perform the same functions in each, it is immaterial what grade or individual we select with which to illustrate our argument. Upon this subject Mr. Darwin says: "In what manner the mental powers were first developed in the lower organisms is as hopeless an inquiry as to show how *life* first originated. These are problems for the distant future, if they are ever to be solved by man." ("Descent of Man," vol. i. p. 35.) Conceding the problems of the origin of *mind* and *life* to be of equal importance, if we show the origin of the latter to be incompatible with evolution, that of the former must also be; for no one will contend that the first man, or any of his successors would ever have had a thought if he had never lived; consequently the mental powers follow and depend upon the living. In fact, the mental powers have no existence except in *living beings*. So conscious is Mr. Darwin that neither the mental nor living powers originated in evolution that he is forced to make this admission, which virtually says: "Evolution furnishes no evidence of the origin of life and mind; for as nothing but a living being can produce another living being; and as nothing but a living being thinks, and as thinking depends upon living, and this upon physical conditions —the possession of vital organs—therefore neither could have come into existence by evolution."

On page 154 he says again: "Undoubtedly it would have been very interesting to have traced the development of each separate faculty from the state in which it exists in the lower animals to that in which it exists in man; but neither my ability nor knowledge permits the attempt." Here it is taken for granted that the faculties of life and thought possessed by man were derived from the lower animals but in a rudimentary state. Now, rudimentary faculties of life and thought are not faculties at all; for faculties imply capacity of performing functions. For example, lungs have the faculty of breathing, but rudiments of lungs cannot breathe; if they breath they are not rudiments, but lungs. The difference, therefore, between faculties and rudiments is that the former perform functions, the latter do not. The first animal, therefore, must not only have had lungs, but every other vital organ, performing precisely the same functions as they do at the present day in every moving thing of life as well as in man; for no animal, no matter how simple its organization, can live or ever could have lived had one of these organs been omitted or had it been a mere rudiment. Hence the first animal was as perfectly organized as any succeeding one, or as man himself is at the present day.

We mean to be understood that this must have forever been the organic condition of everything, from the lowest insect up to man, that had the power to move from one spot to another, or that of *voluntary motion*. To demonstrate this principle of nature, remove the lungs or that apparatus with which some of the lower orders of animals are endowed, answering the same purpose, from any animal, the lowest or the highest, or supply their place with rudiments—that is, with lungs which have not the faculty of breathing—and will the animal live? If it does not live, can it produce a living faculty, or even a rudiment of one? If it had not lived could it have developed mental powers?

If Mr. Darwin has ever considered these facts and their sequence, he endeavors to divert attention from any effort to investigate the conditions of life and reproduction by the sophism that because we cannot comprehend life or the operations of the mental faculties, therefore evolution might have produced them ; whereas the physical conditions of life and mental power—the exercise of faculties—are just as well known as it is known that man cannot breathe without lungs or think without brain. Thus we see that the first and lowest animal must have emerged from the gelatinous mass (if it ever did so emerge) a perfect living organization without a rudiment. This mass, according to Huxley, is the foundation of all life, and as these facts and principles of well-known science remove the foundation —the structure ghost of science—evolution falls with it ; or, as it never had any foundation, it never began to be built.

If he had said that this mass was the material out of which the living God made the living animals of the world, he would have announced the only scientific solution of the problem. Or if Darwin had so far yielded as to have called his primordial "God," he would have presented the only cause adequate to the performance of the work, and which the nature of things makes a necessity. Here, too, Tyndall comes in and boldly asks "Whence came the primordial." In answer we may say, It did not come from his fanciful nebulous matter by the play of atoms ; than which theory nothing can be more absurd, as we have already shown.

The Primordial A Perfect Creature.

Our proposition is that the conditions of life were not the work of evolution, but of creation. It is a fact of physiology that all the involuntary organs of the animal economy are employed in the manufacture [to use a mechanical phrase] of arterial blood from the food taken into the stomach and the air inhaled by the lungs. It is another physiological fact that there is a continual wear and waste of every organ and faculty of the system in the performance of their several functions, and that the waste is repaired from this blood, which must therefore contain all the chemical properties, and in sufficient quantity to meet the demand. When all the organs called vital are in a state of requisite activity, having sufficient material of food and air upon which to work, the blood is in a condition to make the reparation, and the result is health; but let either of these organs become impaired and weak, losing its tone of action, and sickness is the result; and if it entirely ceases its function, death takes place. This demonstrates that the primordial emerging from the gelatinous matter possessed every vital organ in healthy activity, leaving no place for rudiments.

Let us notice some of the more prominent facts in the wonderful operation of the vital machinery. By the mastication of food it becomes mixed with the fluid secreted by the salivary glands, favoring deglutition or swallowing, as well as digestion. By the action of the stomach the nourishing part of the food is reduced to a fluid called chyme. The chyme is again changed into chyle by being mixed with the gastric juice, produced by a peculiar set of secretories in the mucous membrane of the stomach, which is also one of the agents of digestion, after which the chyle is forced into the circulation. The liver secretes its bile from the blood, and discharges it by the common duct into the duodenum. The bladder secretes its gall, etc. As it is the function of these various organs to give the blood chemical affinity for every part of the animal system through their secretories and excretories, it follows that when a kind of food is taken into the stomach containing more of these properties than demanded at a particular time by those parts of the system for which they are appropriate, the organ whose office it is to attend to the distribution of that particular substance secretes the over-plus for use when there is not the usual quantity in the food.

The blood thus formed still lacks two substances to endow it for its work—oxygen and electricity, or animal magnetism. Electricity is the agent of the voluntary and involuntary motions of the whole system, and is inhaled with the air and stored in the two brains for these purposes, and the oxygen to give the blood its color and vitalization. The lungs decompose the air inhaled, retaining these substances for the most part, and exhaling the other atmospheric constituents. These charge the blood, rendering it a chemical and electrical positive in relation to all parts of the system, and with the magnetic expansion and contraction of the heart compel it to circulate. Upon this point we quote the following from Lee's Physiology.

"The blood, as it goes the round of the system, leaving a little bony matter here, a little muscular there; supplying the nails, the hair, the skin, and everything, with the particles which, in the wear and tear of the machine, they have lost; by degrees loses its bright arterial color, and by the time it comes round again to the lungs, it is no longer fit to perform its duty; it has been robbed of all its principles most essential to life, and must be renewed and prepared afresh before it can be of any further use. This is done in the lungs: and this process is what physiologists call the vital part of respiration." (Page 253).

By this it will be seen that the circulation of the blood is an indispensable condition of life, and though it was chemically prepared to meet and repair the waste of the system, without the circulation life would not be possible; from which it follows that every element, organ, and faculty employed in the circulation are *essential parts of the great law of life itself.*

The application of these facts to evolution proves that if a single one of these organs, or the performance of its function, had not existed in the organization of the primordial, it never could have begun to live ; or had either of them been a rudiment, the result would have been the same : from which we conclude that perfect organic beings existed at the beginning, and hence were creations.

We quote further from the same author : "It should be borne in mind that the office of respiration is to bring the blood in contact with the air, and accordingly, the lungs are so constructed as to allow the largest possible quantity of deteriorated blood to enjoy the fullest intercourse with the largest possible quantity of vital air ; *and all the mechanism of bones and muscles which I have described are only subservient to this end.*" Hence, life results from breathing—this from perfect lungs.

The Wonderful Structure of the Lungs.

"It has been calculated by Hales, that each air-cell of the lungs is the one-hundredth part of an inch in diameter, and that the amount of surface furnished by them collectively is equal to twenty thousand square inches. Such is the structure of the vessel which conveys the air to the blood ; now let us examine how the blood gets to the air. This is effected by means of the pulmonary artery, which springs from the right ventricle of the heart, divides into two branches, one from each lung, and again subdivides and ramifies through the organ in a manner precisely similar to the bronchial tubes. Every bronchus, or branch of the trachea, has a corresponding blood-vessel, which traces it through its entire course until it reaches the air-vessels, upon the surface of which the minute vessels expand and ramify, forming a net-work, so beautiful that the anatomist who observed it called it 'The wonderful net-work.' Thus the air is on one side, and the blood on the other, of an immense surface of membrane, finer than the most delicate lace or gauze ; and as such membranes are permeable to air and other gases, the oxygen of the air penetrates it and unites with the blood, while a portion of carbon and water are given off by exhalation. Thus does the blood lose its dark, venous character, and assumes a florid, arterial hue and becomes fitted to carry vigor to every part of the system.

"Thus we see that the lungs and all their complicated machinery of bones, ligaments, muscles, and cartilages, were formed for the sake of these little air-cells; for it is through their agency that the blood undergoes the necessary changes and alterations. When we reflect upon the relative extent of the actual respiratory surface, compared with the dimensions of the lungs themselves, that a structure of blood several hundred feet in surface is exposed to a stratum of air still more extensive, and compressed within the compass of a few inches, we are filled with admiration and astonishment at the wisdom displayed in such a structure, and search in vain among all the contrivances of human skill and genius for a counterpart. [And, we may add, how much more wonderful is that displayed in the structure of the human mind.]

"The oxygen consumed by a man in a minute is about thirty cubic inches. He breathes twenty times in a minute, and at every breath takes into his lungs fifteen cubic inches of atmospheric air, which contains three cubic inches of oxygen, so that one-half of that which is inspired disappears in every act of respiration. This will amount to about 2,000 cubic inches in an hour, and 45,000 cubic inches in twenty-four hours. Thus one man will consume, in twenty-four hours, all the oxygen in a space of 312 square feet." [How delicate the mechanism to perform such work!]

Amount of the Flow of Blood.

Dr. Southwood Smith gives us the following as the result of his experiments: "The volume of air ordinarily present in the lungs is about twelve pints. The volume of air received by the lungs at an ordinary inspiration is one pint. The volume of air expelled from the lungs at an ordinary expiration, is a little less than a pint. Of the volume of air received by the lungs at an inspiration, only one-fourth of it is decomposed at one action of the heart, and this is decomposed in five-sixths of a second. The blood circulates through the system and reaches the heart in 160 seconds of time, which is exactly the time in which the whole volume of air in the lungs is decomposed. The circuits are performed every eight minutes; 540 circuits are performed every twenty-four hours. The whole volume of air decomposed in twenty-four hours is 221,882 cubic inches, exactly 540 times the volume of the contents of the lungs. The quantity of blood that flows to the lungs to be acted upon by the air at one action of the heart is two ounces, and this is acted on in less than one second of time. The quantity of blood in the whole body of the human adult is twenty pounds avoirdupois, or twenty pints. In twenty-four hours fifty-seven hogsheads of air flow to the lungs. In the same time twenty-four hogsheads of blood are presented to the lungs to this quantity of air. In the mutual action that takes place between the quantities of air and blood, the air loses 328 ounces of oxygen and the blood ten ounces of carbon."

All these organs, functions, and processes are so absolutely interdepending that not one can be omitted and life be possible; from which it follows that life is not a single, abstract, mysterious thing; but the result of all the organs and functions we have been considering, united in a single body; or, in other words, the *embodiment is a living animal*.

These facts of physiological science perfectly negative the assumption that organic beings first appeared in rudimentary form. In his lectures of animal rudiments, illustrated by the evolution of the horse from the bird, Huxley confined himself to the parts which were not vital, such as the shape and size of the limbs, toes, wings, etc., arguing that successive generations developed more perfect ones. He might as well have argued that because a man was born with six fingers on each hand and as many toes on each foot (and we have seen such a man), he had, therefore, been developed beyond a man, and was a type of a higher species. Upon the same principle, if he had been born with but one leg or one arm, or no hands, he would not be a man, but a lower link in the animal chain. Had Prof. Huxley told us that the original horse had only rudiments of lungs, heart, or stomach, and yet that he lived, his American audiences would have laughed him to scorn. More ridiculous still would he have appeared had he told them that the horse, with rudiments in the place of vital organs, was in process of development : only give the lifeless thing time and he would become a veritable horse. The identity, however, of the equine species, or that of any other animal, is not in his limbs, toes, tail, size, or color, but in the vital organization ; and we have shown that he never was a horse until all of these were vital, and they were not vital until the animal breathed and therefore lived. If an animal emerged from Huxley's gelatinous nebula, let us inquire what must have been the conditions of emergence. As it is a fact that all living animals have substantially the same vital organs, as perfectly formed, connected, and dependent on each other, the primordial might as well have been man as the most tiny animalcule.

Philosophic necessities bringing the Primordial into existence.

To begin, then, there must first have been produced a shell of a body, with limbs as instruments of locomotion, to enable it to go in quest of food, and to feed itself when found. This anatomy or bone frame-work must have been of the size and shape of the forthcoming animal. The bones must have been clothed with a perfect set of muscles including ligaments holding the bones together at the joints. The muscles must have been intersected with two sets of nerves, one of voluntary and the other of involuntary motion, and another set also of sensation. There must have been a brain, as the source of all these nerves. There must also have been a complete set of arteries and another of veins, with their capillaries, forming a system of tubes for the circulation of the blood, without a break or a barrier. There must also have been two sets of membranes, mucous and serous, the one lining all the cavities of the body and opening into the air, the other lining the closed cavities or sacs of the body.

Here is the anatomical frame, which must have been filled with those organs whose functions are essential to the manufacture of the blood to support animal life, which we have been considering. These are called vital organs; but they are no more so than the blood itself, the air inhaled, or than the nerves of involuntary motion. Divide the eighth pair of these leading from the spinal marrow to the stomach and the stomach is immediately paralyzed, and digestion ceases. This shows that the existence and connection of brain, spinal cord and nerves with the stomach are each as vital as the stomach itself. If the medulla oblongata be injured, breathing immediately ceases. The reason why division of the spinal marrow from the eighth pair of nerves, or par vagum, connecting the heart, lungs, larynx, etc., causes death, is the fact that one of the functions of the par vagum is to carry to the brain the sense of the want of air, or a feeling to respire. This stimulus reacts upon those parts of the spinal cord giving rise to the action of the respiratory nerves of the chest. Or if we divide the pulmonary artery or jugular vein, death also instantly results. Hence the heart or lungs are no more vital organs than these nerves, this vein or artery, or than any other part of the system the removal or paralysis of which causes death. Neither is one or any limited number of them vital, or living; but life results from the existence and connection of all, and in any considerable degree the unimpaired condition of all. The only true definition, therefore, of life, is that it is a combination of organs, each capable of performing a function, so arranged and related in a single body as to give it the power of voluntary motion. In other words, *life is a living animal.*

Here we have the embodiment of every faculty essential to life; but if there be no blood in the arteries and veins, breathing would be impossible, and there would still be no life; and the sensation of the want of air giving rise to this, being the *result of life*, shows it can still have no existence. The fifteen pounds of atmospheric pressure to the square inch might enter the lungs through the nostrils; but its oxygenation would not take place, as this requires the previous existence of the blood upon the outside of the lungs to abstract the oxygen from the fresh inhalation. It is evident, therefore, that had nature succeeded in this perfect formation of an animal, still it would have been without life because without blood. This physiological fact is expressed by Moses thus : " The blood is the life thereof."

To meet this emergency, if nature formed a living animal, she must have provided vegetable or animal food (and at this time neither of these existed, as we are dealing with the first organic existence), and have forced it into the mouth and stomach of the animal; but when there it would have remained undigested; for digestion requires the action of the stomach, which is the *result* of life, which did not itself exist. The only other method nature could have pursued in the performance of this task would have been to select from the environment every ingredient or chemical property of which arterial blood is composed, oxygenate and electrize it (each of these must be in the exact proportion as though produced by the living organism itself), and then open an artery and force it into the whole arterial system. Quite a task for dumb unthinking *nature*.

Nature Incapable of Producing Life.

Thus we see that the conditions of life do not permit the absence of one of these parts, or that one should be in a nascent or rudimentary state. No matter how nearly it may be approximated, the power to perform its appropriate function in the animal economy is wanting, and hence there can be no life. If lungs breathe, they are lungs; if they do not breathe, they are not lungs; though they may be rudiments, as they were while God was forming them, or afterward while they are in the process of parental formation. It only remains to express the conclusion in regard to the coming into existence of this wonderful piece of mechanism—namely: That as the gelatinous or nebulous matter was incapable of forming the first living animal, and as such animal did come into existence, therefore it was the work of a Being of intelligence and power equal to its accomplishment; and for the enlightenment of mankind its Author has caused it to be announced thus: "And the Lord God formed man of the dust of the ground, and breathed into his nostrils the breath *of life*, and the *man* became a living soul." (Genesis 2: 7.) Mark: He did not breathe *life* into his nostrils, but the *breath of life*, which was and is the air with its due proportion of oxygen. Deprive a man of air for ten minutes and he will die. Neither did He breathe a soul into him; but, forcing the vital air into his nostrils, the *man himself* became the *living soul*, are the Maker's own words.

Prof. Huxley further says: "The whole process of evolution may be strictly compared to that wonderful series of changes which may be seen going on every day under our eye, in virtue of which there arises out of that semi-fluid, homogeneous substance which we call an egg the complicated organization of one of the higher animals. That is what is meant by the hypothesis of evolution." That we may see the futility of such a comparison, see "Stern's Reflections" p. 264.

What a loose play of the imagination, to see in any operation of blind, unknowing matter the faculty of producing such marvelous mechanism as is involved in the egg, or to suppose that less than infinite wisdom was required to bring it into existence—and that, too, only assuming it to be capable of reproducing its identical kind. How much greater would be the marvel were matter endowed with the principle of giving life to a superior creature—say a man from a monkey. But Mr. Huxley says, "The whole process of evolution may be strictly compared to this wonderful series of changes." He calls the contents of this egg, "a homogeneous substance, which means composed of atoms of the same chemical quality."

It was necessary to give this definition to the original nebulous matter; for had its atoms been endowed with variety of chemical affinities it would have implied the work of wisdom, and therefore of creation; but it is a gross misstatement of the nature or composition of the matter in the egg to call it homogeneous, which has in it all the chemical properties of the hen, as one of the higher animals; and all animals are known to possess nearly, if not quite all, the chemical properties of the universe. To demonstrate the error of Huxley's definition, make a pin-hole in the shell of an egg, letting out its contents, and fill it with any homogeneous substance, covering the hole with plaster of Paris. Then set a hen on it for three weeks, and if a chicken is hatched, every one will believe in evolution and its advocates.

Hence, to compare the process of hatching a chicken from an egg with the evolution of the first animal from no egg, and from matter of a single element, when the egg possessed all the elements of nature, presents the very acme of absurdity. And this Prof. Huxley calls one of the strict comparisons of evolution! The embryonic chicken was first involved before it could have evolved from the egg. Can a thing be taken from where it is not? Evolution, as we have argued before, implies prior involution; and involution implies creation, and this again a creator. As we have seen, Prof. Huxley admits that evolution, when strictly defined, means being born. Behold, how far he is now from the animal emerging from his nebulous cloud! It is, however, another of his sophistries put forth in order to appear to obtain a starting-point for his evolution machine.

Similar appearance no proof of Species.

Huxley, in common with all the evolutionists, thinks that were the wide gaps between living and extinct animals, such as between the monkey and man, filled up by slight and regular grades from the lowest to the highest, the doctrine of evolution would be established. But the identity of species, and the persistence of each to produce its kind, without regard to similar appearance, demonstrate that were this easy and regular gradation shown it would not furnish the least evidence in proof of the theory. The fox, wolf, and dog appear to be thus graded; the hare and rabbit also, as well as the horse, zebra and ass; yet by the transmissible organization of these animals each is known to be of a different species; as by crossing they not only will not produce their kind, or another species, but will not produce at all, not even a rudiment.

Without a knowledge of these facts, obtained by thousands of experiments, one of these animals might be claimed as the descendant of another; but such knowledge proves hybridization impossible, and also proves that the first pair of each were creations, and that no organic thing ever came into existence by evolution or upon any other hypothesis than that of the Mosaic Genesis. The more profoundly the subject is investigated, aided by the philosophic and scientific light afforded by the nineteenth century, the deeper will become the conviction that the Bible statements respecting the manner of creation and the time covering the work are the ultimate truth.

However lightly any man may esteem the importance of the questions involved in this discussion, we heartily agree with Prof. Max Muller when he said, "The question of the descent of man may be called *the question* of the nineteenth century, and it requires all the knowledge of the century to answer it." And also with Prof. Tyndall when he says, "The religious sentiment which has incorporated itself in the nature of man, is the problem of problems of the present age." One of the greatest hindrances to true religion grows out of the supposition on the part of its defenders that things called science are such when they are not, and that as these conflict with the statements of the Bible, therefore the words employed in the Bible must be changed, or substituted for others in harmony with the false science.

Would it not be a complete abandonment by the advocates of the teaching of nature—which modern scientists hold cannot be reconciled with the Bible statements—to give the words they employ to convey their meaning such flexibility or latitude of interpretation as to convey quite an opposite meaning, in order to accommodate them to the teachings of the Bible? So also to change the phraseology of the Bible in order to make it appear to teach those vagaries, called science, would be an equal abandonment of its revelations, both of nature and religion. The remedy for both evils is to obtain by impartial investigation, a correct understanding of the revelations of nature and of the Bible; and if both books originated in the same mind, all will be found harmonious.

Prof. Tyndall's Belfast speech reviewed.

At a meeting of the British Association in August, 1874, Prof. Tyndall, who had been called to the presidency for the ensuing year, said, "The impregnable position of science may be described in a few words. All religious theories, schemes, and systems, which embrace notions of *cosmogony* [the creation of the world], or which otherwise reach into its domain, must, in so far as they do this, submit to the control of science, and relinquish all thoughts of controlling it. Acting otherwise proved disastrous in the past, and is simply fatuous to-day. Every system which would escape the fate of an organism too rigid to adjust itself to its environment must be plastic to the extent that the growth of human knowledge demands. When this truth has been thoroughly taken in rigidity will be relaxed, exclusiveness diminished. Things now deemed essential will be dropped, and elements now rejected will be assimilated. *The lifting the life is the essential point*; and as long as dogmatism and intolerance are kept out, various modes of leverage may be employed to raise life to a higher level. Science itself not unfrequently derives motive power from an ultra-scientific source [and never was there a more prominent illustration of this fact than the extreme ultraism of this very speech, which in evolution outdoes Darwin himself, as we shall see].

"Whewell speaks of enthusiasm of temper as a hindrance to science; but he means the enthusiasm of weak heads. [If ever enthusiastic temper carried a head off its equipoise, it was that of the man who said, 'I go beyond the experimental evidence.'] There is a strong and resolute enthusiasm in which science finds an ally; and it is the lowering of this fire rather than a diminution of intellectual insight, that the lessening productiveness of men of science in their maturer years is to be ascribed. [We think this fact is to be ascribed to the other fact, that young men are apt to think—because they have not thought deep enough or long enough—things are science which are not; and they have had to abandon so many theories which their maturer years have discovered to be errors, that their superior insight makes them cautious as to what they accept as science. Also, that young and enthusiastic men think they know a great deal more than they do, which fact is discovered when they reach the age of wisdom.] Mr. Buckle sought to detach intellectual achievements from moral principles; but if so, the intellect would be poor indeed.

"We come now to the question of the organization of life. The fact of the modification of species is undoubted; the evidence in support of it collected by Mr. Darwin is overwhelming. The theory is not perfect—Mr. Darwin himself is aware of a weakness—but this is a matter of investigation. There must be no more check put upon scientific investigation. In our day wide generalizations had been reached. [But the details do not warrant any of them.] The origin of species is only one of them. There was that other doctrine of the conservation of energy, of wider grasp and more radiant significance; the constancy and indestructibility of matter, which had long been affirmed, and later experience has justified the affirmation. Later researches have extended the attribute of indestructibility to force. This idea has gradually been extended from inorganic to organic life, and from the vegetable to the animal world.

"There was also physical life asking for a solution. How are the different grades and orders of mind to be accounted for? What is the principle of growth of that mysterious power, which, on our planet culminates in reason? In this also there were development and modification of faculties going on. The adjustments between the organization and the environment had an influence on our constitution and formation which reached far back, and could not yet be properly estimated. What, then, was the ultimate origin? Mr. Darwin had suggested what he calls one primordial form: but how came this form there?" This is the vital question; and now let us see how much light is thrown upon it by this great scientist?

Tyndall Abandons Disguise and Becomes Atheistic.

"Abandoning all disguise, the confession I feel bound to make before you is, that I prolong the vision backward across the boundary of experimental evidence, and discern in that matter which we in our ignorance, and notwithstanding our professed reverence for its creator, have hitherto covered with opprobrium, the promise and energy, form and equality of life. The human understanding itself is a result of the play between organism and environment, through cosmic ranges of time; but there are things and influences woven into the texture of man, such as the feeling of awe, reverence, and wonder which had incorporated itself in the religions of the world; to yield this sentiment reasonable satisfaction is the problem of problems at the present hour.

"Finally, I would set forth equally the inexorable advance of man's understanding in the path of knowledge, and the unquenchable claims of his emotional nature which the understanding can never satisfy; and if still unsatisfied, the human mind, with the yearning of a pilgrim for his distant home, will turn to the mystery from which it has emerged, seeking so to fashion it as to give unity to thought and faith, the enlightened recognition that ultimate fixity of conception is here unattainable, and that each succeeding age must be left free to fashion the mystery in accordance with his own needs. Then, in opposition to all the restrictions of materialism, I would affirm this to be a field for the noblest exercise of that which is in contrast with the knowing faculties of man. Here, however, I must quit a theme too great for me to handle, but it will be handled by the loftiest minds ages after you and I, like streaks of morning cloud, shall have melted away into the infinite azure of the past."

Since this lecture was delivered and the criticisms it provoked were published, Prof. Tyndall says: "I look forward to a calmer future for a verdict, founded not on imaginary sins, but on the real facts in the case. Those who accuse me of ignoring the existence of God, should be content to say, 'Our God.' I do not claim that the doctrine of material atheism is a satisfactory solution of the *great mystery in which we dwell, and of which we form a part.*" He evidently wishes to be understood that he does not repudiate the idea of God entirely, but conceives it to be the God of the pantheist, confounding him with the universe; *pan*, all ; *theos*, god,—"all in God,"—as taught first by Orpheus, a Grecian philosopher ; afterward by Spinoza, its greatest defender. This is also indicated by the expression, "Of which we form a part," as well as by the quotations he has placed at the beginning of his published lecture ; which are more explicit than anything else in his preface.

The first of these is from Xenophon, running thus: "There is one God supreme above all other gods, diviner than mortals, whose form is not like unto man's. [How does this heathen philosopher know this ? If he knew of what form God was not, he must have known of what form he was, as the one implies the other. If I know God is not the form of man, I know it by comparison, the only method of obtaining knowledge ; hence I must know the real form of God, so that I may compare it with the form of man, by which the difference or similarity will be seen], and unlike his nature. [The same argument holds good as to God's nature. If I know God's nature is not like that of man, I must know what the nature of God is, whereby the difference may be seen;] but vain mortals imagine that gods, like themselves, are begotten, with human sensations, voice, and corporeal members. [His god, then, had no members, or incorporeal, immaterial ones, which cannot be embodied or occupy space, and no "voice." He could not, therefore, speak so as to be heard ; but man can speak, therefore he is the greater,—the "diviner."] So if oxen or lions had hands and could work in man's fashion, and trace out with a chisel or brush their conception of godhead, then would horses depict gods like horses, and oxen like oxen,—each kind the diviner, with its own form and nature endowing."

Modern Scientists Quote Heathen Philosophers as Guides.

What strikes us as a most unaccountable phenomenon is, that these modern scientists go back to Socrates, Plato, his pupil, and Xenophon, Plato's pupil, and to Aristotle —all heathen philosophers—to obtain ideas about God, the nature of man, and his destiny, with which to elevate the standard of the knowledge of the nineteenth century! No, Mr. Tyndall, your disguise is too superficial to conceal your design, which is nothing less than the renewal of the attack of Pagan philosophy upon the Christian religion. It is the same old war of the gods of heathenism against the living God of the Bible and its revealed religion ; but the gospel met and vanquished this very philosophy in the zenith of its glory, although defended by the wisdom of Greece and the civil power of the Roman Empire ; and it must be opposed now by the same gospel, and not by the modern compromise with this very philosophy ; for how can Satan cast out Satan ?

The other quotation of Tyndall is from Lord Bacon : "It were better to have no opinion of God at all than such an opinion as is unworthy of him ; the one is unbelief ; the other contumely."

That Tyndall cannot draw Lord Bacon in as a defender of his godless philosophy, ridiculously stigmatizing Christianity as "The Mystery," is shown by another of Lord Bacon's sayings :—"Though a small draught of philosophy may lead a man into atheism, a deep draught will certainly bring him back again to the belief of a God." It is evident that Tyndall has taken the small draught ; let us hope he may take the deep one. In order to do this he will be obliged to take his conception of God from Jesus Christ, "who is the express image of his person" (Heb. 1, 3) ; and "God manifest in the flesh" (1. Tim. 3, 16). Here he will find manhood elevated and the godhead lowered in order to assist the limited comprehension of man to an appreciative conception of the only living God. If this fails to "lift the life of man to a higher level," as the essential thing to be done by science, as Tyndall expresses it, he will still be left to seek among the beasts of the earth and creeping things for gods to worship, with whom even Socrates said, "it was never supposed dwelt virtue ;" and at whose shrines Orpheus, Aristotle, Socrates, Plato, and Xenophon paid their Pagan devotions.

These sarcastic flings, borrowed from heathen philosophy, at the scientific, philosophic, and Christian idea of God, show the extremity to which Tyndall is driven in making a defense against the charge of ignoring his existence. But even in the quotation, it is clear that the heathen philosopher, not blessed as Tyndall is with the written revelation of this Being, had learned from natural science and natural religion that there existed an embodied godhead, a supreme God in unity—which conception cannot be separated from personality—and it was only the question of his shape that bewildered him. To overlook this point is perfectly consistent with all the methods of the evolutionists, who seize upon any sentiment, though only found in the mythical records of antiquity—and even these they distort—which describe gods and beasts as confusedly herding together, and according to the degrading tendency of this teaching, give oxen, lions, and horses the pre-eminence of being their ancestors.

Evolution degrades its defenders.

How can they avoid becoming gross in their imaginations, while in thought and contemplation they constantly mingle with creeping things, searching among beastly nature for the power that brought them into existence? Pursuing this study, to the exclusion of that of God and his moral nature, how can it be otherwise than that they should rapidly descend to the level of the objects of their regard? Instead, therefore, of Tyndallism being progressive and tending to lift the life of man to a higher level, its contemplation of mankind as a species of the animal evolved from a lower species cannot but degrade him by lowering every motive and aspiration to human happiness and greatness. If the gods of heathenism, always acknowledged to be superior to man, at least in mental and physical ability, have failed, in all times and in all countries where Christianity was unknown, to elevate man, how can evolutionism—which sees no greater or better being in existence than man himself after whom to aspire, and everything lower—how can this, we say, lift the life to a higher elevation?

Such an assumption is in conflict with the universal law of moral and intellectual assimilation; and by the teachings of human experience and the facts of moral philosophy we are driven to the reversal of Tyndall's order, and are compelled to say that every theory and system called science must relax its arrogant rigidity and become plastic to the degree that will make its brutal sentiments and godless ideas yield to the advance of human knowledge, which finds in the real science and real philosophy of nature a Great Personal God, to whose handiwork the universe owes its origin. The assumptions of evolution being incompatible with Christianity—which the history of the world shows is the only power able to elevate the standard of human excellence—and not being plastic enough to be harmonized with it, must be abandoned now, as they have been in the past.

Besides, nothing is more certain than that all the systems of heathen religion (including the Mohammedan) and the gods they worship are corruptions of the worship of the true and living God as revealed in the Holy Scriptures, which worship was conceived and performed by Abel the second, and Enoch the seventh man born into the world. In confirmation of this, it must be remembered that the human family has, twice in its history, branched off from a single family, and that while a certain line of descendants have maintained this worship unchanged and uncorrupted, the branches from these centers, naturally wishing to be free from the restraints which the laws of God impose, yet possessing an innate disposition to worship, in succeeding generations lost the knowledge of the living God of their ancestors, and made gods for every human passion, whose worship consisted in their indulgence. Hence heathen gods are as corrupt as their worshipers, while the worship only perpetuates and increases the corruption. That the various heathen religions thus originated is seen in the striking features of resemblance, such as the animal sacrifices, the priesthood, the interceding interpreters of the mind of the gods, and the belief in future rewards and punishments.

· The pupil of Plato, whom Tyndall quotes as the critic of the god-makers because they fashioned their gods in the form of man, it may be supposed had some conception of Tyndallism, or Tyndall of Xenophonism, for his mind had become so far darkened, like all his heathen prototypes, in regard to moral and religious aspirations, as to transfer his worship from the living God to living brutes, and even to the original matter out of which he himself supposed he emerged. And why should he not show respect for his ancestors, or do reverence to the earth that begat him, and give expression to it, as we have seen Tyndall do?

Radical changes in systems of so-called science so rapidly succeed each other, that in the space of about thirty years three different geneses of the world have been established, and all by the same authors. In view of which, what can be more certain than that the truth of the literal interpretation of the Mosaic Genesis of creation must and does at the present moment stand upon impregnable ground? For according to the well-known principles of science and natural philosophy involved in matter, motion, and organic life, nature always was incapable of bringing the simplest plant or animal into existence. The course hitherto pursued by the defenders of the Bible, of subjecting its words and teaching to forced and violent interpretation, in order to make them appear to harmonize with all the upstart notions of skeptical scientists, must also be abandoned, and everything assumed to be science investigated and criticised to the very last degree.

If a statement or theory is alleged to be a fact, we must ascertain whether it is such, and whether the teaching claimed for it is legitimate and logical. In such a controversy, as a believer in the Bible we shrink from no investigation and dread no conclusion. Let us have light! Let us have truth! Even a heathen philosopher looks frowningly down upon those so-called scientists who question the existence of a great First Cause.

> "If there's a God above, and that there
> Is, all nature cries aloud. If not,
> Whence this pleasing thought, this
> Fond desire, this longing after immortality?
> 'Tis the divinity that stirs within!
> 'Tis Heaven itself that points out an
> Hereafter, and intimates eternity to man."
> *Addison's Cato.*

An Appeal to Evolutionists:

> If in thy ruminations thou dost descend
> Where naught than thyself is greater,
> Then dost thou become thy most
> Exalted god, devotions paying
> Within thy little selfish shrine.
> Behold the idol and the worshiper, in one!
> Were it not better thou shouldst, like
> The deist, as high aspire as the sacred
> Temple within thine own cranium,
> Where his god, Reason, sits enthroned,
> Tribune of first and last appeal?
> But if thou wouldst rise above, asking
> To be informed, this revelator with
> His finger pointing upward will
> Respond; No god am I, but myself
> Wast made: come, learn with me
> The God who lives above, beyond,
> And reverence only him.
> If too proud for this, then by the
> Law of similes, thy wings for

Higher flight are closely clipt,
And by downward gravitation
Still must thou descend.
There, among thy brothers in migratory
Crawl, search the ancestral line whence
Thou wast derived, and joining an ancient
Ally sing, "These be thy gods, that brought
Thee up from naught." Thus we leave thee,
Revolving 'mong the dead for life.
     But if thou wouldst help
To raise thyself and fallen brothers,
Contemplate nobler things, e'en
Jupiter, of Persian, Greek, and Roman faith ;
Or Hercules of great renown. Try
To conceive these, who were to their
Worshipers but half-way aids to the Great Supreme.
Fix before thee some nobler imagery
Than thy little self. But if in thy
Groveling feebleness thou canst not
Measure so high, or soar on lofty wing
To catch a reverential glimpse of the one
Central mind of universal nature's
Revelation, then try to scan his
Lowest image—Christ the Man.
Be brave enough the invitation
To accept. "Learn of me ; I am meek,
Lowly in heart ;" and the reflex of his
Great thoughts, moral similitude
Shall be thine. Noble likeness ! grand
Transfiguration ! close associate with
Infinity itself ! Behold what thy destiny
May be. These neglect, and thou
Art a failure : " Better hadst thou not been born."

CHAPTER XII.

PROF. PROCTOR'S NEBULOUS, FIERY ORIGIN OF THE
SOLAR SYSTEM, UNSCIENTIFIC.

Prof. Proctor holds that the matter composing the sun and the planets of the solar system was once in a nebular state, that this was composed of the gases, that the gases fused, and that from the action of the molten, fiery mass the whole system was formed; or that by the simple process of burning and cooling, which is still in operation, its present regular structure has been produced; and that the sun and planets are of different ages, amounting to many millions of years. In one of his lectures, delivered in New York in Nov. 1879, Mr. Proctor said : "In my last lecture I endeavored to give some idea of the immensity of space, and in this I will try to give you some comprehension of the vastness of time, and to afford some idea of the age of the earth as compared with the other planets of the solar system ; the age of the planets as compared with the sun ; and the age of the sun as compared with the worlds of the interstellar spaces. In considering the vastness of the time which has elapsed since the universe had a beginning, the mind is lost in absolute wonder, and utterly fails of comprehension."

After giving some of these incomprehensible periods for the cooling of the earth's crust so as to render it a suitable habitation for living beings, he says : "But back of all this lay the time occupied in the gradual cooling of the earth's crust, when the earth was a fiery, molten mass, whirling through space—a mass of molten and gaseous matter very many times larger than it is now. As to the duration of this period, when the crust was slowly forming, it was very much longer than the subsequent one. According to Bischoff's calculation, the time occupied in the formation of the earth's crust could not be less than 350,000,000 years, and this, the lecturer thought, erred rather on the side of deficiency than excess. But this did not fully measure the time since the earth began, for back of the molten condition there lay still another period, the *vaporous stage, when the whole solar system was a mass of nebulous vapor*. This could only be obtained by approximating, and perhaps a period of 500,000,000,000 years may be assigned as the duration of this time. Adding these figures together, it gave the age of the earth. And this cannot be considered as an exaggerated estimate of the duration of the earth from the beginning, and when taken in reference to the other members of the solar system, the earth must be accepted as one of the shortest lived planets. [Since no data are given this must be taken as a good big guess].

"The planet Jupiter being 340 times larger than the earth, it took seven times as long as the earth to cool, and this would give the enormous period of 3,500,000,000 for the formation of the crust of Jupiter. With the exception of the moon, the planets are at such distances that they cannot be very easily studied ; but, in the case of the earth's attendant satellite, we can study her surface very closely. The earth's mass is eighty-one times larger than the moon, and her cooling surface thirteen times greater. Dividing eighty-one by thirteen would seem to furnish an approximate idea of the age of the two planets, and indicates that about 420,000,000 years ago the moon was passing through the same stages of development that the earth is now experiencing ; and taking the duration of the earth at 2,500,000,000 years, the moon may be considered as representing the condition which the earth will reach in the next 1,000,000,000 years—when she will have attained unto a period of decrepitude and planetary death. Thus we gather from the planets like Jupiter and the moon what the past was and the future of the earth will be, but we must remember that the calculations are based upon certain assumptions [yes, and the assumptions have not a particle of evidence to rest upon], and that the time may be shorter or longer, and the age of the earth may be 2,500,000 instead of 1,000,000,000 years ; but whether we take the longer or the shorter period, it does not matter."

As one of these periods is 400 times shorter than the other, each being based on assumption, either period may be taken as the correct one. It is admitted to be mere assumption, and surely it can be nothing else, because it admits of a discrepancy of 400 times less. Based upon such vague premises, we have as good reason for saying that whether the earth is 2,500,000 years old or only 6,000 years, the latter being a little less than 400 times shorter than the former, it makes no matter ; and this brings it approximately near the truth.

The Nebular Hypothesis Stated.

In reference to this theory Prof. Proctor says : " It has been found that the sun and the whole solar system —the earth, the moon, and the planets—are moving in one direction, and this uniformity of movement would seem to indicate *a community of origin* [yes ! and a simultaneous commencement of motion as well], that at some time the same influence was at work to set it in motion in the same direction. It is at this point, when we look into the heavens for a solution of the mystery, that we come upon the nebular hypothesis ; " [a still greater mystery]. In regard to this uniformity of movement in the planetary system, we may remark that the spurious hypothesis of Laplace gives not the least hint of explanation, and the only other alternative is that the influence at work in originating it was the living Creator, whose existence we have proved was a philosophical necessity, and that He created the world. Unity of design is no more exemplified in the motions of the stellar bodies than in every phenomenon of the physical globe, including its vitalized productions and inhabitants. As Darwin, Lyell, Tyndall, Huxley, and Proctor in common adopt the nebular theory of Laplace, it is of vital importance that we should understand in what it consists. As invented and taught by this skeptical scientist, "it supposes that the bodies composing the solar system once existed in the form of nebula ; that this had a *revolution on its own axis* from west to east ; that, by the *effect of gravity*, the matter composing the nebula gradually became condensed toward the center ; that the exterior portions thus had the velocity of their revolution increased, until by the centrifugal force they were separated from the mass, and left behind in the form of a ring ; that thus the material of each of the planets was separated, while the *main body was condensed toward the center, forming the sun ;* and finally, that each of the planetary rings, by a similar process, deposited other rings, out of which by condensation its secondaries, or satellites, were formed."

Prof. Proctor says the nebular hypothesis of Laplace has been very generally accepted, with some modifications, as explaining the origin of the solar system from one of those masses of nebulous or gaseous matter which we see floating in the interstellar spaces. "The gradual accumulation of the particles of the mass into centers by the influence of gravity, the motion upon the axis, and the cooling of the outer surface faster than the interior, would create a kind of crust which would break off, forming a ring, which would form a mass by itself, and move in the same direction as the parent body. The breaking up of the outside ring into particles would create a large number of bodies floating through space, and if there was not enough attraction to gather them together in one mass, they would revolve through the heavens in the same condition as the ring of asteroids which circle about our own sun and form parts of our planetary system."

It is here assumed that this matter called nebular was that out of which nature, not God, formed the solar system ; that the matter is described as being vapor, cloudy and gaseous ; that this matter took fire, and was one mass of molten liquid, a great sea of fire ; that this fusion was essential to its motion, and the motion to the formation of the planetary system. As the system is said to have originated in this universal conflagration, and the time of the cooling was that consumed in bringing the several planets and the sun into existence, if we prove that the burning never took place, then there was no cooling. If the process did not take place then it consumed no time. Therefore, all these immense periods, measuring the fiery ordeal that brought the earth and the other members of the solar system into existence, are mere figments of fancy. The fact must be ascertained that the house burned down, before the time it consumed in burning becomes a subject for intelligent discussion.

Hypothesis is not science, but mere assumption. Science is based upon fact, but if ever there was an imaginary thing, purely hypothetical, that thing is the famous nebula theory of Laplace, on which modern scientists account for the origin of the world, and which is adopted by Proctor and all the evolutionists. Every fact must have its phenomenon capable of being tested by the senses, or whose existence is susceptible of demonstration by a process of reasoning. A fact must also have its philosophy. The fact may exist, but any theory as to the manner of its existence, or how it came to exist, must be shown to be adequate to cause that existence. If a man says the solar system came into existence through igneous or aqueous causes, he must show that these parts of the system are capable of producing it as a whole.

For example, let him collect a quantity of all the gases of which bodies in the solar system are known to be composed, and which will fuse or burn, and then set them on fire, and if a miniature solar system is produced by the burning and cooling process, then Proctor's astronomy is true science. This would require but a very short time. The theory is that the time of cooling and consequently of burning is in proportion to the size of the body, and if the earth took 2,500,000 years to cool, $\frac{1}{2500000}$ of the whole mass would cool in one year. Indeed, the quantity of the gaseous matter consumed may be so reduced that the smallest planet would not be larger than a pith-ball, and the sun the size of an apple. Such an experiment would be scientific, and would conclusively settle the question. Let these star-gazers whose telescopes pierce the intersteller spaces betake themselves to substantial investigation, and give us either matter-of-fact experiment or logical argument.

We proceed now to test the Nebular Hypothesis by the well-known facts and principles of natural science.

Facts of Natural Science prove the Nebular Hypothesis false.

We remark in the first place that our planet is known to be composed of certain simple elements. This knowledge has been obtained by dissolving compound bodies. The number of elements has increased as more powerful solvents or dissolving agents have been discovered. Another fact is that fire will decompose so great a proportion of earthy compounds that its intensity might be increased to such a degree that in time every compound body would be dissolved into its elements. Now if the globe, including its atmosphere, were exposed to such a heat, every body composed of two or more elements would be decomposed or burned up, and this would be its total destruction. Therefore, instead of its being possible for our earth to have had a nebulous or fiery origin, it would have been completely destroyed, if it had been as perfect as it is now before the fusion commenced.

Another fact is, that simple elements are not susceptible of fusion; in other words, nothing but compounds can burn. If, therefore, the nebulous matter was homogeneous—a mass of simple elements—as is claimed for it, then it could not have burned at all, and could never have been in a state of fusion. Burning, or fusion, is simply decomposition; and the process can only last until this effect is reached. In fact, if there were no compounds, the fire could never have begun to burn; and of course if it did begin, it found formations upon which to feed, and the fiery process continued until all were transformed—dissolved—burned to ashes or cinder, when all fuel having been exhausted, the fire went out of itself, and, of course, could never have begun again to burn. At this point too all motion would be at an end. Hence there could have been no origin of the solar system by the nebular fiery process.

The nebular matter is called gaseous, but if so it could not burn. All earthy compounds are a union of gases, and all matter can be reduced to these by the action of fire. Gases enter into combination with each other, according to certain fixed proportions. Oxygen is the gas which constitutes the principle of animal life and flame. Things are combustible, therefore, in a greater or less degree, as this element enters into their formation. Oxygen renders carbon combustible by entering into carbonized bodies. Nitrogen extinguishes both life and flame. Common air is composed of about 27 parts of oxygen to 73 of nitrogen. The air thus composed is not inflammable, its oxygen being balanced by the larger quantity of nitrogen.

If the gaseous nebular matter was air, only 27 per cent. of it could have been in a state of fusion or molten liquid fire. And even this could have been only upon the condition that the oxygen was separated from the nitrogen; and this presupposes the prior existence of heat to produce the decomposition, while as yet, there had been no heat. Hence the gaseous air could never have been a fiery, molten mass. Besides, had nature succeeded in dividing the nitrogen from the oxygen, and then set the oxygen on fire with a friction match, the flame would have continued until every particle of oxygen was consumed. The fire would then have gone out for want of combustible material. It would make no difference whether this burning mass whirled in space or not; indeed, if it moved it would only have consumed the faster. Nor would it have carried a particle of nitrogen with it; for if it had this affinity for nitrogen after having been thus set on fire, it would never have separated so as to have rendered burning possible. But supposing nature to have been such a fool as wantonly to have burned up all her oxygen, she would thereby have been deprived of the capacity of making a world or a solar system in which light, heat, and life would have been possible; as without oxygen neither of these can exist; and how much less possible in the nascent condition of a planet?

Nebular Matter Vapor—It could not Burn.

We have seen that Prof. Proctor declares that the first condition of nebular matter was vaporous. Vapor is water slightly expanded, but unchanged in its chemical composition. Water is a compound of oxygen and hydrogen. The ingredients are one-ninth of hydrogen and eight-ninths of oxygen. It is a well-known fact that heat expands water into vapor, and cold condenses it again into water, and this presupposes a variety of temperature; but when the whole matter of the solar system was nebulous vapor, there was no law to produce change of temperature; for there can be no heat without the motion of matter to produce friction or light; and at this period all was vapor, not a particle of which would ever move except by heat and its absence, cold, and these terms imply matter moving, or expansion and condensation, which is the effect of its motion, and not its cause.

The conclusion from which is, that if all the matter of the solar system was once vapor, such must it have ever remained, so far as the ability of nature was concerned. If it could have condensed into water, it would prove that it was approximating an ice period instead of a molten state. The fact that a large proportion of the globe is now covered with water, all of which, according to the nebular theory, was once vapor, goes to prove that the cloudy period was followed by a colder one, instead of one of fire, as cold would be required to condense vapor into water. It is evident then that this vaporous compound could no more have caught fire, supposing it to have been in the gaseous condition it is now, than can the Atlantic Ocean or our atmosphere take fire. The only possibility of the nebulous vapor taking fire would be by the separation of its gases; and this could only be done by the application of extraneous fire, which did not exist, as the nebula was first.

Let us, however, suppose that the one-ninth of its hydrogen was separated from its eight-ninths of oxygen, and that dead, unknowing nature should have set the oxygen on fire with a friction match. One of two results would follow: either the fire must be quenched, or all the oxygen would be consumed. The first could not have occurred, for the one-ninth, the hydrogen gas of water or vapor, could not stop the burning of eight-ninths of its oxygen gas. Besides, hydrogen gas being of less specific gravity than oxygen, it would ascend into space never to return. The hydrogen would also become so expanded by the heat produced by eight-ninths of the matter out of which nature was to make the solar system that it would be driven off in space, beyond the power of nature to combine it again with the oxygen, even supposing it had not been consumed.

But nature could not work in these opposite directions —separating gases and then recombining them—and that violently, too, because it must have been done while the burning was going on. If the conflagration could not be arrested, then the other result must follow —namely, the whole of the oxygen would be consumed —that is, eight-ninths of the material out of which nature was going to make or evolve the solar system would be totally destroyed. Now she finds to her cost that she had made a fatal blunder in attempting to make a system of planets and a sun upon the red-hot nebular hypothesis, having only one-ninth of the matter necessary left, and not a particle of oxygen to give light and heat wherewith to produce and continue animal and vegetable life. Poor, foolish nature! to begin making a world by burning up her essential materials!

If Homogeneous—Could Not Burn.

Professor Huxley defines nebular matter to be homogeneous, which means of the same kind—atoms of a single element, having no chemical or electrical peculiarity. There was not, according to Prof. Proctor and the Laplace school, a particle of oxygen, hydrogen, nitrogen, or carbon in all the matter out of which the solar system emerged. Had these existed, which constitute the widest extremes of material elements, and in some of their modifications include the matter of the whole world, then it was not homogeneous. If the claim advanced be abandoned in order to avoid this fatal conclusion, then the philosophers of this school must take the other horn of the dilemma—namely, that instead of the matter being nebulous cloud it consisted of all the chemical solids and fluids which now exist, especially in the inorganic world.

Let some power endow the atoms of the nebulous homogeneous matter with these gaseous forms giving them affinity for each other, and being in a liquid state they would embrace each other, and all the solids and fluids of inorganic nature would almost instantaneously be formed. The operation would necessarily consume no more time than the incorporation of a quart each of alkali and acid when put together, for the endowment must have been universal, as the subsequent formation of the compounds is universal. This endowment gave birth to the laws of nature, which are not abstract myths existing before nature, but inhere in the atoms themselves, according to which they now combine. This endowment, this cosmogony, was a work of which the matter knew nothing, and was incapable of performing. This therefore necessitates and introduces a creation and a Creator. This theory of a beginning of things alone gives us the solution of their existence, and is demanded equally by science, philosophy, and the Bible record, and vindicates the axiom, "From nothing nothing comes."

There is not an atom of matter in our planet that is not endowed with an affinity for some other atom. Combinations of this variety of matter constitute things, not the simplest two atoms of which did nebular matter possess: it was simply *one thing*. As things exist, they could not have come from the nebulous matter which did not possess them; for things cannot evolve unless they were first involved: they must therefore have come from the hand and mind of a living, intelligent Being, with power adequate to their production. We have therefore formulated two axioms deduced from the facts and phenomena of this great subject of creation:

From nebula nothing comes that is.
From God all things come that are.

We have seen that, according to Prof. Proctor's theory of the cooling of the sun and planets, or the Laplace theory, which he adopts, the congelation began on the surface, and continued toward the center. We propose to show that this theory is exactly opposed to the natural law of cooling liquid bodies, which invariably cool first at the bottom; and if the body be a globe having a center of gravity, this center is the bottom, and therefore the first part cooled. It is a law of temperature that heated particles of fluid or liquid, from water to the most sublimated ether, ascend, and that cold ones descend. When the water in a steam-boiler begins to boil and bubble on the surface, you can place your hand on the crown-sheet without injury, though it is here the whole of the water is heated. Supposing the boiler to be without tubes, the water is always of a lower temperature next the bottom than anywhere else, and regularly increases as the surface is approached.

So with the steam,—the vapor: the hottest, dryest, and most expanded steam, and therefore the furthest removed from a solid, is in the dome, and at the highest part of that. The philosophy of it is that as fast as the particles of water lying upon the crown-sheet become heated in the least degree higher than those above them, they rise, while the colder particles descend to take their place, which in turn also heat and rise. Thus all the water in the boiler is thrown into motion, describing circles. As the heated particles rise and the colder ones descend, it follows that those on the surface will be first heated, and will continue to be the hottest, as cooling does not reverse this natural law.

If liquid fire, the earth cooled first in the center.

If the vaporous nebula was once all in a state of fusion —a molten sea of liquid fire, which cooled and hardened before it was consumed—then the part first cooled and hardened was at the center of gravity, or in the exact center of the molten earth ; while that part which was hottest and most expanded was the surface, therefore the furthest removed from hard formation, and never could become hard until the entire mass below was first solidified. So it is with the atmosphere. The hot air in our dwellings rises to the ceiling, while the cold currents descend by being displaced. So also is it with the heating of the atmosphere by the sun. The stratum of air lying upon the surface of the earth has the highest temperature. The rays of the sun coming first in contact with the particles of air on the outer verge of the atmosphere heats them first, which speed their way below, displacing the colder particles until the air on the surface of the earth is heated the highest, and every degree of ascension shows a lower temperature.

We have used the phrases above and below, but it must be remembered that the moving force is not in the cold particles or regions, but wholly in those heated. It is the heat which gives rise to their motion, and compels them to seek their natural cold temperature, where they may recover their lost equilibrium. The motion of the cold particles is produced by their being forced out of their place in space. They must always move toward colder ones than those which displaced them, and always move in circles. Thus we have seen that the hypothesis of the nebulous, fiery origin of the planets and their subsequent cooling is in palpable contradiction to the well-known facts of science, and therefore is wholly fanciful and false.

Prof. Proctor assumes that the mass of fiery nebular matter was endowed with the principle of gravity, and moved on its axis. This mass was the sun, whose origin was the work of fire, whose cooling and gravity gave it motion on its axis and made it the sun as we now behold it. The argument is that the sun has a motion on its axis, and that its gravity was produced by the cooling of its crust, and this because it was previously a mass of fire. But as these are results that depend upon the prior existence of the nebula on fire, and as we have shown that it never was on fire, therefore Prof. Proctor's whole theory of the origin of the solar system is erroneous. But for the sake of argument, let us suppose the fiery nebula to have existed: the question is, Did it have gravity, and did that gravity produce the diurnal motion of the shapeless mass from west to east upon its axis?

It must be borne in mind that all the moving bodies in space are spheres, globes, leaving us to conclude that this form is essential to their regular motions, and we shall presently show that the sun and planets must be spheres, in order to perpetuate the reciprocal motions which they perform. Make a cube of one of them, or give one a flat surface, and that instant it would cease to be a sun or a planet; and as a consequence to have rotary motion. The notion that the revolving of the planets, moving at the rate of speed they do, made them round is absurd—that is, supposing them to have been a plastic nebular mass to begin with; for the high velocity would have given them the form of an arrow or a tube. That the sphericity of the earth's atmosphere, being fluid and gaseous, is not thus destroyed by its motion, proves that the earth never received its shape by its diurnal motion.

The theory, therefore, that the bodies in the solar system became globes by revolving on their axes cannot be true, as they must have been globes before they could have thus moved; and if they had been of any other shape, and were set in motion by any extraneous power, they would have ceased their motion on the withdrawal of that power. It must be remembered that the reciprocal forces of the planetary system did not exist at the time we are considering, as the planets themselves did not exist. We are dealing with the origin of the sun, which first existed, and by whose motions the planets of our system were produced—according to Proctor. In order to give any degree of plausibility to the theory of the fiery origin of the solar system, the sun should have been first formed, and should have had a diurnal revolution on its axis; but this motion no body with a surface of an equal temperature like that of the sun can have.

The sun, from whence proceed the rays which produce the light and heat equally from its entire surface, can have no other gravity than that which holds itself together. Though its entire surface may be a body of electricity (and probably is), yet this does not give it polarity, or negative and positive poles, without which it is not a magnet, to be which it must have attraction as well as repulsion. So far, therefore, as gravity is concerned, the sun is only a positive, and continually repels all the planets in the solar system; and were there not attractive forces in the planets themselves which impel them toward the sun, they would be thrown, by its superior power of repulsion, beyond its influence, and our solar system would cease to exist. But the planets have the endowment of inductive magnets.

Laws Governing Magnetics.

It is a well-known law of magnetics that two positives resist each other; another law is that two negatives resist each other, while the negative and positive attract and come together unless resisted by an equally strong positive. This law likewise governs heated and lighted bodies : the higher temperature resists the lower; and experiments go to show that light and heat play a very important part in the electrical phenomena of the universe—not only destroying the adhesive attraction of all compounds, separating them into their atoms and elements, but also the electrical polarity of bodies. Heat a horse-shoe magnet cherry red, and you destroy its polarity; nor does it regain that quality by cooling. In order to restore its polarity, it must be heated red-hot, then cooled by plunging it suddenly into water or other liquid, and then magnetized by a battery. This piece of steel has now a negative at one extremity and a positive pole at the other. If now you divide it into two, or subdivide it into a thousand or any number of fragments, each piece will exhibit the same phenomenon of a negative and a positive pole. The following experiment illustrates all the phenomena of the solar system except the planetary revolutions.

Fasten pith-balls by threads to an insulated rod charged from a galvanic battery, and they will become suspended, and will surround the rod at equal distances from each other. Thus we have the rod as the sun, from whence proceeds the repellant force, and the planets in the shape of pith-balls. If you cut the threads by which they are held, they will be thrown from their orbit by the repulsion of the rod center. If while suspended you place a lighted candle near one of these pith-planets the ball will recede from the candle as far as the thread will permit: so we have suspension, repulsion, and attraction, by electricity and heat—the centripetal and centrifugal forces, if you please, of the solar system.

Remember, now, that two lighted and heated bodies are positives, and repel each other; that the lighting and heating of the solar system emanate from the central sun; that the sun has the same electrical surface on every side, as well as that which produces light and heat; that one-half of each planet is always lighted and heated, because one-half the face of each is always presented to the sun. Being positives, the sun and planets continually repel each other. The planets would therefore be thrown off into space by the sun, beyond her influence, were there no attractive force equal to the repellant; but this repellant force is counterbalanced by the electrical condition of the half of the planets turned from the sun, which are always cold and dark, and consequently negative; and as negative and positive attract each other, this gives the planets their tendency to move toward the sun. Thus we see that as exactly one-half of each planet is lighted, heated, and electrified by the sun, while the opposite half of each remains dark, cold, and demagnetized; therefore each planet is a magnet, with the two poles equally divided, holding each in its exact orbit. This negative endowment of the planets solves another problem of the phenomena in the solar system—namely, the suspension of the sun in the center of the system. The negative pole of each planet draws the sun toward itself, and forms a balance of power around the central orb and holds it in place—the sun being always and uniformly positive. This is upon the principle that negative and positive bodies attract each other.

The knowledge we receive from these laws, it will be observed, is absolutely limited to the facts of suspension, attraction, and repulsion, and affords not a ray of light as to whence came this organized mechanism, or the impulse which first set the planetary system in motion. Upon the theory of the negative and positive poles of a planet we can also understand the continuance of its motion on its axis, and its annual revolution after having been set in motion, which motion we hold could only have originated in a living being possessed of mind. For instance, as the earth turns on its axis, one extremity of its dark side is being continually lighted and heated, while the other extremity is becoming cold and dark— the one negative and the other positive—which forces being exactly equal, perpetuate its motion. For example, that part of the earth which the sunlight is leaving is the strongest positive, because it has faced the sun all day; while that upon which the sun is rising is the strongest negative, because it has been deprived of the sun's rays all night; and as the strongest positive and the strongest negative have the greatest affinity or inclination for each other, they therefore impel these extreme sections to chase each other, and hence to keep the earth whirling on its axis. Of course, what is true of the earth is true of every other planet in the solar system. From these facts we draw the conclusion that as it is the light, heat, and magnetism of the sun which make magnets of the planets, and as these are essential to planetary motion, both diurnal and annual, therefore the whole system was made simultaneously, and as perfect as it now is—the organization producing the susceptibility of planetary motion, and not, as Proctor says, the motions producing the organization.

Nor is it true that the sun, as a body of nebulous fire, ever had or has now a motion on its axis, as no body of equal temperature and magnetic surface—which is known to be the condition of the surface of the sun—can have. This fact alone is fatal to the theory of the nebulous origin of the solar system, the starting-point of which is that the sun itself became a globe by revolution on its axis ; by this motion also from time to time she threw off from her surface portions of herself, out of which were formed all the planets. These are results, let it be remembered : if the cause never existed, neither did these as its effects.

All Power is Mental.

This conclusion naturally suggests the question, Whence is the power derived which nature manifests? We answer, In mind. In vindication of this proposition we introduce the common argument of cause and effect. Nothing is more universally conceded than that there must be a cause for every effect. It is another axiom that the cause must be adequate to produce the effect. It is also equally true that all secondary or more remote causes are themselves effects—effects of effects. This fact is as comprehensive as the phenomena of the world. That is, there is not a thing that moves or is susceptible of being moved by some other inorganic element, or that which is lifeless, but what is an effect of some other such composite thing; it matters not whether it is the simplest atom, forming a part of our world, or the largest and grandest stellar orb.

If, then, all things are effects, it is evident there is no cause, strictly speaking, in all nature. Hence, the Cause which gave things this endowment and susceptibility of affecting and moving each other must be both supernatural and of prior intelligent existence. To state the argument concisely, we say: Nature exists, and everything she contains is susceptible of motion. These motions are interdepending, from the lowest to the highest. Motion or inclination to move (pressure) manifests power; but as motions are results growing out of prior endowment, they did not originate the power: it must have had its source in the mind of a Being capable of forming and endowing the atoms, or any combination of them, which includes all natural existences, with the chemical and electrical peculiarities they possess.

To the argument we may add, that this endowment gave rise to what are called the Laws of Nature, giving them birth, which, being the results or effects of the things of nature, never originated anything. The solar system moves, and every atom it contains possesses gravity and pressure, which induce or incline them to move; but these qualities are inherent, and therefore must have come from a cause outside of nature. By these acts nature was born, after which, but not before, it is proper to say, things are changed and modified by the laws of nature, or affect each other according to inherent and fixed principles. The endowment of the atoms and their various combinations, forming the bodies of the solar system and the subdivisions they contain, gave birth to science and called philosophy into existence.

To illustrate the fact that power is mental, let us suppose a case. A man has observed that heat expands water into steam; that by confining water in a boiler with fire under it, pressure is produced; that to let the steam escape and come in contact with a piece of iron or other object moves that object, and that its motion is power, which will be felt if it is resisted. There he sits at a table, with paper and pencils before him. He thinks, he calculates, he makes marks, and finally draws upon paper the draught of a five thousand horse-power steam-engine. Supposing him to be a practical mechanic of sufficient skill to make all its parts according to the drawn dimensions, he constructs the engine and boiler which, when put on board the ocean-steamer, drive her through the water with a power equal to that of five thousand horses; and yet this was the result of the thought of one man. Hence his mind exerted upon this vessel the power of five thousand horses; yet this is a manifestation of what is called physical power. It is evident, however, that there is no reason for making the discrimination. Although we here see an exhibition of mental power, yet it is not original force, as man himself is a creature whose whole physical, moral, and mental organism is an effect, and not a cause, and therefore derives all its phenomena and susceptibility from the sole first cause, resident in the mind of the Creator.

Relation of cause and effect demonstrates Creation.

It is evident, from this view of nature and her laws, that the origin of molecular motion, organic and inorganic, the result of which is power, is mental. This includes the motions of every intelligent creature in the universe as well as the phenomena of the entire solar system, each of which is but an effect following another effect, and as such cannot exist without an adequate cause. These effects are so many fingers, pointing with unerring certainty to the prior existence of the great first cause, who involved in nature all her peculiarities and possibilities, every movement of which, from the falling of a leaf to the rolling of the planets, is but an unfolding of these involved mental dynamics. The comparative superiority of the machinery of nature over that made by man, although involving the same principles—for there is not a movement in human mechanics that is not borrowed from nature—is seen in the fact that nature's machinery needs no human or angelic hand to set it in motion.

As an illustration of the production of one of God's machines from seed, let us take the peach. Like all other seeds, this has incorporated in it the embryo tree, yet not an atom of it would ever move of itself, and is not therefore a law of nature. Neither is the soil such a law, nor yet the light and heat received from the sun. The soil may contain all the chemical properties adapted to form the seed, and it may be environed by the requisite atmospheric agencies; but if the seed was not planted in the soil, still there would be no germination; but if so planted, the circle is closed and we get a partial view of the law of vegetable reproduction—the essential elements of which are the organic soil, light, heat, moisture, and the atmosphere, with its carbon, all of which are charged with electricity.

But to obtain even an imperfect knowledge of this wonderfully complicated law, it must be understood that plant growth and maturity imply the existence and motions of the earth as an astronomical body; and this also implies the perfect existence and motion of the whole planetary system, as well as those of their central sun. Suppose the seed was planted on that side of the earth turned from the sun, and that the earth did not revolve on its axis. As that side of the earth would therefore be always dark and cold, not one of the particles of the planted seed would ever move, except possibly to decompose and thus move toward death instead of toward organic life. Not an atom of its shell or kernel would expand, which in order to germinate requires a sufficient degree of heat to burst the shell. To thus expand the kernel requires a substance which will pass freely through the pores of the shell without expanding it; for if each were expanded equally there would still be no bursting of the shell, and consequently no growth.

Atmospheric air cannot penetrate the walls of the seed, else the kernel would have been decomposed in a few days after it had fallen ripe from the tree, just as the rest of the peach was decomposed. The substance which penetrates the shell and expands the kernel must be some one of the modifications of electricity, whose particles are so minute that they penetrate and permeate every atom in nature. Coming thus in contact with the atoms of the kernel, it expands each one of them. This expansion moves them, the motion creates friction, and the friction produces heat, which added to the expansive force bursts the shell, giving the properties of the kernel access to those the soil contains, which are chemically and electrically attracted to itself, giving rise to germination. Thus life begins: the germ commences and continues to grow, and when the plant reaches the surface it absorbs atmospheric carbonic acid, and finally becomes the mature tree.

The tree has the faculty of decomposing the air and of retaining the carbon after having changed it into carbonic acid gas, and also of rejecting the greater part of its other constituent gases. This operation produces the motion of all the atoms of the contiguous air, whose friction against each other creates heat. This expands them, sending off the colder particles and returning the warmer, each forming a current and seeking to restore the atmospheric equilibrium of temperature and chemical affinity. This motion of the air is what is called the blowing of the wind, of course on a small scale; but its cause is the same as that which produces the hurricane or the tornado.

We have supposed the peach seed to have been planted on a perpetually dark side of the earth; and as sunlight is essential to vegetable growth, the diurnal revolution of the earth is a necessity, and therefore introduces this motion of the planet as another of the elements in the great law of vegetation. We have also supposed the seed to have been planted in a dry soil. But as moisture is essential to vegetable growth, dew or rain must fall to prepare it to do its work. But these can only come from the atmosphere, and as water is not one of the constituents of air, it must be drawn into it by some principle adapted to the purpose. Hence atmospheric evaporation by the agency of the sun. Water is thus taken up, principally from the seas, lakes, and rivers, until the air becomes so highly saturated that its gravity precipitates it to the earth, and we say it rains. But the water would fall again directly into the bodies from whence it had been taken up, were it not for the movement of the clouds. This movement is produced by the unequal expansion of the air principally resulting from the ecliptic motion of the earth, giving it its seasons, while its revolution on its axis perpetually warms and cools different sections unequally.

These interdepending functions of nature—and they comprehend its whole machinery in motion—present us with two fundamental facts of natural science: First, that not the simplest plant could have lived in any nascent or half-formed condition of the globe or solar system, or in one less perfect than that which now exists:

and without vegetation for animal food animals could not have existed, and could not now. The second fact is, that the laws of nature are not abstractions, susceptible of having existed before the formations and organizations of nature, but chemically and electrically they grow out of the formations themselves. In a word, they are the reciprocal effects which all atoms or compound bodies produce upon each other, and give rise to their various motions, the result of which is power; but the endowment being an effect necessitates a prior cause, and as the effects manifest intelligent adaptation, therefore He who endowed nature thus was intelligent. Here we have the only philosophic and scientific cause of all things,—a Creator to whose Mind must be ascribed all the power the solar system exhibits, giving us the demonstration that all power is *mental*, and all nature is the work of God.

CHAPTER XIII.

PSYCHOLOGIC TRANSMISSION OF DISEASE.

Contiguity Produces Races.

IN considering the natural causes which affect the variation of species into races, that of sensible psychological impression applying to animals, and of sympathetic impression producing similar effects among plants, have been entirely overlooked by naturalists. In relation to plants, it is well known that contiguity of planting modifies vegetable production. Plant two kinds of potatoes, differing in size, shape, and color, in close proximity, and the product will be unlike either, but a mixture of both. Plant red and yellow tomatoes together and the product will be red and yellow striped. So it will be with corn and beans, and indeed with all vegetables and plants of the same species. Notwithstanding these marked varieties, not a single vegetable ever lost its substantial identity; men have never yet "gathered grapes of thorns, or figs of thistles." That question was thus decided scientifically by the Great Naturalist, more than 1,800 years ago, and it so remains. That certain species of plants are adapted to certain climates and latitudes presents no objection to the theory of simultaneous and perfect creation, as well as production in a certain locality, from which all succeeding generations have been distributed over the face of the earth, and with this local exception, all are exotics. The following poetic passage so fully and naturally explains the phenomenon of seed and plant distribution that we here introduce it:

PSYCHOLOGIC TRANSMISSION OF DISEASE. 371

> Thus the soil was formed, plants of
> Every species set therein, blooming
> With ripe and luscious fruit, all in
> Finished perfection, ready to
> Entertain the new-made living man.
> Seed precipitate from these, carried
> By the moving winds of heaven
> And commerce of the world to every
> Clime of earth, lodged in every
> Soil and clime, but alone productive
> In those congenial, thriving within
> The clime for which they were designed.
> The Torrid Zone received and
> Nursed her own. They lived, and
> After their kind yielded fruit whose
> Seed was in itself.
> The Frigid Zone received the same;
> They chilled, more weakly grew,
> And then extinct became.

The differences among races of plants are not so marked in feature as those of animals, and this fact finds its solution in the animal endowment of organs of sense, which give the power to receive and transmit mental impressions. This brings us to the consideration of these faculties, which we find to be the common possession of every living thing having the power of self-motion. We remark in the first place that every animal or insect, however high or low its rank in the scale of being, having the faculty of self-motion, possesses intelligence; the differences among them being not in kind but in degree. In this assumption we include man as well. To draw lines, therefore, of demarcation, on one side of which intellect is ranked, and on the other instinct, we hold to be without justification either in science, philosophy, or Holy Writ. In proof of this, it is only necessary to understand the conditions of self-motion : for as motion is an effect, it must have its antecedent cause. Essential to this phenomenon is the possession of at least one of the five senses, which are the channels of communication between the brain, as the organ of the mind, and external objects.

A man, or any other animal, is touched by a coal of fire, and instantly the nerves of sensation are affected, which act as telegraphic wires, conducting the electric force to all parts of the body, and convey an impression to the brain that some nerve is attacked. The mind thinks about it, and as the result a pain is felt which would not be the case if the mind were inoperative, as in sound sleep. In cases of suffocation during sleep, before the impression becomes sufficiently strong to awaken, it is often too late for escape. Now, by a mandate of the will, the same force is dispatched through the voluntary nerves, having their source in the intellectual organs of the brain, or physiologically speaking, "the brain proper." The force dispatched is of sufficient strength to move the part menaced or the whole animal from the seat of danger and pain. This is done by the electric agent of the mind contracting the muscles of the body to which it is adapted, just as though the muscles of the arm were brought in contact with the negative and positive poles of a charged galvanic battery. The motion is the result of the motive to be relieved from further danger. The consciousness of the pain, or that it was pain, was the result of the appreciation of its nature which an unknowing, inanimate thing could not possess.

It is evident that the operation above described involves the action of the intellectual faculties, such as casualty, comparison, and will, necessitating volition, which are the prominent manifestations of mental action, and are precisely the same whether they exist in man or the lower animals. As all are similarly constructed, with nerves of sensation and volition, organs of sense and the two brains, and as all act exactly alike in similar circumstances of exposure, all are intellectual. Indeed, to call the same action instinct in the lower animals and intellect in man is to give the animals the pre-eminence, ranking them as gods, who are supposed to know without thinking, or ever having learned. Note also the fact that the faculty called instinct in the lower animals is equally the possession of the human infant. As the child becomes more intelligent, at what point does instinct cease and intellect begin?

Comparative Order of Mind.

As it is through the mind that physical peculiarities are transmitted to offspring, it follows that that species of animal possessing mind in the highest degree will present the greatest differences of physical feature; and as man is the animal thus distinguished, his offspring must be thus characterized; and facts bear ample testimony to the truth of the theory. Because various classes of animals have vertebral formations Mr. Darwin concludes that they therefore all had a single progenitor. Speaking of this he says: "The homological construction of the whole frame in the members of the same class is intelligible, if we admit the descent from a common progenitor." (Descent of Man, vol. i. p. 31.) On the same principle it might be argued that the moon was once a star, and that these again were the sun, because all are spherical and shine; but let us see if this similarity of structure is not intelligible on other grounds, and upon other principles. If twenty houses were built all upon the same architectural plan, would that prove them to have had a common progenitor, or that one man built them all?

There are certain fundamental principles of architecture common to every house—a foundation, roof, and walls. To leave any one of these out, whatever was made it would not be a house. If there were no foundation for walls there could be no walls; if there were no walls to support a roof, there could be no roof, and if there was no roof there could be no house. Without a roof it might be a walled yard, but that is all. To make a house, therefore, without all these would be as impossible as to make two hills without a hollow between. So every living animal that has power to move must be endowed with vital organs, organs of sense, brain, nerves, and instruments of locomotion. It is quite immaterial how widely animals may differ in shape, size, or color, or however peculiar may be their mode of motion—none could exist and lack one of these faculties, though in general construction they may differ as much even as a man and a lobster. For instance, can a being be made,without an eye and yet be able to see? Or can a thing of voluntary power be made without instruments of locomotion?

If intelligence cannot do this, can blind nature, not having the sense of an insect, make a thing without eyes and yet that can see? without faculties to move, and yet that can move? If not, could the power that brought living creatures into existence have proceeded upon any other principle of construction than that of endowing all varieties with such faculties? and if they perform the same functions would they not be substantially the same? In the philosophy of mechanics it is a well established axiom that the same result cannot be produced without the employment of substantially the same principle. In the construction of machines—say steam engines—one may be made to vary from another in so marked a manner that a novice might suppose another principle of construction was adopted; but let a keen-eyed mechanic inspect them and he would at once point out their substantial similarity.

We therefore conclude that the substantial organic similarity of structure and peculiarity of shape, size, color, etc., pertain to races and not to species, and demonstrate them to be in harmony with the law of unity and identity of species, each having a progenitor differing as much from each other as their offspring have differed in all generations. No matter who or what brought the originals into existence, he or it was compelled by philosophic necessity to construct all after a common model, a physiological and fundamental basis, and the preserved distinction of each species through successive generations demonstrates the existence of such distinction in the first progenitors.

In contradiction of this Mr. Darwin says, that because all animals are similarly constructed, at least the vertibrates, those which have a spinal column or backbone, as commonly called—as, for example, a man's hand and a bat's wing, or the backbone of a monkey and that of a man, therefore the hand of man came from the wing of a bat, and man was once a monkey. Indeed, he claims that everything of vegetable and animal kind evolved from a single living thing, thus flatly denying the well-known fact of universal experience, that different species will not reprodue another species by crossing. If Mr. Darwin had called the first progenitor God, and ascribed to Him the creation of the first progenitors of each species, their natural organic existence requires and proclaims—we say it with due respect for his ancestors —he would not so nearly have proved the legitimacy of his pedigree. Behold, how, by bold declamation, and in defiance of the best known principles of philosophy, he reverses the whole order of nature, by claiming that the less produces the greater ! Thus, a fish evolves a bird, a bird a bat, a bat a monkey, and a monkey a man. In a word, a living, moving universe came of itself, from inorganic, dead matter.

He argues by implication that if there was no similarity of construction manifested among animals, they might have had no common progenitor; in such a case God might have created them. He evidently supposed God to be a poor workman. If a monkey could have been made without brain, spinal column, nerves, eyes, ears, hands, or feet, then his theory might not be true, not seeming to see that such a creature of the imagination would have been no monkey at all. It would not even have been the simplest anamalcule, which can only be seen by the aid of the microscope, not a species of which is not endowed with as perfect organs as those possessed by the elephant. Indeed, according to the theory of evolution, the elephant's progenitors was one of these little creatures, a thousand of which have ample swimming room in a single drop of water. The argument in proof of this assumption is that these little animals, as well as the large ones, have backbone, joints, eyes, and instruments of locomotion.

The fact of similar construction proves simply this: that the Creator desired a variety of animals for different purposes, to answer which they must be made peculiar in form as well as in their vital, transmissible organization, so that these peculiarities might be inherited by their offspring, and yet so similar that the organs of life for one species would be the organs of life for all ; and the instruments of locomotion, to enable one species to go in quest of food, would be so substantially similar that they would serve the same purpose for all.

Does it any more prove, because all vertebrate animals have a similar structure, that all came from a single progenitor, than that because all animals have eyes they therefore had a common ancestor? There is much greater similarity in the structure of eyes than of backbones; besides, eyes are the universal possession of animals. It would therefore have been more consistant and plausible if Mr. Darwin had claimed that, because of the homological structure of eyes, all animals that can see evolved from a common progenitor; and to carry the argument to its legitimate conclusion as Tyndall and Huxley claim it should be carried, this progenitor with eyes evolved from one which was inorganic and had no eyes. The argument of similar structure proving descent from a single original stock, occupies a large portion of Mr. Darwin's two-volume "Descent of Man," and in view of this exposure, we ask whether it has the least foundation in science, philosophy, or is sustained by logic or truth?

Mr. Darwin's Shallow Reasoning.

In further efforts to establish his theory Mr. Darwin says: "No other explanation has ever been given of the marvelous fact that the embryo of a man, dog, seal, bat, reptile, etc., can at first hardly be distinguished from each other." We suppose the reason why no explanation has ever been given of this fact is to be found in the other fact, that no one ever assumed the ludicrous position that the eggs of all animals, whether of fish, flesh, or fowl, were homogeneous, or of the same nature, until Mr. Darwin thus distinguished himself. Everybody else seems to have understood that if they found an egg which seemed different from any other egg with which they were acquainted, or if appearing similar yet was found under peculiar circumstances, in order to know the nature of the possible animal within, it would be necessary to wait until it was hatched, or be informed by some one who knew what kind of an egg it was.

Because the egg of a turkey and of a goose resemble each other, are we to infer that the embryos they contain are not as dissimilar as the turkey and goose which may be hatched from them? Thus we have the argument of the "marvelous similarity of eggs, or embryos," and it is easy to see that it is marvelous only because it floats in Mr. Darwin's marvelous brain, very marvelously mixed up with similar wonders. It however furnishes another glimpse of the same science (falsely so-called) which is used in the attempt to disprove the identity of each species, and is arrayed equally against true science, true philosophy, and the facts of experience, as well as those of both profane and sacred history.

Mr. Darwin says (p. 31): "In order to understand the existence of rudimentary organs, we have only to suppose that a former progenitor possessed the parts in question in a perfect state, and that under changed habits of life they became greatly reduced, either from simple disuse, or through the natural selection of those individuals which were least encumbered with a superfluous part, aided by the other means previously indicated." In order to expose the false theories of these so-called naturalists it is only necessary to quote them against themselves and each other. It is claimed that because animals having no eyes have been found in caves where perpetual darkness reigned, their progenitors came into existence in these caves; and the caves being the result of modern convulsions, therefore they could not have been created according to the Mosaic genesis. Here is a chronological case made out. To sustain the argument of rudiments, however, this fact is used for an opposite purpose, and to teach quite another idea. Because perfect organs may be lost by disuse, it follows that the ancestors of the eyeless animals might have had good eyes, and therefore might have been created according to the Mosaic genesis.

It is easy to see from the manner in which Mr. Darwin states this argument that it not only furnishes no proof to sustain the theory of rudiments and of development, but that it points to degeneracy rather. To be used for his purpose, he should have stated it, and adduced facts to sustain it, thus : In order to understand the existence of rudimentary organs, you must suppose that a former progenitor did not have them, and therefore all his organs were perfect, or that he had no organs at all, and therefore did not live, and consequently could transmit nothing to offspring, and was therefore no progenitor at all. It is unquestionable that not only rudimentary organs, but those of full and perfect development, may be lost in the course of successive generations simply by disuse.

How the eyeless animals became such.

In order to account for the loss of eyes by certain animals, we must understand the natural law of adaptation. We suppose the progenitors of the eyeless animals when entering the dark caves had perfect eyes ; but amid perpetual darkness, they became useless, in consequence of which the next succeeding generation had weaker and smaller eyes, and the eyes of each succeeding generation became still more imperfect until at length there appeared those not only without eyes, but without the least rudiments of eyes. It is one of the best known laws of physiological science that use or exercise of any organ of sense, mind, or motion, if not carried beyond a certain point, increases both the size and vigor of that organ. We have no doubt that, if a number of generations should succeed each other of persons having no use for arms, or making no use of them, there would at length be born children without arms, or with the faintest rudiments of arms. Also that if in the succession of generations men should educate themselves and children into the belief that there was nothing in existence greater than themselves—and it is impossible to venerate a being or thing unless it is supposed to be superior—the faculty of veneration would not only degenerate, but become extinct, with not a rudiment remaining, leaving man a mere selfish savage.

It is surprising that Mr. Darwin sees in this principle of physical transmission evidence of the doctrine of evolution from the less to the greater—from rudiments to organs, and from no rudiments to rudiments; when in fact its whole operation is toward the degeneracy and loss of organs; it is transmutation and destruction. Let us suppose that by disuse or any other cause a generation of a species should lose any of its organs, would that deficiency change it into another species? If the organ lost was a vital one, the animal would soon cease to live at all, and therefore could not reproduce its kind or any other kind. Hence the argument precludes the possibility of another species coming into existence.

Thus we are forced to the conclusion that any vital change, such as one species must undergo while passing into another, implying functional modification, renders successive generations impossible. For instance, that organ in animal evolution which preceded lungs, ceasing to perform its function, whatever that was, the animal would immediately die; and if its function was breathing, then it was not a rudiment, but lungs, and perfect lungs—for it requires perfect lungs to breathe so as to continue animal existence—and if it was so rudimentary that it did not breathe, then the animal had no life, as animals cannot live without breathing; and, not being alive, it could evolve nothing. In the absence of all other proof, this argument is fatal to evolution.

In order to establish the doctrine of evolution it must be shown that by use or otherwise one species became possessed, not of rudiments (for with these it could not live, and if it did not live it could not have been a progenitor at all), but perfect organs, which no progenitor possessed. These must have been perfect in order to be vital and generative, both of which functions are incompatible with a single dead rudiment—as a heart which cannot perform its office in the circulation, a stomach which will not digest food, lungs which will not breathe. If they do not perform these functions they are rudiments, and as these were the rudimentary organs in the progenitor, no progeny ever came from the dead thing. On the other hand, if it was a progenitor it must have possessed all the vital organs in perfection, and therefore was a work of creation; for no evolutionist ever claimed that Dame Nature had the ability to bring into existence a perfect living animal at once, just as such are born of parentage. It must also be shown as a result of disuse, natural selection, or generative transmission, that a succeeding generation had become so far changed in its vital structure that it could not produce its own species; and having thus failed, how could it produce another? Instead of this, it would become extinct at death; for if such qualities allied themselves with any succeeding generation, they must have been involved in the original progenitor, as evolution implies prior involution: a thing cannot be taken out of another which does not possess it, at least in embryo.

If, therefore, there was but a single progenitor, as Mr. Darwin claims, which as we have seen was constitutionally incapable of evolving another species, then there never was but a single species. Each individual of a species might by circumstances be made to differ, in size, shape, and color, from every other, forming numerous races ; but as long as the variations did not affect the vital organization, disqualifying it for reproducing its kind, there would still exist but a single species ; and if the change did thus affect the vital organs, the result would have been that when that single species died, all would have become extinct, and evolution would have had to begin again, but with no better chances of success than before.

This, however absurd, is not the end of the absurdity ; for in the same passage Mr. Darwin reaches the conclusion that because animals lose perfect organs they acquire them by habit and natural selection. In the argument he assumes the untenable position that animals have superfluous organs otherwise than as monstrosities. For example, if eyes had become superfluous, because of being surrounded by total darkness, precluding the possibility of exercise, a generation would be born without eyes ; therefore the common progenitor of all species had no eyes itself ; but yet in the succession of generations transmitted good eyes to its offspring, because of being surrounded by light.

As this principle extends equally to all physical organs, therefore a generation succeeding another, and dwelling in noiseless solitude, would in time so physically degenerate that there would come one having no ears. This is a valuable hint to the deaf. If sound, by natural selection, will develop new and perfect ears, it certainly should repair defective hearing. Those afflicted with deafness, therefore, should go where there is plenty of thundering noise. We were about to say that Darwinism reverses all the physical laws of voluntary and involuntary transmission of organic qualities ; but in fact it does not go deep enough into the philosophy of the laws of nature to comprehend them : at any rate, if any of these self-styled naturalists have done so they have not given publicity to the discovery, which proves either that they wish to deceive or that the charge of superficiality is just.

The absurdity of "Natural Selection."

As the loss of organs is the result of disuse and distaste, it follows that the gaining of new ones is by exercise and taste. Taste exists upon one of two conditions : First, seeing something in the possession of another which the beholder covets ; or, secondly, by conceiving something which does not exist, but which we would desire to possess. In regard to the first, we remark that it presupposes the existence of some physical peculiarity which the original progenitor desired to possess, and which, if the desire existed at all, could have had no effect upon it, as there were no animals but itself in existence ; it was therefore confined to the necessity of transmitting its exact likeness to its offspring. As this similarity must be perpetual, therefore natural selection could never have had a starting-point, even though the original progenitor existed. And this is the fundamental principle upon which all the varieties of animals and their peculiarities have come into existence !

But suppose a start were made, according to the theory of natural selection, from a number of animals, of the same species, then its practical operation would be as follows : A monkey sees another with a shorter tail than his own, and falls in love with him on this account, though he has often felt the necessity of having a longer one whereby he might clamber more safely among the branches of the trees, coiling it round which he could reach or swing further out in gathering his food. What a foolish monkey, to indulge such a desire! And this is one of our nearest relations, about which Darwin so gravely discourses! But suppose the monkey should see another who by some accident had lost his tail altogether, and should fall in love with him. According to the theory of natural selection, the offspring of the tailless monkey would be born without tails, provided the male had succeeded in convincing his female companion of the superiority of tailless monkeys, which, we may easily imagine, would require a very ingenious discourse on the beauty of short tails, or rather of no tails. His mate might object on practical grounds.

Would they not be much more liable to fall from trees, and be compelled to cling closely to the trunk or large limbs, while the food they desired was far out on the branches, which their long-tailed brothers could safely reach. Would not the lady monkey have the best of the argument?

Is it any more likely that monkeys should desire their offspring to be born monsters—as they would be without tails—than that human parents should desire theirs to be born without eyes? But whatever modifications might have been effected and transmitted by taste, they were limited absolutely to those organs coming within observation, and in no case or degree could have affected the involuntary vital organs. To modify these by evolution and natural selection would require the monkey to understand the shape and function of lungs, for example, which did not exist, and that her offspring should be born with rudiments of lungs—for perfect lungs to come in a single generation would be creation—and if thus gratified they would be born dead, as rudimentary lungs cannot breathe.

Let us illustrate this idea by the animal without eyes.

We have already referred to the fact that exercise enlarges and increases the vigor of any organ of the animal system; but here is one that has no organs or eyes to exercise, and how can the animal begin the operation? Suppose, further, that the animal had embryonic or rudimentary eyes, with which, of course, it could not see; how could it exercise these when seeing is the only exercise of which the eyes are capable? Such exercise, being voluntary, could only be induced by motive, which could only arise from an appreciation of light and color, and this appreciation can only result from observation which it never enjoyed. Hence, as the original progenitor had no eyes, though it might have had rudiments, it could never have acquired them by exercise, nor by natural selection, as the one implies the other, though it had millions of centuries and as many generations for the operation, and that simply because it implies natural impossibility. As another example take the man we have supposed without arms, whose condition must once have been that of the original progenitor, and how was it possible for him to obtain arms by the exercise of no arms, not even rudiments of arms?

Mr. Darwin prophesies that all will be evolutionists.

In behalf of such an absurdity Mr. Darwin has the hardihood to conclude : " We can understand how it came to pass that man and all other vertebrate animals have been constructed on the same general model, why they pass through the same early stages of development, and why they contain rudiments in common, consequently we ought frankly to admit their community of descent. To take any other view is to admit that our own structure, and that of all animals around us, is a mere snare laid to entrap our judgment; but the time will come before long when it will be thought wonderful that naturalists, who were well acquainted with the comparative structure and development of men and animals, should have believed that each was the work of a separate creation." That is to say the time will soon come when all naturalists will renounce belief in the Bible, especially that part which declares that God created, by an especial act, the original progenitors of each species, and endowed them with the faculty of reproducing their kind. This is to reject equally the whole Bible and the Christian religion. In fact, there is no worship compatible with Darwinism, as it denies the existence of anything superior to man himself; for worship is only conceivable upon the concession of a superior being.

But we have the same right to prophesy that Darwin has; and we venture the prediction that those who will know and do know the most about the teachings of the Bible will and do know most about the science and philosophy of nature : who have already found the one to be the complement of the other. Indeed, the statements contained in the Bible concerning the phenomena of nature have always been and are to-day vastly in advance of scientific discovery, and the book of Genesis especially contains the only true account of the manner in which the world came into existence. We also predict that Mr. Darwin's children, if he has any, will degenerate into monkeys in that same indefinite period, wherein will be realized the fulfillment of his prophecy.

It may with propriety be asked, Why has not the genius of evolution developed beautiful mansions for the accommodation and comfort of man, beginning with the rudimentary caves as their inorganic types? Surely this is not so difficult a task as to have evolved the man himself, or the great globe as his dwelling-place, only on a larger scale. It may be replied that this work was purposely left for man himself, in order to develop his physical faculties. *Wonderful sagacity! inanimate nature capable of elaborating abstract ideas!* We know of no reason why everything of life or motion, voluntary or involuntary, animate or inanimate, connected with our world, which either directly or indirectly work out results, should not be considered *machines*, among which may be mentioned the solar system, the earth, gravity, the atmosphere, electricity, heat, light, water, clouds, every plant and every animal. The fact which gives them this character is that each works out some definite purpose; yet in truth they are only secondary causes, in other words effects of a Great First Cause.

There are certain facts and principles connected with the existence of all machines, the most prominent of which are as follows: Every machine must have had a maker, as no machine could have made itself, much less its superior; everything producing a certain effect was constructed by intelligence and design. Whether the agents working out these results are secondary causes, or effects of effects, or the only cause, merely proves their organizations to be more or less complicated: the more direct the simpler. The smallest atom endowed with polarity and chemical affinity is as much a machine as a plant formed of an aggregation of atoms; only the plant performs a more important purpose in the universe. These truisms concerning some of the phenomena of nature simply indicate those grand divisions known and classified as the mental and physical sciences.

Nature cannot be Arrayed against Herself.

That any of the natural sciences should antagonize another, or should draw its conclusions without reference to or by ignoring any other—as geology does by declaring it has nothing to do with the origin of things, or any theory of cosmogony, which involves the foundation of all science, viz: mind—its source—shows a superficiality of investigation, a narrowness of view, and a bigotry of spirit, which could otherwise hardly be conceived. History might as well say she had nothing to do with dates or events, astronomy with calculations, chemistry with affinities, or physiology with bones. The steam-engine, if asked whence its origin, might as well answer, I came, or, I evolved, and the answer would be just as satisfactory. If the hypothesis of evolution is true, is it obligatory on its advocates to show where the independent link in the chain of being lies?

Man, it is said, drew upon the monkey for his existence, the monkey upon the reptile, the reptile upon the fish, the fish upon the bird, the bird upon the plant, and the plant reaches down, not only to the very simplest thing that grows, but to the gelatinous, homogeneous, or nebulous matter, as it is variously designated. But to the inquiry, From what did this lowest thing spring? geologists virtually answer, While we are absorbingly interested in the most minute form and peculiar construction of every other link, and all about how it came to be possessed of the nicest shade of organic difference, yet as to how the second link came to be connected with the first, we have nothing whatever to do. Indeed, we only use the comprehensive phrase, "Primordial form," as a screen, supposing it will have the effect of preventing the embarrassing question being pressed as to how it came to exist. Just as the evolutionists had become thus securely settled down, and seemed by the use of this sophistical answer to be relieved from further molestation upon this vexed point, out comes Professor

Tyndall with the cry, "Whence came the primordial form?" As the question has elicited no reply, either from Darwin, the reputed father of the theory of organic evolution, or from Lyell, the father of inorganic evolution, we must still hold their school responsible for its arrogance in pretending to have no interest in the search after the First Link in the chain, which interdepending Nature, her adjustable uniformity, and finished workmanship, declare to be the Living God, the creator of all things, whose wonderful skill and power are as clearly manifested in the formation of the smallest animalcule that swims in the drop of bog-water as in the most gigantic living creature. Indeed, perhaps the former excites our just admiration in a greater degree ; for when we examine, by the aid of the microscope, an object which is so small and delicate that the unassisted eye cannot discern it, and which the point of the finest needle would destroy in an instant, and yet find it perfectly beautiful in all its organic parts and functions, our wonder is increased until the mind is filled with astonishment.

It is here that the science of mind as an integral part of nature comes to our assistance, and if our conceits are not too groveling to comprehend it, it will reveal to us half of nature's secrets. Indeed, all the beautiful arrangements and adjustments of the world, whether of nature or art, reflect the skill of the minds whence they have emanated, from God downward. To him who ignores this science, nature will forever remain an impenetrable mystery.

How preposterous the notion that the grosser things of the world should rise in rebellion against the mind that made them ! Better might geological evolution deny the existence of its inventors. As well might every link in the interdepending chain of being protest against the existence of the next higher, as the second against the first; or as well might one of those marvelously organized animacules—supposing it to be the first link —declare that it made itself, or that it evolved, or what is worse, that it should manifest its ingratitude by declaring that it had no interest in its father—indeed, that it never had any father. Such sentiments might be pardoned in the insect, but the utterance of such absurdity by a man would make him a fit companion of those from whom he confesses his ancestors sprung—the monkey. It is claimed by the advocates of evolution that the finding anywhere on the surface of the earth of a piece of flint suitable to be fixed into a split stick, as the handle of an ax, is as certain evidence of the prior existence of man in such locality as though his footprints had been discovered in the sand. This claim is founded on the fact that the construction of the ax exhibits intelligence, and not evolution; but why not attribute its peculiar shape to the genius of evolution, rather than to the skill of art? It surely would be more reasonable to conclude that the ax itself, with its piece of sharp flint projecting from one side, near the end, evolved from one a little more crude and a shade less resembling a work of art, than that man himself evolved from a thing which did not possess even his embryo.

 Let us suppose that a hundred of these axes were found in the same locality, and that the structure of each varied in such nice shades and degrees that any two of them nearest each other could not be distinguished, and yet that the two most unlike bore no more resemblance to each other than a man does to a lobster; why, then, might not the simplest ax be considered a mere work of nature, the handle itself having gradually turned to stone? Now the whole ax is stone, but still retains something of the form of the most perfect implement.

In order to account for the extreme difference which these axes exhibit, one of two conclusions is inevitable —either, that a man made each of them, one after the other, or that he made the first and rudest, and endowed it with the faculty of producing and reproducing from itself the other ninety-nine. If the latter, was not the making of every ax as much the direct act of the workman, who involved all in the first, as though he had made each separately, the succeeding ones being evolved by the necessities of its own mechanical structure? And does not its organization display infinitely more ingenuity in its adaptation to its purposes than though the artificer had made each ax separately, without this power of propagation.

Man one of God's Machines.

Upon this principle, the first man was one of God's machines, whom He made from the dust of the earth, and in that act involved in his structure all the beings susceptible of evolving from him. Now, was not each of these as much an act of direct creation as the first man himself,—in fact, an organic part of the first? And how much greater skill and wisdom were thus displayed than though each man had been made separate. In fact, the skill manifested is in proportion to the endowment of each with the power to produce offspring; if the progeny are the exact fac-simile of their parents, the mechanical structure is proportionally simpler than though it evolved superior offspring. Thus we reach the conclusion that the most perfect organisms existed first; even if all evolved from a single one primordial form, that form was the most perfect of all, and each succeeding generation has been growing simpler and simpler, and man, the last, is the simplest of all. The hypothesis of Darwin is thus demonstrated to be erroneous.

As the same facts and principles are applicable to inanimate objects, why have there not, in the ample time which has elapsed since man appeared upon earth, been evolved beautiful dwellings for his comfort, and everything else essential to his highest development and civilization? It is no answer to say that houses not being organized according to the laws of vegetable or animal life, do not produce offspring, and therefore cannot modify them: for this was the condition of all nature before the primordial form was evolved. If, therefore, inanimate and inorganic matter was considerate enough to evolve such a being as man, incorporating in him certain needs and desires, why should it not have evolved the simpler things to meet those needs, especially dwellings for his shelter and comfort?

Here, however, common sense, reason, science, and philosophy are rudely set at naught by the assumption of the arrogant position, that though the finding of the ax or flint hatchet demonstrates the prior existence of man, and that he was the artificer of the hatchet, yet the existence of man himself, the grandest embodiment of artistic skill of all, is no evidence of the prior existence of an intelligent Being as his architect and maker, who must have been as much superior in skill to plan and in power to execute, as manifested in the man he made, as the man was superior to the ax or dwelling, the work of his art. The philosophic necessities in these cases demonstrate that the Being who made the man was as abstract from the man made, as the man was separate from the hatchet and dwelling he made.

This assumption of the evolutionists reverses another fundamental principle of both nature and art—namely, that the order of mind is revealed by what it produces. If a work bears the stamp of the simplest character, the mind that made it was of the simplest endowment. As the house of a beaver manifests the degree of intelligence of the beaver, so also the architectural skill involved in the construction of a work of art reveals the greatness of the intellect that conceived and the skill that executed the work, and as a consequence demonstrates the prior existence of the beaver and man. So also with the universe: the construction and interdependence of all the members of the solar system, presenting a vast and complicated mechanism, equally reveal the independent, prior existence of its Creator, possessing powers of conception and execution equal to those displayed in its works. But the silly hypothesis of evolution makes the house of the beaver bring the beaver himself into existence—the mansion evolve its maker—and, to carry the argument to its legitimate conclusion, it makes the unknowing world produce the knowing Being who made it.

Tyndall's admiration for his Ancestral Matter.

It is admitted that there is a vast break in the chain between men and monkeys; but the break, it is said, is only apparent, as the connecting links have not yet been discovered, which only implies further investigation. Prof. Tyndall, however, throwing off all disguise, plants himself squarely and frankly on the assumption, not only that one organic (which means living) being evolved another, from the lowest up to man (as the limit of Darwinism), but that inanimate, inorganic matter, simpler in form than any which now exists, had the faculty of uniting and forming living beings. Says he: "I discern in that matter which we in our ignorance have hitherto covered with opprobrium, the promise, potency, form and quality of life." It is easy to see that the Professor's reverence has undergone a complete metamorphosis —from God to the discernment in dead matter of a god susceptible of being thus disgraced. This, however, is only another illustration of the universal tendency of mankind to worship something. In the case of this scientist we see reverence paid to poor abused matter, the god of energy, potency and wisdom that made him. This puts us in mind of a people who once made a golden calf and sung to it, "These be thy gods, who brought us up out of the land of Egypt."

With such an object of groveling admiration before the mind, how is the life of himself and of the rest of mankind to be lifted to a higher level, which Tyndall declares is to be accomplished by the new science of evolution? He is also seconded by Prof. Huxley. We have the right, therefore, to interpret the theory of evolution as comprehending the production of inanimate as well as animate things, without the existence of any primordial. If the works of art have evolved from the brain and the mechanic powers of man, and man himself from an inorganic thing, or simple particles of matter, comprehending in the original all the powers and susceptibilities of his nature, does it not follow that things which have no life are equally the subjects of evolution? First, the living man evolved from dead matter, and secondly, from him evolved dead things, called works of art, as well as living beings like himself. In this work of reproduction is there not displayed contrivance of infinitely greater intelligence than though the hills, mountains, and plains were so constructed that they would produce, without seed or germ, men, implements of manufacture and dwellings of the most perfect kind, all in complete maturity, but too simple to reproduce others?

For instance, would it not require less mechanical skill and power to make a locomotive engine, simply capable of doing its ordinary work, than to so construct it that when once set in motion it would make and turn out other locomotives, more beautiful, powerful, and perfect than itself, as the theory of evolution requires? Beholding the display of such a wonderful machine, what must be the mental caliber of the man who should deny that the original locomotive was made by a skilled mechanic? Does not the merest novice in the study of the mechanism of nature know that every species of vegetable and animal kind, from the lowest to the highest, including man, is endowed with this mechanic power of reproduction? and does not the fact demonstrate all this knowledge and power to have been the exclusive possession of the Being who constituted the organizations of the globe, just as it demonstrates the fact that the mechanic who made the first locomotive made at the same time all its capabilities, including every form and degree of power and susceptibility? And is there not infinitely greater mechanic skill displayed in the construction of the simplest plant of the field than in the most beautiful and perfect device ever projected and made by man?

The common experience of mankind is that if a stupendous work of art or intellectual achievement is required, we do not look for help to the minute insect, but seek for it in the greatest artistic skill and the highest intelligence, with capacity adequate to the task ; but evolutionists reverse all this and recommend us to go to the insect, as the best qualified for the work, as the greater comes from the less. In the absence of all other proof, such transcendent folly seems sufficient to brand its ostentatious pretensions as the mere dreams of the wildest speculations, alike incongruous, and repugnant to the clearest deductions of reason and philosophical science.

CHAPTER XIV.

DETERIORATION, NOT PROGRESS, THE ORDER OF NATURE.

A MAN is an intellectual, moral, physical, and religious being, and as all these departments are interdependent, it follows that permanent progress implies an equal development, and therefore an equal cultivation, and that an excessive cultivation of any one of these endowments must be accomplished at the expense of the rest. If the constitution of man were so balanced that he would be disposed to cultivate equally each of his faculties, and if the circumstances of social and civil life were also favorable, then the order of nature might be that of progress. But when the exigencies of life demand so much time for obtaining mere animal sustenance, there is little left for other purposes; therefore, the facts and environments render man a victim of deterioration.

Bearing these facts in mind we remark that, no matter how wise any man or generation may be, if each succeeding one manifests increasing physical weakness, it presents a condition of things incompatible with increased wisdom or morality. Hence if such are the facts at the present time, the human species are marching toward extinction instead of progressive development, and any seeming progress may be real degeneracy. For example, if the intellect of a generation is developed at the expense of physical vigor, increasing weakness is entailed, and a predisposition to disease which renders it less able to sustain the same amount of mental application. Were it a fact that mankind progressed, then there would come a generation among whom sickness and disease would be unknown—one whose intellectual attainments would be so great, and all the laws of health and life be so fully understood, that there would be no ignorant violations ; and an equal degree of moral and religious advancement would forbid the commission of crime against body, mind, or Maker. No matter how slow the progress such a generation must come, and each one manifest its degree of the advancement.

The longevity of such a generation would be counted by hundreds instead of tens of years. As inconsistent with progress, we may refer to the fact that diseases increase in each succeeding generation, and of course physicians multiply in the same ratio. This is especially true of the last few generations, and they are virulent and fatal in proportion to the extent of the derangement; from which it follows that new diseases, or more virulent phases of old ones, indicate new phases of prior organic derangement. If these are in the air, it argues new phases of atmospheric disorder, which demonstrates, in the absence of all other proof, the final extinction of man.

Cavendish devoted an immense amount of time to the study and analysis of the atmosphere, making no less than five hundred experiments. He came to the conclusion that the composition of the air was constant, and subject to no variations, going to show that all attempts to determine the quality of the air by chemical analysis in order to detect impurities were futile. Later experiments have developed unexpected results, but only to the effect that impurities in the air depend upon so small quantities or variations of its constituents that they were overlooked by earlier investigators, owing perhaps to the imperfection of their methods and instruments. This variation for a long time was considered of little or no significance. These later refined processes, including hundreds of analyses—made of air of the same locality by day and by night, in all weathers and at all seasons of the year, on the earth's surface, and on the tops of mountains, at different altitudes by balloon ascensions, and upon land and ocean—shows a spirit of investigation which has led men to devote years of labor to the solution of the problem. The result shows that though the variations of the constituents of the air are important, yet they are so minute that the difference must be represented not even by hundredths, but thousandths, even hundred thousandths.

The following is an extract from a recent work by Dr. Angus Smith, an English chemist: "Some people will probably inquire why we should give so much attention to such minute quantities of oxygen as one hundred and ninety in a million. In a gallon of water there are 70,000 grains. Let us put into it an impurity at the rate of 190 in a million, and it amounts to 13½ grains in the gallon. This amount would be considered enormous if it consisted in putrefying organic matter, or any organic matter usually found in water. But we drink comparatively a small quantity of water, and the whole thirteen grains would not be swallowed in a day, whereas we take into our lungs from 1,000 to 2,000 gallons of air daily."

Diseased air and Mental Impression.

There is perhaps no terror incident to the present life of so fearful portent as that which locates disease in the air. If poison is in a certain kind of meat we may refrain from eating it. If contagion is apprehended from too close vicinity of the diseased, we may preserve a healthful distance. From miasmatic localities we may remove to more salubrious ones; but if impurity floats in the air which we must inhale or die, or perhaps die if we do inhale, the most appalling fact possible of contemplation is presented. In the great plagues of the world it has been alleged that the infection was in the air. Observers of the course of the Asiatic cholera have uniformly agreed that the disease was carried in the air from one country to another. Not only has this theory prevailed as to the march of epidemics, but the belief in the prevalence of bad air in large towns in warm weather is so extensive that every summer the cities are thinned out, and the rush to the sea-side and mountains has become an almost universal mania.

It must however be confessed that very much of the evil effects of what is supposed to be impure air results from mere mental impression, otherwise the imagination. Groundless fears derange and depress the vital forces through the organs which the mind controls. Danger is thus shifted from the deadly air to the equally, if not more, fatal influence of a terrified mind, which augments rather than mitigates the evil. This power of physical derangement often produces death even in the absence of all other causes. There are so many facts illustrative of this power (the philosophy and physiology of which we have considered elsewhere) of deranging every vital function of the human system attended by fatal consequences that we might fill volumes with their records; but the following examples must suffice for the purpose.

The St. Petersburg *Medical Journal* published the following account of an experiment tried in that city when it was first visited by cholera: "Three convicts who had been condemned to suffer death were given beds to sleep on for one night, upon which persons had just died of Asiatic cholera, without the beds being cleaned, and without their knowledge of the fact. After a sufficient time had elapsed for the disease to have manifested itself, if taken, and finding they had not been in the least affected, they were then told they were to sleep in beds on which persons had just died of cholera, when in fact the beds were new and were furnished for the experiment. The result, however, was that all three took the disease, two of whom died in twenty-four hours, and the third barely survived."

We may relate a fact of our own experience, to show that even a consciousness that evil effects are being produced by the power of mental impression is no protection. The last time the cholera visited this country (1849) the disease for a few days was very fatal in the city of New York. On one of those days we were in the city, and were given a room for the night on the fifth story of a hotel. Retiring at an early hour, I rested the first part of the night as well as usual, but was aroused from sleep by troublous dreams about cholera. The question came with overwhelming force, Suppose I should be attacked now with the disease? Every attempt was made to banish the thought, but in spite of all efforts, like Banquo's ghost, it would not down. Here are no friends to administer to me, and the disease demands immediate attention; I might even die here before morning, and among total strangers. I made desperate efforts to reject every suggestion with which I was haunted as if with so many malignant specters. It was now about midnight. Soon I not only had other symptoms of the disease, but was seized with the violent cramps accompanying cholera. I rose and dressed, and hoping to divert my attention from the dreadful subject, took the paper of that day's issue and sat down to read, all this time being perfectly conscious that the trouble was wholly the result of mental impression. But this knowledge only increased the agony both of mind and body;

besides the paper seemed to contain nothing but accounts of the ravages of the cholera. Casting it down almost in despair, the question returned with redoubled force, What must be done? I had with me no medicine of any kind, and nothing within reach except brandy, in which I had long since lost confidence as a remedy even in such cases. At about three o'clock in the morning came from some good source what proved to be a life-saving thought to me: If brandy will not cure your body, it will lock up your thoughts if you take enough of it. This was just what I wanted. Down into the bar-room I went, roused up the barkeeper, and drank nearly a tumblerful of brandy. I went back to bed as courageous as a hero, and in a few minutes had lost all realization of the situation, and did not awake until about eight o'clock in the morning, as well as ever, with the exception of a headache from the effects of the brandy.

We may also mention the following experiment, but have forgotten the authority: "A criminal condemned to die accepted bleeding as the manner of death. He was laid upon a dissecting table, his arm bared and pricked, and, as he supposed, a vein opened, but he lay in such a position that he could not see the arm. At the same moment a stream of water which he could hear, but not see, was set running from a vessel. The result was, the man grew pale and weak, and died in just as short a space of time as though the running water were his own blood, when in fact not a drop of blood had been taken from his veins."

As a general illustration of this power of physical derangement, let us suppose that on the first appearance of typhoid fever the whole medical profession had agreed in pronouncing it incurable, giving publicity to the decision, and describing the symptoms in the most minute details, adding that no person feeling any of these need look for medical aid, as the physicians themselvse would immediately take the disease ; besides, that they knew of no method of relief. Suppose, further, that the infection was declared to be in the common air, and was everywhere diffused. Who does not know that such a report, though false in every particular, would produce one of the most malignant and extensive plagues that ever scourged the human family. It is therefore from considerations of prudence that all honest physicians discountenance the belief that the germs of disease float in the air, and they do so often against their own convictions. They do so also in order to counteract impressions of fatal diseases in the minds of their patients.

If then it be a fact that the most extreme physical derangements are produced by psychological power, set in motion by mere mental impression and fixed upon the vital organs, may not any of the ordinary diseases thus originate ? Another cause of physical deterioration is mental excitement (which is but another phase of the same philosophy), and each succeeding generation seems more susceptible to its influence, whose inevitable result is the exhaustion of the nervous forces, which are of course transmitted, rendering the system less and less able to sustain the increased strain. This weakness predisposes to disease, as well as renders diseases more virulent and difficult to cure when taken. Some of the most marked results of the increased nervous excitement in our age are as follows: Almost universal neuralgia; a vast increase in the number of cases of what is popularly known as softening of the brain; a corresponding increase in deaths from apoplexy. Continuous strain upon the cerebrum, the source of the voluntary nerves, creates feverish excitement and prostration, when suddenly an unlooked-for and embarrassing event is sprung upon the already overtaxed brain. The brain being unable now to expel the circulating fluids governed by its electric forces, thus deranged and called to the seat of reason and to the anterior brain, the seat of vitality, instantly the man falls paralyzed in death.

There is also in the present generation a vastly increased liability to heart disease. It is well known that the circulation of the blood is materially accelerated by mental excitement. Whether we consider the heart as merely the regulator of the circulation or the motive power, its mechanism is not susceptible of enduring the shocks of a violent and sudden rush of blood through its delicate valves, adapted only to ordinary circulation, which therefore interferes with its healthy action and compels irregular motion. Hence any mental excitement, causing the blood to suddenly rush to the brain and as violently through the heart, creates disease, or weakness, which is its predisposition, and the course of the disease will be rapid in proportion as such shocks are numerous and violent, until at last, on the least extraordinary exertion of the body or excitement of the mind, the heart gives way, and in an instant the man falls dead. The suddenness of death may possibly result from the neutralization of the arterial or positive blood and the venous or negative blood around the heart.

To the above causes of human deterioration may be added insanity. That this disease may be transmitted to offspring is a fact too well known to need proof here. Instead, however, of its becoming less frequent and violent, which human progress would seem to require, the fact that increased brain strain in any age causes an equal increase of excitement demonstrates that the cases of insanity must also increase, and in the same ratio; each new case where ancestors were not thus affected forms a new center from which to send out its seed of deterioration and death. Consumption is another fearfully devastating scourge of the human species, and no one will question the fact that it is transmitted from family to family, from generation to generation, in continually widening streams of desolation; every new case in a family, like that of insanity, furnishes a new radius of death. It is within the memory of the oldest of our generation that the first cases of what is called quick consumption were known; prior to this the duration of the disease was nominally seven years.

Scrofula is another disease more extensively developed at the present than at any former period. Its virus is unquestionably inherited. Of course it is not fatal in so short a time as consumption; but it spreads over the whole system, affecting every vital organ, but locating generally on the weakest, simply because it is the weakest. Hence, it is like a cold, susceptible of inducing almost every disease; and for the same reasons that other hereditary diseases become more numerous and virulent, so must this. We are thus presented with a fearful picture of "The court of death"—and who will say it is in the least overdrawn?—which furnishes an unanswerable argument in proof of the deterioration instead of the progressive development of mankind.

What is meant by the inheritance or transmission of disease is not that because the parent has consumption, for instance, his children will be born with that disease, or because the brain of the parent is affected that his children will be born insane; but that the lungs or brain in the offspring will be comparatively weaker, giving a greater predisposition to disease. It follows also that the diseased branches of descent increase in the ratio that the children are more numerous than the parents.

Hence, those afflicted with organic diseases—and all diseases are organic—must transmit to their offspring corresponding weakness and liability to disease, no matter what their name or nature, rendering each successive generation less able to resist similar attacks.

The saying is no more proverbial than true, that " Every generation grows weaker and wiser." This, then, is our subject, with the limitation as to the increased wisdom in our day, which we will presently consider. Successful mental effort implies a vigorous brain, and a vigorous brain means a sound nervous system. From which it follows that a diseased nervous system hinders the increase of knowledge ; and if this is true of individuals, it must be also true of generations which are made up of individuals. And a generation has for its weakness no escape, no remedy. The conclusion therefore is that there will come a generation the true description of which will require the proverb to be amended, thus : " Every generation grows physically weaker and therefore mentally weaker." Indeed, it seems to us that we have already reached the generation in which general and substantial knowledge is on the rapid decrease. Question our business men in regard to solid reading, sound thought, or substantial mental acquirements, and the large proportion will frankly admit that they have no time for them ; that their business makes such demands upon their attention that they can only read the newspapers or some light literature. What is true of them is true in a greater degree of the wives and daughters, especially in regard to light literature. In corroboration of this statement we have only to refer to the demand for and spread of this style of reading at the present day.

In view of such a state of facts we ask if we have not

already reached the generation to which the amended proverb will forcibly apply? It is within our remembrance that the subjects of lyceum lectures were of a scientific, philosophic, or historical character. Now they generally consist of the biography of popular novelists, discussion of courtships, theatrical readings, "peculiar people," etc.—something to please the fancy for the moment; but nothing to tax the mind, leaving it to starve for the want of food, or overtax it with excitement.

Among other causes which tend to degenerate the civilized nations of the world, especially our own, we may mention the fact that there are vast numbers of people who do not marry young, if at all. On the part of the males this in a great measure is owing to the expense of a family being beyond their means. Of course the same reason prevails largely with a corresponding class of females: they demand husbands who can support them according to the expensive style of the day, and are not willing, like their mothers, and much more their grandmothers, to make the necessary sacrifices and perform the requisite labor, in common with their husbands, to obtain a start in the world.

On the other hand the laboring classes, often with small and uncertain wages, marry and take the chances, and many of them far outstrip the others in the acquisition of a competency, and even wealth. But among this class are principally the ignorant and vicious, with large families, the children naturally imitating the vices instead of the virtues of their parents, thus reversing the doctrine of development by natural selection.

Another matter connected with this subject, and one for serious consideration—one we mention with reluctance—is implied in the question of how to avoid the expense of bringing up children. We allude to the practice of embryonic infanticide, whereby the offspring of those who should live to improve the generation in morals, intellect, and religion, is reduced to the very smallest number consistent with living according to the esteemed respectable standard. Another fact closely connected with this matter is that this class of mothers are physically feeble, and therefore predisposed to disease, principally through the want of bodily exercise or muscular labor which is essential to physical development. The servant-girls have sound bodies as the result and reward of housework, the natural vocation of woman. According to the law of transmission, the children of modern ladies are endowed with large brains, giving the impulse to intense mental and moral activities, but with enervated physical systems, too weak to sustain their indulgences, or to prolong life to man's allotted period of "three-score years and ten."

This retrogressive tendency might be remedied in the course of several generations by the well-directed energies of the children of those who had been servants, were it not that they are generally born in poverty, where deprivations and surrounding bad examples render them vicious and therefore weaker and sicklier than the other class; and being compelled to labor at an early age, they do not improve mentally. There is one other class to which we must refer in order to complete the picture—namely, the sons of the rich. A large number of these come to mature age without a feeling of responsibility, when generally it is too late to learn the lesson. They are spendthrifts and often dissipated, in consequence of which, they die early. Others are interested in nothing but making money. They can talk fluently about money, if about nothing else. Indeed, to be a successful money-maker, especially in this age, whose standard of riches is among the millions, constant study and unflagging devotion are demanded, no time being left for the physical labor necessary to counteract the enormous strain upon the mind. Consequently from this class come the victims of heart disease, paralysis, and apoplexy, and when important financial reverses occur, the suicides. We do not point to these evils which deteriorate mankind as peculiar to our age ; but as they are now increasingly prevalent and aggravating, it is impossible to avoid the conclusion that they palpably reverse the theory of the evolutionists and of all others who expect the coming of a better generation of mankind upon earth.

There are various other causes which obstruct the progress of mankind ; which have destroyed the civilizations of the past, and are reaching fearful proportions in most of the civilized countries at the present day. The most prominent among these, and the one which we propose briefly to consider, is that which relates to the demand and supply of food ; upon which we introduce the following extract from the writings of E. D Mansfield, the great economist : " Malthus long since stated that population was limited by food, and hence that marriages must diminish where food is scarce. This proposition startled many persons, who seemed to think it was in some degree in opposition to the law of God, that people should be multiplied and society built up.

" They forgot that each law of God is consistent with every other law, and that while the earth may have capacity to feed innumerable millions, it may not have capacity when there is a concentration of population in small districts, while a very large part of the earth remains uncultivated. In a word, can half of mankind be *non-producers* in cities and towns without elementary decay ? To build up vast cities and fill them with monuments of art and luxury which we call civilization ; and justly, because the word is derived from *civis*, city.

"The question is whether civilization is not self-destructive? Is it not in fact one of the real causes of the destruction of nations; and as long as civilized nations hold ideas they now hold on the nature of civilization, must not the life of nations be limited, and our most civilized nations decay and perish, as did the great nations of antiquity? [If the most civilized of generations perish, as the history of the world shows they have done, must they not have degenerated first, or sickened before death? If such is the fate of the most enlightened, what must be the fate of the lower classes?] This is a question of the greatest importance to society, religion, and philosophy. It is not one which concerns Europe, China, or India, and at some future period, but it is a question which at this very moment is pressing upon us in the United States, young as we are.

"Apparently the economists of this country have not begun to think that if the non-producers continue to gain on the producers as rapidly as at present, notwithstanding all the aid of agricultural machinery, (and it is already immense, and which has itself resulted from the great demand for food, on the principle that necessity is the mother of invention) there will come a time, by mathematical ratios, when population must press against the limits of food, and by necessity population must diminish.

"You say, 'No matter: that will be beyond our time —ages hence.' Perhaps so. But you may be startled to find that in some places it is upon you now. There are evident signs of an approaching crisis of some sort, though we cannot tell exactly what shape it will take. . . . Look at the condition and at some facts of the United States and other countries. The city of London is now importing its food from Russia and America, hundreds and thousands of miles off. Is there not danger of one of those 'providential accidents,' as we may call them, occurring, when the supplies of London will be cut off for a time? and may it not occur at any time? Look at Ireland, which in three years lost two millions of people! that was not very long ago. You may say that Ireland depended upon potatoes alone. So

London is depending upon Russia and America for food. There are evident signs of a pressure for food in the great cities; and although the multitudes may be asleep on the subject, yet it will be well for thoughtful minds to consider it. When we find beefsteak 15 cents a pound in Cincinnati, 25 cents in New York, and 30 cents in London, where it was not half that forty years ago, it calls for investigation, if not for wonder.

An approaching Crisis.

"In New York and Cincinnati there is a rise of 100 per cent. in the price of meats in one generation (thirty years). It is evident enough that the next generation cannot stand a similar rise. But this is only one and a small sign of the *great food trouble*. We find, notwithstanding the working-men have far higher wages both in Europe and America than ever they had before, yet they complain, and combine for higher wages, and the whole body are in fermentation, and we cannot but see that there is something wrong in the relation of food and labor. If food has been relatively scarce, then just such effects as we see here will be produced—higher prices of food and discontented workmen—which is simply cause and effect. The business of philosophers is to discern the reason why the phenomena exist. To me the cause seems very evident; but I do not so clearly see the remedy."

The writer then gives a table showing that the population of the three central States, New York, Pennsylvania, and Ohio, increased in the cities and towns sevenfold in comparison with the increase in the rural or producing districts in the same time, and continues: "Now it is impossible to continue this relative increase of civic over rural population without ultimate starvation. Hence, we can come to but one conclusion, that the city and town population of this country must cease to increase or we shall increase the price of provisions to an insupportable rate, and finally to failure. In a word, the present condition of things we call civilization cannot continue much longer."

It is not to be wondered at that this writer, viewing the present, should infer the future portentous evils which he has described, and should not so clearly see the remedy. The only remedy he suggests is in the dispersion of population to the unoccupied regions, and their becoming producers of food. The practicability of such a scheme, however, grows more hopeless every day, indicating the continuance of the present state of things until the struggle between the starving poor and the rich is reached. This struggle is as sure to come as that like causes produce like effects. If, then, we must have the contest, and the revolution be as extended as the evil, it will embrace the whole civilized world. The question then arises, Which party will triumph? History answers, The starving poor. When bread panics occur, the people, urged on by the desperation of hunger and long oppression, set all law at defiance, and help themselves.

It is true we have had few bread riots in this country, and these on a small scale, which have been speedily suppressed by overwhelming numbers; but the riots here contemplated comprehend the cities of the civilized world, connected as they are by telegraphic communication, and imply an equally extensive organization. The poor will be arrayed against the rich, not because of enmity, but because they hope thereby in some way to obtain the necessities of life for themselves and their children. The vast majority being the poor, is it not certain that they will succeed in the work of ruin and survive, for this is all it could eventuate in, while the cultivated, refined, and progressive will be obliged to succumb? Such was the result during the French Revolution, in the days of Louis XVI., when Paris was in the hands of the riotous mob, and the streets ran with the blood of the rich, the intellectual and the moral. Such contests must be as widespread and ruinous as the parties are numerous and extreme in social position.

Just as sure, therefore, as human nature remains the same, must history repeat itself. There is but one remedy for these threatening evils and dangers, and that is the voluntary abandonment of combinations and monopolies of wealth and power. By social upheavals the progress of ages may be destroyed in a month. According to this philosopher there is no remedy for the state he so gloomily depicts. For how can the poor of the large eastern cities occupy the distant uncultivated lands, be they never so fertile and cheap? to say nothing of the purchase of farms and of the means of subsistence until they should get a start. They have not even money enough to pay for the transportation of themselves and families to the nearest of the unoccupied western lands. Hence the impracticability of the remedy suggested by this political economist for the evil of overcrowded cities. Therefore—the struggle must come; and it is easy to foresee the result—the survival of the *unfittest*—thus completely reversing the doctrine of progress.

With such a picture to contemplate—and we have no fears that any observing man will say it is overdrawn—we would ask if it does not lend tenfold force to the scientific and philosophic demonstrations already advanced against Darwin's theory of progressive development? Indeed, does it not point, as surely as the needle to the pole, to the final extinction of mankind as inhabitants of the earth in its present form?

Evolution Atheistic Science.

Evolution is emphatically atheistic science. Before its discovery, science, especially that of astronomy, was acknowledged to be in the defense of theism; and progress from the less to the more perfect, although not then a well-defined question of discussion, was virtually denied by atheists, as being inconsistent with the idea that things had no beginning, because development from lower orders implied a commencement which was fatal to atheism ; and its adoption necessitated the complete abandonment of the endless existence theory of things, and the admission that nature had a beginning. It is clear, therefore, that the investigation has forced atheism from its position of no beginning to a beginning of the universe, and we have demonstrated that the beginning was by creation. It is true that the mongrelism of atheistic evolution employs the phrase progressive development, but not *endless* development ; for the ideas of endless progress, as applicable to the present world, are incompatible with each other.

Pure atheism requires that there never was any progress, retrogression, modification, or succession of things in the universe—no coming in and no going out of existence—no being born and no dying—no beginning and no ending. That everything moved in circles, and not in geographical or chronological lines. In a word, that everything in the universe was characterized by fixed unchangeability ; but as all this is refuted by the facts and order of the universe, it demonstrates the atheistic sentiment of their endless theory of things in the past false ; and as we have proved that the progressive development theory of evolution is contrary to all science, all philosophy, and all history, written in the rocks and elements of nature, atheists cannot use it for the confirmation of their cherished obliteration of God from His universe. Hence, the only alternative it leaves—and that, too, as a scientific and philosophic necessity—is the great truism of nature as well as Scripture :—

"𝔍𝔫 𝔱𝔥𝔢 𝔟𝔢𝔤𝔦𝔫𝔫𝔦𝔫𝔤 𝔊𝔬𝔡 𝔠𝔯𝔢𝔞𝔱𝔢𝔡 𝔱𝔥𝔢 𝔥𝔢𝔞𝔳𝔢𝔫 𝔞𝔫𝔡 𝔱𝔥𝔢 𝔈𝔞𝔯𝔱𝔥."

CHAPTER XV.

NATIONAL DEGENERACY THE VOICE OF HISTORY.

Darwin's Assumptions Refuted.

IF Darwin's assumption is true, that progress is the invariable rule among mankind, it would be vindicated by the history of nations as well as that of generations, and especially of those nations that have successively held the empire of the world. Were the assumption true, we repeat, we should have as a reason for the overthrow of one nation by another the fact that that power which triumphed was better fitted to elevate and improve the condition of the people; and whenever such a change took place the new rulers would be very careful not to destroy the works of art, learning or refinement; and that the agencies and records of human advancement—the laws, standards of virtue, and monuments of noble characters and deeds—would be preserved and adopted. But as the exact reverse of this is the history of the past, therefore Darwin, Tyndall, Lyell and Huxley stand rebuked by the universal voice of mankind.

If the moral sentiments of human nature were equally balanced between virtue and vice, right and wrong, then bad books, bad examples, and their teaching would be no more pernicious than those of an opposite character would be influential for good. In such case moral evolution would have an equal chance of success; but when it is as obvious as man's existence that he gravitates toward vice and wrong, does it not follow that natural selection, if unchecked, would develop a generation so morally corrupt, so mentally and physically enervated, that it would be unable to reproduce itself, and therefore the human species would become extinct? What was it that destroyed the great nations of the East? We answer, War, with its usual accompaniments, pestilence and famine. While it is admitted that some nations have derived temporary and even permanent advantages by aggressive warfare, yet these are exceptions, and it is questionable whether even they have advanced the standard of civilization in the world at large. In the life and march of nations, each has in turn become affluent, corrupt, supine, and impoverished, thereby falling an easy prey to a smaller yet stronger one, though the latter may not have had a single superior element other than that of mere physical force. The victor in turn travels the same road from affluence to poverty, from power to weakness, the survivors in no case showing any mark of mental, moral, and physical progress—for progress implies an equal advance of all departments and phases of human nature. Improvement of one of these at the expense of the other is real degeneracy. Excessive cultivation of the intellect at the expense of the moral nature only qualifies a villain to be more villainous. The transmission of pernicious sentiments and bad examples, if equally imitated, lowers the moral standard in the same degree as good ones elevate it. It is sadly true that though God made man upright, he has "sought out many inventions," and for the prosecution of infamous purposes. Every perpetration of a new or greater crime only makes its repetition easier, and in an advanced state of civilization its publication in a book or newspaper, or its exhibition in a theater, is itself a crime. So also every new instance of noble virtue renders its imitation easier; hence, as the standard of individual goodness and greatness is elevated, vice and crime become more and more atrocious. But the history of the world shows that the instances of great villainy are far more numerous, and if sent abroad with those of eminent virtue and sacred truth, then might they have something of an equal chance of success; but while the latter perish in obscurity and are forgotten, or at best are brought into notice by accident, the former are emblazoned in song and story and travel on the wings of every wind. The masses purchase largely and eagerly devour fiction and error, and even professed Christian publishers often give them to the public in preference to sound and healthy reading because of their love of money. The young and misguided usually sympathize with the moderately wicked, while only here and there is found one who seeks after truth and the most exalted virtue, without regard to the selfish question whether it will pay in the present world, looking only to the hope of reward which Christianity holds out as inducement to sacrifice the present life for one of eternal duration.

Evolution, on the contrary, sees nothing in mankind but a common brotherhood with the beasts that perish—alike in life, death, and eternity,—and in the nature of things presents no example for imitation higher than man himself, and that too in his lower fellow animal nature. We need not wait for such degrading sentiments to develop their legitimate fruit in order to determine its character. It may be seen in the lowest savage that roams the earth, whose ancestors refused to retain God in their thoughts until they had lost all conception of His existence—moral accountability, or of the possibility of their own future existence.

Blot out man's hope of endless association with his Maker in a coming world, a fitness for which its gospel alone gives, and he rapidly degenerates to the condition of the savage. This is the legitimate tendency of Darwin's teaching and that of his school; for if God did not make man, He is not his proprietor, and is under no responsibility to Him. Man may therefore fly to the indulgence of every vile passion and the perpetration of every degrading act, and all will be the same in the end. Thus is sown the seed of a prolific harvest of vice and immorality more dangerous and deteriorating to mankind than that scattered by all the infidels, deists and atheists since the world began; and oh, what a harvest will be gathered if the false reasonings and subtile sophistries of the so-called modern scientists are not effectually exposed!

For our part, we cannot see how it is possible for a man to avoid becoming more or less skeptical if he reads the latest works of Darwin, Lyell, Tyndall, or Huxley, unless he is so well grounded in natural science and philosophy as to be able to reach deeper and see further into their fundamental principles than they have done. So, whether we consider the doctrine of evolution according to natural selection in the light of mental, moral, or physical science, or as applicable to individuals or communities, its tendency is equally to degenerate mankind. Sir Charles Lyell quotes many ancient and modern writers touching the nature and appearance of the geological formations, all of whom in the earlier stages of the study of the rock verified the Mosaic account of creation and the deluge by the facts they discovered. Coming down to later times, a few began to diverge from that hypothesis, until finally the theory of Lyell and Darwin was developed; and of course, as it declares, it is the fittest to survive. But what is it that has thus far survived? We answer, A pestilent and rank growth of skepticism. Whether these teachings are good or bad, whether they are to advance or retard the elevation of man, depends upon whether they inculcate the Christian idea of God and the Bible. Every one who is at all acquainted with the history of civilization knows that in its march the highest development has kept exact step with Christianity. Hence it is no more true that "Westward the march of empire makes its way," than that westward the march of Christianity makes its way; for the latter has always preceded the civil elevation of mankind.

It is equally true that in those countries where Christianity was first planted, and flourished side by side with Grecian and Roman civilization, when Mohammedanism and paganism stifled and extinguished its light, civilization went out with it. Indeed civilization, in its most exalted sense, as well as what we call humanity, are but the reflex of Christianity, and can no more shine or be seen without it than can the moon without the sun.

In Lyell's and Darwin's rejection of the Mosaic account of creation, both as to the manner and time of the work, thus denying its inspired authority, we find them quoting from the Indians and the records of other ancient peoples in corroboration, if not vindication, of their views, showing that in their opinion its authority is of less importance. With regard to Egyptian cosmogony Lyell says: "We gather much information from writers of Grecian sects, who borrowed almost all their tenets from Egypt, and among others that of the former successions, destruction, and renovation of the world. We learn from Plutarch that this was the theme of one of the hymns of Orpheus, so celebrated in the fabulous ages of Greece. It was brought by him from the banks of the Nile; and we find in his verses, as in the Indian systems, a definite period assigned for the destruction of each successive world. The returns of great catastrophes were determined by the period of the Annus Magnus, or great year—a cycle composed of the revolutions of the sun, moon, and planets, and terminating when these return together to the same sign whence they were supposed at some remote epoch to have set out. The duration of this great cycle was variously estimated. According to Orpheus, it was 120,000 years; according to others, 300,000; and Cassander makes it 360,000. [These estimates bear the true stamp of geological calculation of definite periods—immense length and great discrepancy—and all founded upon an event which was supposed to have occurred at some remote period. Again he says:] We learn particularly from the Timaeus of Plato that the Egyptians believed the world to be subject to occasional conflagrations and deluges whereby the gods corrected the career of human wickedness and purified the earth from guilt."

If these accounts are true, then the human species never progressed, but always degenerated, and that to such a degree that the gods were obliged to destroy the whole generation and commence with a new one. Of course the most perfect was always first, which reverses the principle of evolution.

Heathen Philosophy Corruptions of Scripture.

Here we have certain information brought by Orpheus and Plato, both Grecian writers, from Egypt. This relates to the destruction of the world by a flood, in order to correct the wickedness of men; and also its destruction by conflagrations in order to purify it. The question arises, If these Greeks obtained this information from the Egyptians, from whence did the Egyptians obtain it? We answer, From the Hebrews, who resided in Egypt four hundred years, and made their exodus from it more than two thousand years before Orpheus or Plato was born—before even Greece existed. These Hebrews knew that their God once destroyed the world by a flood, and all but eight of its human inhabitants perished; and that it was done because of their great wickedness.

The history of this destruction is recorded in the 6th and 7th chapters of Genesis, and the determination is thus expressed: "And God saw that the wickedness of man was great in the earth, and that every imagination of the thoughts of his heart was only evil continually. And it repented the Lord that he had made man on the earth, and it grieved him at his heart. And the Lord said, I will destroy man, whom I have created, from the face of the earth; both man, and beast, and the creeping thing, and the fowls of the air; for it repented the Lord that he had made them." (6 : 5–7).

The Hebrews also knew that their God had rained fire and brimstone from heaven upon Sodom and Gomorrah, and the cities about them, destroying both them and their inhabitants for their wickedness by a mighty conflagration. This catastrophe happened in the days of Abraham, the grandfather of Jacob, who went into Egypt at the commencement of this four hundred years, and from whose family the Hebrew nation sprung. The account of this conflagration is recorded in the 19th chapter of Genesis. At the 24th and 25th verses we read: "Then the Lord rained upon Sodom and upon Gomorrah brimstone and fire from the Lord out of heaven; and he overthrew those cities, and all the plain, and all the inhabitants of the cities, and that which grew upon the ground, and behold, and lo, the smoke of the country went up as the smoke of a furnace."

The Hebrews had also the prophecy of Enoch, the seventh person from Adam born into the world, by which at this early period God made known his determination to purify the world from the curse and power of the wicked. It was revealed to the apostle Jude, who wrote it, thus : "Enoch also, the seventh from Adam, prophesied of these, saying, Behold, the Lord cometh with ten thousand of his saints, to execute judgment upon all, and to convince all that are ungodly among them of all their ungodly deeds which they have committed, and of all their hard speeches which ungodly sinners have spoken against him." (Jude 14). This coming of the Judge and judgment is associated in the Bible with the conflagration of the world yet to come.

Now, what was more natural than that the Hebrews should have taught the Egyptians about the flood and these conflagrations, and the object for which God had thus punished and intended to punish mankind, and that subsequent to this last world-wide conflagration he was to make of its ashes a new world in which righteousness will forever dwell? Hence it is evident that the traditions of these Greeks concerning floods and conflagrations inflicted for the wickedness of men came from the Scriptures of truth ; and thus does Lyell inadvertently confirm the historic statements of Moses by heathen mythologists. Lyell calls it a wonderful conception of heathen mythology, and of very great importance in fixing the data for his speculations, especially that relating to the creation. He says:

"One remarkable fiction of Egyptian mythology was the supposed intimation of a masculo-feminine principle, to which was assigned the development of the embryo world from chaos, somewhat in the way of incubation. When the first chaotic mass had been produced by a self-dependent and eternal being [A self-dependent being must be an intelligent being, and an intelligent being must be a living being; therefore it was, even according to this heathen mythologist, a living God who produced the first thing.] it required the mysterious functions of this subordinate deity to produce the mundane egg from which the world was hatched. Aristophanes, alluding to this Egyptian fable, which had been engrafted by Orpheus on the Greek mythology, introduced the chorus in his comedy of the birds, singing in solemn hymn:

"' How sable-plumed night conceived
In the boundless bosom of Erebus,
And laid an egg from which sprung
Love, resplendent with golden pinions.'

"Love fecundated the dark-winged chaos, and gave origin to the race of birds."

But why should Lyell consider this hymn of Orpheus singing about the subordinate deity hatching the world from an embryonic, mundane egg, so wonderful a fiction, when he adopts Darwin's more marvelous conception that the world, the solar system, and all they contain were hatched into existence without an egg, or without a hen to sit on it? Again he says: "It is not inconsistent with the Hindoo mythology to suppose that Pythagoras, whose opinions will presently be mentioned, might have been found in the East. Not only the system of universal and violent catastrophes and periods of repose in endless succession, but also that of periodical revolutions, effected by the continual agency of ordinary causes. [Will Mr. Lyell please inform us how such 'violent catastrophes' could have been produced by 'ordinary causes?'] For Brahma, Vishnu, and Siva, the first, second, and third persons in the Hindoo triad, severally represented the creation, the preserving and destroying powers of the deity. The co-existence of these three attributes, and in simultaneous operation, might well accord with the perpetual but partial alterations, finally bringing about a complete change."

DEGENERACY THE VOICE OF HISTORY. 423

Lyell's Inconsistency in ignoring the Bible Record

How much more consistent would the inference be that these views originated in the mind of the great Creator, Preserver, and Destroyer of the world, as revealed in the Bible hundreds of years before Pythagoras or any Hindoo Brahma existed, and which had been thus corrupted by the traditions of those whose ancestors had sprung from the family of Noah! The inference also is hardly legitimate that the gods were such slaves to the things they made that they must continue to change and destroy; for in that case they would have destroyed themselves. Neither could the catastrophes here mentioned have been brought about by slow degrees and ordinary changes, for such would have been no catastrophes at all.

The fact is, Lyell here endeavors to use these mythological fictions for two opposite purposes: First, he gives them full credit for the long definite periods which intervene between the catastrophes, as this suits his pet theory of making the world older than the Bible declares it to be; and he very carefully endeavors to show that the catastrophes were not catastrophes, for the reason that another of his opinions is that there never were any catastrophes, as creations or destructions, and never will be. Behold this great scientist so hard pressed for evidence in defense of his theories that he seizes upon the periods from the pagan myths to prove the events they describe, but tells the poor gods the events themselves never occurred! It is like saying it is three hundred years since the Reformation, but there never was any reformation.

He continues: "The fiction expressed in the verses from Menu, of eternal vicissitudes in the vigils and slumbers of Brahma, seems accommodated to the systems of general catastrophes, followed by new creations and periods of repose." Observe how mythological fiction is exalted at the expense of Bible truth, betraying the secret animus of men of his school to undermine the authority of the sacred Scriptures—searching among heathen fables for evidence to contradict Moses. But even this citation from Hindoo tradition Lyell perverts by attributing to Brahma the authorship of the catastrophes, while in Hindoo theology Brahma is only one of the three whom God created, by whose co-operation the world was formed.

If uniform progress has marked the civilizations of the world, then we should find the rudest peoples among the earliest nations, and the highest among those of the present day. That such is not the fact will appear by referring to the degeneracy and degradation of the once elevated standards of the civilization of the beautiful countries of Asia and Africa, which were once the seats of the learning, wealth, art, virtue, power, and refinement of the world. Where are Thebes and Memphis, the proud cities of Egypt, whose standard of learning was so high that when the apostle wished to convey an adequate idea of the intelligence of the great Hebrew leader, he declared that "Moses was learned in all the wisdom of the Egyptians."

Where is Troy, once the mistress of Asia? Where is Babylon, the capital of the great Chaldean monarchy, the first to wield universal dominion? Where the Medo-Persian monarchy, which in turn swayed the scepter of the world, as in the days of Cyrus and Darius? Where also is Greece, with her Thales, Solon, Lycurgus, Demosthenes, and Socrates? In order to show the conceptions which the Grecian philosophers entertained of what human societies and states should be, and what they endeavored to make them, we introduce the following passage from "Rollin's Ancient History," vol. i., p. 290, 291:

"Plutarch describes an entertainment which Priander gave to the illustrious seven wise men of Greece. At supper, one of the company proposed this question: Which is the most perfect popular government? That, answered Solon, where an injury done to any private citizen is such to the whole body. That, said Bias, where the law has no superior. That, said Thales, where the inhabitants are neither too rich nor too poor. That, said Anarcharsis, where virtue is honored and vice detested. That, said Pettacus, where dignities are always conferred upon the virtuous, and never on the wicked. That, said Cleobulus, where the citizens fear blame more than punishment. That, said Chilo, where the laws are more regarded and have more authority than the orators."

Though the element of religion is not here directly mentioned, only implied by the expressions "vice and virtue," "the wicked and the virtuous," which only exist as deviations from or obedience to a religious standard, and presupposes the existence of the standard as one of the essentials of the social state; yet every one who is acquainted with the sentiments of these great men knows that religion was inculcated as a fundamental principle. For example, it is said that one of the maxims which Bias particularly taught and recommended was: "To do all the good we can, and ascribe all the glory of it to the gods." It is unnecessary to say that these grand sentiments constitute the very highest form of civilization, and when entertained by the great minds of a nation they must go very far toward molding the character of the people, and controlling their lives.

National Progress Not the Rule.

Now, if progress is the "invariable rule," why did not Greece, whose people were once so highly developed, continue to exist as a nation? Being the fittest to survive, why must we now sing of her in the image of Powers' "Greek Slave:"

> In chains she stands, and proudly frowned:
> Tell not the fallen Greek she's bound;
> 'Twill lighten every cursed link—
> Fetterless still her limbs to think.
> Greece, like this sculptured slave,
> Thy heroes, poets, wise and brave—
> The marshaled world's embattled plain
> Swept by the Macedon's swift-winged train.
> Yes! mighty Greece, where Homer's song
> In lyric numbers flowed along
> O'er Mars' proud hilltops' ancient dome,
> And crimsoned fields of Marathon.
> Her likeness now clad in this chain,
> Sadly bent o'er ruined fame.
> It breathes not yet, there life must be—
> So formed in nature's melody.
> She weeps o'er Grecia's fallen state,
> The helpless tear sheds o'er the great.
> Her heart bled deeply ere she fell,
> So seems the image form to tell.
> Greece yet in chains, though Byron weep,
> The artistic type doth still repeat;
> Her star of freedom's faded light,
> Moonless, rayless, quenched in night,
> Entombed within the grave of time,
> With national sepulchers there to chime
> The noiseless dirge that wakes no more
> To song or freedom, chains or war.

That such exalted sentiments were not confined to Greece alone, and to her golden age, is shown by the fact that the standard of Scythian progress, long before Scythia formed a part of the Grecian kingdom, indeed, before Greece was a kingdom, was still higher and nobler than that of Greece. The Scythians inhabited a country in the North of Europe. Rollin says, vol. i. p.

314 : "Let us acknowledge, to the shame of ancient philosophy, that the Scythians, who did not particularly apply themselves to the study of wisdom, carried it to a greater height in their practice than either the Egyptians, Grecians, or any other civilized nation. They did not give the name of goods or riches to anything but what, humanly speaking, truly deserves that title : as health, strength, courage, the love of labor, sincerity, an abhorrence of all fraud and dissimulation. In a word, all such qualities as render a man more virtuous and valuable. These were their riches." This historian beautifully adds : " If to these happy dispositions we could add the knowledge and love of the true God and of our Redeemer, without which the most exalted virtues are of no value, they would have been a perfect people."

How far do these sublime pictures of human advancement excel those of any modern country or nation, even in this boasting age of ours, either in England or America ! Greece was conquered by Rome in an aggressive warfare, and history shows that she never equaled, much less excelled her, in a single element of human greatness—not even in her Augustan or golden age. In her decline and fall, Greece became inferior only to Rome in stratagem, intrigue, and selfish ambition ; and if a people animated by these debasing principles are better fitted to survive, then the theory of natural selection may be true. While the conquest seemed to elevate the Romans by the new Grecian association, in the same degree it corrupted the Greeks and lowered the national standard of virtue and intelligence.

When Rome was mistress of the world, disposing of nations and individuals at her pleasure—and she always took pleasure in it—it would seem that the only protection against indignity was to become a Roman citizen; but the privilege cost so much that few could obtain the distinction, and all the rest were slaves. It is true that in Athens, the cradle of Grecian greatness, the authorities suffered conspirators to put Socrates, the father of moral philosophy, as he is called, to death, for no crime; but when the plot was discovered the conspirators paid the penalty, which was the forfeiture of their own lives; but Rome sent her soldiers to crucify Christ without the least crime being proved against him, at the instigation of a murderous mob of infatuated Jews, and nothing was ever done to the conspirators.

These facts demonstrate that the march of nations, instead of being progressive in that which ennobles man, is steadily toward degeneracy. If it be true, as claimed, that mankind constantly advance, then why have all the splendid empires of the world perished, to give place to such nations as Great Britain and the United States, whose moral and civil standards are so low that places of power and trust are bought and sold for money? If the claim be true, then the present generation should have inherited a virtuous and noble mind from Greece, incorruptible morals from Scythia, an elevated patriotism from Sparta, and a vigorous body from Rome. In contrast to this we have almost universal covetousness. Treachery and deceit are so common that man has no faith in man. It is the generation of the "almighty dollar." Almost universal fraud has taken the place of honor. Had Shakespeare intended by the following lines to describe this characteristic of the present generation, he could scarcely have done so more accurately.

> "What is honor? A word. What is
> That word? Honor. What is
> Honor? Air. A trim reckoning.
> Who hath it? he that died on

> Wednesday.
> Doth he feel it? No. Doth he hear it?
> No. It is insensible then? yea,
> To the dead. But will it not live
> With the living? No. Why?
> Detraction will not suffer it.
> Therefore I'll have none of it."

Rome never equaled Greece in Virtue or Intelligence.

In the year 30 B.C. the Roman republic became a monarchy under Octavius. Before this Julius Cæsar set fire to the city of Alexandria, and destroyed a library containing 400,000 volumes. How does such an act show Roman civilization to have been superior to that of Greece or Africa, and therefore fitter to survive? In the year 83 A.D. the Emperor Domitian banished all the philosophers from Rome and suppressed their schools. Does this show Rome to have been superior to Greece as the leader in the van of human progress? Let us come down to the period when the Roman Empire was itself overrun and divided among the barbarian tribes of northern Germany. The city of Rome was sacked and burned by the Goths under Alaric, 410. A.D. The conquest of Spain and Gaul by the Vandals and the permanent settlement of those countries by them took place 412, A.D. They also planted themselves firmly in Toulouse in 414. In fact, nearly all Europe was overrun by the Visigoths at this period. About the same time, also, Attilla, the Hun, known as the "Scourge of God," ruled an immense empire stretching from China to the Atlantic. Genseric also established a Vandal kingdom in Africa, took Carthage, and plundered Italy in the year 439.

These barbarous tribes had not an element of civilization which could be compared with that of Rome in the Augustan age, distinguished for that in which Christ was born, much less a civilization equal to that of Greece. If it be asked, Why, then, did these tribes succeed in such mighty conquests? we answer, Because they were more savage, and therefore had less, in fact no respect, for the rights and interests of others. Here we see the most unfit survives, and the world retrogrades instead of progresses. In the year 393, after the death of Theodosius, all classes of the people degenerated, and from this date may be reckoned the fall of the Roman Empire. Its decline, however, followed the reign of Antoninus. The effeminate and luxurious habits of the nobles and citizens, the vices of the emperors, the means by which they rose to power, the disposal of the sovereignty by the military, the recruiting of the army from Germany and other barbarous countries, the increasing numbers and audacity of the foreigners—all combined precipitated Rome from the eminence which she had attained during the consulate and the first years of the empire. Such, in brief, is the history of the rise, maturity, decline, and fall, not only of Rome, but of the whole family of nations, which in each case is marked by the waxing and waning of human culture and greatness. To assume that any generation has advanced mentally, morally, and physically is to assume that which the historic facts do not justify.

In a national contest for subjugation, if the survivor could and would take up the standard of the vanquished, and steadily advance it, then indeed the world might boast of progress; but when a child at birth can have transmitted to it as a natural inheritance all the knowledge and experience of its parents, then it will be possible for a nation just emerged into life to select and assimilate all the elements calculated to ennoble man which the conquering power finds in possession of the fallen, whether in sentiment or practice, and adding these to its own, thus give birth to a new civilization, a new humanity. Or if it were a fact, which is quite otherwise, that when the nation most advanced in human progress made war upon another it would only subjugate the lower and more vicious, expunge all the bad sentiments written in its books, and cheerfully adopt whatever was found which would elevate its own standard, preserving it without tarnish or compromise, then might evolution have grounds for defense. Such a nation would have ingrafted on her own stock a higher taste in art, more exact methods in science, truer principles of philosophy and more elevated sentiments of religion ; or, if found to be better, adopt them as a whole. This would indeed be progress, and had this been the result of the wars between nations, each contest would have blessed instead of having cursed mankind ; but alas ! how the march of nations and of generations has reversed all this !

Had such been the case, then those hardy tribes of Germany who divided the Roman Empire into fragments and possessed themselves of them would have energized the people by the infusion of physical strength into Roman weakness, and diffused among them the spirit of patriotism and love of liberty which characterized them in their barbarian homes. Instead of this, however, these very events hastened the decline and culminated in the fall of the Roman Empire.

Had progress been the rule, the barbarians would have maintained every virtuous trait of national character which they brought from their rude German homes, and would have absorbed the advanced civilization and learning of the empire ; but not even a healthy compromise was the result of the union.

From the fall of Rome down through the mediæval, or emphatically the Dark Ages, ensued a period which all agree in characterizing thus : Galileo was condemned for teaching that the earth revolved. Although the earth was held to be a sphere two thousand years before, it was now held to be flat by the teachers of the age. Thus did science and philosophy retrograde instead of having progressed. At the beginning of the sixth century Mohammedanism had its advent, which has also degraded and cursed the human family. Within its dominions it had not only blocked every wheel of the car of progress, but thus rolled it centuries backward, and to-day it holds possession of the countries which once were the most civilized and Christianized of the world, and which had established an empire stretching from the Ganges to Morocco, embracing a vast number of populous islands in one direction, and from the southern extremity of Arabia to the borders of Hungary in another, including a very large proportion of the inhabitants of the world. Even at the birthplace of the Saviour the Crescent is elevated, and the sign of the Cross has been banished for hundreds of years. Jerusalem, even all Palestine, Athens, Constantinople, and all Egypt lie under the withering curse of Islam, and have for more than eleven centuries.

The tenets of its religion convey the best idea of the extent of the degeneration of the people of those countries. They teach the utter abhorrence of all who do not embrace them, and that the Koran contains everything worthy of being known. When the Saracens, under the command of Omar, A.D. 642, took the city of Alexandria, they seized a library of 700,000 volumes, which they committed to the flames. They heated the water of their baths for six months with burning books.

Some one remonstrated with Omar for destroying the books. He asked if what they contained was all in the Koran. In reply he was told it was not. "Then," said he, "it ought to be burned;" and if it was all in the Koran then there was no use for it."

A People Never Rise Above their Religion.

We may remark that a people never rise above their religion, and very seldom come up to its standard; and we ask, What element of civilization has not Islam strangled? What feature of progressive development has it ever manifested to vindicate its fitness to be established or to continue to exist? Here is a moral, civil, and religious monstrosity, which has blotted out all the civilizations of the East, as well as its Christianity, and has survived for forty generations, furnishing another gigantic fact in palpable contradiction to the claim that the world progresses. We may add another fact in this connection—namely, that England, claiming to be in the van of progressive evolutionary development, has kept Mohammedanism in existence for centuries. But for England's interference Russia would long ago have destroyed it as a civil power, which would have gone very far toward the destruction of its foolish and bloody religion, which sends immediately into Paradise all who die in warring for the civil or religious rights of Mohammed. We repeat: if human progress were the rule, then the wisdom developed by the experience of nations and generations would be adopted by those succeeding, while that which was foolish and pernicious would be always rejected; but in the march of nations and generations the reverse of this is sadly apparent.

As an example, take the teachings of Plato, the pupil of Socrates, who, living late in Grecian history, may fairly be supposed to have been learned in all the wisdom of Greece. In his cosmological theory he taught the existence of a Supreme Being, but that in consequence of the apparent imperfections of organic and inorganic nature, and because the Supreme Divinity could make nothing but the most perfect, committed the creation of the world and its inhabitants to a subordinate Deity. To make the world and set it in motion, this god plunged himself into the ocean of chaotic matter, when, testing his powers, he shook the mighty whole, and turning rapidly on himself, drew after him the world obedient to his efforts. Here originated the doctrine of Pantheism. Whatever its god may be conceived to be, he is confounded with the matter of the universe he made, which in fact makes the world itself a living animal.

It is easy to see that this notion tends to degrade mankind by enslaving their maker by the material world, and that this idea has reached its lowest depth in the theory of evolution, whose advocates simply shift the deityship from Plato's Logos to the "Laws of Nature," in the latter case leaving the Supreme Being entirely out of the question. As the scientists consider mankind the most exquisite workmanship turned out by the evolution machine, their conceptions of greatness can reach no higher than themselves, and consequently they are incapable of the exercise of veneration or acts of devotion. They can not even enjoy the poor solace of natural religion, which supposes nature to be greater than man.

Then there is Plato's doctrine of natural immortality, which, in its various modifications and phases, has wrought endless confusion in the theological world, being confounded with the immortality promised by Christ to His saints, and the immortality of Plato who said that the subordinate deity mixed soul matter in a cup, of which he made an immortal soul for every man who was to be born into the world, but none for women—women have no souls. These he reserved in a soul-storehouse, ready for distribution among male children as soon as born. He also taught that the human body was nothing but a carcass, which, when it dies, is dead forever, at which event the soul is released from the body as from a prison, and is received on high, where it lives without a body to all eternity.

Plato also taught that if a man died unpardoned by the gods, his immortal soul was sent into a place of punishment, where by the influence of his living friends he might be purged of his guilt, and afterward also received above among the gods. This philosopher saw the difficulty of transmitting immortal souls from parents to children, rendering it necessary that the mother, at least, should possess as many immortal souls as she had children, and yet the theory gave the mother no soul at all; but he avoided this difficulty by having all the souls made at once, and at the beginning of the world.

With him also originated spiritualism, and a host of kindred errors which have hung like a nightmare both upon Christianity and human progress, and which enslave the minds of the present generation, even of scientists and philosophers, the most advanced specimens of whom in their conceit have concluded their ancestors were baboons.

Plato's Doctrine of the Divine Essence (Deism).

Then we have the mysterious and mischievous doctrine of the "Divine Essence," which also originated with Plato, as the following sketch of his views will show. In his discourse on the formation of the world he says:

"And now the author of all things addressed the genii, to whom he had confided the government of the stars: Ye gods, who owe to me your birth, listen to my sovereign commands. You have not a title to immortality, but you may partake in it by the power of my will, more potent than the bonds which unite the parts of which you are composed, to fill with inhabitants the sea, the earth, and the air. Were these creatures to receive life from me they would be exempt from the empire of death, and become equal to the gods themselves. I therefore commit to you the care of producing them. Delegates of my power! unite to perishable bodies the germs of immortality which you shall receive from me; and form those beings who may command over other animals to remain subject to you; let them receive birth at your command, live to increase by your benefactions, and after death let them unite to you and share in your happiness.

"He said, and immediately pouring into the cup, in which he had mixed the soul of the world, the remains of what he had reserved of that soul, he composed the souls of individual creatures, adding to those of man a portion of *divine essence*, and annexed to them irrevocable destinies. Then it was decreed that mortals should be born, capable of knowing and serving the divinity; that the man should have the pre-eminence over the woman; that justice should consist in triumphing over the passions, and injustice in yielding to them; that the just after death should pass into the stars, and there enjoy unalterable felicity; and that the unjust should be changed into women, or, if they remained unjust, transmigrated into different animals, and that they should not be restored to their primitive dignity until they should become obedient to the voice of reason. After these immutable decrees, the Supreme Being disseminated souls into the different planets and commanded the inferior gods to clothe them successively with mortal bodies, to provide for their wants and to govern them. The immortal and rational soul was assigned its place in the brain, the most elevated part of the body, to regulate its motions."

Plato flourished about 388 B.C., and from this condensed presentation of his views it will be seen that he may be called the first pantheist, the first deist, the first spiritualist, and the first evolutionist, except that so far as the last is concerned, he began with the existence of a Supreme Being, who, however, was only the author of all things, as he made the soul, or genii that made the world, by clothing himself with all its material. So far as the world is concerned, he began with man, the most perfect, and thence on down to woman, thence also to the lower animals—exactly the reverse of Darwin's theory. If there is science or sense in either, it attaches to the teaching of Plato.

We have said that modern deism originated in the philosophy of Plato. The *divine essence, the immortal divinity or soul*, his philosophy located in the human brain, to which he ascribed the faculty of reason. That the deists consider this the only god to be worshiped and the only guide to be consulted in all human relations will be apparent by the following extract from an address delivered a few years since by Jules Favre at the French Academy in Paris, who was called to the professorship as successor to Victor Cousin. After pronouncing an eulogium on M. Cousin, whom he declared to be the great expounder and translator of Plato, the successful philosophic writer, a peer of France under Louis Philippe, and Senator in the time of Louis Napoleon, he proceeded with his peroration thus : " But the god of whom my immortal soul possesses the indelible image—the god who reveals himself to my conscience by my reason —is a god of intelligence and truth, and the first law which he has imposed upon me is respect for my intelligence and my liberty. [This is self-worship.] I am faithful to him in obeying my reason [his god], which he has given me for my guide. My duty is, therefore, to judge and to choose, and to refuse what my reason rejects."

The idea that every man has a little, immortal deity,

or *god-essence*, enthroned in his brain, to be worshiped and consulted as the first and highest duty, the dictates of the *god-essence* being an infallible guide to faith and practice, is demonstrated by the honest and yet palpable contradictions manifested by the mental, moral, and religious sentiments of mankind, to be one of the most extravagant and monstrously absurd notions ever conceived by a credulous mind. The pernicious influence of the deistical sentiments of the French Academy are strikingly exemplified in the deplorably low standard of Parisian religion and morality, and its rank skepticism.

It were better that the seed thus sown by these ancient heathen authors had died with their inventors than that they should have survived not to advance, but to degenerate and curse mankind. As blighting and demoralizing as these evil opinions have been, they can only be considered as having paved the way for the doctrine of evolution—the quintessence of all the deceptive sophistries and lying wonders of the world, reducing man to a common brotherhood with the brutes around him. Admitting the existence of no being higher than himself after which to aspire, the possibility of his elevation is precluded, and as it is an inherent law of his being to imitate and to worship, he becomes like the lower things he studies, and prostrates himself in the groveling worship of the ancestral monkeys and the creeping things through which he has crawled into existence.

Cook, of Boston, adopts Plato's Doctrine of " Life."

Mr. Joseph Cook, of Boston, also teaches this deistical doctrine of the divine essence as taught by Plato. Cook calls it the life, and the life was first—that is, before the organization—and produced it. He represents the brain as the keys of the instrument upon which this living, intelligent creature, residing in the man's head, but not confounded with it, plays. It is no more a part of the brain than a player on the keys of a piano is a part of the piano itself; but just as the musician plays upon the keys of the instrument, so this inhabitant of the head plays upon the organs of the brain. This creature is in possession of all the thoughts and intelligence the man will ever have, because all knowledge begins within, and then dispenses it by playing upon brain-keys, just as the musician dispenses music by playing upon the keys of the piano; or, as the spiritualist expresses it, "the spirit uses the organs of the man, as those of speech, by which to make its revelations." If the human organic keys are in any wise deranged or disorganized, in the same degree will the intelligence be vague or incoherent, just as the music of the instrument will be discordant if the strings are out of tune.

Here, however, the analogy ceases; for while all music is impossible upon an instrument with every string broken, and the whole thrown into a state of disorganization, as are those of the dead, yet complete disorganization of the organic brain and of the whole man only releases the player and qualifies him to discourse more beautiful music, higher and more profound thought; so that the want of rational thought is no more to be attributed to the intelligent being who sits back of the brain than the bad music is to the player who attempts to perform upon a piano the strings of which are all out of tune or broken. The error of this hypothesis is easily shown by the conclusions which it necessitates, some of which are as follows:

First: this inward being did not obtain his knowledge from or through the medium of the organic brain, but only dispenses it as its own thoughts, first to the man himself, and secondly, through his bodily organs, to others, as best it was able through the service of so poorly made instruments.

Secondly : If this intelligent tenant of man's head did not receive his knowledge through the brain or organic senses, he must have possessed it before he took possession of the tenement. This is the doctrine of Plato and Cook ! " The life produced the organization."

Thirdly : Human intelligence (argues Mr. Cook) is not the result of learning from books or other outward sources, in which case the five senses and the brain might not have existed at all, as these could not think, and therefore could convey no thought to thinking spirit or soul, or divine essence—call it what you will. This spirit is in possession of all the knowledge, and by playing on the brain-keys lets it out to the man himself, and through him to others, by the organs of speech, by writing, or by signs ; and were the man dumb and had never heard, he could write of sound and music just as well: for his music teacher within knew all about the art, and having the brain to play on he could give the man himself appreciable thought of music ; and controlling the organs of speech, which are entirely independent of his ears or auditory nerves, he could sing or speak equally as well as though he had always heard.

If this doctrine is true, then there need never have been books, schools, or teachers, as the intelligent spirit or " divine essence " does not receive thoughts through material organs, which are incapable of forming any, but only plays upon organic brain-keys to convey its thoughts, originating within itself, first to the house, or man in which he resides, and thence through his bodily organs to society. Even this does not make society any more intelligent ; for each of its members has his knowing creature, his instructor, in his own head, who cannot receive thought from the outward world, as thought must be formed before it can be communicated to the intelligent resident of the head ; and as the material organism is incapable of thinking, therefore all outward teaching is absolutely impossible upon this hypothesis. This is skeptical materialism in its worst form. The logical result of this theory is that all human knowledge was in possession of these living divinities before they entered the brain of mankind, and being abstract and independent of the human organization, living before and producing it, they will survive its dissolution, remaining as intelligent as before. If they do thus exist, and thus survive, their prior, living, intelligent existence to the bodily organization is demonstrated.

Cookism destroys Moral Responsibility.

Fourthly : From such a condition of being it also follows that man is not responsible for his ignorance, as it is the natural weakness or derangement of the organic brain, which prevents his natural resident genius from dispensing the instruction he possesses to the carcass in which he lives. The man is equally irresponsible for his moral conduct, and for the same reason—namely, the weakness of the moral organs of the brain.

Suppose the lower passions to be very largely developed in an individual, the play upon which would cause the man to become a drunkard, to rob, and murder, is it not plain that the material, organic man was not to blame for having such a disposition, or for the perpetration of these acts, but that the responsibility rests wholly upon the resident in the interior, who played upon the bad keys, as the bad music was the work of the player upon the untuned piano? The resident gentleman had no business to play on the bad organs of the brain. He, therefore, is the culprit, and not the man; and it is as great a piece of ignorant and heartless presumption to punish the man—the mere instrument who is thus forced to act—as to hold the untuned stringed instrument responsible for the bad music the player makes. No; it is the player who is the delinquent and sinner in both instances.

It is to be hoped that the microscopical and surgical sciences will soon reach a degree of perfection that will enable students to remove the skull, detect and bring out these mysterious, impious, and vicious wretches, and administer to them due punishment for their bad deeds, as well as reward them for their good actions; for nothing can be more unjust and cruel than the infliction of penalties upon human beings for their apparent bad deeds, or to award them honor for seeming good conduct. Nor should any man be censured for his ignorance or esteemed for his wisdom. As it is an indisputable fact, a demonstration of philosophical science, that human intelligence is the result of physical organization, it follows that there never would have been any had organic man not existed. In such case the little myths of "divine essence" would never have been seen or known.

But as human intelligence begins, and is therefore an effect, its existence must depend upon conditions. Let us suppose, then, the main condition to be the prior existence of this other intelligent being residing in the brain of man, and remembering also it has been found that the existence of organic brain and organs of sense are essential to its manifestation as well as its reception, we are given as a consequence the fact that this second person, this knowing resident, must also be endowed with similar organs by which he himself is rendered capable of communicating his, intelligence to the body or the man surrounding him, and through which he himself became intelligent, or able to form thoughts. But as these organs of the second person must be composed of brain and nerves, or their equivalents—for it is immaterial of what kind of substance they are made, provided it is of a nature capable of presiding over and employing such organs as its instruments of manifestation—he must himself be as really an organic, sentient being as the first; and for the same reasons the third, fourth, fifth, and so on, must be living, sentient creatures, each independent of the other. From this complication and involvement we can never arrive at the original; and until we find him we shall never reach the source of intelligence and of responsibility; everything is instrumental, and moved by inherent fatality.

What can be more preposterous than the notion that such a myth—too small or too sublimated to be seen by the most powerful microscope—has the faculty of producing all the power man manifests, and of possessing all his knowledge, and that, too, before conveying it to the man himself?

This attempt to involve, as a resident, another intelligent being among the organs of man's organic brain in nowise accounts for the living and mental phenomena of the man; and even were the hypothesis true, it would only shift the conclusion from that of being the result of two organizations, of which the second (the man) is only the instrument, of the first (the divine essence,) the fundamental principle being that material human organization is indispensable to thinking, of which thought or intelligence is the result. With these, and similar views respecting the nature of man entertained at the present day, and substantially adopted from the most ancient heathen philosophy and science, with what consistency can we boast of progress, or that the fittest survives?

The Lower Animals depend upon Man for Subsistence and Existence.

One of the commonest and most formidable objections which atheism, and especially scientific atheism, makes to the Bible is that it regards man as the great object for which the world was created, delegating to him supreme dominion, and of course making all animals and other living things subservient and depedent. Man's desire to survive death—to live again—and his hope of eternal being are attributed to his pride; for he has, it is said, really no more grounds for indulging this hope than have the lower animals. As with these, so with him: death ends all. Indeed, modern science completely reverses this relation, and not only makes man dependent upon the lower animals for his subsistence, but provides for him a long line of ancestors from among these lower living things through whom he has evolved into being.

Our position in answer to this objection is, that the subsistence and therefore the continued existence of the lower animals, including fish and fowl, for any considerable length of time—say five hundred years—depends upon the labor and existence of man, so that his extinction would result in their extermination. If, therefore, the extinction of man would cause the extinction of the lower animals, the fact would seem to be demonstrated that man and the lower animals came into existence simultaneously. This fact alone completely disproves the hypothesis of evolution according to natural selection.

The Biblical declaration upon the subject is as follows : " And God said, Let the waters bring forth abundantly the moving creature that hath life, and fowl that may fly above the earth in the open firmament of heaven. And God created great whales, which the waters brought forth abundantly, after their kind : and God saw that it was good. And God blessed them, saying, be fruitful, and multiply, and fill the waters in the seas, and let fowl multiply in the earth. And God said, Let the earth bring forth the living creature after his kind, cattle, and creeping thing, and beast of the earth after his kind : and it was so. And God made the beast of the earth after his kind, and cattle after his kind, and every creeping thing upon the earth after his kind ; and God saw that it was good.
'· And God said, Let us make man in our image, after our likeness : and let them have dominion over the fish of the sea, and over the fowl of the air, and over the cattle, and over all the earth, and over every creeping thing that creepeth upon the earth. So God created man in His own image, in the image of God created He him ; male and female created He them. And God blessed them, and God said unto them, Be fruitful, and multiply, and replenish the earth, and subdue it : and have dominion over the fish of the sea, and over the fowl of the air, and over every living thing that moveth upon the earth." (Gen. 1 : 20–28). " And out of the ground the Lord God formed every beast of the field, and every fowl of the air ; and brought them to Adam to see what he would call them : and whatsoever Adam called every living creature, that was the name thereof." (Gen. 2 : 19). "And God said, Let the earth bring forth grass, the herb yielding seed, and the fruit tree yielding fruit after his kind, whose seed is in itself, upon the earth : and it was so. (Gen. 1 : 11). " And God said, Behold, I have given you [man] every herb bearing seed which is upon the face of the earth, and every tree, in the which is the fruit of a tree yielding seed ; to you it shall be for meat, and to every beast of the earth, and to every fowl of the air, and to every thing that creepeth upon the earth, wherein is life, I have given every green herb for meat : and it was so." (Gen. 1 : 29–30).

We see that the terms herb and fruit as here employed comprehend the meat (food) for all living things. Animals have been divided into classes according to the kinds of food upon which they naturally feed, as frugivorous, herbivorous and carnivorous. The herbivorous are such as feed on herbaceous plants, soft and succulent, which perish annually down to their roots, or what are generally comprehended in what we call vegetation. The carnivorous are those animals which naturally prey upon other animals; of these are the lion, tiger, wolf, and dog. These, however, prefer the flesh of herbivorous to that of carnivorous animals, hut devour both. The frugivorous and herbivorous animals have outnumbered the carnivorous in about the proportion that civilized and semi-civilized man has outnumbered the savages. We think we may safely advance the opinion that there is a greater number of domestic animals in ten cities of the United States than there are carnivorous animals in the whole world besides.

Another important fact which goes very far toward the establishment of our position is, that man is the only animal who clears the land of trees and cultivates the soil—he only sows seed, plants fruit-trees, and reaps harvests. There is no account of a race of men so savage that they did not clear land, sow seed, and reap harvests, nor one that did not rear and keep domestic animals. Another fact is that trees will grow wherever there is soil enough to sustain any kind of plant, and also that they will be numerous in proportion to the richness of the soil. It is likewise a fact that no cereals or fruit will grow in a dense woods, not even grass for hay; also that it does not require fifty years to grow a forest of oaks, and not half that time for one of various other kinds of trees. It is also a fact that a large proportion of vegetable matter produced upon the earth is washed into the rivers, lakes and seas by the rains of heaven, which supplies the food for the smaller fishes, while the larger prey upon and devour the smaller.

It is a fact that the birds or fowls feed on fruits, vegetables, fish, and carrion, and also that the birds of prey devour the smaller ones and the domestic birds and fowls.

The World with Man Extinct.

Let us now suppose the sudden extinguishment of mankind, and what would be the result. Take this continent for example—and of course what would result here would equally upon every other continent and island on the face of the globe. Suppose the time of the catastrophe was early spring, too soon to sow or plant. That spring not a seed is sown or planted on the face of the earth, and as a result no harvests are reaped in the fall. By the next spring almost all the domestic animals have died by starvation and exposure, especially those who depend on the harvests of the field for food. The carnivorous and birds of prey have fattened and increasingly multiplied during this period. Ten years pass, and not a domestic animal lives on the continent. Let us look ahead to the end of the century, and see in what a condition are all the cleared lands and the rich, cultivated farms. All are covered with dense woods · not a square rod of land which would produce grass for cattle can be found uncovered by wild brushwood or trees. The fruit-trees, overtopped and choked by wild-wood, long since became extinct.

The herbivorous animals flourished for a time on the prairies, where the unbroken winds sweep over and destroy the young trees before they obtain sufficient size and strength to resist their fury. Here for a time the contests raged between the wild and tame animals, but in less than twenty-five years none but carnivora survived, and long before the hundred years had ended the last two of these had met in deadly conflict; the survivor fed on the vanquished and laid down and died by starvation. The flowers, vegetables, fruits and animals, the food for insects, being gone, they too had ceased to be. The smaller birds, which fed upon these, have joined the number of the dead. Those birds of prey which depended upon insect-feeding kind for food have devoured the few that remained, and finally also died of starvation.

Those birds which preyed upon the small fishes living close to the shores and in shallow waters have also perished for lack of food. These fishes fed upon the living and dead insects, also upon the vegetable matter washed from the cultivated farms, but in less than a hundred years the supply had been exhausted, and the insects and small fishes had become extinct. Upon these smaller fishes the larger ones of the deep had depended for their food; the supply being cut off, they too had preyed upon each other, and the last dread contest had taken place between the two surviving monsters of the deepest seas. The stronger and more savage had killed and devoured his antagonist and himself had died by starvation. Universal death reigned.

There are scores of other causes which we might mention and which would accelerate the extinguishment of the animal life of the world after man was gone; but those we have named are so absolutely interdependent, and therefore consequent, that it needs but the statement of the facts in order to demonstrate our position, that without the labor of man the world is worthless—

that he not only holds dominion over all other living things, but that they can no more live without his labor and care than can an infant without a nurse. If one hundred years is not sufficient time wherein to complete the extinction of animal life under the circumstances we have supposed (which we believe to be abundant) then extend the time to five hundred years. Surely no animal could have existed five hundred years; much less could they have come into existence and maintained themselves hundreds and thousands of years before there was a living man upon earth, as evolutionists teach. The supposition is rendered still more impossible when we take into consideration the claim of these skeptical scientists that before the animals appeared there was a period of luxurious vegetation called that of the "carboniferous," covering millions of years. As we have seen in the case of animals the most savage and unfit survive, so also is it with vegetation. Without the existence, labor and care of man the grain fields and fruit orchards succumb while the choking weeds, wild brushwood, and dense forests prevail and take their place. This gives us the conclusion that if man had not come into existence before vegetation had obtained this destructive march, and with his labor and art to have beaten back the devourer, neither he nor the lower animals could have maintained their existence, thus completely reversing the theory of geological evolution according to the doctrine of natural selection, that the fittest survives. These facts and their legitimate teaching not only confirm, but demonstrate the Bible statements of the creation that all organic beings and things, plants and animals, with man at their head, came into existence simultaneously. It is the voice of universal observation—of scientific and philosophic necessity.

It seems to us that no man who understands the science and philosophy of the universe contained in the " Scriptures of truth " and the revelations of nature can be indifferent to the consummation of the great object of the Creator in bringing them into existence, namely, the re-creation of the present temporary world and system into one of endless duration and absolute perfection. " The world to come whereof we speak."

THE END OF VOLUME ONE.

TESTIMONIALS.

Observers have noted—some with alarm, others with indifference—the rapid spread of infidelity within the past few years. How to check its growth, or at least how to counteract its influence, is a question which had engaged the attention of many thoughtful minds. The clergy, though loudly called upon to defend their faith and put down the common enemy, have generally maintained studied silence. Such as have responded to the call have done so with such indiscretion that they, too, might better have kept silence. Mere denunciation is more likely to repel friends than to convert or restrain foes. I note, however, one remarkable exception. The Rev. Thomas Mitchell, of Brooklyn, marches boldly into the enemy's country and fights him on his own ground, and with his own weapons—the truths of science.

He has in press a work in two volumes, entitled COSMOGONY, wherein he attacks, with great skill and spirit, the positions and theories of the evolutionists, geologists, astronomers, chronologists, and the whole school of atheists who masquerade in the garb of science.

I have read the manuscript of Mr. Mitchell's work, and I am bound to confess that, though I had pretty nearly acquiesced in the doctrine of evolution, with all its ridiculous and grotesque conclusions—I say, I freely confess that Mr. Mitchell's arguments have caused me to hesitate and doubt. For he certainly has presented problems which men of science have not yet even attempted to solve; nor does it seem possible that they can be solved upon any other known modern scientific principle.

In dealing with Mr. Robert Ingersoll, Mr. Mitchell employs no velvet words, and uses no gloved hands. Indeed, he directly charges him with untruth and misrepresentation, and what is

TESTIMONIALS.

more, he seems to prove his charges. The work is to be sold by the American News Company, New York; which means, of course, a large sale. However that may be, the book ought to sell on its own merits. Whoever will read it, whatever may be his opinions, cannot fail to gain new ideas, and to see familiar facts presented in a new light.

CHARLES HUNT.

Mr. Hunt was thirteen years on the New York *Tribune*, and part of that time on the editorial staff.

Brooklyn, Feb. 15, 1881.

PROFESSOR MITCHELL,

Dear Sir :—I know you to be a sincere and zealous inquirer after Truth. You are well qualified by your learning and training as a thinker and biblical critic to investigate those subjects to which your time and attention are directed. Though my opinions in regard to certain doctrines of Scripture are different from yours, yet I highly approve of your efforts to defend the truth as you believe and understand it.

Your COSMOGONY is a work of great merit. It displays research, learning, and thorough acquaintance with the Sacred Volume. The facts are well arranged, the illustrations are apt and striking,—all expressed in clear and forcible language. Such a work is much needed. It will no doubt have an extensive circulation—as a book ought to have, the object of which is "to demonstrate that the Scriptures have emanated from a mind seeing the end from the beginning." With kind regards,

Yours very truly,

DAVID SYME, A.M.

The Rev. David Syme was Professor of Mathematics, Natural Philosophy, and Chemistry, in the Grammar School of Columbia College, New York.

To Rev. THOMAS MITCHELL :

Dear sir :—From your discussions, of which your promised COSMOGONY is an epitome, and from the examination of the table of contents I should judge that the book will be one much needed in the field of theolegical science at the present day, its aim, scope, and effect being the elucidation of *Truth* suited to the comprehension of the masses as well as furnishing mental food for the most intellectual, and must become a work long felt to be a necessity among the people.

J. B. JONES, M.D.,
Brooklyn, N. Y.

Feb. 1881.

Having read some of Rev. Thomas Mitchell's books, and heard him discourse agreat many times upon scientific, philosophic, and religious questions, with the whole range of which he seems to be familiar, tracing and elucidating their connection and dependence upon each other, and the able manner in which all are reduced to one great circle of harmony, each part occupying its appropriate place; thus reaching conclusions which not only seem to be logical, but unanswerable. In view of which I have no hesitation in giving it as my opinion that his forthcoming COSMOGONY will be hailed as a most valuable accession to the literature of the world, and peculiarly applicable to these times, as it meets the pretended scientific objections to the Holy Scriptures and Christianity, as well as those of the skeptical and atheistic world. I cannot, therefore, but anticipate for it a very wide circulation.

ELIPHALET NOTT, M.D.

Dr. Nott is a graduate of Union College, New York, and educated under the care of his grandfather, the late Dr. Nott, who was sixty-one years president of the college.

www.ingramcontent.com/pod-product-compliance
Lightning Source LLC
Chambersburg PA
CBHW022133300426
44115CB00006B/168